ADDITIONS AND CORRECTIONS

TO THE

W.P.A.

INVENTORY

OF

MONTGOMERY COUNTY, OHIO:

DAYTON

Jana Sloan Broglin

HERITAGE BOOKS
2025

HERITAGE BOOKS

AN IMPRINT OF HERITAGE BOOKS, INC.

Books, CDs, and more—Worldwide

For our listing of thousands of titles see our website
at
www.HeritageBooks.com

Published 2025 by
HERITAGE BOOKS, INC.
Publishing Division
5810 Ruatan Street
Berwyn Heights, MD 20740

(Originally Titled)
INVENTORY OF THE COUNTY ARCHIVES OF OHIO

Prepared by
The Ohio Historical Records Survey Project
Division of Community Service Programs
Work Projects Administration

No. 57. MONTGOMERY COUNTY (DAYTON)

Columbus, Ohio
The Ohio Historical Records Survey Project
1941

International Standard Book Number
Paperbound: 978-0-7884-4313-8

Foreword... vi-vii
Preface
      Preface 2nd Edition....................................... viii-ix
      Preface 1st Edition .... x-xi
Abbreviations, Symbols, and Explanatory Note..................... xii-xv
Historical Sketch... xvi-xxxi
Governmental Organization and Records System .... xxxii-lxiv
Housing, Care, and Accessibility of the Records................. lxv-lxxvii
Floor Plan of County Courthouse............................. lxxviii-lxxxi

County Offices and their Records

County Commissioners... 1-30
      Minutes. Institutions and relief. Financial records. Miscellaneous. Sanitary department. Aid for the blind. Relief administration: case records; WPA and CCC records; NYA records.
Recorder 31-44
      Real property transfers: deeds and registers; leases; mortgages; liens; registered lands; plats and surveys. Personal property transfers. Incorporations and partnerships. Grants of authority. Miscellaneous.
Clerk of Courts 45-61
      Court proceedings. Judgments and executions. Jury and witness records. Motor Vehicles. Commissions and licenses. Partnerships. Elections. Financial records. Coroners' inquests. Miscellaneous.
Court of Common Pleas 62-89
      Civil Cases. Criminal cases. Naturalization.
      A. Division of Domestic Relations
            Divorce records. Juvenile court: delinquents; aid to dependent children.
      B. Assignment Commissioners.
      C. Probation Department.
Supreme Court 90-92
Superior Court.. 93-98
      General court proceedings. Jury and witness records. Judgments and executions.

Court of Appeals 99-105
       District court. Circuit court. Court of appeals.
Probate Court 106-128
       Civil cases. Criminal cases. General court proceedings. Estates and guardianships: wills; appointments, bonds, and letters; inventories, sale bills, and claims; accounts and settlements; inheritance tax. Assignments. Dependents. Naturalization. Vital statistics: Births and deaths; marriages. Licenses and certificates. Financial records. Miscellaneous.
Jury Commissioners 129-130
Grand Jury. 131-132
Petit Jury 132-133
Prosecuting Attorney 134-138
Coroner 139-140
Sheriff. 141-152
       Court orders. Jail records. Financial records. Miscellaneous.
Dog Warden 153-154
Auditor 155-181
       Property transfers. Plants, maps, and surveys. Taxes: Real property; personal property; adjustments; delinquent; inheritance; utility; excise. Financial records: budgets and appropriations; general accounts; special accounts; bills and claims; vouchers and warrants. Licenses. Enumerations and statistics. Bonds. Weights and measures. Miscellaneous.
Treasurer 182-195
       Taxes: real property; personal property; adjustments; inheritance; excise; collections. Financial records. Bonds. Miscellaneous.
Budget Commissioners 196-197
Board of Revision 198-201
Board of Trustees of the Sinking Fund 202-203
Board of Elections 204-207
       Minutes. Registrations and votes. Financial records.
Board of Education 208-211
Board of Health. 212-217
       Minutes. Case records. Immunizations. Contagious diseases. Inspections. Vital statistics. Miscellaneous.

Board of Trustees of the Stillwater Sanatorium 218-223
    Admissions and registers. Case records. Statistics. Financial records.
    Personnel.
Superintendent of the County Home. 224-230
    Minutes. Case records. Financial records. Personnel. Miscellaneous.
Board of Trustees of the Children's Home. 231-236
    Minutes. Case records. Financial records. Miscellaneous.
Board of County Visitors 237-238
Soldiers' Relief Commission 239-240
Soldiers' Burial Commission 241-242
Blind Relief Commission 243
Board of Aid for the Aged 244-249
    Applications and investigations. Case records. Miscellaneous.
County Engineer (Surveyor). 250-256
    Surveys, plats, and maps. Improvements: roads, bridges, and ditches;
    contracts. Financial records. Miscellaneous.
Board of Directors of the Miami Conservancy District 257-268
    Property and tax records. Financial records. Maps and photographs. Orders
    and contracts. Miscellaneous.
Agricultural Society 269-272
Agricultural Extension Agents 273-276
    Conservation and crop control. 4-H clubs and home demonstration.
    Correspondence.

Bibliography 277-282
Roster of County Officials 283-293
Addresses and Websites 294-296
Index to Inventory Entries. 297-317

The *Inventory of the County Archives of Ohio* is one of a number of bibliographies of historical materials prepared throughout the United States by workers on the Historical Records Survey Program of the Work Projects Administration. The publication herewith presented, an inventory of the archives of Montgomery County, is number 57 of the Ohio series.

The Historical Records Survey Program was undertaken in the winter of 1935 -1936 for the purpose of providing useful employment to needy unemployed historians, lawyers, teachers, and research and clerical workers. In carrying out this objective, the project was organized to compile inventories of historical materials, particularly the unpublished government documents and records which are basic in the administration of local government, and which provide invaluable data for students of political, economic, and social history. Up to the present time more than 1,700 guides, inventories, and indexes have been issued by the Survey throughout the Nation. The archival guide herewith presented is intended to meet the requirements of day-to-day administration by the officials of the county, and also the needs of lawyers, businessmen, and other citizens who require facts from public records for the proper conduct of their affairs. The volume is so designed that it can be used by the historian in his research in un-printed sources in the same way he uses the library card catalog for printed sources.

The inventories produced by the Historical Records Survey Program attempt to do more than give merely a list of records–they attempt further to sketch in the historical background of the county or other unit of government, and to describe precisely and in detail the organization and functions of the government agencies whose records they list. The county, town, and other local inventories for the entire county will, when completed, constitute an encyclopedia of local government as well as a bibliography of local archives.

The successful conclusion of the work of the Historical Records Survey Program, even in a single county, would not be possible without the support of public officials, historical and legal specialists, and many other groups in the community. Their cooperation is gratefully acknowledged.

The Survey Program was organized by Luther H. Evans, who served as Director until March 1, 1940, when he was succeeded by Sargent B. Child, who had been Field Supervisor since the inauguration of the Survey. The Survey Program operates as a Nation-wide series of locally sponsored projects in the Division of Community Service Programs, of which Mrs. Florence Kerr, Assistant Commissioner, is in charge.

Howard O. Hunter
Commissioner

PREFACE
2nd Edition

In 1929 after the stock market crash along with the Great Depression, crop failures and drought, which followed, President Herbert Hoover and his successor Franklin D. Roosevelt formulated relief projects, the most successful was the establishment of the Works Progress Administration (WPA).

Established as the Works Projects Administration in 1935, the WPA was the largest of the many programs developed during Roosevelt's "New Deal." In 1939, the agency's name was changed to Works Progress Administration, and continued as such until its demise in 1943.

The Federal Writers' Project, a division of the WPA (known as Federal Project Number One), created jobs for many unemployed librarians, clerks, researchers, editors, and historians. The workers went to courthouses, town halls, offices in large cities, vital statistics offices and inventoried records. Besides indexing works, many records were transcribed. One of these many projects was the *Inventory of the County Archives* which has benefitted genealogists and historians. The inventories listed the records, either by volumes or file boxes and years per record type, within the office. Although the WPA oversaw this project, the information for each volume of records may differ significantly by the information submitted.

Information regarding the CCC (Civilian Conservation Corps), WPA, and NYA (National Youth Administration) are mentioned in this volume for Montgomery County. For more information about these programs, see: NYA **https://en.wikipedia.org/wiki/National_Youth_Administration;** CCC: **https://en.wikipedia.org/wiki/Civilian_Conservation_Corps;** and WPA: **https://en.wikipedia.org/wiki/Works_Progress_Administration.**

The information herein is verbatim except for obvious spelling errors. Records listed may have met the requirement for retention and have been destroyed as per the records retention act, while other records are considered permanent records. (*See:* **https://codes.ohio.gov/ohio-revised-code** Ohio Revised Code, sections 149.31 and 149.34). Records once considered "open" to the public, such as lunacy, idiotic, and juvenile cases, may be "closed" due to a revision of state laws. However, the records may be opened to family members with adequate proof of lineage.

2nd Edition

　　The addresses and website section of this edition list an up-to-date location guide to each office mentioned, if located.

　　This project was to encompass all of Ohio's 88 counties although approximately 30 of these inventories have been located while others may be missing or never done.

　　Mention is made of the Ohio State Archaeological Society now known as the Ohio History Connection, 800 East 17th Avenue, Columbus, Ohio, **www.ohiohistory.org.**

Jana Sloan Broglin
Fellow, Ohio Genealogical Society
Swanton, Ohio
2025

PREFACE
1st Edition

The Historical Records Survey of the Work Projects Administration began operation in Ohio in February 1936. The Project was organized and operated by the district supervisors of the Writers' Project until November 1936 when it became an independent part of the Federal Project No. 1. With the termination of the Federal Projects in September 1939, the Ohio unit became the Ohio Historical Records Survey Project, sponsored by the Ohio State Archaeological and Historical Society. On August 3, 1941, the Ohio Historical Records Survey Project became a unit of the Consolidated Records Assistance Project in Ohio, sponsored by the Ohio State University.

One of the purposes of the Survey in Ohio has been the preparation of complete inventories of the records of the state, county, and municipal records. The *Inventory of the County Archives of Ohio* will, when completed, consist of a set of 88 volumes numbered according to the position of the county name in an alphabetical list of Ohio counties. Thus, the inventory herewith presented for Montgomery County is number 57. Inventories of state archives and of municipal and other local records constitute separate publications.

The principle followed in the inventory of the county records has been to place a record in the office of origin rather than in the office of deposit. The records are arranged with those of the executive branch of government first, followed by judicial, law-enforcement, fiscal, welfare, and miscellaneous agencies. Minor agencies are placed in the general arrangement according to function rather than according to constitutional or statutory responsibility to a major subdivision. The legal development of each office or agency has been treated in a prefatory section preceding the inventory of the records of the office. Although a condensed form of entry is used, information is given as to the limiting dates of all extant records, the contents of individual series, and the location of records in courthouse, statehouse, or other depository.

The work of the Historical Records Survey was begun in Montgomery County in 1936. Since February 9, 1938, the project has been operated under the direction of Mr. James L. Graham, District Supervisor. The project personnel is entirely responsible for the accuracy of the inventory. The Board of County Commissioners of Montgomery County, serving as a contributing co-sponsor, provided the materials for the publication of this volume. The project is also grateful for the valuable assistance given by the various county officials and their office staffs. The State office staff under the immediate supervision of Miss

Winifred Smith, Assistant State Supervisor, arranged, edited, and indexed the volume.

The volumes comprising the *Inventory of the County Archives of Ohio* are issued in mimeographed or printed form for free distribution to state and other public officials and to public libraries in Ohio, and to a limited number of libraries outside the state. Requests for information concerning particular units of the *Inventory* should be addressed to the Ohio Historical Records Survey Project, Room 216, Clinton Building, Columbus, Ohio.

Lillian Kessler
State Supervisor
Ohio Historical Records Survey Project

Columbus, Ohio
December 1941

ABBREVIATIONS, SYMBOLS, AND EXPLANATORY
NOTES

ADC . . . . Aid to Dependent Children
adm. . . . . administration
am.. . . . . amended
Arch.. . . . . Archaeological
Art. . . . . Article
c.. . . . . copyright
capias . . . . a warrant or order for arrest of a person,
typically issued by the judge or magistrate in a case.
CCC.. . . . . Civilian Conservation Corps
certiorari. . . . . to be more fully informed
chap(s). . . . . chapter(s)
comp. . . . . compiler
Const. . . . . Constitution
ed(s). . . . . editor(s)
et al. . . . . (et alii), and others
et seq . . . . and the following
(et) passim . . . . and here and there
ex officio . . . . as a result of one's status or position
et seq. . . . . and following
fee simple . . . . full and irrevocable ownership
G. C. . . . . General Code
habeas corpus . . . . protection against illegal imprisonment
ibid. . . . . the same reference
loc. cit. . . . . *(loco citato)* in the place cited
N. P. . . . . The Ohio NISI PRIUS REPORTS
n. p.. . . . . no place of publication shown
n. s. . . . . new series
nolle prosequi . . . . notice of abandonment by a
plaintiff or prosecutor of all or part of a suit or action

NYA . . . . National Youth Administration
O.L. . . . . *Laws of Ohio*
op. cit. . . . . *(opere citato)* In the work cited
posse comitatus . . . . a group of citizens called upon to assist the sheriff
praecipes . . . . a written request for action
prima facie . . . . on the first impression
pro rata . . . . in proportion
procedendo . . . . sends case from appellate court to a lower court
pt. . . . . part
quo warranto . . . . by what authority or warrant
replevins . . . . return of personal property
                                              wrongfully taken or held by a defendant
R.S. . . . . Revised Statutes
sec(s) . . . . section(s)
sic . . . . thus, following copy
supersedeas . . . . a stay of enforcement of a judgment pending appeal
v. . . . . versus
venires . . . . a group of people summoned for jury duty
vol(s). . . . . volume(s)
WPA . . . . Works Progress/Projects Administration
writ . . . . a formal, legal document, a decree
x . . . . by
— . . . . current, to date
4-H . . . . (Four - H)

ABBREVIATIONS, SYMBOLS, AND EXPLANATORY NOTES

Each chapter or section of "County Offices and Their Records" consists of an essay describing the legal status and functions of one department of county government and an inventory of the records of that department.

Each record constitutes a separate entry. Entries are arranged under topical headings and subheadings.

Each entry sets forth, insofar as applicable, the following:

1. Entry number. Entries are numbered consecutively throughout the inventory.
2. The exact title as it appears on the record, or if the record has no title a supplied title in brackets. If the title of the record is non-descriptive, misleading, or incorrect an additional title (in capitals and lowercase letters), also enclosed in brackets, has been supplied.
3. Dates show inclusive years or parts of years covered by the record. Breaks in dates indicate that the record is missing or was not kept between dates shown. A dash in place of the final date indicates an open record. If no current entries have been made the date of the last entry is noted. Where no statement is made that the record was discontinued at the last date shown, it could not be definitely established that such was the case. Where no comment is made on the absence of prior and subsequent records, no definite information could be obtained.
4. Quantity, given in chronological order wherever possible.
5. Labeling. Numbers and letters within parentheses indicate labeling on volumes, file boxes, or other containers.
6. Variations in title. The current or most recent title is used but significant variations are shown with dates for which each was used.
7. Change of agency. Occasionally a record is discontinued as a county record and kept by some other agency.
8. Description. A statement of the nature and purpose of the record and of what the record shows. As the contents of a record may vary, over time the description may differ somewhat from the record at any one period. Wherever feasible, changes in content are shown with dates. In map and plat entries the names of author and publisher and the scale are omitted only when not available.

9. Arrangement. Records said to be alphabetically arranged are frequently alphabetized only as to initial letter of the surname. This is true especially where there is a secondary arrangement.
10. Indexing. Self-contained indexes are described in the entry. Separate indexes constitute separate entries with cross references to and from the record entry.
11. Nature of recording. Changes are indicated with dates.
12. Condition. No statement is made if good or excellent.
13. Number of pages. Averaged for the series.
14. Dimensions show size of volumes, maps, file boxes, or other containers and are expressed in inches in every instance. The dimensions of volumes are given in order of height, width, and thickness; of file boxes in order of height, width, and depth.
15. Location. Rooms referred to are in the county courthouse unless some other building is specified.

Title line cross references are used to complete series where a record is kept separately for a period of time or in other records for different periods of time. They are also used in all artificial entries which are made to show, under their proper office, records kept in the same volume or file with records of another office. In both instances, the description of the master entry shows the title and entry number of the record from which the cross reference is made. Dates shown in the description of the master entry are for the part or parts of the record contained therein, and are shown only when they vary from those of the master entry. Artificial entries show only title, dates, and description.

Separate third paragraph cross references from entry to entry, are used to show prior, subsequent, or related records which are not a part of the same series. If, however, both entries are under the same subject headings, no third paragraph references are made. "See also" references from subject headings refer to entries in the same department which contain records logically belonging under that heading but which have been classified under an equally appropriate heading.

Montgomery County, named for General Richard Montgomery who was killed in the assault on Quebec, December 31, 1775, was created by an act of the Ohio General Assembly passed March 24, 1803[1] and was erected and organized May 1, 1803. Created from part of Hamilton County, Montgomery originally embraced all of the territory extending northward from Butler and Warren Counties to the state line and extending westward from Greene County to the Indiana boundary. It was diminished by the formation of Miami, and Darke Counties, and assumed its present boundaries in 1812.[2] Its present area of 455 square miles contained a population of 273,481 in 1930, sixth largest in the state. Dayton, the county seat, had a population at the 1930 census of 200,982, and at the 1940 census of 210,718.[3]

Montgomery County was apparently a favorite habitat of prehistoric Indians. The valley of the Great Miami which flows through the county is particularly rich in archaeological remains. Near Miamisburg is located the largest mound in Ohio, an example of the Adena culture, standing 68 ft in height and more than 800 feet around the base. All together 111 prehistoric sites have been uncovered, including 76 mounds, 14 enclosures, 12 single burials, six village sites, and three cemeteries.[4]

In the historic period the territory which is now Montgomery County lay in the land of the Shawnees and, particularly, the Miamis.[5] The Great Miami River was a potential highway between the Ohio Valley and Canada, and therefore important in the rivalry of the French and English for possession of the West. In 1749 Celoron de Bienville, on behalf of France, toured the region of the Ohio and planted lead plates to denote possession. One of these plates was planted at the mouth of the Miami River which he ascended on his return to New France. [6]

---

1. *Laws of Ohio*, 1, 10.

2. Randolph Chandler Downes, "Evolution of Ohio County Boundaries," *Ohio State Arch. and Hist. Quarterly*, XXVI (1927), 340-477.

3. U. S. Bureau of the Census, *Sixteenth Census of the United States, 1940, Population, First Series, Number of Inhabitants, Ohio*. 17.

4. William C. Mills, *Archaeological Atlas of Ohio* (Columbus, 1914), 57: E. F. Greenman, "Excavation of the Coon Mound and An Analysis of the Adena Culture," *Ohio State Arch. and Hist. Quarterly*, IV (1905), 446-447.

5. H. C. Shetrone, "The Indian in Ohio," *Ohio State Arch. and Hist. Quarterly*, XXVII (1919), 273-510.

6. A. A. Lambing, ed., "Celeron's Journal," *Ibid.*, XXIX (1921), 336-396.

Two years later, in 1751, Christopher Gist and his companions, Andrew Montour and George Groghan, explored the Miami Valley. Gist reported in his Journal that it was a "fine, rich level land, well timbered . . .well watered. . .and full of beautiful natural meadows. . .and abounds with Turkeys, Deer, Elks, and most sorts of Game particularly Buffaloes. In short it wants nothing but cultivation to make it a most delightful Country."[7] By the treaty of 1763 France gave up her claims to the Ohio Country.

When American frontiersman began to settle in Kentucky in the 1770s, Indians from above the Ohio continually molested the whites. In 1782 George Rogers Clark led a thousand Kentuckians on a punitive expedition, skirmishing with the Indians on the site of Dayton. Four years later Colonel Logan again defeated the Indians on the same spot.[8] The settlement of southwestern Ohio began in 1788 under the auspices of the land speculator, John Cleaves Symmes. At first, settlement was restricted to the shores of the Ohio River. However, the pressure of population in Kentucky, Pennsylvania, and other frontier regions, the promotion of land speculation, the attractiveness of cheap lands, and the virtual removal of the Indians from southern Ohio by the Treaty of Greenville (1795), led to rapid migration northward. Pioneers of frontier communities, especially of Kentucky and Pennsylvania, filtered into the back country.[9]

In June1789, Major Benjamin Stites, John Stites Gano, and William Goforth bargained with Symmes for a tract around the mouth of the Mad River where they planned to build a town called Venice. The scheme fell through, however, because of the Indian uprisings.[10] Wayne's victory at Fallen Timbers in 1794 and the subsequent treaty of 1795 opened a "golden age" for land speculators.[11]Just 17 days after the Treaty of Greenville was signed, General Arthur St. Clair, Governor of the Northwest Territory, General James Wilkinson, notorious for his intrigues with Spain and with Aaron Burr, Jonathan Dayton, soldier, statesman, and also a friend of Aaron Burr, and Major Israel Ludlow, "prince of the

---

7. William M. Darlington, ed., *Christopher Gist's Journals*. . .(Pittsburgh, 1893), 47
8. John F. Edgar, *Pioneer Life in Dayton and Vicinity* (Dayton, 1896), 14-15.
9. Randolph Chandler Downes, *Frontier Ohio, Ohio Historical Collections,* III (Columbus, 1935), 59, 61, 65.
10. John W. Van Cleve, "A Brief History of the Settlement of the Town of Dayton" *Journal of the Historical and Philosophical Society of Ohio*, No. 1 (1838), 64-70.
11. Downes, *Frontier Ohio*, 79.

Miami surveyors and land speculators,"[12] contracted with Symmes for the purchase of the entire seventh and eighth ranges between the Great and Little Miami Rivers, on condition that they establish three settlements, one to be located at the mouth of the Mad River.[13] Surveyors were immediately dispatched to survey and locate the boundaries of the tract, and in November 1795 Ludlow finished laying out the town of Dayton,[14] where early in 1796 a settlement was made under the direction of surveyors John Dunlap and Daniel C. Cooper.[15] About the same time settlers arrived on the site of Miamisburg, and soon after some families located their homes on the Mad and Miami Rivers above Dayton.[16]

Symmes claims, based on his original contract,[17] included all the territory between the Miamis, extending northward to a line between the heads of those rivers.[18] Symmes' surveyors subdivided his land into six-mile townships, sections, and ranges on the rectangular plan. However, unlike the system elsewhere in the United States, rows of townships running east and west, instead of north and south, were called ranges. Townships were numbered east from the Great Miami, starting with number one at the river, resulting in considerable irregularity for both township and range numbers within the district.[19] The lands west of the Great Miami in Montgomery County were among the first Congress Lands to be surveyed under the law of 1796. Townships were numbered west from the Great Miami in this instance.[20]

When Symmes failed to meet his financial obligations to the federal government, his grant was limited by a patent of 1794 to 311,682 acres for which he had paid, located in the lands of present Hamilton, Butler, and Warren Counties.[21] The contract of 1795 for the seventh and eighth ranges between the Miamis was, therefore, an illegal transaction.

----

12. *Ibid.*, 145.
13. Van Cleve, *loc. cit.*
14. *Ibid.*
15 Downes, *Frontier Ohio*, 80.
16. Van Cleve, loc. cit.
17. John Cleves Symmes, "The Trenton Circular," *Quarterly Publication of the Historical and Philosophical Society of Ohio*, V (1910) 3, 82-92.
18. Downes, *Frontier Ohio*, 66.
19. C. E. Sherman, *Original Ohio Land Subdivisions, Final Report*, III, *Ohio Co-operative Topographic Survey* (Columbus, 1925), chapter vi, 69.
20. *Ibid.,* 123.
21. William E. Peters, *Ohio Lands and Their Subdivision* (2d ed. Athens, Ohio, 1918), 279.

An act of Congress in 1796 raised the price of public lands. Those who have settled in Dayton or in the seventh and eighth ranges found himself in a difficult situation. They had no legal title to the lands for which they had already paid a dollar or less, and in order to establish a title they had to repurchase at the relatively high price of two dollars.[22] In 1799 Congress passed an act granting the right of preemption to the settlers of lands above the limits of Symmes' patent.[23] A series of acts followed reducing the minimum number of acres which could be purchased from 640 in 1796 to 168 acres in 1804, and extending the time of payment.[24]

In 1801 two land offices opened at Cincinnati, one to sell to those with preemption rights, the other to sell Congress Land which was west of the Great Miami.[25] At that time, St. Clair and other proprietors relinquished their claims because of the two-dollar price.[26] Whereupon Daniel C. Cooper, in accordance with the agreements with the settlers and by the purchase of preemption rights, became the titular proprietor of Dayton and much of the surrounding country.[27] For many years the title of cooper's land, a title upon which many of the settlers were dependent for their own titles, was subject of considerable litigation. From 1807 to 1813 St. Clair and original proprietors kept cases in courts against Cooper but these were finally won by Cooper and there was a withdrawal of all charges against him.[28]

The confusion of titles and price of lands restrained the settlement of the region about Dayton. Until 1801, when the land offices were opened, all settlers in Montgomery County were squatters. The first settlers included Scotch, Scotch-Irish, English, and Germans who emigrated especially from Kentucky, and also from Pennsylvania, Maryland, Virginia, and the Carolinas. Many of the first migration were transients who squatted until they were required to pay for their lands when

---

22. R. Pierce Beaver, "The Miami Purchase of John Cleves Symmes," *Ohio State Arch. and Hist. Quarterly*, XL.
23. Clarence E. Carter, ed., *The Territorial Papers of the United States* (Washington, 1934), III, 16 *et seq.*
24. *Laws, Treaties and Other Documents Having Operation and Respect to the Public Lands* (Washington, 1810), 139-157.
25. A. W. Drury, *History of the City of Dayton and Montgomery County, Ohio* (Chicago and Dayton, 1909), I, 86-87.
26. Beverley W. Bond, Jr., "Memoirs of Benjamin Van Cleve, *Quarterly Publication of the Historical and Philosophical Society of Ohio*, XVII (1922). 66.
27. Edgar, *op. cit.,* 34.
28. Drury, *op. cit.,* I, 89-91.

they moved on to other unsettled regions.[29] The first settlers of Twin Valley, in the southwestern part of the county, came chiefly from Kentucky, once they had migrated from Pennsylvania, Maryland, Virginia, and North Carolina. Among these squatters were some four or five German families.[30]

     After the opening of the land offices in Cincinnati permanent settlers began to arrive, and most of the squatters moved away practically in a body.[31] Even those Kentuckians who remained in German County, that is, in Twin Valley, were in a few years bought out by the permanent settlers.[32] Predominant among the permanent settlers were the Germans who emigrated from Pennsylvania, especially from Berks County. Among the first Germans to arrive in Montgomery County were Dunkers from Virginia.[33] In 1804, 24 German families abandoned their homes in Berks County, Pennsylvania, and migrated in a group to Twin Valley where Germantown was founded by them within a few years. A steady stream of settlers followed in the next four years, mostly from Pennsylvania, but some also from Maryland and Virginia.[34] By 1810, Twin Valley was thickly populated and the land was selling at from $25 to $50 an acre.[35] All the other townships and the town of Dayton likewise received many Germans during this period of heavy immigration.[36]

     The county's population grew rapidly after the land offices were opened and by 1810 it had reached a total of 7,722.[37] During the War of 1812 Dayton became a supply station and a thoroughfare for the American troops. This movement of troops affected an excellent market for farm produce. The evidence of prosperity and the fertility of the region were attractive to many including soldiers, who proceeded to make their homes in Montgomery County.[38]

---

29. Downes, *Frontier Ohio*, 72-75; Edgar, *passim;* W. H. Beers and Co., pub., *History of Montgomery County* (Chicago, 1882), 156 et seq.

30. J. P. Hentz, *Twin Valley* (Dayton, 1883), 35-40.

31. *Ibid.,* 43; Beers, *op. cit.,* 28.

32. J. P. Hentz, *History of the Evangelical Lutheran Congregation in Germantown, Ohio* (Dayton, 1882), 9.

33. Drury, I., *op. cit.,* 707-709.

34. Hentz, *Twin Valley*, 50-60.

35. Hentz, *Evangelical Lutheran Congregation of Germantown*, 9-10.

36. Beers, *op. cit., passim.*

37. U. S. Bureau of the Census, *Compendium of the Eleventh Census, 1890,* I, 35.

38. Edgar, *op. cit.,* 160; Van Cleve, *loc. cit.*

The depression following the War of 1812 also led to migration from east of the Allegheny Mountains to the westward.[39] By 1820 the population increased to 15,999. The construction of the Miami Canal during the following decade resulted in a considerable growth of the population, Dayton expanded 195 percent and Montgomery County reaching a total population of 24,362 by 1830.[40] The 1830s and '40s saw an increase in the German population as a result of the immigration from Germany following the unsuccessful revolutions of 1830 and 1848, and saw the immigration of the Irish who fled their native land during the famine years of the late 40s. In 1860, 28 percent of Dayton's population of 20,081 was of foreign birth.[41]

The economic and industrial revolutions following the War Between the States were accompanied by an astounding growth in Montgomery County as is shown in these figures: 1860, 52,230; 1880, 78,550; 1890, 100,852; 1900, 130,146; 1910, 163,673. The expansion of the World War period and the era of prosperity experienced in the 1920s were accompanied by a population increase of almost 67 percent.[42] The expansion of Dayton, whose population increased more than 72 percent from 1919 to 1930, of course accounted for most of the county's growth.

Throughout the years the Germans have continued to be the predominant group of the population. Of the 10,979 foreign-born whites in the county in 1870, 7,386 were German and 2,008 were Irish.[43] 20 years later in 1890 there were 14,695 foreign-born, of whom 10,096 were Germans and 2,552 were Irish.[44] At the same time there were in Dayton alone 15,878 natives who had been born of German parents and 3,310 natives born of Irish parents.[45] At the 1930 census there were 14,055 foreign-born whites in Montgomery County, including 4,785 Germans, 1,334 Hungarians, 869 Russians, 780 English, 708 Poles, 668 Italians, 628 Canadians, 622 Irish 505 Yugoslavs, and 200 to 400 each from Scotland, France, Austria, Czechoslovakia, Lithuania, Romania, and Greece. Nearly 37,000 residents were born of foreign parents whose nationality was as follows: German 19,387

---

39. Frank P. Goodwin, "The Rise of Manufactures in the Miami Country," *American Hist. Review*, XII (1906-1907), 761-775.
40. U. S. Bureau of the Census, *Fifteenth Census of the United States, 1930, Population*, 10.
41. Geo. H. Porter, *Ohio Politics During the Civil War Period* (New York, 1911). 14.
42. U. S. Bureau of the Census, *Fifteenth Census of the United States, 1930, Population*, 10.
43. U. S. Bureau of the Census, *Compendium of the Ninth Census of the United States*. 1870, 430.
44. U. S. Bureau of the Census, *Eleventh Census of the United States, 1890 Population* I, pt. vi. 650.
45. *Ibid.,* 708.

Irish 3,944; English 2,065; Hungarian 1,436; Polish 1,148; Russian 1,108; Canadian 1,045; French 1002; and between 500 and 1,000 each of Italian, Lithuanian, Austrian, and Scottish.[46] In addition to these elements there were 18,313 Negroes, 6.7 percent of the total population, 17,077 of whom were located in Dayton.[47]

In the early years the energies of the people of Montgomery County were devoted primarily to farming. At the 1930 census however, only 5,378 persons which was less than five percent of those in all industries were engaged in agricultural pursuits.[48] During the War of 1812 agriculture prospered, only to suffer a severe slump in the years immediately following. In Dayton in 1822 flour sold for $2.50 a barrel, butter 45 cents a pound, chickens for 50 cents a dozen, beef for one to three cents a pound, ham for 2 to 3 cents a pound, corn for 12 and one-half cents a bushel, and wheat for 25 cents a bushel.[49] The lands of the Miami Valley are fertile and rich and by 1853 the assessment value of farmland in Montgomery County was the highest in the state.[50] In the eight years from 1860 to 1867, Montgomery County produced more wheat than any other county in Ohio[51] and she still retains her rank among the leading agricultural counties in the state. In 1930 approximately 80 percent of the total area of the county was in farms, the value of which including land and buildings was $37,474,135, a value which was exceeded only in Wood and Franklin Counties. In the same year the value of all farm products which were sold, traded, or used was $6,375,491, seventh in Ohio.[53] A heavy producer of a large variety of agricultural products, on only one tobacco, was Montgomery County a leader. In 1930 she ranked second to Darke County in the production of tobacco, was 6,067,480 pounds.[54]

---

46. U. S. Bureau of the Census, *Fifteenth Census of the United States, 1930 Population*, III, pt. ii, 500, 504.

47. *Ibid.*, 482, 492.

48. *Ibid.*, 511.

49. Drury, *op. cit.*, I, 132-133.

50. Commissioner of Statistics of Ohio, *Third Annual Report, 1859*, 45, 108.

51, Ohio Secretary of State, *Statistical Report, 1868*, 12-14.

52. U. S. Bureau of the Census, *Fifteenth Census of the United States, 1930, Agriculture*, II, pt. I, 288-293.

53. U. S. Bureau of the Census, *Fifteenth Census of the United States, 1930, Agriculture*, II, pt. I, 301,

54. *Ibid.*, 435.

The production of an agricultural surplus furnished the West with the means of buying store merchandise. Thereupon, merchants established themselves and began importing from the East and from Europe. The expense and inconvenience caused by poor transportation facilities led to the development of local manufactures. By 1815 the Miami Valley had expanded to a size to support industries on a larger scale than household or small-shop, and mills and factories began to rise. Markets for the products were found not only in the Northwest but also in the Lower Mississippi Valley and shortly in the whole South.[55] When Benjamin Van Cleve first went to Dayton in 1796, flour cost $9 a barrel, plus $2.50 per hundred weight for transportation from Cincinnati.[56] The first industries of Montgomery County, as would be expected, were milling and conveyances for transportation. In 1799 Cooper built a corncracker, a sawmill, and a stillhouse[57] and William Hamer built a grist mill in the same year.[58] Within the next three decades many establishments arose, among them were factories for the production of furniture, cloth and clothing, shoes, nails, guns, iron, leather, chairs, wagons and carriages, glass, stoves, clocks, and hardware.[59]

In 1800 David Lowry constructed a flat boat at Dayton and carried a load of grain, pelts, and 500 venison hams to New Orleans. Each year after that saw fleets of flat boats loaded with such produce and also pork, flour, and whiskey sailing down the Western rivers.[60] In 1809 a regular freight line was established to Lake Erie by the way of the Miami and Maumee Rivers.[61] 1813 the first bank, the Dayton Manufacturing Company, was organized with a capital stock of $61,055.[62]

55. Goodwin, *loc. cit.*; David C. Shilling, "Relation of Southern Ohio to the South During the Decade Preceding the Civil War," *Quarterly Publication of the Historical and Philosophical Society of Ohio*. VIII (1913), 3-28.
56. Bond, "Memoirs of Benjamin Van Cleve," *loc. cit.*
57. Edgar, *op. cit.*, 34.
58. Joseph W. Sharts, *Biography of Dayton* (Dayton, 1922), 11.
59. United Brethren Publishing Co., pub., *History of Dayton, Ohio* (Dayton, 1889), 391, *et seq.* Hereafter cited, *History of Dayton.*
60. Beers, *op. cit.*, 555; Daniel Drake, *A Natural and Statistical View of Cincinnati and the Miami Country* (Cincinnati, 1815), 148.
61. Edgar, *op. cit., 138.*
62. *Ibid.,* 172-173.

The protective tariff system, the development of the steamboat, and the opening of the Miami Canal to Dayton in 1829, to Piqua in 1837, and to Toledo in 1845, resulted in an economic boom in the Miami Valley, except during the panic years. Dayton was admirably situated for water power which was used to run numerous factories. The first mill race was constructed by Cooper as early as 1799 and within the next few years other mill races were built. In 1830 James Steele built a dam across the Miami River above Dayton and cut a race. In 1838 and 1845 two large hydraulics were built.[63] By 1860 there were 298 manufacturing establishments in Montgomery County, employing 2,120 laborers at an annual cost of $712,770 and producing goods for the year valued at $4,425,374.[64]

The economic revolution which followed the War Between the States was felt in Dayton in the rise of large industries who used steam for power and the railroads for transportation and marketed their products on a national basis. Among these were the Barney and Smith Car Works (1855), which imported Hungarians for its labor supply, the National Cash Register Company (1884), the Davis Sewing Machine Company (1888), the Day-Fan Electric Company (1889), the Ohmer Car Register Company (1898), and in the present century, the W. P. Callahan Company, manufacturers of gas and gasoline engines, the Ohio Foundry, the Delco Light Company, The Green and Green Company, The Dayton Rubber Manufacturing Company, The Wright Airplane Company, and many others. In 1888 there were 149 manufacturing establishments in Dayton, employing 9,514 wage earners. In 1900 there were about 350 manufacturing plants, in 1910 about 400, and in 1918, 411 establishments in Dayton.[65] With the end of the world war in 1919 came the end to local independence of many Dayton Industries. Prominent among the international concerns which were established was General Motors which took over the Delco Light Company and established the Frigidaire Corporation. The Dayton Sewing Machine and Dayton Scale companies were merged with eastern combines. The National Cash Register and Mercantile Corporation head large international monopolies.

---

63. Sharts, *op. cit.*, 30-31.
64. U. S. Bureau of the Census, *Eighth Census of the United States, 1860, Manufactures,* 467-468.
65. Charlotte R. Conover, ed., *Dayton and Montgomery County Resources and People* (New York, 1932), II, 481-505.

In 1929 the Dayton Industrial Area, coextensive with Montgomery County contained 521 manufacturing establishments who employed 42,591 wage earners at total annual wages of $64,793,012 and there were 855 salaried employees who received a total of $21,023,503 for the same year. The value of the products manufactured was $330,318,581.[66] As industrial development has taken place, the wealth of the county has increased correspondingly. In 1846 farmlands and buildings were evaluated at $6,782,134 and urban property at $2,815,701. In 1880 for the first time the evaluation of urban property which was $16,026,029, surpassed that of $15,393,696 of the rural sections.[67] Since the opening of the twentieth century the tax duplicates of Montgomery County increased from $64,763,860 in 1900 to $294,314,570 in 1920 and $531,899,820 in 1930. The years of the depression saw a reduction of that figure to $367,981,155 in 1935 at that time the fifth largest tax duplicate in the state.[68]

At least as early as 1801, Benjamin Van Cleve and others petitioned Governor St. Clair to erect a new county with Dayton as the seat of justice.[69] Shortly after Ohio was admitted into the Union the first legislature created Montgomery County with Dayton as the temporary seat of government and soon the permanent seat. The first court was held in the upper room of George Newcomb's Tavern on July 27, 1803. In 1805 the courthouse was located in rooms at Hugh McCullum's new tavern, the rent of which was $25 for the year. In the winter of 1807-1808 a new brick courthouse was occupied. A stone courthouse, built in the form of a Grecian Temple, was completed in 1850 and still stands.[70] The present courthouse was erected in 1881-1884 at a cost said to have been $174,945.[71] An annex to this building was voted in 1935.[72]

The city of Dayton as incorporated in 1805 was governed by a board of seven trustees, a collector, a supervisor, and a marshal, all elected. The board,

---

66. U. S. Bureau of the Census, *Fifteenth Census of the United States, 1930, Manufactures*, III, 397, 413.
67. Beers, *op. cit.*, 536.
68. Ohio Auditor of State, *Annual Report, 1935*, 552.
69. Bond, "Memoirs of Benjamin Van Cleve," *loc. cit.*
70. Edgar, *op. cit.*, 78-84; Beers, *op. cit.*, 301-308, 462.
71. *Laws of Ohio*, III, 266.
72. Commissioners' Journal, vol. 16 [1935], 686.

known as the "Select Council of the Town of Dayton," chose one of its members as president.[73] He also served as mayor. All expenditures were authorized by a public vote of the freeholders and householders. For the first year's government the total expense was $72.[74] During the nineteenth century various changes in the municipal government transformed Dayton into the regular mayor-council form. In the era of reform which opened with the dawn of the twentieth century the demand for better government was heard in Dayton when a movement led by John H. Patterson, president of the National Cash Register Company, was set on foot to establish a commission-manager form of government. The Dayton Bureau of Municipal Research was established in October 1912, and produced a body of facts for the campaign for a commission charter.[75]

The movement was bitterly fought by the local Socialist Party who argued that it was a scheme to perpetuate the control of the city by local big business interests. The Socialists had become a powerful element in Dayton politics in 1911 when two of the party candidates were elected to the city council.[76] Similar to the situation when Galveston, Texas, accepted the commission system, the Dayton flood of 1913 assisted the movement in the city, when a specially appointed commission, headed by Patterson, efficiently administered the government during the flood and the reconstruction period. In 1914 the commissioner-manager form of government, somewhat similar in form to the original trustee system, went into operation in Dayton, the first large city to adopt it. Since then Dayton has, on the whole, experienced and efficient administration. Partisan politics have not been eliminated, and the Socialists have consistently opposed the administration, demanding the restoration of democratic institutions and procedure and wide powers of municipal ownership.[77]

In the Northwest Territory the Federalist Party was enthroned. Governor St. Clair, Secretary Winthrop Sargent, and Judge Jacob Burnet were all supporters of Federalism.[78] In the election of 1803, Jeremiah Morrow, the Republican

---

73. *Laws of Ohio*, III, 266.
74. Edgar, *op. cit.,* 106-107.
75. Conover, *op. cit.,* I, 325.
76. Sharts, *op. cit.,* 111.
77. Conover, *op. cit.,* I, 320-321; Sharts, *op. cit.,* 113-118.
78. Homer C. Hockett, *Western Influences on Political Parties to 1825. . .* Ohio State University *Bulletin*, XXII, No. 3, (1917), 54-55.

candidate for Congress, carried Montgomery County.[80] During the next several years Ohio Federalism tended to merge into Republicanism, and there was little division in Montgomery County politics until the War of 1812. At that time, however, the expansionist Republicans carried the county, favoring Madison over Clinton and electing a strong supporter of war to the state legislature.[81]

In 1824, when the old Republican Party began to break up, Montgomery County cast its vote for Jackson over Clay and Adams.[82] Developing business interests, especially in Dayton, due to the construction of the canal, and anxiety over Jackson's veto of the Maysville Road Bill in 1830, perhaps were the reasons why Montgomery County people choose National Republicans to the legislature in 1830.[83] Party division, however, was close during the transitional period of party politics occasioned by the rise of the Whigs. In 1832 two Democrats were elected from Montgomery County to the state legislature.[84] In 1840 the Whigs reached their greatest strength. During the campaign a great rally, attended by William Henry Harrison, was held at Dayton and is said to have attracted between 100,000 and 300,000 persons.[85] In that year the Whigs carried the county.[86] Again in 1842 a large Whig convention in Dayton, attended by Clay, was said to have attracted around 100,000.[87]

In the 1830s the slavery question now occupying the center of the political stage caused much dissension in Ohio cities, particularly in Dayton. In 1826 a colonization society was formed in the city, and in 1839 an anti-slavery society was organized. Anti-slavery leaders, James G. Birney, Reverend John Rankin, Dr Hibbard Jewett, Reverend Thomas E. Thomas, and ex-Senator Thomas Morris, were mobbed when they tried to lecture in Dayton. During the forties Montgomery County as a whole remained a Whig county. In 1855 it returned to the Democratic

---

80. Beers, *op. cit.,* 302.
81. *History of Dayton*, 143.
82. Eugene H. Roseboom, "Ohio in the Presidential Election of 1825," *Ohio State Arch. and Hist. Quarterly,* XXVI (1917), 153-224.
83. *History of Dayton*, 160; Eugene Holloway Roseboom and Frances Phelps Weisenburger, *A History of Ohio,* (New York, 1934), 154.
84. *History of Dayton*, 164.
85. Henry G. Hubbart, *The Older Middle West* (New York, 1936), 10
86. *History of Dayton*, 493.
87. Edgar C. Holt, *Party Politics in Ohio, 1840-1850, Ohio Historical Collections*, I (Columbus, 1931), 182.

fold,[88] probably due to the reaction of the Germans against the anti-foreign Know-Nothing Party which had gained strength in the election of 1854. By 1859 Montgomery County had again switched its support to the rising Republicans.[89] In the elections of 1860 and 1861 Montgomery County remained in the Republican column, but in 1862 its allegiance was to the Democrats.[90]

The South had furnished a market for many of the products of the Miami Valley, especially of manufactured goods and foodstuffs. It was believed by many, particularly those having family ties in the old south, that the continuance of the slaveholding system in the southern states was necessary for the continued prosperity of the Miami Valley.[91] During the War Between the states, Dayton became the center of the Peace Democrats, led by a Dayton citizen, Clement L. Vallandigham, who openly opposed the Lincoln administration and the war. Likewise, Dayton became a hotbed of the secret societies whose members were sympathetic to the South, the "Knights of the Golden Circle," the "Order of American Knights," and the "Sons of Liberty," of which Vallandigham became Supreme Commander in 1864.[92] The end of the war and the era of reconstruction found Montgomery County's citizens fairly equally divided in their adherence to the major political parties. In the county in 1868 Vallandigham defeated Schenck for Congress by a vote of 6,557 to 6,440, although the latter carried the third district which included Montgomery County. At the same time Grant received 6,502 votes to Seymour's 6,113 for the presidency. In 1869 the county gave 6,420 to Pendleton, the Democratic candidate for governor, and 6,163 to Hayes, the Republican.[93] Since that time the voting strength of the Democratic Party has slightly exceeded that of the Republicans in the county. Seven times since 1876 a majority of the votes have gone to the Republican candidate for the Presidency and eight times to the Democratic candidate. In 1920 James M. Cox, a citizen of Dayton and Democratic candidate for President, was defeated in his own county. Montgomery County gave President Roosevelt a decisive majority in 1932 and a far greater one in 1936.[94]

---

88. Porter, *op. cit.*, 17.
89. *Ibid.*, map, p. 26.
90. Shilling, *loc. cit.*
91. Hubbart, *op. cit.*, 156.
92. Mayo Fessler, "Secret Political Societies in the North during the Civil War," *Indiana Magazine of History*, XIV (1918), 183-286.
93. Ohio Secretary of State, *Annual Report, 1869*, 68, 97.
94. Ohio Secretary of State, *Election Statistics, 1932*, 102; *Dayton Journal*, Nov. 5, 1936.

The early settlers of Montgomery County brought with them the various religions of their communities. The Scotch and Scotch-Irish of the Pennsylvania, Kentucky, and other frontiers introduced Presbyterianism. The Beulah Presbyterian Church was organized in 1798 by John Patterson and a group of Kentuckians who settled on Beaver Creek in the southwestern quarter of Van Buren Township. In 1803 the influence of the Kentucky Revival of 1800 reached Beaver Creek, and the prominent evangelists, Robert Marshall, Richard McNemar, John Thompson, and James Kemper, all Presbyterians, held a great camp meeting. At this time it split occurred in the congregation, and the community divided into three sects, Presbyterians, New Lights, and Shakers.[95] The First Presbyterian Church at Dayton was organized probably in 1800.[96] Methodism, also carried by the Kentuckyans, reached the county as early as 1798, when the Reverend John Kobler preached the first sermon in Dayton and organized a class with eight members.[97] The Miami Circuit was organized in 1798, extending along the Miami and Little Miami Valleys as far north as the Dayton region.[98] The Baptists penetrated the valley and organized the Miami Baptist Association in 1798 and the Mad River Association in 1811.[99] Quakers, particularly from North Carolina, settled north of Dayton in Randolph Township and organized their church in 1807.[100]

German immigrants introduced the Dunker Church at least as early as 1801, when Jacob Miller, a minister, settled in the county.[101] The immigration of Germans to Twin Valley resulted in the establishment of the Lutheran, German Reformed, and United Brethren Churches in Montgomery County. In 1809 the Lutheran congregation, one of the oldest in Ohio, was organized.[102] Bishop Philander Chase established the Episcopal Church in Dayton about 1817, the Catholic Church was organized about 1831, and the Jewish Church was organized about the middle of the century. By 1860 the Methodists reported 44 churches; the Lutherans 11;

---

95. Edgar, *op. cit.*, 242.
96. Beers, *op. cit.*, 552.
97. Robert W. and Mary D. Steele, *Early Dayton* (Dayton) 1896), 233.
98. Beverley W. Bond, Jr., *The Civilization of the Old Northwest: A Study of Political, Social, and Economic Development, 1788-1812*. (New York, 1934), 475-476.
99. *Ibid.*, 471.
100. *Ibid.*, 474; Beers, *op. cit.*, 59.
101. Drury, *op. cit.*, I, 709.
102. Hentz, *Twin Valley*, 133, 173.
103. Beers, *op. cit.*, 659, 673-674.

Dunkers eight; Baptists seven; Presbyterians and German Reformed, each five; Christians, Catholics, and Unionists, each four; Quakers, two; and Shakers, Congregationalists, and Episcopalians, each one.[104] At the 1926 federal census of religious bodies Montgomery County had 104,556 church members, including 31,065 Roman Catholics; 12,921 United Brethren in Christ; 10,902 Lutheran; 10,013 Methodist (Episcopal); 8,012 Baptists; 5,351 Reformed; 3,993 Presbyterians; 2,392 Brethren (Conservative Dunkers); 1,889 Christians; and 1,871 Episcopalians.[105]

Benjamin Van Cleve opened the first school in the county in the Dayton blockhouse in 1799. Other schools were soon opened until by 18:10 it is estimated there were 10 in the county.[106] In 1808 the Dayton Academy was incorporated, the second secondary educational institution chartered in the state.[107] During the early years of Ohio's existence Montgomery was one of the leading counties in promoting educational legislation. People from Hamilton, Butler, and Montgomery Counties were the chief sponsors of the acts of 1803, 1805, 1810, 1817, and 1820 which prescribed the administration of Section 16 reserved in each township for educational purposes.[108] In 1836 a convention in the interest of free schools was held in Dayton, a part of the popular agitation taking place over the whole state. The first school houses in the county were built about 1838, and in 1840 three large school buildings were erected in Dayton under the leadership of Robert Steele.[109] In 1844 German schools were made a part of the regular city system, and in 1849 a special school for Negroes was opened.[110]

104. U. S. Bureau of the Census, *Eighth Census of the United States, 1860, Statistics*, 447, *et seq.*

105. U. S. Bureau of the Census, *Religious Bodies, 1926*, I, 656, *et seq.*

106. Beers, *op. cit.,* 309; Robert W. Steele. *The Public Schools and Libraries of Dayton* (Dayton, 1889), 6.

107. Edward A. Miller, "The History of Educational Legislation in Ohio," *Ohio State Arch. and Hist. Quarterly*. XXVII (1919), 1-21.

108. William McAlpine, "The Origin of Public Education in Ohio," *Ohio State Arch. Hist. Quarterly,* XXXVIII (1929), 409-447.

109. Steele. *The Public Schools*. 6, 16-17.

110. *Ibid.,* 21-22.

Among other educational and cultural influences was the Dayton public library, incorporated in 1805, the first to be chartered in Ohio. Although it was closed in 1835, it was reopened in 1847.[111] The first high school was established in Dayton in 1850. A normal school was set up in 1869. The Bonebreak Theological Seminary, a United Brethren institution, open in Dayton in 1871, and the Central Theological Seminary, a training school for ministers of the Reformed Church on the United States, was moved to Dayton in 1908. In 1860 the Miami Commercial College was founded, and about 1880 the Jacobs Business College was set up.[112] The University of Dayton, a Roman Catholic institution, was established in 1851. The German population of Dayton promoted an interest in music and perhaps caused the introduction of music to the public school curriculum in 1849. The consolidation of the Saengerbund and the Frosinn Society resulted in the formation of the Harmonia Society. In 1874 the Philharmonic Society was organized.[113] The interest in music has been great enough to support the Miami Valley Conservatory of Music, located in Dayton.[114] Another cultural contribution to Dayton and the surrounding community has been the erection of the Art Museum within recent years and the procuring of a valuable collection for it.

Dayton is perhaps best known as the home of the Wright brothers. During the World War, Dayton was the center of the aircraft industry of the War Department. Wright and Patterson Fields, northeast of the city, are well-equipped War Department fields. Wright field especially is devoted to experimental and testing work. Montgomery County has attained fame for its achievements in flood control. After the 1913 flood an extensive system of dams and reservoirs, administered as the Miami Conservancy District, was constructed at a cost of $33,000,000.[115] Among the public institutions located in the county are the Dayton State Hospital for the Insane and the National Home for Disabled Soldiers, also located at Dayton.

---

111. *Ibid.*
112. Drury, *op. cit.,* I, 437, 454, 466-469.
113. Robert O. Law Co., pub., *Memoirs of the Miami Valley* (Chicago, 1919), II, 106-107.
114. *Ibid.,* 113
115. William M. Gregory and William B. Guitteau, *History and Geography of Ohio* (Boston, 1922), 117.

The county as a political institution and as a subdivision of the state for purposes of political and judicial administration is of ancient origin.[1] In a form substantially similar in all general features and functions it has existed in England since early times, and in America since its settlement. As the tide of migration moved westward, following the American Revolution, the institutions of the seaboard states were transferred to the newer west, undergoing such alteration as best suited frontier conditions.[2]

The earliest provision for the organization of counties in what is now the state of Ohio was contained in the Ordinance of 1787, by which the government of the Northwest Territory was directed to "lay out the parts of the district in which the indian [sic] titles shall have been extinguished, into counties and townships, subject, however, to such alterations as may thereafter be made by the legislature."[3] The organization of county government, therefore, began before the organization of the state and before the adoption of a state constitution. Prior to statehood nine counties were organized, the first county lines were drawn in 1788.[4] The last county lines were altered in 1888, exactly 100 years later.[5]

The establishment of local government in the Northwest Territory was one of the first concerns of Governor St. Clair. The Ordinance of 1787 furnished the framework, but details of institutions had to be constructed. All county officials, under the provisions of the Ordinance, were made appointive by the governor. St. Clair, a former resident of Pennsylvania, in providing for local administration depended in a large part upon the Pennsylvania Code, which, in some instances,

---

1. Edward Channing, *A History of the United States* (New York, 1905), I, 425-426.

2. Beverly W Bond, Jr., *The Civilization of the Old Northwest: A Study of Political, Social, and Economic Development, 1788-1812* (New York, 1934), 58-59.

3. Clarence Edwin Carter, ed. and comp., *The Territorial Papers of the United States* (Washington, 1934), II, 44.

4. *Ibid.,* III, 279.

5. *Laws of Ohio,* LXXXV, 418; Randolph Chandler Downes, "Evolution of Ohio County Boundaries," *Ohio State Archaeological and Historical Quarterly,* XXXVI, (1927), 449.

was altered to meet the needs of pioneer communities.[6] The provisions for local administration were, for the most part, simple and effective. In each county the court of general quarter sessions of the peace, composed of three or more justices of the peace, served as a fiscal and administrative board of the county, estimating county expenditures, appointing tax commissioners, and providing for highway and bridge construction.[7] By the end of the decade the court was authorized to enter into contracts for building and repairing the county jail and the courthouse.[8] Other county officials appointed during the territorial period included a sheriff, a coroner, a recorder, a treasurer, a license commission, and justices and clerks of the various courts.[9]

Officers having been appointed, the next step in the organization of government was the establishment of a system of local courts. Evidence seems to indicate that the judicial system for the county had been carefully planned. The court of common pleas, composed of not less than three no more than five appointed judges, was an inferior court having general common law jurisdiction in the various counties with that of the supreme court.[10] The court of general quarter sessions, besides serving as a fiscal and administrative board of the county, had jurisdiction in lesser criminal cases.[11] A probate court, composed of a single judge, was given jurisdiction in probate and testamentary matters.[12]

---

6. The governor and judges were given power to "adopt and publish in the district such laws of the original states" as they thought necessary and these laws were to remain in force unless disapproved by Congress. In many cases the governor and judges had not adopted laws of the original states, as the ordinance stipulated, but had passed measures that conformed in spirit. Since there was some question of the legality of these laws St. Clair, in 1795, after the lower house of Congress disapproved of the laws passed at the legislative session by 1792, called a legislative station to revise the territorial Code. The commission, after sitting for three months, completed Maxwell's Code, named in honor of the printer, W. Maxwell. Few changes were made in the Maxwell Code by the territorial assembly which was elected in 1798. Carter, II, 43. The minutes of the legislative assembly are reproduced in *The Ohio State Archaeological and Historical Quarterly,* XXX (1921), 13-53.
7. Theodore Calvin Pease, comp., *The Laws of the Northwest Territory, 1788-1800,* 4, 36, 337; 69-70; 467-468; 74, 77, 453, 456, 485
8. *Ibid.,* 485.
9. *Ibid.,* 8, 24-25, 61, 68-69, 197.
10. *Ibid.,* 7.
11. *Ibid.,* 4-7.
12. *Ibid.,* 9.

In1795, following St. Clair's revision of the territorial code, circuit courts were established an orphans' courts were instituted.[13]

In the meantime the local government was further developed by the organization of civil townships. The governor and judges adopted a law from the Pennsylvania Code requiring the justices of the court of quarter sessions to divide each county into townships and appointed each a constable to act in townships and the county, a clerk, and one or more overseers of the poor.[14]

The territory entered the second stage of administration when, in 1798, the population having reached the requisite five thousand, the governor ordered the election of a representative assembly.[15] The system of local government continued as established by the governor and judges, and the transition was achieved without a disturbance of local administration. The admission of Ohio as a state did not, in the main, materially affect county organization and administration. The system of local government having been organized by the governor and judges and the legislature of the Northwest Territory, the basic offices were continued. Except for the provision for the election of a county sheriff and a county coroner in each county, two officials of utmost importance in pioneer communities, the constitution was silent on such matters as titles, number, and duties of officials.[16]

It devolved, therefore, upon the legislature to confer powers upon the county. In 1804 the legislature made provision for a board of county commissioners, composed of three members elected for a three-year term.[17] The board of county commissioners, supplanting the court of quarter sessions, became the administrative and fiscal board of the county. In 1803 the legislature, recognizing the need for a more adequate system of land records, provided for a recorder to be appointed by the court of common pleas for a seven-year term and for a surveyor to be appointed by the court of common pleas.[18]

---

13. *Ibid.*, 157, 181-188.
14. *Ibid.*, 37-41, 338. The system of local governmental administration was the result of sectional compromise, since it combined the county system of the southern and middle states with the elements of the New England town. Dwight G. McCarty, *The Territorial Governors of the Old Northwest: A Study in Territorial Administration,* (Iowa City, 1910), 53-54.
15. Carter, *op. cit.,* III, 514-515.
16. *Ohio Const., 1802,* Art. VI, sec. 1.
17. *Laws of Ohio*, II, 150.
18. *Ibid.,* I, 136, 90-93

Another act authorized the appointment of a county treasurer by the associate judges; a later one provided for his appointment by the county commissioners.[19]

The legislature also provided during its first session for a prosecuting attorney to be appointed by the supreme court to prosecute cases on behalf of the state.[20] In 1805 the appointing power was transferred to the court of common pleas.[21]

A new office was created in 1820 that of county auditor, first appointed by the legislature, had as his duty the preparation of the tax duplicate.[22] The county board of revision, the purpose of which was to correct some of the inequalities of assessments, was established in 1825. The first board of revision or equalization, as it was sometimes called, was composed of the commissioners, the auditor, and the assessors.[23]

The judicial power of the state in matters of law and equity was vested in the supreme court, the court of common pleas, and the justices' courts. The articles of the constitution provided for a court of common pleas to be composed of a president and associate justices. The members of the court, appointed by a joint ballot of both houses of the general assembly, were to hold court in three judicial circuits into which the state was to be divided by the legislature.[24] The court was assigned common law and chancery jurisdiction in all cases as provided by law.[25] To the court was assigned jurisdiction in probate and testamentary matters and in the appointment of guardians, functions performed during the territorial period by the probate court.[26] Finally, the court was authorized to appoint a clerk.[27]

The county offices created by the legislature were designed to transact the business of a state as yet unaffected by transformations wrought by industrialism and the problems presented by large urban areas. Aside from the maintenance of

---

19. *Ibid.,* I, 97-98; II, 154; XX, 264.
20. *Ibid.,* I, 50.
21. *Ibid.,* III, 47.
22. *Ibid.,* XVIII, 70.
23. *Ibid.,* XXIII, 68-69.
24. *Ohio Const., 1802,* Art. III, secs., 3, 8.
25. *Ibid.,* Art. III, sec. 3.
26. *Ibid.,* Art. III, sec. 5; Pease, *op. cit.,* 9.

county poorhouses, the county had no functions in the administration of public welfare.

As the wave of democratic philosophy swept across the country in the eighteen twenties and thirties there arose a demand not only for an extension for the franchise but also for the election of public officials. Accordingly the auditor became an elective official in 1821, the treasurer in 1827, the recorder in 1829, and the prosecuting attorney in 1833.[28]

While the legislature responded to the general demand for the election of county officials, there arose a further demand for a revision of the constitution which failed to meet the needs of an expanding state. This movement came as a result of dissatisfaction with the judicial system which place the burden of judicial administration upon four judges who had the task of holding court each year in all the counties.[29] Then, too, there arose a demand for the election of all public officials, for the prohibition of charters that granted special privileges, and for a limitation on the power of the legislature to create a state debt. In February 1850 the legislature, following a favorable popular vote on the proposition, called for the election of delegates to meet in convention in May. The constitution drafted by the delegates, was approved by special election on June 17, 1851. The constitution of 1851, like the constitution of 1802, failed to provide a definite form of government and administration. Aside from the constitutional provision for the election of a county treasurer, sheriff, and clerk of courts and recreating the probate court which had existed during the territorial period, the organic instrument was silent on the administrative duties of the county.[30] Again all matters pertaining to county government were entrusted to the legislature. While the legislature conferred certain powers upon the county, it was limited by constitutional provision which required all laws of a general nature to be uniform throughout the state.[31]

---

27. *Ibid.,* Art. III, sec. 9.

28. *Laws of Ohio,* XIX, 116; XXV, 25-32; XXVII, 65; XXXI, 13-14.

29. J.V. Smith, rep., *Official Reports of the Debates and Proceedings of the Ohio State Convention . . . held at Columbus commencing May 6, 1850, and at Cincinnati commencing December 2, 1850,* 597 *et seq.* [Jacob] Burnet, *Notes on the Early Settlement of the north-Western territory,* 356. See also the *Ohio State Journal,* December 11, 1840.

30. *Ohio Const. 1851,* Art. X, sec. 3; Art. IV, sec. 16; Art. IV, sec. 7.

31. *Ibid.,* Art. II, sec. 26.

The present administrative organization of Ohio county government presents a picture of extraordinary complexity. Each county quadrennially elects, besides the board of county commissioners, nine administrative officials: recorder, clerk of courts, probate judge, prosecuting attorney, coroner, sheriff, treasurer, auditor, and county engineer. While these officials conduct a major portion of the country's business, there is a variety of appointive officers and boards, as well as ex-officio commissioners. For convenience the work the county government may be classified under the following general heads: administration, judicial system, law enforcement, finance and taxation, elections, health, public welfare, and public works.

Administration

The board of county commissioners is the central feature of the present structure of county government. The functions of this board touch either directly or indirectly every other branch and department. The board is the agency in whose name actions for and against the county are brought. This board is empowered to determine certain matters of policy for the conduct of county affairs such as adoption of the budget, establishment of services left optional by law, and the authorization of improvement.[32] Thus, in a limited sense it constitutes the legislative branch of the county. The commissioners, however, had no ordinance-making powers. The board also functions as the central administrative body although much of the administration, centered in other elective offices, is beyond its immediate control. The county auditor was originally made secretary of the board and still functions as such in a majority of the counties.[33] Later provisions of the law permitted the board to appoint its own clerk, thus removing the duty from the auditor.

---

32. General Code, sec. 2421.
33. G. C. sec. 2566.

Judicial System

The constitution of 1851 made significant changes in the composition of the court of common pleas. The judges, heretofore appointed by the legislature, were made elective for a term not to exceed five years. For the purpose of electing judges the state was divided into nine districts. Each district was divided into three parts; one common pleas judge was to be elected in each division. Court was to be held in every district or county with such jurisdiction as should be provided by law.[34] The legislature made provision for the districts that left a jurisdiction of the court much as it had been in the earlier years of its existence.[35] The constitutional amendment of 1912 abolished the divisions and subdivisions provided by the constitution of 1851, and authorized the election of one or more common pleas judges in each county.[36]

The judicial system was extended in 1851 by the creation of district courts composed of one supreme court justice and several common pleas judges in each district.[37] For administrative purposes the nine common pleas districts were apportioned into five judicial circuits.[38] The courts were assigned original jurisdiction in the same matters as the supreme court and such appellate jurisdiction as might be provided by law.[39] The district courts, abolished by the constitutional amendment of 1883, were superseded by the circuit courts which were given the same jurisdiction as their predecessors. The state was divided into seven circuits. In each circuit three judges were to be elected.[40] The judicial system was again altered in 1912 when, by constitutional amendment, the circuits were renamed courts of appeals.[41] The state is divided into nine appellate districts. There are three judges in each district selected by the people of the district for a six-year term.[42]

---

34. *Ohio Const. 1851,* Art. IV, secs. 3, 4.
35. *Laws of Ohio,* LI, 145.
36. *Ohio Const. 1851,* (Amendment), Art. IV, sec. 3.
37. *Ohio Const. 1851,* Art. IV, sec. 5.
38. *Laws of Ohio,* L, 69.
39. *Ohio Const. 1851,* Art. IV, sec. 6.
40. *Ibid.,* Art. IV, sec. 6.
41. *Ibid.,* Art. IV. Sec. 6.
42. G. C. sec. 1514.

The constitution of 1851 re-created the probate court, which, existing during the territorial period, was abolished by the first constitution, its authority and jurisdiction being then vested in the courts of common pleas. Each county has one probate judge elected by the people for a four-year term.[43] By constitutional provision, the probate judge has original jurisdiction in probate and testamentary matters, the appointment of guardians, the settlement of the accounts of the executors, administrators, and guardians,[44] and the issuance of marriage licenses. An amendment to the constitution of 1912 authorized the common pleas judge, when petitioned by ten percent of the voters in counties having a population of less than sixty thousand, to submit to the voters at any general election the question of combining the probate and common pleas courts.[45] This combination exists in Adams, Henry, and Wyandot Counties.

Because of an increased amount of juvenile delinquency, the legislature, in 1904, authorized the judges of the court of common pleas, the probate court, and the insolvency courts where established to appoint one or more of their members as juvenile judges to hear cases involving neglected, dependent, and delinquent children.[46] In most Ohio counties the probate judge serves as judge of the juvenile court. In counties which have a court of domestic relations, as in Montgomery, the judge of that court serves in this capacity.

Law Enforcement

Closely related to the courts are the agencies of law enforcement in the county. Law enforcement is conducted by four officials: sheriff, prosecuting attorney, coroner, and the dog warden. These officials are concerned primarily with the enforcement of state laws, and leave the enforcement of municipal ordinances, and, in some instances, of state statutes in urban centers to municipal law-enforcement agencies.

---

46. *Laws of Ohio*, XCVII, 561-562.

The county sheriff, whose duties have been materially curbed by municipal law-enforcement agencies and the state highway patrol, has as his duty the enforcement of state laws.[47] He serves as custodian of the county jail,[48] and as an executive agent of the courts.[49] It has been estimated that approximately one-half of the sheriff's time is devoted to duties connected with the courts. The sheriff is restricted by lack of scientific equipment which has become essential to law enforcement.[50]

The county prosecuting attorney, the most important agent in the enforcement of criminal law, is directed by law to "inquire into the commission" of crime within his county, and to prosecute on behalf of the state all complaints, suits, and controversies to which the state is a party.[51] In conjunction with the state attorney general, he prosecutes in the supreme court cases arising in his county.[52] He acts also in a civil capacity as legal counsel for the commissioners and other county officials.[53] The prosecuting attorney may institute proceedings against an individual, but as a rule charges must be filed against the offender before action is taken. The prosecuting attorney has certain administrative duties such as serving as a member of the county budget commission and as a member of the board of sinking fund trustees.[54]

The county coroner has the ancient duty of determining the cause of death where death occurs under suspicious circumstances or by unlawful means,[55] the

---

47. G. C. sec. 2833. The sheriff's authority extends to all parts of the county, although for obvious practical purposes he rarely makes an arrest in incorporated areas.
48. G. C. sec. 3157.
49. G. C. sec. 2834.
50. *The Reorganization of County Government in Ohio*: *Report of the Governor's Commission on County Government,* 104. The sheriff system worked admirably in rural communities. From the standpoint of police administration, it is unsatisfactory in areas of dense population. In such areas there is need for a force of officers whose duty it is not merely to apprehend law violators but to prevent the infraction of the law by patrolling the territory. For an interesting discussion of some of the newer problems confronting law-enforcement agencies see Donald C. Stone, "The Police Attack Crime," *Nat. Mun. Review,* XXIV, (1935), 39-41.
51. G. C. sec. 2916.
52. G. C. sec. 2916.
53. G. C. sec. 2917.
54. *Laws of Ohio,* CXII, 399-400; CXV, pt. ii, 412; CXVI, 585; CVIII, pt. i, 700-702.
55. G. C. sec. 2856.

making of the proper distribution of property found on or about the deceased,[56] and the management of the county morgue.[57] It has been suggested, by authorities on county administration, that the office be abolished in the duties transferred to a medical examiner appointed by the prosecuting attorney.[58]

Another law-enforcement agent existing within the county is the dog warden. This official is appointed by and is responsible to the county commissioners. No special qualifications are required for the office. The dog warden has as his duty the enforcement of sections of the General Code relative to the licensing of dogs, the impounding and destruction of unlicensed dogs, and the payment of compensation for damages to livestock inflicted by dogs. The dog warden and his deputies, and in performance of their legal duties, have the same "police powers" as those conferred by statute upon sheriffs and police.[59] Prior to 1927 the duties now performed by the dog warden were performed by the county sheriff.[60]

Law enforcement in the county is defective in two respects: first, there is little or no co-ordination between the four agencies of law-enforcement, and second, there is little or no responsibility for neglect of duty. Evidence seems to indicate that the present inefficient and antiquated system could be corrected by consolidating all law-enforcing agencies into a county department of law enforcement under the immediate supervision of the county prosecuting attorney.[61]

The administration of criminal justice in the county has grown up in more or less hit-or-miss fashion and is for the most part unsatisfactory and extremely cumbersome. Arrests are made by the sheriff, or other police officer, who are theoretically officers of the state, but who are under little or no supervision. The accused person is brought before a local magistrate for a preliminary hearing. In the

---

56. G. C. secs. 2863, 2864.
57. G. C. sec. 2851-1.
58. W.F. Willoughby, *Principles of Judicial Administration,* 165-173. According to a recent act, effective June 8, 1937, only a licensed physician or a person who shall have previously served as coroner is eligible to fill the office. G. C. sec. 2856-3.
59. *Laws of Ohio,* CVIII, pt. I, 535; CXII, 348; G. C. sec. 5652-7.
60. *Laws of Ohio,* CVII, 535.
61. *Report of the Governor's Commission,* 117-122.

event the accused is committed, it is necessary, in most cases, to receive an indictment before a grand jury.[62]

Finance and Taxation

There are three types of financial functions performed by county officers: tax administration, handling of the fiscal affairs of the county, and the trusteeship of funds held for individuals in court procedure. The principal financial authorities are the board of commissioners, the auditor, and the treasurer. The commissioners levy taxes, appropriate funds, and authorize payments.[63] The auditor's primary duties are the keeping of accounts, the issuance of warrants, the valuation of real estate, and the preparation of the tax list.[64] The treasurer collects taxes, receives and has custody of county money, and disburses it upon warrant from the auditor.[65] Other functions relating to county finance are performed by the board of revision, budget commissioners, and board of sinking fund trustees.

During the early years of Ohio history, the principal sources of state and county revenue were the general property tax, the poll tax, and the fees received from licenses and permits to engage in certain kinds of business.[66]

A tax law enacted by the first territorial legislature (1799) designated certain types of property as taxable for county purposes. All houses in towns, town lots, out-lots, all water and wind mills, ferries, cattle and horses, were put on the county duplicate. A tax on land subsequently used also for county purposes, was originally devoted exclusively to the needs of the territorial government. County

---

62. For a criticism of the administration of criminal justice, see Edwin H. Sutherland, *Principles of Criminology,* chap., xiv; Willoughby, *op. cit.,* chaps. xi, xiv, xxxvi.

63. G. C. secs. 5630, 5637, 7419.

64. G. C. secs. 2570, 2573, 2583-2589.

65. G. C. secs. 2649, 2649-1, 2656, 2674.

66. An act of 1825 levied a tax on the income of attorneys, physicians, and surgeons for state purposes. Amount of tax was determined by the court of common pleas. Salmon P. Chase, comp., *The Statutes of Ohio and of the Northwest Territory, 1788-1883,* 1471. This act was repealed in 1852, Maskell E. Curwen, comp., *Public Statutes at Large of the State of Ohio,* 1755. The poll tax was perpetually abolished by constitutional authority in 1802. *Ohio Const. 1802,* Art. VIII, sec. 23.

officials were to assist in the administration of this tax as well as that of the county levy.[67]

In the course of time many additions were made to the original list of taxables. Taxable property came to include capital employed in merchandising (1826), and by exchange brokers (1825), pleasure carriages (1825), money loaned at interest (1831), and stock in steamboats.[68] In the latter year dividends of bank, insurance, and bridge companies were also made taxable.[69] The first act of a general nature directing the taxation of railroads was passed in 1851.[70] In 1862 a tax on the gross receipts of express and telegraph companies was enacted.[71] A levy on capital stock of freight lines was authorized in 1896.[72] Subsequent enactments brought into the category of "general property" the possessions of public utilities in general. By such accumulations "property," by the end of the nineteenth century, had become a much more inclusive term than it had been one hundred years earlier.

County agencies became even more useful with the discovery of new tax sources. When, at the opening of the twentieth century, the general property tax lost its importance as a revenue source for the state, taxes on inheritance and cigarettes, then, later, on gasoline, liquid fuel, liquor, retail sales, malt, and the like, took its place.[73] County officials continued to administer the general property tax, which was devoted henceforth to the uses of local governments, and they assisted in the administration of a number of those newer taxes as well.

The assistance rendered by county officials has been equally extensive in the system of issuing licenses and permits. The issuance of marriage licenses began during the territorial period (1788).[74] An act to license merchants, traders, and tavern keepers was passed in 1792.[75] Ferry licenses were authorized in 1799.[76]

---

67. Chase, *op. cit.*, 267-279. Previous acts of 1792 and 1795 were temporary in nature.
68. Chase, *op. cit.*, III, 1517, 1476; *Laws of Ohio*, XXIX, 272-280.
69. *Laws of Ohio*, XXIX, 302-303.
70. Curwen, *op. cit.*, 1647.
71. J. R. Sayler, comp. *The Statutes of the State of Ohio*, 301.
72. *Laws of Ohio*, XCII, 89-93.
73. Ohio Tax Commission, *Financing State and Local Government in Ohio, 1900-1932,* (mimeographed, Columbus, 1934)2.
74. Chase, *op. cit.*, I, 101.
75. Chase, *op. cit.*, I, 114-115.
76. Chase, *op. cit.*, I, 219.

With the passage of time one license after another has been required until unlicensed businesses have become something of an exception rather than the rule. Even with the increasing assumption of licensing authority by the state, county officials had continued to issue certain licenses assigned to their jurisdiction long ago.[77]

Under the early laws (1792) commissioners were to list the male inhabitants above the age of 18, stocks of cattle, yearly value of land, and other property. Valuation of this property was made by township and village assessors, appointed annually by the court of common pleas.[78] These local assessors, who became elective in 1795, were again appointed in 1799.[79] In 1825 the property valuation was assigned to a new official, the county assessor, also appointed by the court of common pleas.[80] This official, who became elective in 1827, was succeeded in turn, in 1841, by a township assessor to be elected annually.[81]

In conjunction with these administrators a system of real estate reappraisal was initiated. In 1846 county commissioners were directed to divide their counties into suitable districts and to appoint an assessor for each whose chief function should be to revise the valuation of real property.[82] An act of 1863 made these officers elective and provided for reappraisal every tenth year.[83] This was subsequently changed (1868) to every fifth year and in 1878 returned to the 10-year interval.[84]

In 1913 the assistance of county officers in tax administration was temporarily dispensed with and their duties were given to state officials. The county was again made an entire assessment district but district (or county) assessors were now to be appointed by the governor. The tax commission (established in 1910) was enjoined to supervise and direct the assessment of real and personal property.[85]

---

77. See pp. 34-35, 110, 129, 154, 207-208.
78. *Laws of the Territory of the United States Northwest of the River Ohio*, (Philadelphia and Cincinnati, 1792-1796), II, 17-18.
79. Chase, *op. cit.,* I, 169, 273.
80. Chase, *op. cit.,* II, 1477.
81. Curwen, *op. cit.,* 775-779.
82. Curwen, *op. cit.,* 1269.
83. Sayler, *op. cit.,* 413.
84. Sayler, *op. cit.,* 1641; *Laws of Ohio*, LXXV, 459.
85. *Laws of Ohio*, CIII, 786-787.

This attempt at unification of authority in the state was partially abandoned, however, in 1915, when assessment was returned to the county auditor and to elected township, village, and ward assessors.[86] In 1925 the latter officers were discontinued and the duties of assessment devolved upon the county auditor alone.[87]

The advent of the state tax commission brought no great alteration in the process of assessment. The county remains the basic unit and the county auditor continues to serve as an agent of the state. Though the state commission now assesses certain forms of property, certification is made to the county auditor. For example, public utilities are now assessed by the commission and proportional shares of the revenue are apportioned to the counties which contains such property.[88] Financial institutions report directly to the commission which certifies to each county auditor the assessment of each taxable deposit.[89] Intangible property owned by individuals and corporations, not otherwise accepted, is listed and valued by the county auditor. Returns showing more than $500 of taxable income are forwarded to the commission for appraisal and certified by it back to the county auditor.[90] From these certifications of the commission, the personal property lists returned to him by individuals, and the real estate assessment for which he is personally responsible, the auditor makes up the grand duplicate of real and personal property taxes.

The county continues to be the basic unit also in the matter of budgeting and the levying of taxes on property. In 1792 the courts of general quarter sessions were directed to estimate the sums needed to defray the cost of county government, specifying as nearly as possible the purpose for which such sums were necessary. This budget was to be laid before the governor and judges and approved by the legislature. Commissioners annually appointed for the purpose were to apportion or levy the tax.[91] In 1799 it became the duty of these commissioners to ascertain the

---

86. *Ibid.,* CVI, 246 *et seq.*
87. *Ibid.,* CXI, 486-487. Revaluation of real estate was required in 1925 and every sixth year thereafter.
88. G. C. sec. 5430.
89. G. C. secs. 5412, 5412-1.
90. *Report of the Governor's Commission,* 75.
91. Chase, *op. cit.,* I, 118-119.

probable expenses of the county as well as levy the tax–a duty which continued until refinements in administration were made necessary because of the increasing number of taxing authorities.[92]

In order to achieve some systematic arrangement in the county fiscal system, the function of estimating expenses, or budgeting, was consolidated in recent years in the hands of a county budget commission. Since the Ohio legislature, in 1911, established a tax rate limitation, it was necessary to establish a commission vested with authority to reduce the amounts set up in the annual tax budgets when the overlapping districts required more than the aggregate maximum tax rate permits.[93] Organized in 1911 the county budget commission was composed, for a time, of the auditor, the mayor of the largest municipality, and the prosecuting attorney. Taxing authorities in the county were directed to submit their budgets to this body through the agency of the auditor.[94] The board was authorized to make adjustments in the budgets, alterations which the taxing authority might appeal to the tax commission. The budget commission, directed in 1911 to certify its action to the auditor, was subsequently instructed to make such certification to the various taxing units which should themselves authorize the necessary tax levies and certify them to the auditor.[95] In 1927 the composition of this board was altered when the county treasurer replaced the mayor.[96]

Early appeals against unjust assessments (1792) were heard by judges of the general territorial court, common pleas judges, or justices of the general quarter sessions court.[97] After 1795 petitions for redress were directed to the county commissioners.[98] This appeal agency was superseded in 1825 by the board of equalization, composed of the commissioners, assessors, and auditor.[99] This agency continued to function through the following years with occasional changes in personnel.[100]

---

92. Chase, *op. cit.,* I, 276-277.
93. G. C. sec. 5625-3. Since 1934 there has been a limitation of ten mills on the dollar. G. C. sec. 5625-2.
94. *Laws of Ohio,* CII, 270-272.
95. G. C. sec. 5625-25.
96. *Laws of Ohio,* CXII, 399.
97. *Laws of the Territory . . . Northwest of the Ohio River,* II, 20-21.
98. Chase, *op. cit.,* I, 171.
99. Chase, *op. cit.,* II, 1476-92.
100. The county surveyor became a member at times, in 1868, for example Sayler, *op. cit.,* 1642.

With the reorganization of property tax administration in 1913 the function of tax revision was taken away from the county officers. In each district (county) the tax commission was directed to appoint three persons for the term of three years to form a district board of complaints.[101] An act of 1915 abolished this plan, however, and returned the function of revision to the care of county officials. A board composed of the treasurer, prosecuting attorney, probate judge, and the president of the board of county commissioners, was directed to appoint a county board of equalization.[102] This plan, too, was soon dispensed with. An act of 1917 constituted the county treasurer, the auditor, and the president of the board of commissioners as the county board of revision.[103]

The history of tax collection is equally intricate. The fiscal duties of the county treasurer, who now collects the property tax, comprised, in the very early period, only the receipt and custody of revenue funds. The actual collection was performed by other agencies. Due to the fact that in earlier years there were two district tax levies–one on land for territory and later the state, and one on other property for county purposes–tax collections involved a double operation and duplicate officials.

The collectors of the county levy assessed in 1792 were appointed by the judges of the court of common pleas who were empowered to designate the sheriff, constable, or any other suitable person to perform this function.[104] By provisions of an act of 1795 township collectors were appointed by tax commissioners and assessors.[105] From 1799 to 1805 taxes for county purposes were collected by county collectors.[106]

---

101. *Laws of Ohio*, CIII, 790-791.
102. *Ibid.*, CVI, 254-255.
103. *Ibid.*, CVII, 40; G. C. secs. 5580, 5596. See also pp. 242-244. Highest appellate jurisdiction, held originally by the general court and later (1805) by the associate judges of common pleas, was given, in 1825, to a state board of equalization composed of the state auditor and one member from each congressional district. With the establishment of the state tax commission that agency was made the final appeal. *Laws of Ohio*, III, 111; Chase, *op. cit.*, 1481; Curwen, *op. cit.*, 1784; G. C. sec. 5625-28.
104. Chase, *op. cit.*, I, 119.
105. Chase, *op. cit.*, I, 171.
106. Chase, *op. cit.*, I, 277.

An act of 1805 designated the township listers as collectors of the county levy but, in 1806, the commissioners were permitted to appoint a county collector instead if they believed such a course to be expedient. This arrangement remained in force until 1825.[107]

The statute of a general nature providing for a tax on land for territorial purposes was enacted in 1799. From 1799 to 1804 the collectors of county tax were to collect the territorial tax also.[108] In 1804, however, the county sheriff was specifically designated as the collector of the state tax.[109] From 1806 into 1816 the county commissioners were again permitted to use their own discretion as to whether a county or township collector should be appointed.[110] The county collector of the land tax mentioned in the statutes from 1816 to 1825 was, in all probability, the same official who collected the county tax, though due to a lack of definite terminology it is impossible to be certain.[111]

In 1825 the arrangement for a separate tax duplicate for state and county purposes was abolished and levies for both were made on the same property. In 1827 the office of county collector, who had performed that function in the intervening two years, was abolished and the treasurer, henceforth to be an elective officer, was given the duty of tax collection.[112]

The collection of certain taxes other than that on general property is performed by county agency. Thus, for example, inheritance taxes, authorized by the legislature in 1894, are computed by the auditor, adjusted by probate court, collected by the treasurer, and distributed to the proper agency by the auditor.[113] County auditors certify to the tax commission lists of persons licensed to engage in the business of selling cigarettes. County treasurers are the agents of the state treasurer for the sale of cigarette tax stamps.[114]

---

106. Chase, *op. cit.,* I, 277.
107. Chase, *op. cit.,* I, 471, 527; II, 771, 1384-85.
108. Chase, *op. cit.,* I, 270.
109. Chase, *op. cit.,* I, 415.
110. Chase, *op. cit.,* I, 537, 727; II, 973.
111. Chase, op. cit., II, 973, 1370-71.
112. *Laws of Ohio,* XXV, 25.
113. G. C. secs. 5338, 5341, 5348-11.
114. G. C. sec. 5894-1 *et seq.*

The tax on wines, cordials, and beer is collected by means of the sale of stamps by county treasurers in a manner similar to that employed in collecting the cigarette tax.[115] The tax on brewers' wort and malt is collected in an identical manner.[116]

The dispersal of administrative functions among county agencies is demonstrated more effectively, perhaps, in the issuance of licenses and permits which furnish a source of revenue for both the state and the county. The county auditor has issued, collected, and accounted for dog licenses from 1917 to the present;[117] he has issued and the treasurer has collected the fees from cigarettes (1893—),[118] malt (1933—),[119] peddlers' (1862—),[120] and show licenses (1827—).[121] Hunting and fishing licenses have been issued by the clerk of courts since 1904 and 1919 respectively.[122] In addition, the clerk has issued for the court of common pleas ferry licenses (1805—),[123] auctioneers' licenses (1818—),[124] and peddler's licenses (1810-1862).[125] Marriage licenses, issued from 1803 to 1851 by the clerk of courts, since the latter date, have been in the jurisdiction of the probate court.[126]

The establishment of a board of trustees of the sinking fund (1919) was a logical development in the county fiscal administration. This board, composed of the auditor, treasurer, and prosecuting attorney, has as its principal function the payment of bonds issued by the county and the investment in bonds of moneys credited to the sinking fund.

---

115. G. C. sec. 6064-42.
116. G. C. sec. 5545 *et seq.*
117. *Laws of Ohio,* CVII, 534.
118. Jay F. Laning, comp., *Revised Statutes of the State of Ohio,* (Norwalk, 1905), 1513.
119. G. C. sec. 5545-5 *et seq.*
120. Sayler, *op. cit.,* 273; G. C. sec. 6349.
121. Chase, *op. cit.,* III, 1582; G. C. secs. 6374, 6375.
122. *Laws of Ohio,* XCVII, 474; G. C. (Page and Adams) sec. 1430.
123. *Laws of Ohio,* III, 96; VIII, 107; XXIX, 447. Ferry licenses were issued by associate judges, 1803-1805. *Ibid.,* I, 94.
124. Chase, *op. cit.,* II, 1040; G. C. secs. 5864, 5869.
125. Chase, *op. cit.,* I, 670.
126. Chase, *op. cit.,* I, 354; *Ohio Const., 1851,* Art. IV, sec. 8.

Bonds issued in the process of county borrowing must be recorded in the office of the sinking fund trustees and signed by the auditor, as secretary of the board. The trustees certify to the board of commissioners the rate of tax necessary to provide a sinking fund for the payment of the principal and interest of the bonded indebtedness. The trustees are required to keep a full and complete record of transactions and a complete record of the funded debt of the county.[127]

Elections

During the first nine decades of Ohio history the county sheriff was charged with the duty of announcing the time and place of holding elections, providing ballot boxes, ballots, and other supplies, and the township trustees served as judges of the elections.[128] With slight alterations designed to facilitate the conduct of elections in municipalities, this system was continued until 1892. At that time there were created the offices of the state supervisor of elections and deputy state supervisors of elections with duties prescribed for the conduct and supervision of all elections in the state.[129] The secretary of state, designated as the state supervisor of elections, was authorized and instructed to appoint four deputy supervisors for each county, who, in turn, appointed in all precincts four judges and two clerks of elections.[130]

Under the present election laws, provision is made for a chief election officer, a board of elections in each county, and judges and clerks in each precinct. The board of elections in each county consists of four qualified electors in the county, the members of which are appointed by the secretary of state, two of such members being appointed on the first day of March in the even-numbered years to serve a four-year term.[131]

---

127. G. C. sec. 2976-18 *et seq.*
128. *Laws of Ohio,* I, 76-77; III, 331-332; VII, 113; XXIX, 44; L, 312; LXVIII, 68.
129. *Ibid.,* LXXXIX, 455. This act, however, did not apply to the election of school directors.
130. In 1870 each township, exclusive of the territory embraced within the limits of a municipal corporation which was divided into wards, composed an election precinct. See *Laws of Ohio,* LXVII, 47. An act of 1891 provided for the division of precincts in which 500 or more voters had been polled. *Ibid.,* LXXXVIII, 464.
131. G. C. secs. 4785-6, 4785-8.

In making appointments to the membership of the board, equal representation is given to the political party polling the highest and next highest number of votes for the office of governor in the last preceding state election. In this connection provision is made for party recommendations of persons for such appointments.[132]

Under the early election law the canvassing board was composed of the clerk of the court of common pleas and two justices of the peace called by him to his assistance.[133] The practice continued until 1892 when the board of state supervisors of elections succeeded to the duties formally performed by both the clerk of the court of common pleas and the county sheriff. The sheriff, however, continued to announce the time and place of holding elections in the county until January 1, 1930 when the board of elections assumed this historic duty.[134] The duty of canvassing the returns, under the present statutes, is performed by the board of elections. The board in each county is required, within five days after each general or special election, to canvas the returns, and to prepare abstracts of the votes cast.[135] A certified copy of the abstract is to be transmitted to the secretary of state, and another copy filed in the office of the board.[136] The board is required also to prepare and transmit to the president of the senate a separate abstract of the returns of election of governor, lieutenant governor, secretary of state, auditor of state, and attorney general.[137]

---

132. G.C. sec. 4785-9. Under the Ohio election law, it is the duty of the secretary of state to appoint persons so recommended, unless he has reason to believe that such a person would not be a competent member of the board.

133. *Laws of Ohio*, I, 83; III, 336-337; VII, 119-120; XXIX, 49; L, 316; LXI, 68; LXXXII, 30.

134. G. C. sec. 4785-5; *Laws of Ohio*, LXXXIX, 455; CXIII, 307. The election laws of Ohio were revised and recodified by an act of the general assembly, passed April 5, 1929. *Laws of Ohio*, CXIII, 307-413.

135. G. C. secs. 4785-152, 4785-153.

136. G. C. sec. 4785-153.3

137. *Ohio Const. 1851*, Art. III, sec. 3; G.C. sec. 4785-154.

Health

Prior to 1919 the county had few responsibilities regarding health administration. With the development of urban centers with congested areas the problem of health administration was brought to the attention of the legislature. Prior to the enactment of the present health code in 1919, jurisdiction in matters of health was vested in the cities villages and townships. Under the act of 1919 all villages and townships in the county were combined into a general health district under the supervision of a board appointed by the advisory council composed of the mayors of villages, and chairman of township trustees. Each city in the district is organized as a separate health district. Two general health districts or a general health district and the city health district located within such a district may combine.[138] All physicians are required to report communicable diseases to the district health commissioners who impose quarantines.[139]

The legislature has placed on the county commissioners the responsibility in the treatment of tuberculosis. Any county, regardless of its size, may employ nurses, operate clinics, and care for patients in private, municipal, or county sanatoriums. Any county having a population of 50,000 or more inhabitants may with the consent of the state department of health, erect and operate sanatoriums, and two or more counties may form districts for the same purpose. The sanatoriums are operated by special boards appointed by the county commissioners.[140]

Besides establishing sanatoriums for the treatment of tubercular patients counties are authorized to operate general hospitals. The county hospital is operated by a board appointed by the county commissioners.[141] Evidence seems to indicate that the county is a proper unit for hospital administration.

---

138. *Laws of Ohio,* CVIII, pt. I, 238; CVIII, pt. ii, 1085-86.
139. *Ibid.,* CVIII, pt. ii, 1088-89.
140. G. C. secs. 3148-1, 3148-3.
141. G. C. secs. 3127-3138-4.

Public Welfare

The administration of public welfare is one of the most complex and one of the most expensive functions of county government. The administration of institutional and outdoor relief is delegated to eight boards and commissions operating independently and with little regard for efficiency.

The administration of the county home is vested in the county commissioners and a superintendent appointed from a list of names of persons eligible under civil service regulations. Employees are appointed by the superintendent.[142]

Although provision was made for the institutional care of the county's indigent as early as 1816, it was not until after the conclusion of the War between the States when hundreds of Ohio children were left homeless, that the legislature enacted measures for the care of dependent children.[143] Prior to the act of 1865, the trustees of the poorhouses were authorized to apprentice dependent children. The administration of the children's home is vested in a board of trustees, appointed by the commissioners, and a superintendent appointed by the board of trustees.[144]

The board of county visitors, an agency for the examination of county institutions, was created by the general assembly in 1882. Until 1906 the board was appointed by the court of common pleas and after that date by the probate judge.[145] The board consists of six persons appointed for a term of three years.

In 1886 counties were required by law to provide relief for indigent soldiers and sailors and their dependent wives, children, and parents.[146] Soldiers' relief is administered by a commission consisting of three persons appointed by the court of common pleas for terms of three years. This commission, in turn, selects township and ward committees.[147]

In 1884 the legislature made provision for soldiers' burial committees in each county.[148]

---

142. G. C. secs. 2522, 2523.
143. *Laws of Ohio*, III, 276; VIII, 223-224.
144. G. C. secs. 3081, 3084.
145. *Laws of Ohio*, LXXIX, 107; LXXIII, 174; XCVIII, 28; G. C. secs. 3082-1.
146. *Laws of Ohio*, LXXXIII, 232-234.
147. G. C. secs. 2930, 2933.
148. *Laws of Ohio*, LXXXI, 146-147.

The administration of soldiers' burials is vested in committees consisting of two persons in each township and ward appointed by the county commissioners.[149]

Counties maintain a system of pensions for the needy blind. Prior to 1936 blind relief was administered in the county by the probate judge (1904-1908), by a blind relief commission appointed by the probate judge (1908-1913), and by the county commissioners (1913-1936).[150] The present system originated in 1936 when the legislature accepted the provisions of the Federal Social Security Act. Blind relief is financed by federal, state, and local funds and is administered in the state by the Ohio commission for blind and in the county by the county commissioners, whose decisions are subject to review by the Ohio commission for the blind.[151]

Prior to 1932 the county confined its relief activities to the institutional care of the indigent. Outdoor relief, except for those persons lacking a legal settlement, was provided and administered by the townships and cities. With the coming of the economic depression the resources of the municipalities and township proved inadequate for financing relief activities. Accordingly, in 1932, the legislature conferred on all counties the authority to care for the poor in their own homes. Funds for such purposes were provided by the issuance of bonds and by a diversion of gasoline taxes for financing such services. While the state relief commission, created for administering state relief, is required to pass upon local relief budgets, the county relief offices, administered by the county commissioners, provide relief services in the county.

Today old age pensions are relieving the counties of the increased burdens of institutional relief. This system, originating in 1933, provides for persons sixty-five or more years of age. No person may be granted a pension if the net value of his property is in excess of $3,000 or his annual income is in excess of $480.[152] The old age pension system is financed by state and federal funds and is administered by a division of the department of public welfare through county boards of aid of the aged.[153]

---

149. G.C. sec. 2950.

150. *Laws of Ohio,* XCVII, 392-394; XCIV, 56-58; CIII, 60.

151. *Ibid.,* XVIV, pt. ii, 195-200. See also pp. 3-4, 106, 260.

152. *Laws of Ohio,* CXV, pt. ii, 431-439; CXVI, pt. ii, 86-88, 216-221.

153.*Ibid.,* CXV, pt. ii, 431-439.

Under the provision of the initial act the county commissioners served as ex-officio members of the board of aid for the aged in the county. Since May 1, 1937, the chief of the division has been required by law to appoint an advisory board in each county consisting of five members. This board, appointed for a two-year term, succeeded to the duties formerly performed by the county commissioners.[154]

Aid to dependent children, although provided by the legislature in 1913 in the form of mothers' pensions, assumed a new significance, when, in 1936, the legislature accepted the provisions of the Federal Social Security Act. Aid to dependent children is financed by federal, state, and local funds. The administration of the act in the state is delegated to the department of public welfare and in Montgomery County to the probate judge serving as juvenile judge.[155]

Public Works

The responsibility for the administration of public works in the county rests with the board of county commissioners, county engineer, and sanitary engineer. The county commissioners, since the inauguration of county government, have had the responsibility with authorization and financing of public works. With the immense development of highway improvements, occasioned by the introduction of automobiles and trucks as means of transportation, public works became one of the most important functions of the county commissioners and consequently the county engineer, who, during the first one hundred and twenty years of his office, had as his principal duty the surveying of lands, received new duties and responsibilities with respect to the construction of roads, culverts, ditches, and in most cases bridges.[156] Within the last two decades the township roads, under the joint authority of the county and the township trustees, have been gradually absorbed by the county state system of highways.[157]

---

154. G. C. sec. 1359-12.
155. *Laws of Ohio,* CXVI, pt. ii, 188-196.
156. *Laws of Ohio,* XCVIII, 245-247; CVIII, pt. I, 497.
157. The centralization of highway construction was guaranteed under the road law of 1915. The township trustees, at one time one of the most important agencies in local highway construction, have become a local improvement board with powers to authorize but not to supervise road construction. *Laws of Ohio,* CV, 589-594.

The Ohio counties were formed to meet the needs of rural pioneer communities with a population spread relatively uniformly over the entire state. Recent decades have brought remarkable changes. Many sections of the state have become thoroughly industrialized, and, as a result of the change, have been forced to treat of such problems as housing, health, sanitation, police administration, scientific transportation, and sewage disposal. These problems with which the county organization has been unable to cope are rapidly taking the forms of city problems.

When it is considered that in 1930, of the 1,201,455 persons in Cuyahoga County 900,429 were in Cleveland, of the 361,055 people in Franklin County 290,564 were in Columbus, of the 589,356 people in Hamilton County 541,160 were in Cincinnati, and that of the 347,709 people in Lucas County 290,718 were in Toledo, it is not strange therefore that demands were made for a reorganization of county government to eliminate the waste and confusion occasioned by overlapping jurisdiction of county and municipal functions.[158]

In view of the growth of large cities and the confusion occasioned by the conflict of county and municipal powers, there has been an attempt to have a more satisfactory relationship between the two organs of local government. This took the form of a constitutional amendment, which, defeated in 1919, was placed on the ballot in 1933 by initiative petition and adopted by the electorate. The amendment provides:

"The general assembly shall provide by general law for the organization and government of counties, and may provide by general law–alternative form of county government. No alternative form shall become operative in any county until submitted to the electors therefore and approved by a majority of those voting thereon under regulations provided by law. Municipalities and townships shall have authority, with the consent of the county, to transfer to the county any of their powers or to revoke the

---

158. U. S. Bureau of the Census, *Fifteenth Census of the United States, 1930, Population*, III, pt. ii, 518, 520, 521, 525, C.A. Dykstra "Cleveland's Effort for City-County consolidation," *Nat. Mun. Review,* VIII (1919), 551-556.

transfer of any such power, under regulations provided by general law, but the rights of initiative and referendum shall be secured to . . . every measure . . . giving or withdrawing such consent."[159]

The constitutional amendment of 1933 altered the status of the county. Where the status of the county was formerly fixed by statute, it is now subject to local determination in the same manner as municipalities.

The arguments advanced in favor of the system fall under three heads;

1.   It makes possible a different form of government for urban centers where political, social, and economic conditions differ from those of rural counties.

2.   It promotes efficiency and economy by the elimination of duplicate officers and employees.

3.   It promotes efficiency by the centralization of power and responsibility.[160]

A commission on county government was appointed by Governor White in 1933 to formulate optional plans by county government for submission to the legislature.[161] Accordingly, in 1935, the commission submitted to the legislature ten bills embodying its recommendation as to matters of county reorganization. The major bills authorized three optional forms of county government, subject to adoption by local electorate: (1) a county manager plan, (2) the elective plan, (3) the appointed executive plan.[162] Of the ten bills presented, two became laws. One of these authorized the transfer to the county of any local governmental activity by voluntary agreement between the county and a local subdivision within the county. This measure, of course, opened the way for the consolidation of such activities as welfare, police, and sewer construction which need unification in counties having a large urban population.[163] The other act authorized the charter county to take over health administration, noninstitutional relief, and park construction.[164]

---

159. *Ohio Const. 1851,* (Amendment, adopted November 7, 1933), Art. X, sec. 1.
160. *The Ohio State Journal,* Art. X, sec. 1.
161. R. C. Atkinson, "County Home Rule Developments in Ohio," *Nat. Mun. Review,* XXIII (1934), 235.
162. R. C. Atkinson, "Ohio–Optional County Legislation, *Nat. Mun. Review,* XXIV (1935), 288.
163. *Laws of Ohio,* CXVI, 102-104.
164. *Ibid.,* CXVI, 132-135.

While the amendment offers an opportunity for the improvement of local government in counties in which large municipalities, no use has been made of it.[165] Present Franklin County with a population of 361,055 has essentially the same type of county government as Vinton County with a population of 10,287.[166]

While unsuccessful attempts have been made to correct some of the defects of county administration in areas containing large urban populations, little consideration has been given to rural counties where, due to a constant decline in population, the old governmental organization has become unduly expensive and ill-suited to the needs of the population. This is particularly true in the counties located in the southeastern and northwestern portions of the state where the population has steadily declined since 1880. There is a question as to whether the services of modern government in such counties can continue to be maintained without the consolidation of contiguous territory for purposes of administration. The Ohio Constitution, from its beginning in 1802, has contained a restriction upon the legislature regarding the minimum area of counties. None could be formed with less than 400 square miles–or reduced below that size.[167] With the development of modern means of transportation and communication this area is ridiculously small. The combination of administrative purposes by sparsely populated counties, having common social and economic interests would eliminate waste, overhead, and duplication of personnel.

Governmental service is constantly requiring the employment of better trained officials. Evidence seems to indicate that only by enlarging the size of the administrative area to make possible the specialization in work can the requisite degree of training and skill be secured in the performance of public service.[168]

---

165. Home rule charters were submitted to the voters in Hamilton, Cuyahoga, Lucas, and Mahoning Counties. Advocates of home rule attributed the defeat of these measures to politicians who saw in the scheme the destruction of the spoils system. See R.C. Atkinson, "Ohio– County Charter Elections," *Nat. Mun. Review,* XXIV (1935), 702-703.

166. U. S. Bureau of the Census, *Fifteenth Census of the United States, 1930, Population,* III, pt. ii, 520, 531.

167. *Ohio Const. 1802,* Art. VII, sec. 30; *Ohio Const. 1851,* Art. II, sec. 3.

168. Cf. H. Eliot Kaplan, "A Personal Program for County Service," *Nat. Mun. Review,* XXV (1936), 596-600.

The relation of the county to the state is also a matter of importance. As a result of radical changes in economic life, matters which were once a purely local interest and concern have become of state-wide importance. During recent years the old type of county organization has proved inadequate to meet the needs of modern civilization. Recognition of this fact is found in the steady growth of state control of such matters as public accounting, health and welfare administration, and law enforcement.

At the same time the county has definitely supplanted the township as the administrative unit. This is particularly noticeable in the substitution of the general health district for the township district, and the transfer of tax assessment from the township assessors to the county auditor. The county-state administration of highway maintenance and public welfare has been affected. Although many deplore the passing of the little red schoolhouse, the substitution of the county school district for the township area has resulted in better educational advantages for children residing in rural areas.

It is significant that modern invention has removed the necessity for the rural administrative units of such small proportions. The transfer of power from the smaller to the larger unit has arisen out of the desire for better service and economy. Little remains to justify the retention of the township.

Records System

It has been the duty of most officials since the beginning of county government to keep a record of the business of their offices. Differences in population between counties however, forced a wide variance and the recording as evidenced by the fact that several types of records were kept in the same book in some counties, and in others were kept in separate books. As indicated in detail in the office essays, preceding the records of each office, the legislature eventually prescribed not only what records were to be kept but also the content. In this field there was a remarkable advance following the adoption of the constitution of 1851. Such legislation assured some uniformity in the county records' system.

There are three county officials whose work is wholly or largely clerical, consisting mainly in the preparation and custody of records: the reorder, the clerk of courts, and the judge of probate court. They each have some part in the recording of instruments affecting the title of property and of other documents presented for record. The clerk of courts serves as clerk of both the court of common pleas and the court of appeals, and the probate judge maintains the records of his own court.

It is the duty of the county recorder to copy, index, and file documents authorized to be recorded in his office. The system of recording is prescribed in detail by law. In most counties recording is done by typewriter with considerable use of printed forms. The photographic method of copying is in use in Clark, Hamilton, Lucas, Montgomery, and Summit Counties. Deeds, mortgages, plats, and leases must be copied into separate books, and indexed by direct and reverse indexes.[169] The recorder is required, also, to prepare daily an alphabetical index to each instrument.[170]

The principal records of the clerk of courts are prescribed by statute. They include an appearance docket, trial docket, execution docket, journal, and a complete record of proceedings, a system of indexes, and a file of original papers.[171] The clerk is responsible for a variety of non-judicial records work of which the filing and indexing of certificates of title to motor vehicles is the major item. The act effective January 1, 1938, requires the clerk to issue certificates in triplicate and to file a duplicate of them.[172] At present the clerk of courts may act as the agent of the state for the sale of hunting, and fishing licenses.[173] He also issues auctioneers' and ferry licenses.[174]

The clerical office of the probate court performs the following services: the recording of miscellaneous instruments, including marriage licenses[175] and certificates of physicians, surgeons, and nurses which authorize them to practice their professions in the state.[176] The court record system of the office, originating in 1853 and continued by the probate code of 1931, is prescribed by statute and involves the proper keeping of papers in each case and copying materials in appropriate record books.[177]

---

169. G. C. secs. 2757, 2764.
170. G. C. secs. 2764, 2766.
171. G. C. secs. 2878, 2884, 2885.
172. G. C. sec. 6290-6.
173. G. C. sec. 1432.
174. G. C. secs. 5868-5869, 5947-5950.
175. *Ohio Const. 1851,* Art. IV, sec. 8.
176. *Laws of Ohio,* XCII, 45-47; XCIX, 499; CVI, 193.
177. *Ibid.,* CXIV, 321-322.

Few records are prescribed for the law-enforcement agencies. The county sheriff is required by law to keep at least three books: a foreign execution docket,[178] a cashbook,[179] and a jail register.[180] Indexes, direct and reverse, to the foreign execution docket were prescribed in 1925.[181] The system of recording is prescribed by statute. The county coroner's records consist of two: reports of findings in cases of unlawful death,[182] and an inventory of articles found on or about the body of the deceased.[183] Such records are required by law and the contents of the records minutely prescribed.

The number and type of records kept by county prosecuting attorneys vary widely. In Montgomery court records and delinquent tax records are kept, but in many of the counties in the state, no records or files are kept and individual memoranda are disposed of by the incumbent. In some of the counties, however, the records of the prosecuting attorney are kept on standard forms and include such records as a grand jury docket, a grand jury testimony record, and a criminal court docket. Since the prosecuting attorney is vested with large discretionary powers, there is need of special records and files. Such records according to authorities on judicial administration should include, among others, a permanent record of the names and addresses of witnesses, the deputy or division handling the case, and the reason for failure to prosecute, and the reason for which a *nolle prosequi* was asked and granted.

The records of the financial agencies of county government are prescribed by statute. Although records were kept in the earlier years, it was not until 1902 that the matter of keeping and the content of such records attracted the attention of the legislature. It was evident that accounts had not only been poorly kept but there had been little uniformity among the counties of the state. Accordingly, in 1902, the legislature enacted the most important and far-reaching laws on the subject. This act provided for a uniform system of accounting, auditing, and reporting, under the supervision of a newly-created bureau of inspection located in the office of the auditor of state. The act further provided for the annual examination of all finances

---

178. G. C. sec. 2837.
179. G. C. sec. 2839.
180. *Laws of Ohio*, XLI, 74; G.C. sec. 3158.
181. *Laws of Ohio*, CXI, 31.
182. G. C. sec. 2857.
183. G. C. sec. 2859.

of all public offices.[184]

The governor's commission on the reorganization of county government, after studying the county records' system and noting the illogical combination of administrative, judicial, and financing functions, made the following recommendations:[185]

1. County charters and optional forms of government should provide for a department of records and court service to take over the functions of the recorder and clerk of courts, the non-judicial record work of the probate court, and the functions of the sheriff as a court officer.

2. The issuance of licenses should be transferred from the clerk of courts to the department of finance.

3. Wider use should be made of the photographic process of recording in large counties.

4. Legislation should be adopted permitting the destruction of chattel mortgages and automobile bills of sale after they have ceased to have effect.

5. The requirement of three systems of indexes of cases in the clerk's office should be eliminated from the code and only the index of pending suits and living judgments should be required.

6. Provisions should be made in the rules of the common pleas court for service of process by mail and that method should be brought into general use.

Concurrently with the development of a record system, steps were taken to assure the proper restoration of damaged or dilapidated records treating of lands and surveys. The county engineer, when directed by the county commissioners, is required by law to transcribe any and all dilapidated maps and the records of plats and field notes of surveys from the records of the court of common pleas, auditor, recorder, or other officer in the state where they may be procured.[186] Similarly, the

---

184. *Laws of Ohio*, XCV, 511-515.
185. *Report of Governor's Commission,* 186-187. See also R.E. Heiges, *The Office of Sheriff in the Rural Counties of Ohio,* 55-56, 60-61.
186. G. C. sec. 2804.

county recorder, when authorized by the county commissioners, is required to transcribe from the records of the counties all deeds, mortgages, powers of attorney, and other instruments of writing, for the sale, conveyance, or encumbrance of lands, tenements, or hereditaments, situated within his county.[187]

The large accumulation of county records, occasioned by increasing governmental services, presents a serious problem. It is important, on the one hand, valuable space in county courthouses and other county depositories be not cluttered up with vast quantities of useless materials. On the other hand, it is important that every precaution be taken to prevent public officials from destroying valuable public records in order to make space for current business.

Within recent years photography has become an increasingly important aid in archival administration. The Ohio legislature, following the modern trends in recording, has enacted measures looking forward to the conservation of space in the county courthouses by permitting county officials to destroy records which have been reproduced photographically. Under this act, passed in 1937, any county official charged with keeping public records may, when the space requires it, have such records copied or reproduced by any photographic process and destroy the original papers. The original records, however, must be preserved until the time for filing legal proceedings based upon the documents shall have elapsed.[188]

While the legislature has attempted to enact legislation looking forward to the conservation of much needed space in county courthouses, a significant trend is to be observed in the increasing interest which is being displayed for a department of county archives where all noncurrent records may be properly housed, classified, listed, and made more readily accessible to those interested in consulting them. The arguments advanced in favor of such a system are: (1) that the preservation of county records should be viewed as a distinct function of county government, (2) that the administration of county archives should be under the direction of those qualified to serve efficiently and effectively both the needs of the administration and historians, (3) that the construction of county archives buildings for noncurrent records would make available more space for current business, which, at present, is seriously curtailed.

---

186. G.C. sec. 2804.
187. G.C. sec. 2763.
188. G.C. sec. 32-1.

In the field of archival administration the state, rather than the county, has been the experimental laboratory and the results have been eminently successful.[189]

---

189. For an interesting and informative article on the administration of state archives, see Charles M. Gates, "The Administration of State Archives," *The Pacific Northwest Quarterly,* XXIX (January 1938), No. 1; also in *The American Archivist,* I (July 1938), 130-141.

Even before Montgomery County was created, Dayton was recognized as the temporary seat of justice for the surrounding district. Therefore, with the establishment of the county, May 1, 1803, the three commissioners appointed to make the decision chose Dayton as the permanent county seat. The home of George Newcomb was selected as the scene of the first court[1] but the following year sessions were transferred to the house of Hugh McCullum.[2]

In 1806 a contract was let to Benjamin Archer for the erection of a courthouse at the northwest corner of Third and Main Streets. It was a two-story brick building, 38 by 42 feet, fronting on Main Street. In the rear facing Third Street stood the temporary jail, a one-story log structure, 16 by 30 feet. The courthouse cost $4,760[3] and was ready for occupancy in 1807.[4]

To meet the growing demands for more working and storage space, plans were completed early in 1816 for a new courthouse to be erected between the original building and the alley to the north. It was a brick construction, 46 feet wide by 20 feet deep, two stories high, and was completed in 1817 at the cost of $1,149.[5] However, the growth of Montgomery County exceeded its ability to meet the demand for larger public buildings. After razing the original courthouse in 1846 and before the completion in 1850 what is now called the "old courthouse," this second county building was used for most county purposes.[6]

The "old courthouse" which is of the Grecian temple type, has a frontage of 62 feet on Main Street, extends 127 feet west along third Street, and is 44 feet high. It is constructed of Dayton limestone and is fireproof throughout. The courthouse rests on a terrace reached by eight wide, stone steps and another flight of steps leads from the terrace to the portico. The front of the building is ornamented with six massive stone pillars which supports the roof of the portico. Two ornamented iron doors open from the portico into the main corridor. This corridor leads to the rotunda which is 20 feet in diameter and 42 feet high.

---

1. W. H. Beers and Co., pub., *History of Montgomery County*, (Chicago, 1882), 301-308.
2. Road and Commissioners' Record, volume A1 [1804-1823], 7-8.
3. *Ibid.,* 32-35.
4. Beers, *op. cit.,* 302-308.
5. Road and Commissioners' Record, volume, A1 [1802-1823], pp. 239-241.
6. A. W. Drury, *History of the City of Dayton and Montgomery County, Ohio* (Chicago and Dayton, 1909). I, 140.

Around the rotunda a circular flight of stone steps leads to the gallery of the courtroom on one side and to the second floor offices on the other. The courtroom which is now used by the probate court, opens from the rotunda and is elliptical in form. It occupies a space of both stories, and is lighted by a dome, whose eye is 43 feet high. The estimated cost of the building was $63,000.[7]

In 1857 the "old courthouse" became entirely inadequate for the needs of the county, but there were many years of delay because of changes in the plans and conflicting views as to style and utility, before the county building was razed and the "new courthouse" erected. This was completed in 1884 at a total estimated cost of $147, 945.[8]

The "new courthouse" which has a frontage depth of 150 feet and is 85 feet high is ornamented and faced entirely with dressed stone. It is of simple rather than ornate style and has usefulness rather than beauty as the main objective. The ground floor is elevated slightly above the street and is of easy access.[9]

The combined space of the two courthouses was still inadequate and early in 1916 outside space had to be leased.[10] In 1925 the county surveyor needed more space and a small addition was built in back of the new courthouse at a cost of $13,486,[11] in the same year a $10,000 addition for the auditor was constructed at the southeast corner of the building.[12] The clerk of courts required more room and this problem was met, about 1930, by partitioning off the east corridor on the second floor. In 1935 the county was paid a yearly rent of $12,000 for offices and storage space outside the courthouse. Plans were drawn for the construction of an "annex" to the new courthouse[13] and in 1936 the new, modern edition was completed. It is 140 feet long, 38 feet wide, and 65 feet high; made of wire brick and plain in architectural style, following closely the utilitarian style of the new courthouse. The approximate cost was $73,000 paid from the general funds and a federal grant as a Work Projects Administration project.[14]

-----

7. Beers, *op. cit.*, 462.
8. Beers, *op. cit.,* 463.
9. Drury, *op. cit.,* 178.
10. Commissioners' Journal, volume 23 [1916-1917], p. 252.
11. *Ibid.,* volume 31 [1925], p. 372.
12. *Ibid.,* p. 48.
13. *Ibid.,* volume 41 [1935], 565.
14. *Ibid.,* p. 686.

The records of the many county offices formerly stored in the new courthouse attic and in the basement, have been arranged in a systematic and orderly manner in the new record rooms recently constructed in the old courthouse basement. This much needed Improvement makes these older records more accessible to the user.

The location, condition, and facilities for housing and care of the records of the various departments are given detailed treatment on the following pages. Locations, unless otherwise noted, are in the courthouse. Floor plans of both the old and new courthouses and the annex, at the end of this chapter, will facilitate the finding of depositories.

County Commissioners. This office is located on the first floor of the new courthouse, south side of the building, and consists of one room, with two small offices partitioned off, floor space 25 by 50 feet. The bound records are kept on roller type shelves along the walls and roller shelves under the counters. Unbound records are kept in steel file boxes. All records are easily accessible. The rooms are fairly well lighted and ventilation is good. The commissioners' records are housed in this office, in the auditor's office and record room, in the clerk of courts' record room 1, and the older bound records in the commissioners' record room F in the basement. The records of this office were in custody of the auditor who served as commissioners clerk until June 29, 1908, when the county commissioners appointed a full-time commissioners' clerk.[15] The sanitary department has one room west of the commissioners' office; all records of this department are housed here.

Aid for the Blind. The blind relief office, 18 x 24 feet, is on the first floor of the new courthouse on the north side of the building. All records are kept in a steel file cabinet against the west wall. Lighting and ventilation are good. Some older records are housed in the county commissioners' office.

Relief Administration. This department occupies the entire second floor of the Barrar Building which is located on the southeast corner of Fifth and Stone Streets. There are four offices, separated by glass partitions, built along the west wall. All records are kept in steel cabinets and file drawers. In the main room the cabinets are placed back to back in the center of the room. The more active records are kept in file boxes on desks. All records are in good condition.

---

15. Commissioners' Journal, volume 18 [1908], p. 108.

The rooms are fairly well lighted and ventilated. Relief and CCC Records are housed in these offices.

The NYA records are housed in the NYA offices which occupy two rooms in the southeast corner of the second floor of the Beckel Building, 8 North Jefferson Street. The records are all loose-leaf and are kept in steel file cabinets conveniently placed along the east wall of the south room. All records are in good condition, being free from dust and dirt. Lighting and ventilation are fair, and there is ample space available for expansion if needed.

Recorder. This office is in the northwest wing and annex of the new courthouse on the first floor, and consists of three rooms, with a floor area of 106 by 30 feet. Most of the records are kept in these rooms. The bound records are on steel roller shelves along the walls and under the counters. Unbounded records are in steel cabinets. The rooms are exceptionally well lighted and ventilated. A few of the old records are in the recorder's record room in the basement of the old courthouse. Records are all in good condition.

Clerk of Courts. This department is in the northeast corner, second floor of the new courthouse. This suite consists of three rooms and the vault. The clerk's main office, 52 by 32 feet, is divided by a wood counter. Bound records are kept on steel shelving along the walls wherever space is available. These shelves are protected to a certain degree from fire and dust by metal curtains. Unbound records are kept in steel file cabinets, placed near the center of the room, and in other convenient places. This office also has a fireproof vault. All records are in good condition, and are generally accessible. Windows do not provide enough natural light, making it necessary to use artificial light most of the time. Ventilation is good.

The room just south and adjoining the clerk's main office is used mostly for auto registration. The records in this room are kept in steel file cabinets, placed along walls, and some near the center of the room. While the room is not crowded, there is little space left for expansion. Windows furnished most of the light, but artificial light is used in some parts of the room. Ventilation is good. All records are in good condition, and are so placed that they are easily accessible when needed for reference.

The clerk of courts also occupies a small room on the east side of the building. This room was provided by laying a floor in the stairwell between the second and third floors, and building a partition across part of the hall. This room is used for registration of motor vehicle bills of sale. Bound records are kept in steel file cabinets. All records are in good condition, and are easily accessible when needed for reference. The room is very crowded and poorly lighted. Artificial lights are used constantly and two windows furnished the ventilation.

The clerk of courts' record rooms are located in the basement of the old courthouse, on the east and south sides of the building. The records housed in these rooms are old, and seldom used for reference. Bound records are kept on wooden shelves, and most of them are in good condition. Unbound records are kept in steel filing cabinets and heavy fiber boxes placed on wooden shelves. These rooms have no ventilation and artificial light is the only light available. While these rooms are quite crowded, there is still some space available if needed. There are several volumes belonging to the clerk of courts house in the assignment commissioners' office.

Court of Common Pleas. The records of this court are in custody of the clerk of courts. Conditions of housing are described in the paragraphs pertaining to that office.

Court of Domestic Relations. The records of this court and the juvenile court are in the custody of the clerk of courts. Conditions of housing are described in the paragraphs pertaining to the clerk of courts.

Aid to Dependent Children. This office consists of three rooms on the north side of the third floor of the new courthouse; the reception room, 12 by 18 feet; and two offices, 15 by 18 feet and 7 by 13 feet, respectively. The records are kept in steel file cabinets in both of these offices. There are also a few records housed in the clerk of courts' office.

Assignment Commissioners. This office is on the second floor of the new courthouse annex. The room, which is 12 by 10 feet, is shared with the jury commissioners. All records are kept in a large desk and under a steel counter on shelves, and are in good condition. Lighting and ventilation in this office are excellent.

Probation Department. This department has two rooms and is located in the north side of the new courthouse on the third floor. The waiting room has no windows, the only natural light is furnished by a skylight. The room north of the waiting room is the main office and is separated from the waiting room by a partition. This room has two windows which furnish sufficient light and ventilation. The room east of the probation department rooms is the court stenographer's room, but it also houses the records of the probation department. This room which may be entered from the corridor or from the main office of the probation department, has two windows. Probation records are kept in a steel file cabinet, 118 by 134 by 15, which stands against the west wall. Bound records are on shelves, 40 by 27.5 by 15, and unbound records are in file drawers. All records are in good condition and ample space is available for expansion.

Supreme Court. Records of the defunct county supreme court are in the clerk of courts' record rooms in the basement of the old courthouse.

Superior Court. The clerk of courts' record room in the basement of the old courthouse, house the records of the defunct superior court.

Court of Appeals. The records of this court are in custody of the clerk of courts. Housing conditions of these records are described in the paragraphs above devoted to the clerk of courts' office.

Probate Court. The probate court offices occupy the entire first floor of the old courthouse, and the courtroom the entire west end of the building. The courtroom, which is entered from the main corridor, has very little natural light, and is poorly ventilated. However, no records are housed here. The probate office room 1 or clerk's office is located in the southeast corner of the building, just off the main corridor. The unbound records in this room are kept in wooden file cabinets built along the east wall. The bound records are kept on shelves beneath an ell-shaped counter which serves as a desk, and on shelving on the west wall, just between the inside and outside doors. All records are in good condition, and are readily accessible, but the room is small, and there is no space available for additional shelving. Lighting and ventilation are fair. The typists' room, or room 2, which adjoins the clerk's office on the west side is also entered from the main corridor. The unbound records here are kept in steel file cabinets, placed wherever space is available. The bound records are kept beneath and above a short counter just inside the corridor door, against the west wall. These records are in good condition, and are convenient for reference. Lighting and ventilation are fair. A small room west of and adjoining the typists' room is occupied by the deputies. The records in this room are kept in a steel file cabinet placed against the east wall. The room is crowded, inadequately lighted, and poorly ventilated.

On the north side of the corridor are the probate judge's private office and the stenographer's room. The records in the stenographer's room are kept in steel file cabinets placed against the south wall. Both of these rooms are well lighted and ventilated. A corridor connecting the new courthouse with the old, separates these two rooms from the marriage license bureau, which is located on the east side of the building. This room is small, and is very poorly lighted and ventilated, having only one window on the north side. The records housed here are kept on wood shelving built along the south and east walls. All are in good condition. The room is quite crowded, and there is no space available for expansion.

The probate record rooms, four in number, are located in the basement of the old courthouse on the west side of the building. The bound records are kept on wooden shelving. The unbound records are kept in steel file cabinets. All bound records are covered with heavy canvas, and with the exception of the very oldest volumes are in good condition. These rooms have no ventilation or natural light, and at times become damp, but are always kept clean,

Jury Commissioners. Jury commissioners share a room on the second floor, new courthouse annex, with the assignment commissioner. For housing conditions, see the above paragraphs pertaining to that office.

Grand Jury. No separate records are kept by this agency.

Petit Jury. No separate records are kept by the petit jury.

Prosecuting Attorney. This office is located on the second floor of the new courthouse annex and occupies the entire west end of the building. It consists of a reception room, main office, secretary's office, library, and six offices for assistant prosecuting attorneys. The bound records are kept on wooden shelving in the corridor. The unbound records are kept in steel file cabinets and in a movable steel vault in the office of the prosecuting attorney's secretary. All records are in good condition and are readily available for reference. Lighting and ventilation are good. The secretary's room is rather crowded, but all other rooms have available space for expansion.

Coroner. The headquarters of the coroner are in the private office of the incumbent, Dr. Robert D. Snyder, 1019 South Brown Street, Dayton, Ohio. The records are kept in filed drawers on top of a steel filing cabinet. They are in good condition and readily available for reference.

Sheriff. This office, consisting of two rooms with the floor area of 40 by 24 feet, and a vault is located on the second floor of the new courthouse, southeast corner of the building. Unbound records are kept in steel file cabinets and bound records are on steel shelving along the walls on the end on shelves under the counter. A large vault built in the north wall contains some bound and unbound records. Most other records are in good condition, others fair. There is sufficient natural light, but the ventilation is poor. The sheriff also has an office in the county jail which contains no records. Some of the older records of the sheriff's office are in the clerk of courts' record room 1 in the basement of the old courthouse and in a small attic in the county jail. Records in the jail attic are in very bad condition; the room has no ventilation and is very musty and dirty.

Dog Warden. The dog warden's office is located in the Animal Shelter, Patterson Boulevard, Dayton, Ohio. The shelter consists of two rooms, the reception-waiting room and the warden's office. The records are kept in steel file cabinets along the walls and in desk drawers in the office of the warden. All records are in good condition and easily accessible. Lighting, heating, and ventilation are good.

Auditor. This office occupies three office rooms and a vault on the first floor, southeast corner of the new courthouse, with a floor area of 56 by 42 feet. The bound records are kept on roller type shelves along the walls and under the counters. Unbound records are in steel file boxes. Some bound and unbound records are in a fireproof vault on the north side of the inter office. Lighting and ventilation are good.

Some personal tax records are kept in the auditor's personal tax department, a room 12 by 34 feet in the basement of the new courthouse, south side. The bound records are on steel shelves along the walls and the unbound records are in steel file cabinets. Lighting and ventilation are fair. Other tax records are in the auditor's taxation and appraisal department, on the third floor of the new courthouse. The bound records are on steel shelves along the walls; the unbound records in steel file cabinets. Lighting and ventilation are good.

Other depositories of the auditor's records are the vendor's license room in the southeast corner of the new courthouse, the dog license bureau just west of and adjoining the license room, and a record of payment of mothers' pensions in the aid to dependent children's office. Older volumes and unbound records are in the auditor's record rooms in the basement of the new courthouse. These record rooms are fairly well lighted but ventilation is very poor.

Treasurer. This office consisting of two rooms and a vault, is in the northeast corner of the first floor of the new courthouse. The main office has a floor area of 80 by 30 feet; the steel vault, in the southeast corner of the treasurer's office, 8 by 8 feet; and the sales tax department just west of the treasurer's office has a floor space of 16 by 13 feet. All of the current and some of the permanent records are kept in the office and in the vault. The older ones are kept in the auditor's record room in the basement of the new courthouse. All bound records are kept on steel roller shelves along the walls and under counters and in the vault. Unbound records are kept in steel filed boxes. The rooms are fairly well lighted, but the ventilation is poor.

Budget Commissioners. The records of the budget commissioners are kept by the county auditor and are housed in his office and room 3.

Board of Revision. The current records of this board are in custody of the auditor in office room 3 and the older records are in the basement record rooms.

Board of Trustees of the Sinking Fund. Records are in custody of the auditor in office room 3.

Board of Elections. This office which is in the basement of the new courthouse annex, has 4800 square feet of floor space. There are 200 square feet of counters placed along the north side of the corridor, underneath which are 37 file cabinets for the bound records. In the center of the room are 13 steel filing cabinets which contain the unbound records. There is a fireproof vault, 32 by 8 feet, accessible by a steel door in the wall at the south side of the room. The lighting, heating, and ventilation are excellent.

Board of Education. The board of education office consists of two rooms on the second floor of the courthouse, southeast corners; the reception room, 18 by 18 feet; and the office, 18 by 34 feet. Unbound records are in steel file cabinets and the office. Bound records are kept in a steel vault. The vault is a movable type and is at present placed against the west wall of the reception room. All records are in good condition. Lighting and ventilation are good.

Board of Health. The office of the board of health is now located on the second floor in the Cooper Building, northeast corner of the Second and Main Street, Dayton Ohio. This office occupies five rooms, two of which are used as record rooms. The main office is used by clerks, and also as a reception room. Just south of the main office are two small rooms which are occupied by the doctor in charge. Current loose-leaf and card records are kept in fiber file boxes on the desk of the clerks. One wooden file cabinet placed against the east wall of the main office also contains some unbound records. Unbound records and folders, and bound records not frequently used for reference are kept in the two record rooms north of the main office. All records are in good condition.

Large windows furnish sufficient natural light and good ventilation in summer. Steam heat is used in winter. Ample space is available for expansion if needed.

Board of Trustees of the Stillwater Sanatorium. This sanatorium, also known as the District Tuberculosis Hospital, serves Montgomery and Preble Counties and is located on State Route 48, about nine miles north of Dayton. The first permanent building was authorized in April 1916,[16] and was first occupied in April 1918. On January 31, 1938, the board of county commissioners authorized the erection of an entirely modern, fireproof structure on the grounds just south of the old building.[17] The office of the hospital consists of one room located on the main floor at the west end of the building. The bound records are kept on a shelf under the counter and unbound records are in steel file boxes on the counter. Clinical charts and X-ray records, seldom needed for reference, are kept in steel file cabinets in the basement on the south side of the building. One large steel vault located in a small room in the rear of the office, contains all the financial records. All records are in good condition. The card index system of filing makes them easily accessible at all times.

Superintendent of the County Home. This institution was established December 6, 1825.[18] The original site, purchased April 10, 1826, contained 160 acres in the northeast corner of Jefferson Township, three-quarters of a mile south of Drexel, Ohio, now known as 601 Infirmary Road. Since that time additional land has been purchased and the present site contains 244 acres. The original building has been enlarged to meet a growing population and new outbuildings and a laundry added.[19] The admission building was authorized by the county commissioners on June 6, 1908,[20] and a new wing was added, March 12, 1915.[21]

---

16. Commissioners; Journal, volume 23 [1916], p. 30.

17. *Ibid.,* volume 44 [1938], p. 67.

18. Road and Commissioners' Record, volume B [1823-1840], p. 28.

19. Commissioners' Record, volume 4 [1859-1865], p. 326; volume 7 [1883-1894], p. 383; volume 8 [1885], p. 168.

20. Commissioners' Journal, volume 18 [1908] p. 397.

21. *Ibid.,* volume 22 [1915], p. 149.

The records of the county home are kept in the office of the superintendent which consists of one room, just off the main entrance of the administration building. Bound records are kept on open shelves along the wall and unbound records are in steel cabinets placed along the west wall. Most of the records are in good condition. Ample space is provided and all the records are readily accessible. All records are located at the county home except six volumes of minutes of the directors, 1854-1912, which are housed in the commissioners' record room F in the basement of the new courthouse.

Board of Trustees of the Children's Home. The Montgomery County Children's home was established November 28, 1866.[22] On March 23, 1867, land was purchased on Summit Street, Dayton, Ohio, by the county commissioners for the erection of a building to be devoted to the care of indigent children.[23] The site for the present home, a 20-acre tract at 3304 North Main Street, Dayton, was accepted by the county commissioners as a gift from Dr. Shawen, on March 10, 1926.[24] There are ten cottages, an administration building, swimming pool, playgrounds, auditorium, and laundry. The records of the home are in the administration office which consists of one room on the north side of the administration building. The bound records are on steel shelves along the walls and unbound records are in steel file cabinets. All records are in good condition. Lighting and ventilation are excellent.

Board of County Visitors. No separate records are kept by this board.

Soldiers' Relief Commission. This office, located on a mezzanine floor between second and third floors of the new courthouse, occupies two rooms: the reception room, 12 by 18 feet; and the office, 14 by 14 feet. The records, all in good condition, are kept in a 36-cubic-foot metal filing cabinet in the office. Lighting and ventilation are fair.

Soldiers' Burial Commission. This commission keeps no separate records.

---

22. Commissioners' Record, volume 5 [1866-1867], p. 147.
23. *Ibid.,* p. 175.
24. Commissioners' Journal, volume 32 [1926], p. 273.

Board of Aid for the Aged. The office of the board of aid for the aged is located on the fourth floor of the Elk's Building, southeast corner of Third and Jefferson Streets. This office occupies six rooms, all separated by wood and glass partitions. The reception room is just opposite the elevator. Adjoining this room is a typists' room, the intake room, investigators' room, and two private offices. All records are kept in metal filing cabinets, conveniently place so that when needed for reference they are readily accessible, and all are in good condition. The rooms are well ventilated and have sufficient natural light. There is ample space available for expansion.

County Engineer. Office of the engineer is in the west end of the first floor of the new courthouse, and in the sanitary department which adjoins on the east. In the engineer's office, which has a floor area 60 by 50 feet, the unbound records are kept in filing cabinets and bound records are on shelves. In the sanitary department on the south side of the office is a file, 3 by 3.5 feet, for maps. Lighting and ventilation are fair.

Board of Directors of the Miami Conservancy District. This district was established June 28, 1915.[25] It includes portions of the following nine counties: Montgomery, Shelby, Miami, Clark, Green, Warren, Preble, Butler, and Hamilton. The conservancy building, 38 East Monument Avenue, Dayton, consists of three floors. The main floor houses the drafting room on the north side of the building and the director's room just across the corridor on the south side of the building. The front room, facing east, and covering the entire end of the building, contains exhibits of different kinds of rocks and soil, kept in glass cases.

The drafting room records, consisting of maps, tracings, and blueprints, are kept in wooden cabinets and plan files. The card index system is kept in steel file boxes. The system of filing used makes it possible to find readily any map or drawing when needed for reference. All records are in good condition.

The bookkeeping department occupies the entire second floor. It is divided into ten rooms, by wood and glass partitions. Inactive records are in the third floor record room. This room which is somewhat smaller than the rest, is used entirely as a record room. The unbound records are kept in steel file cabinets placed against the walls and bound records are kept in enclosed steel cabinets which are placed on top of the file cabinets containing unbound records.

---

25. Common Pleas Record, volume 90 [1915], p. 222.

These records are in good condition, free from dust and dirt, and are easily accessible at all times. The Conservancy Building is fireproof, well lighted, and properly ventilated.

Agricultural Society. The present Montgomery County Agricultural Society was organized May 15, 1890.[26] The records are kept in the office of the secretary of the Montgomery County Fair board, 709 Reibold Building, Dayton, and in the Administration Building, County Fairgrounds, 1047 South Main Street, Dayton. The records in the Reibold Building are kept in a fireproof vault and those in the Administration Building are in steel file cabinets. All are in good condition.

Agricultural Extension Agents. The office of the agricultural extension service consists of one room on the third floor of the Federal Building, room number 313 on the south side of the building. Records are kept in steel file cabinets, placed against the north and south walls. All records are in good condition, and readily accessible at all times. Lighting and ventilation are good.

Law Library. The library occupies the third floor of the new courthouse annex. Except for a small office in the southeast corner, the entire floor is used for filing of volumes, and for reading, study, and consultation purposes. Housed in a fireproof structure of modern design and construction, the heat, light, ventilation, and other facilities are of adequate and commendable character. From an initial foundation of 200 volumes, its holdings have increased until it now comprises 27,000 volumes. It is maintained and supervised by the Montgomery County Bar Association.

---

26. Commissioners' Record, volume 29 [1890], p. 209.

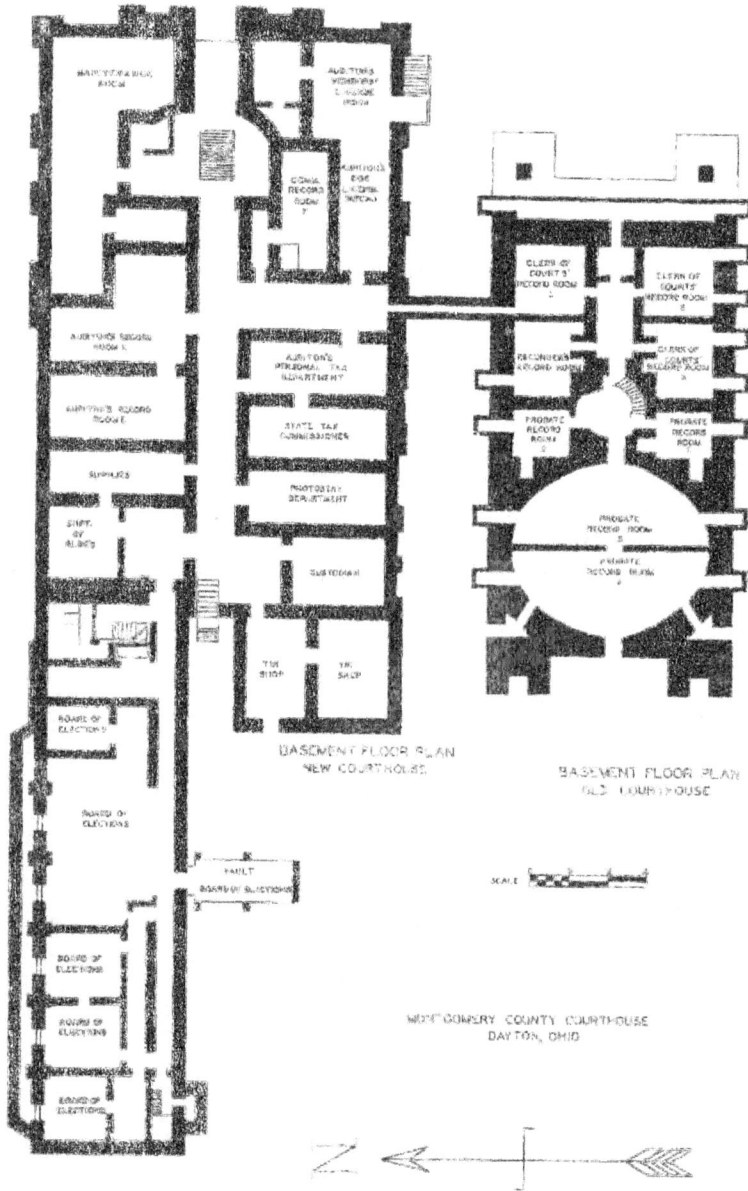

BASEMENT FLOOR PLAN
NEW COURTHOUSE

BASEMENT FLOOR PLAN
OLD COURTHOUSE

SCALE

MONTGOMERY COUNTY COURTHOUSE
DAYTON, OHIO

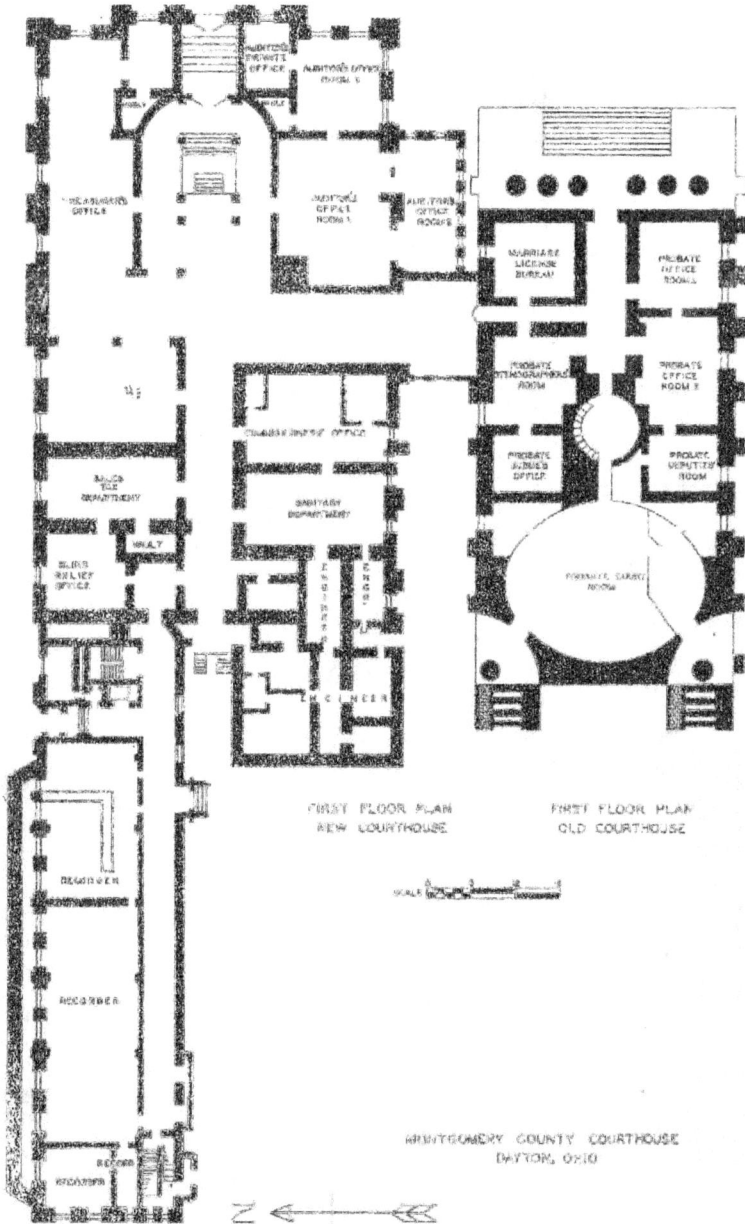

FIRST FLOOR PLAN
NEW COURTHOUSE

FIRST FLOOR PLAN
OLD COURTHOUSE

MONTGOMERY COUNTY COURTHOUSE
DAYTON, OHIO

FLOOR PLAN OF COUNTY COURTHOUSE

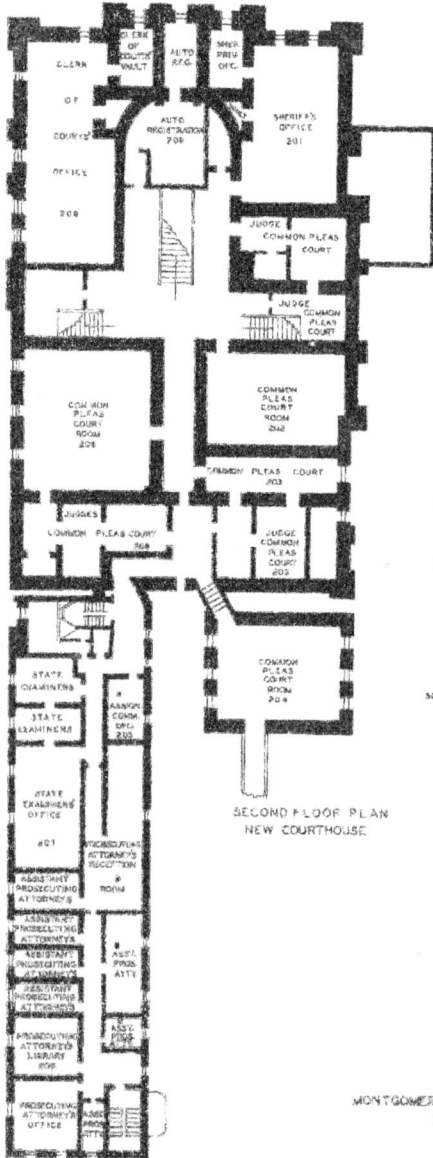

SECOND FLOOR PLAN
NEW COURTHOUSE

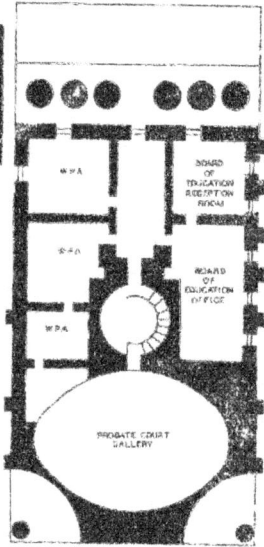

SECOND FLOOR PLAN
OLD COURTHOUSE

MONTGOMERY COUNTY COURTHOUSE
DAYTON, OHIO

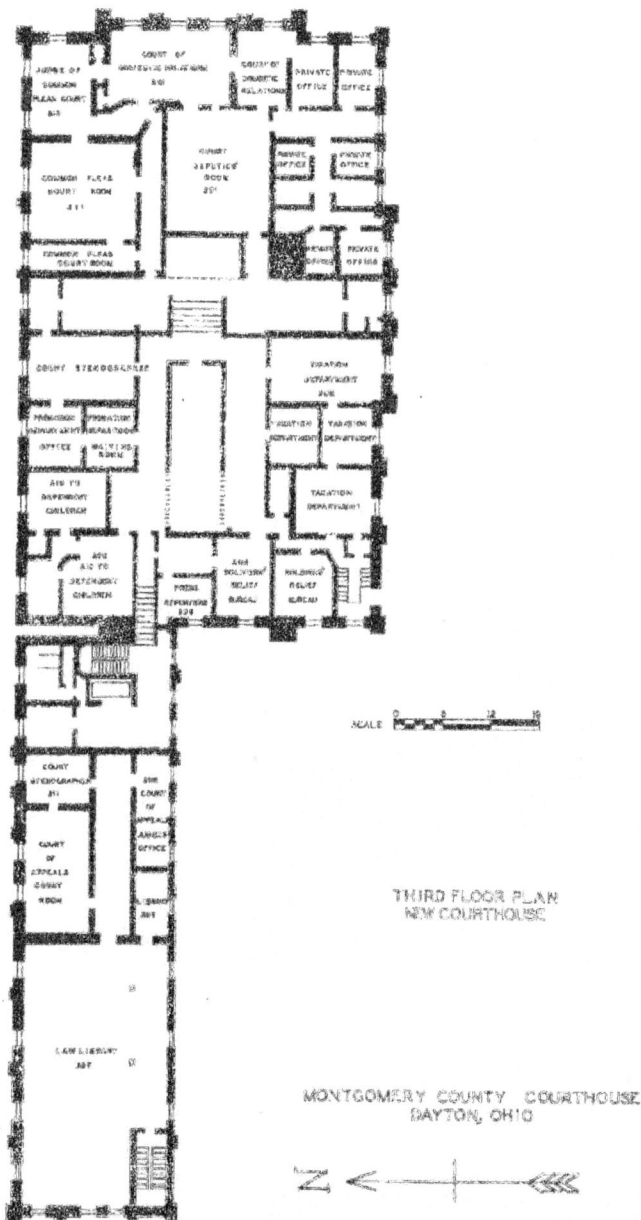

THIRD FLOOR PLAN
NEW COURTHOUSE

MONTGOMERY COUNTY COURTHOUSE
DAYTON, OHIO

The governmental system established in 1802, under the first constitution of Ohio, made no provision for the office of county commissioners and its existence is due entirely to statutory enactment. The board, created in 1804, was the successor of the courts of general quarter sessions, which, during the territorial period, served as the representative agent of the county. The board of county commissioners consisted of three members elected for a three-year term.[1] In 1807 the commissioners were made a corporate body vested with the power to sue and be sued.[2] They were required to keep a record of their proceedings, to levy taxes for the support of the county, appoint a county treasurer, and to supervise the construction of bridges.[3] They were paid on a per diem basis. Moreover, during the early period they were given the task of constructing courthouses, jails, and offices for the clerk of courts, court of common pleas, the sheriff, the auditor, and the treasurer.[4] From 1805 to 1820 the commissioners were required to fix the amounts of tavern and ferry licenses and the rates for transportation by ferry.[5] Of these earlier duties the commissioners retain all but those of fixing the amounts of tavern and ferry licenses and ferriage rates and that of appointing a county treasurer. However, since 1831 they have been authorized to examine and compare the accounts of the county treasurer and to examine the condition of county finances.[6]

Besides the duties regarding county building construction and finance, the commissioners were given the task of constructing local highways when so authorized by the legislature. During the first thirty years of Ohio history the duties of the commissioners in this respect were local in nature. But as the system of road construction expanded they were given the additional duty of converting free turnpikes into state roads.[7] Although numerous plank roads had been constructed by private companies during the eighteen forties, it was not until 1850 that the legislature authorized incorporation for this purpose.[8] When those companies were caught in the stringency of a financial depression in 1857, the commissioners were authorized to purchase their holdings.

---

1. *Laws of Ohio,* II, 150.
2. *Ibid.,* V. 97.
3. *Ibid.,* VIII, 45.
4. *Ibid.,* II, 154-157; XXIX, 315.
5. *Ibid.,* III, 96; VIII, 107; XVIII, 170.
6. *Ibid.,* XXIX, 291. See also G. C. sec. 2644.
7. *Laws of Ohio,* XLVI, 74.
8. *Ibid.,* L, 282; XLVIII, 49.

If such transactions were made, the transfer signed by the president of the company was to be deposited with the county auditor.[9] In 1871 the commissioners, although earlier subjected to regulatory measures by the legislature, were prohibited from levying taxes for roads to exceed three and a half mills on a dollar on the taxable property in the county.[10] Later, in 1885, they were authorized to levy taxes not to exceed five mills on the dollar on all taxable property in the county for the maintenance of roads which have been damaged by excessive wear or were damaged from other causes.[11]

With the development of modern means of transportation, scientific principles were applied to road construction and maintenance. Although the county surveyor, now the county engineer, had in earlier years furnished the commissioners with estimates for bridge construction, it was not until the latter part of the nineteenth century that they were authorized to utilize the scientific knowledge in road construction.[12] At the beginning of the present century the surveyor was directed to appoint a maintenance engineer, with the consent of the commissioners, to supervise the repairing of improved roads in the county.[13]

Although the county commissioners have never been closely associated with the administration of criminal justice, their earlier duties regarding the construction of county jails qualified them, in the earlier period, for additional duties in this respect. During the middle of the nineteenth century the commissioners of Cuyahoga County were authorized to employ persons on construction work who were confined in the county jails.[14] While this provision was repealed by the criminal code, adopted in 1853, other earlier functions applicable to all counties were continued. Since 1843 the commissioners have provided equipment and fixtures for places of incarceration, food and clothing for prisoners, and appointed a county physician.[15] Since 1869 they have been authorized to offer a reward for the detention or apprehension of any person charged with a felony in the county.[16]

---

9. *Ibid.,* LIV, 198.
10. *Ibid.,* LXVIII, 117.
11. G. C. sec. 7419.
12. *Laws of Ohio,* LXXXIX, 172; XCVIII, 245-247.
13. *Laws of Ohio,* CVIII, pt. i, 497.
14. *Ibid.,* XXXVII, 54.
15. *Ibid.,* XLI, 74; LXXXVII, 186.
16. *Ibid.,* LXVI, 321.

Since 1892 the commissioners in any county where there is no workhouse may, under certain conditions, release or parole an indigent person confined in the jail.[17] With the extension of modern crime into the rural areas in the form of small-town bank robbing, the commissioners were given the duty of furnishing motorcycles to the sheriff and his deputies in an attempt to compete with the high-powered equipment used by modern gangs. One of the latest functions in this respect is the contracting with radio stations the broadcasting of descriptions of fleeing criminals.[18]

Besides providing for those who have violated the laws, the commissioners were given the duty of caring for persons who, because of poverty or physical or mental defects, became public charges. Thus, county relief for the indigent, one of the most pressing problems of the twentieth century, was met in frontier Ohio. As early as 1805 an act, modeled from the territorial law, was passed which was similar in all respects to the poor laws of the seventeenth century England.[19] Under the early enactments the township trustees were authorized to appoint overseers of the poor. In 1816 the county commissioners were authorized to construct "poor houses" for the care of the county's indigent. As the system developed in succeeding decades the county was made responsible for those who have become permanently disabled, and for paupers who could not be satisfactory cared for except at the county infirmary, now called the county home. Since 1913 they have been authorized, in any county containing a city which has an infirmary, to contract with the director of public safety for the care of the county's indigent.[20]

The township trustees and officials of municipal corporations were made responsible for providing temporary relief to needy residents of the state, or the county, township, or city. In the event any person became chargeable to a township in which he had not gained legal residence, it was the duty of the overseers, later the township trustees, to remove him to the township where he was legally settled. With slight alterations, the principles of this system continued until the twentieth century.[21]

---

17. *Ibid.,* LXXXIX, 408; CXIII, 203.
18. G. C. sec. 2412-1.
19. *Laws of Ohio,* III, 272.
20. G. C. sec. 2419-1. See also p. 224.
21. For study of the administration of relief in Ohio prior to 1934 see Aileen Elizabeth Kennedy, *The Ohio Poor Law and Its Administration* (Sophonisba P. Breckinridge, ed., *Social Service Monographs* No. 22, University of Chicago Press, Chicago, 1934).

Since 1908 the commissioners have been authorized to issue warrants for the relief of the blind in sums varying from $100 to $400 per year.[22] When the blind relief commission was abolished in 1913 its powers and duties were transferred to the county commissioners who were authorized, on evidence furnished by a registered physician or surgeon that the applicant for blind relief might have such disability benefitted or removed by medical or surgical treatment, and with the written consent of the patient, to expand all or part of a year's relief allowance for this purpose.[23]

Six years later, in 1919, the allowance for blind relief was raised to $200 per person per annum, and the county commissioners were authorized to appoint such clerks as they might deem necessary to investigate applications and to serve at the pleasure of the county commissioners.[24]

In 1927 the maximum benefit for blind relief was increased to $400 per person per annum, but in the event of both a husband and wife being blind and both receiving relief, the total maximum benefit for the two was fixed at $600 per annum.[25]

In April 1936 the state accepted the provisions of the Federal Social Security Act approved August 14, 1935, providing federal grants for state aid to the blind, and the legislature designated the Ohio commission for the blind the administration agency in the state, and the county commissioners were made the administration agency in the county. The county commissioners were directed to appropriate from the general fund of the county a sum sufficient when supplemented by federal and state grants to provide for the blind a substance "compatible with decency and health," and if they failed to make such appropriations the attorney general was directed to bring *mandamus* proceedings against them.

The act of 1936 provides that those entitled to blind relief are persons not less than eighteen no more than sixty-five years old, who have lost their sight while residents of the state, and who have resided in the state for a period of five years in the nine years immediately preceding application, the last year of which period shall have been continuous.

---

22. See p. 241.
23. *Laws of Ohio,* CIII, 60.
24. *Ibid.,* CVIII, pt. i, 421- 422.
25. *Ibid.,* CXII, 109.

Applications for blind relief are filed with the county commissioners who are required by statute to list such claims in their order of application in books kept for that purpose. At least ten days prior to action on a claim the applicant files a duly certified statement, including a certificate from a registered physician "skilled in diseases of the eye" stating to what extent the applicant's vision is impaired, and written evidence from two reputable citizens that they know the applicant to be blind and that "he has the qualifications to entitle him to the relief asked." The county commissioners may allow the examining physician a fee not to exceed five dollars, and may employ an additional physician to examine the applicant. If after such inquiry the county commissioners are satisfied that the applicant is entitled to relief, they are directed by statute to issue an order for such sum as the board finds necessary, not to exceed the maximum fixed in 1927, such sum to be paid monthly from the fund created for that purpose. The ruling of 1913 concerning medical and surgical treatment for applicants remains in effect. Persons whose applications are denied by the county commissioners may appeal to the state commission for the blind which on its own motion may revise any decision of the county commissioners. Both the Ohio commission for the blind and the county commissioners have power to issue subpoenas, compel presentation of papers, and examine witnesses.

At least once a year, oftener if directed by the Ohio commission for the blind, the county commissioners must examine the qualifications, disabilities, and needs of all persons on the list of the blind, and may increase or decrease the amount of relief according to the budgetary requirements within the limits fixed by law. If the county commissioners remove a name from the list of the blind they are required to notify the county auditor and the Ohio commission for the blind as to their action.[26]

In addition to furnishing financial aid to the civilian population the commissioners were authorized, in 1886, to levy a tax for the relief of indigent Union soldiers, sailors, or marines of the Civil War, or if such veterans were deceased, for their dependents.[27] In 1919 the provisions of the original act were amended to include all indigent veterans of the World War.[28]

---

26. *Laws of Ohio,* CXVI, pt. ii, 195-200.
27. *Laws of Ohio,* LXXXIII, 232. See also p. 239.
28. *Laws of Ohio,* CVIII, pt. i, 633.

The commissioners were authorized also, in 1884, to defray the funeral expenses of any honorably discharged soldier, sailor, or marine who died indigent. Ten years later the provisions of the act were extended to include the mother, wife, or widow of any soldier, sailor, or marine; and war nurses.[29]

The humanitarian duty occurring for the county's dependent and neglected children was delegated to the county commissioners. Since 1866 they have been authorized to establish and maintain children's homes. At the beginning of the present century, when the treatment of children was undergoing a remarkable change, they were authorized to place dependent and neglected children in private homes or institutions where they were receive food, clothing, and medical and dental treatment.[30] The development of the juvenile court system added new responsibilities. In order to segregate completely juvenile offenders from adults being tried in the regular criminal courts, the commissioners were authorized to provide a separate building, to be known as the "juvenile court."[31]

The unprecedented depression in the third decade of the twentieth century proved the antiquated, uncentralized system of relief administration entirely inadequate. As a result of the abnormal employment conditions and the crop failures following the drought of 1930, many local subdivisions of the county charged by law to administer support and medical relief to the indigent were unable to discharge their obligations. Accordingly, in 1931, the legislature passed an emergency act authorizing the county, township, and municipal taxing authorities to borrow money and issue bonds for poor relief, providing the state tax commission found that no other funds were available.[32]

During the early months of 1932 the governor, aware of the widespread suffering in the state, called the legislature into special session.[33] At this session the legislature authorized him to appoint a state relief commission composed of five members to study the relief situation. This commission was permitted to cooperate with the national, state, or local relief commission, which, in many counties, had been established and was already functioning. Since the county and township treasuries were depleted, on account of the excessive drain caused by the mounting relief load and a steady decline of tax collections, the legislature authorized an excise tax on utilities, for the year 1932-1937, to be used for relief purposes.

---

29. *Ibid.,* XC, 177. See also p. 231.
30. *Laws of Ohio,* CIX, 533.
31. *Ibid.,* CXIII, 4701.
32. *Ibid.,* CXIV, 11-12.

This state tax was to be allocated to the counties on the basis of population, the tax duplicate, and the value of the utilities property in the county as of 1930. The funds allocated to each county under this act were to be credited to the "county poor relief excise fund."[34]

The county commissioners were authorized to borrow money for emergency relief and evidence such indebtedness by the issuance of negotiable bonds and notes. Upon submission of such resolution to the state tax commission, the commission was directed to estimate the amount which would probably be allocated to the county from the public utility excise taxes and was directed to calculate the total amount of bonds, the principal and interest on which might be paid out of such estimated allocation. The date of maximum maturity of such bonds was to be on or before March 15, 1938. If, in the year 1932, additional funds were needed for poor relief, the county commissioners were authorized, after the state tax commission found that no other funds were available, to issue additional bonds in the amount not exceeding one-tenth of one percent of the general tax list and duplicate of the county. The maturity date of such additional bonds was to be on or before September 15, 1940.[35]

The proceeds of the sale of such bonds were to be placed in a special fund, denominated the "emergency relief fund." No expenditures were to be made from this fund except in accordance with the method and under the uniform regulations prescribed by the state relief commission, and in no case after December 31, 1933. The county commissioners were authorized to distribute, prior to the first of March 1933, portions of the fund to the political subdivisions of the county, according to the needs for poor relief determined by the county and set forth in such an approved budget. The money distributed to the subdivisions was to be expended in them for poor relief, including the renting of lands and the purchase of seeds for gardening by the unemployed.[36] County poor relief included mothers' pensions, soldiers' relief, temporary assistance to nonresidents, maintenance of a county home and the children's home, and work and direct relief. In the townships and municipalities relief was interpreted to be the support of the poor and the burial of persons who died indigent.

---

33. See message of the governor to the eighty-ninth general assembly in *Laws of Ohio,* CXIV, pt. ii, 6-8.
34. *Laws of Ohio,* CXIV, pt. ii, 19-20.
35. *Ibid.,* CXIV, pt. ii, 18-21.
36. *Ibid.,* CXIV, pt. ii, 21-22.

Each subdivision administering funds under the act was expected to require labor in exchange for relief given to any family in which resided an able-bodied wage earner.[37]

In the same year the county commissioners were designated as a board to administer the state law providing aid for the aged.[38] In February 1933 the tenure of the state relief commission was extended to March 1, 1935.[39] In the same year the legislature levied an additional tax stamp on the sale of bottled and bulk beer, malt, cosmetics, and toilet preparations to furnish additional funds for emergency relief.[40] The state treasurer was authorized to appoint the county treasurer as his deputy for the purpose of selling tax stamps to be affixed to such articles.[41]

The commissioners' duties regarding poor relief were further extended in 1935. They were authorized to provide noninstitutional support, care, assistance, or relief for the indigent in the county.[42] In 1935 the state relief commission ceased to exist by reason of the terms of the act creating it. The legislature however, passed a measure designed to co-ordinate and correlate all emergency poor relief work, activities, and administration with the federal emergency relief administration which was authorized to administer and direct the distribution and expenditure of federal funds for relief in the state. Accordingly, all powers previously vested in the state relief commission were transferred to the county commissioners. Whenever in their discretion such action was necessary in order to continue the co-ordination and correlation of state, local, and federal funds they were authorized to appoint, with the approval of the director of finance of the state of Ohio, a representative or representatives of such emergency poor relief.[43] If such an officer were appointed, the representative succeeded to all powers and functions, which, under the act, were delegated to the county commissioners. This representative, however, was subjected to such terms and conditions in respect to auditing, examinations, and reports as were directed by the county commissioners and the federal agency.

---

37. *Ibid.,* CXIV, pt. ii, 17.
38. *Ibid.,* CXV, pt. ii, 431-439. See also pp. 244-245.
39. *Laws of Ohio,* CXV, 22.
40. *Ibid.,* CXV, 642, 649; CXV, pt. ii, 5, 33, 83, 177, 200, 247, 256.
41. *Ibid.,* CXV, 642.
42. *Ibid.,* CXVI, 571.
43. *Ibid.,* CXVI, 571. The first relief director was appointed in Montgomery County, April 21, 1933. Commissioners' Journal, volume 39 [1933], p. 165.

The county commissioners were directed to conduct relief activities outside limits of municipal corporations through the township trustees, insofar as practicable, and were to be guided by the recommendations of the township trustees with respect to relief need in such political subdivisions. Again, as a 1932, the commissioners were authorized, if the state tax commission found that no other means existed to provide funds, to borrow money and issue bonds in the year 1935-1936. The maximum maturity date of such bonds was to be on or before March 1, 1944.[44] Other bonds, in addition to those who secured by the county's share of the excise tax, might be issued not to exceed one-fifth of one percent of the general tax list of the county.[45] If the county was unable to issue bonds by reason of the limitation imposed by the constitution,[46] the taxing authority of each subdivision was authorized to submit the question of issuing bonds to the electorate either at a general or special election.[47]

The year 1936 saw the re-creation of the state relief commission. Consisting of four members appointed by the governor, this body was authorized to serve until January 31, 1937. Again, as in 1932, the commission was directed to study problems of relief, to receive advice from federal, state, and local governmental departments, and to co-operate with agencies of the national and local governments and private agencies engaged in the administration of financial support of direct or indirect relief, to administer moneys appropriated to the commission for poor relief, to examine the conduct of local governmental agencies in administering relief, and to order the distribution and payment of moneys from state treasury.

The county commissioners were authorized to administer all advances by the state to the relief commission and were directed to operate through duly authorized agencies of townships, municipalities, and school districts. Within the appropriations made by the commissioners and subject to the rules and regulations of the state relief commission, the commissioners were instructed to appoint assistants and such other employees as were necessary.[48]

The county commissioners, like the state relief commission, were directed to co-operate with all agencies of the federal, state, and county governments, and with private agencies which were engaged in administering relief or financial support to the needy.

---

44. *Laws of Ohio,* CXVI, 571.
45. *Ibid.,* CXVI, 575.
46. *Ohio Const. 1851,* Art. XII, sec. 2.
47. *Laws of Ohio,* CXVI, 578.
48. *Laws of Ohio,* CXVI, pt. ii, 133-148.

It was made the duty of all county, township, and municipal governments administering relief or assistance to dependents to report to the county commissioners, at their request, the name and address of all persons to whom they were providing aid and the amount and character of aid given.[49]

The principle of issuing bonds and securing them by the county's share of the utility taxes was continued. Moreover, there are appropriated to the state relief commission from the general revenue fund the sum of $3,000,000 which was designated as the "state relief rotary fund." The various counties of the state which had not issued bonds and were not authorized to do so without the consent of the people, were empowered to obtain an advance from the state relief rotary fund in an amount equal to that of bonds which were permitted to be issued under the provision of this act. If the county failed to repay the total of all advances and interest at two percent before June 1936, the state relief commission was directed to refuse to make further allocations or distributions to the county.[50]

In the early months of 1937 the legislature authorized the state relief commission to serve until April 1937. Under this act the county commissioners are authorized to give temporary support and medical relief to nonresidents and to all needy persons possessing legal residence in the county. Funds may be expended for both direct and work relief. However, all persons on relief able and competent to perform labor who refuse to accept private employment under prevailing conditions and prevailing wages, may be dropped from the relief roles. This ruling does not apply, however, to areas where strikes are prevalent. On the other hand, any person receiving relief in the county is permitted to engage in any business without losing his relief status. During the period of such employment, he is required to forfeit the pro rata amount of relief received by him, and is eligible to his former relief status upon the conclusion of such employment.

The county commissioners are required to file with the state relief commission a budget and a detailed statement and plan showing how the funds to be received are to be expended, the purpose for which they are to be used, the nature and kind of work to be carried on, and the number of persons to be aided by such relief.

---

49. *Ibid.,* CXVI, pt. ii, 133-148, 240.
50. *Ibid.,* CXVI, pt. ii, 133-148.

Besides this, the county commissioners must file a complete analysis of their proposed expenditures, together with an estimate of all available resources, including the unencumbered proceeds of any bonds heretofore issued and the amount of bonds which the county commissioners have a right to issue without a vote of the people on the approval of the state tax commission of Ohio as authorized in 1935.

Of the funds allocated to the county by the state relief commission for direct relief, the commissioners may, when they believe that the cost of administration may be reduced, reallocate the funds on a percentage basis of relief requirements of the various subdivisions.[51] The emergency relief measures passed during the period 1932-1937 gave the counties a centralized relief administration for the first time.

In Montgomery County the funds for administering county relief are supplied by the county commissioners and the state of Ohio. For the year 1940 the state supplied 38 percent of the funds and for the year 1941 appropriated 50 percent of the funds. Applications for relief are received in an office of the relief bureau; applicants are interviewed by the intake division and investigated by the case workers, and if found worthy, are certified as eligible for relief. All relief is issued to the client for food, clothing, rent, and other necessary items by orders, as no cash is given.[52]

In addition to other forms of relief the county commissioners provide funds for aid to dependent children.[53] They are required to include in the annual tax budget an amount not less than that computed to yield a levy of fifteen one-hundreds of one mill on each dollar of general tax list of the county. Funds are also provided by the federal and state governments. If the commissioners fail to comply with the provisions of the act relating to appropriations, the state department of public welfare is directed to institute *mandamus* proceedings against them.[54]

While control over relief work has become one of the most important phases of the commissioners' work, particularly in recent years, many other responsibilities have been assigned to them.

---

51. *Ibid.,* CXVII, 13; George C. Trautwein, ed., *Page's Ohio Cumulative Code Service* (Cincinnati, 1937), No. 20, 65-67.
52. See entries 26-35.
53. See p. 41.
54. G. C. secs. 1359-36–1359-45; *Laws of Ohio,* CXVI, pt. ii, 188-195.

The commissioners, by the authority conferred upon them to construct public buildings, were given duties regarding educational advancement. Since 1871 they have been authorized to accept bequests for the construction county libraries, and since 1923 to issue bonds, after receiving the approval of the voters, for the construction of libraries, or to contract with existing libraries for the use of people in the county.[55] Moreover, during the same period, they were authorized to provide and maintain civic centers in the county and to employ an expert director to supervise and administer them.[56]

Other duties not closely related to original ones have been added from decade to decade. For example, in 1850 the commissioners were authorized to subscribe for one leading newspaper of each political party in the county and cause them to be bound and deposited with the county auditor as public archives.[57] The newspapers on file in the auditor's office have not been listed in this inventory as they are to be the subject of a separate publication. An amendment to the original act, passed in 1923, provided for the preservation of such newspapers for a period of ten years, after which they may be removed to the Ohio State Archaeological and Historical Society Library.[58] They have been authorized also to promote historical research by appropriating annually a sum not to exceed $100 to defray the expenses of compiling and publishing historical data for historical societies not incorporated for profit.[59]

During the early years of the twentieth century commissioners were given the duty of providing facilities for county sanitation, which, in previous years had been sadly neglected. In 1917 they were authorized to lay out, establish, and maintain one or more sewer districts within the county. Since 1917 no sewer or sewage treatment works may be constructed outside of any incorporated municipality by any person, persons, firms, or corporations until the plans have been approved by the commissioners.[60]

---

55. G. C. secs. 2454, 2455; *Laws of Ohio,* CX, 242.
56. G. C. sec. 2457-4.
57. *Laws of Ohio,* XLVIII, 65.
58. *Ibid.,* CX, 4.
59. G. C. sec. 2457-1
60. G. C. sec. 5602-1; *Laws of Ohio,* CVII, 440.

In accordance with the provisions of the General Code,[61] the county commissioners of Montgomery County established a sanitary department, December 1, 1924.[62] The department is under the jurisdiction of the commissioners and is delegated the duty of designing, constructing, operating, and maintaining sanitary sewers and water systems in the county sanitary district.[63]

Also during the first decade of the twentieth century, the county commissioners were authorized to provide facilities for the treatment of tuberculosis. In 1908 they were authorized to establish a county tuberculosis hospital and in 1909 to co-operate with the commissioners of the other counties for the establishment of a district tuberculosis hospital.[64] In counties not served by a county or district hospital the commissioners were empowered in 1913 to appoint, with the approval of the state department of health, one or more instructing and visiting nurses to visit homes or places housing tuberculosis patients.[65] Since 1917 they have been authorized to establish tuberculosis dispensaries and provide by tax levies the necessary funds for their establishment and maintenance.[66]

In accordance with the provision of the act of March 1909, the county commissioners of Montgomery and Preble Counties on July 14, 1909, formed a joint-county board to establish and maintain a district tuberculosis hospital.[67] This hospital is located in Dayton, the county seat of Montgomery County, and is known as the Stillwater Sanatorium. The records of this institution are included in the inventory of Montgomery County archives.[68]

Since the middle of the nineteenth century the county commissioners have been active in encouraging agricultural societies and county fairs. The act of February 28, 1846, authorized the formation of agricultural societies and made provision for financial assistance by the county commissioners.[69] Subsequent legislation changed somewhat the original regulations as to organization, membership, ownership of property used for county fairs, and premiums.

---

61. G. C. sec. 6602-1.
62. Commissioners' Journal, volume 30 [1924], p. 710, see entry 1.
63. See entries 15-23.
64. *Laws of Ohio,* XCIX, 62; C, 87.
65. G. C. sec. 3153-1.
66. G. C. secs. 3148-1, 3153-4, 3153-5.
67. Commissioners' Journal, volume 19 [1909], p. 227, see entry 1.
68. See pp. 218-222.
69. *Laws of Ohio,* XLIV, 70.

However, appropriations are still made by the county commissioners to organize agricultural societies and under certain stipulations to independent agriculture fairs.[70] In 1890 the present Montgomery County Agricultural Society was formed and with the exception of three years, 1895 to 1897 inclusive, county fairs have been held each year.[71]

Finally, the county commissioners have acted in a supervisory capacity over other county officials. Since 1850 they have been authorized to compare the annual reports and statements made to them by the prosecuting attorney, clerk of courts, sheriff, and the treasurer; take measures to rectify errors, correct discrepancies, and record in their journal the results of such examinations. Prior to the transfer of the duties of the secretary to the board of county commissioners to a full-time commissioners' clerk, appointed in 1908 under the provisions of the act of 1904,[72] these reports were required to be filed with the county auditor, who had custody of the commissioners official acts and proceedings.[73] In 1896 the commissioners were given their present duty of visiting hospitals, detention homes, private asylums, and any other institution exercising a reformatory or correctional influence over individuals, and reporting on the sanitary conditions and treatment of inmates.[74] Although these reports are required to be filed with the county prosecuting attorney and kept open to the inspection and examination of the public, they were not located in the inventory of Montgomery County records.

The board of county commissioners, which is composed of three members, offers a typical example of an office, which, designated primarily for an agricultural society, has expanded to meet the needs and requirements of modern society. At present the commissioners are elected for four-year term[75] and receive a salary of $3,777.08 per year.[76]

---

70. *Ibid.,* LI, 333; LVIII, 142; XCII, 205; XCIV, 395; XCV, 403; CVIII, pt. i, 381-385; CIX, 240; CIX, 238; CXII, 84; CXVI, 47.

71. Commissioners' Record, volume 9 [1890], p. 209. A. W. Drury, *History of the City of Dayton and Montgomery County, Ohio* (Chicago and Dayton, 1909), I, 806-807. See also p. 269.

72. *Laws of Ohio,* XCVII, 304. In Montgomery County the first full-time clerk to the commissioners was appointed June 29, 1908 and sworn in July 1, 1908. Commissioners' Journal, volume 18 [1908], pp. 408, 410. See entry 1.

73. G. C. sec. 2504; *Laws of Ohio,* XLVIII, 66.

74. *Laws of Ohio,* XCII, 212.

75. *Ibid.,* CVIII, pt. ii. 1300.

76. Ohio Auditor of State *Annual Report, 1939,* 376.

1. COMMISSIONERS' JOURNAL

1804—. 45 volumes (A1, B, 3-45). Title varies: Road and Commissioners' Records, 1804-1840, 2 volumes; Commissioners' Record, 1840-1905. 14 volumes.

Minutes of the board of county commissioners relative to county business, showing date of meeting, names of members present, and a record of action taken on each motion and resolution. Proceedings pertaining to building and repair of roads with complete road record, 1840-March 1841, and petitions and resolutions on same, April 1841—, showing name of road, location, length by rods and miles, names of points to and from, names of owners of property affected, report of viewers and county surveyors, materials, estimated cost, and claims for damages; building and repair of ditches, showing name of ditch, location, specification, and cost; building and repair of bridges, showing name and location of bridge, name of road, specifications and cost; improvements and new county buildings; resolutions and petitions; appointments of appraisers, viewers, tax collectors, and certain county officials including first dog warden,1927; itemized account of bills approved, showing date of bill, name of creditor, amount, purpose, and date of order authorizing payments; proceedings regarding children's home, 1867—; county home, 1826—; tuberculosis hospital, 1908—; establishment of sanitary department for the extension of sewer and water lines, 1924; budgets and appropriations to all funds and departments including blind relief, 1908—; soldiers' relief, 1884—; soldiers' burials, 1884—, showing name and address of decedent, name of undertaker, and amount allowed; emergency relief, 1934—; copies of annual, official reports of county departments and officials, 1850—, showing date of report, name of official or department, itemized account of money received and disbursed, period covered by report; approval of infirmary directors annual reports, June 1829-March 31, 1885, and copies of semi-annual reports of infirmary directors, April 1, 1885-1912, showing dates covered by report, financial and statistical data on the infirmary, and itemize inventory of infirmary property, machinery, tools, and equipment; copies of contracts and agreements, showing date, name of contractor or other principles, terms are contract or agreement, purpose, and amount; and all other official business under jurisdiction of the county commissioners. Also contains commissioners' Journal [Sanitary Department]. 1935—, entry 15. Arranged chronologically by dates of meetings. Indexed alphabetically by names of principals and subjects; also separate index to bridges, roads, and ditches, December 1872-August 1901, entry 2; to bills allowed, December 1872-January 1909, entry 3; to miscellaneous matters, 1901-1909; entry 4.

1804-1910, handwritten; 1911—, typed. Average 500 pages. 18 x 13 x 3. 2 volumes, 1804-1840, Auditor's vault; 34 volumes, 1840-1930, Commissioners' record room F; 9 volumes, 1931—, Commissioners' office.

2. INDEX TO COMMISSIONERS' JOURNAL [Bridges, Roads, Ditches]
December 1872-August 1901. 3 volumes (1-3). Discontinued.

Index to bridge, road, and ditch records entered in the Commissioner' Journal, entry 1, showing full name of all petitioners, name and location of bridge, road, or ditch, date of journal entry, and volume and page numbers of journal. Arranged alphabetically under tabs by names of petitioners and chronologically thereunder by dates of entries. Handwritten. Average 400 pages. 15 x 12 x 2. Commissioners' record room F.

3. INDEX TO COMMISSIONERS' RECORD [Bills Allowed]
December 1872-January 1909. 8 volumes (1-8). Discontinued.

Index to bills allowed as entered and Commissioners' Journal, entry 1, showing full name of creditor, volume and page number of journal, and date of entry. Arranged alphabetically by names of creditors and chronologically thereunder by dates of entries. Handwritten. Average 400 pages. 18 x 12 x 3. Commissioners' record room F.

4. INDEX TO COMMISSIONERS' JOURNAL [Miscellaneous]
1901-1910. 1 volume. Discontinued.

Index to miscellaneous matters entered in the Commissioners' Journal, entry 1, showing subject of the journal entry, names of principals, nature of business, and volume and page numbers of the journal. Arranged alphabetically by names of principals. Handwritten. 400 pages. 18 x 12 x 3. Commissioners' record room F.

Institutions and Relief

5. JOURNAL [County Home]
1913—. 3 volumes. (1-3).

Record of official proceedings of the county commissioners as board of directors of the county home, showing date of meeting, names of members present, and appointments made, giving name of appointee, position, and term of appointment; also approval of bills for supplies, equipment, additions, repairs, salaries, and sundries; also includes records of visits of the board with report of findings and recommendations, and copies of reports of superintendent of county home to the board of directors, showing period covered by report, and statistics on the population of the home. Arranged chronologically by dates of meetings. Indexed alphabetically by subjects or names of principals. Typed. Average 350 pages. 18 x 12 x 2. 2 volumes, 1913-1932, Commissioners' record room F.; 1 volume, 1933—, Commissioners' office.

For prior records, see entry 491.

6. RECORD OF THE COUNTY INFIRMARY
1906-1911. 1 volume. Discontinued.
Record of applications to the county commissioners for admission to the county infirmary, showing name of applicant, age, sex, date of application, reason applied, claim of residence, physical condition of applicant, and disposition of the case. Arranged alphabetically by names of applicants and chronologically thereunder by dates of applications. No index. Handwritten. 350 pages. 16 x 8 x 2. Auditor's room E.

7. REPORTS OF CHILDREN'S HOME
1867—. 1 folder.
Annual reports from the trustees of the children's home, 1867-1912, and the superintendent, 1913—, showing date of report, expenses of operation and maintenance for year, including salaries of superintendent, matron, visiting agents, other employees, medical care and drugs, food, water, fuel and light, wearing apparel, board of children in private homes, funeral expenses, education and recreation (including transportation), repairs to motor vehicles and machinery, traveling expenses of officers, employees, and inmates, and total; also receipts from farm produce and stocks, from other counties for care of children, and sources other than county treasury; statistics, showing daily average number of children, amount of cost per capita, total number of children in home at beginning and end of year, and losses during the year; name of each trustee and expiration of term. Arranged chronologically by dates or reports. No index. 1867-1895, handwritten; 1896—, typed on printed forms. 9 x 11.5 x .5. Commissioners' office.

8.RECORD OF SOLDIERS' RELIEF [Burials]
1884—. 3 volumes.

Reports of burial commission to county commissioners on the burial of indigent soldiers and sailors, their wives, widows, mothers, and children, showing name of decedent, what rank or relationship, date of death, itemized statement of burial expense, copy of report by township or ward committee on claim, and date approved by county commissioners. Arranged chronologically by dates approved. Indexed alphabetically by names of decedents. Handwritten on printed forms. 1 volume 240 pages. 18 x 5 x 3; 2 volumes average 150 pages. 15 x 12 x 1.5. Commissioners' office.

9. EMERGENCY POOR RELIEF VOUCHERS
1934-May 1937. 208 file boxes. (labeled by contained order numbers).

Original orders or vouchers issued and canceled, certifying the receipt of food, medicine, fuel, clothing, housing, and sundries, showing to whom issued, address, kind of assistance, order or voucher number, and amount of order. Arranged numerically by order or voucher number. No index. Handwritten on printed forms. 12 x 18 x 26. Auditor's room E.

10. MISCELLANEOUS RELIEF ORDERS
1928—. 65 file boxes, 1 file drawer. (dated).

Original orders issued by county commissioners to dealers or vendors for food, clothing, rent, coal, or sundries for relief clients, showing name of dealer or vendor, name of recipient, date issued, order number, amount, purpose, and date filed. File boxes arranged chronologically by dates of filing; file drawer arranged alphabetically by names of recipients and chronologically thereunder by dates of filing. No index. Handwritten on printed forms. File box, 18 x 26; file drawer, 6 x 18 x 24. Commissioners' record room F.

Financial Records

11. SHEEP CLAIMS
1887—. 2 volumes. (1, 2).

Record of claims filed with commissioners for sheep killed or injured by dogs, showing date, name of claimant, claim number, number of sheep killed, number injured, amount claimed, amount of allowed, and name of witnesses. Arranged numerically by claimed numbers. No index. Handwritten on printed forms.

Average 250 pages. 12 x 8 x 1.5. 1 volume, 1887, Clerk of courts' record room 1; 1 volume, 1888—, Commissioners' office.

12. MONTHLY FINANCIAL STATEMENT
March 1939. 1 statement. Prior records destroyed.
Monthly statement by the auditor to the commissioners of the finances of the county, showing date of statement, balance on hand in each fund and account at the beginning of the month, amount of receipts to each, amount disbursed from each, balance remaining to the credit of each, and balance of money in the treasury and depository, and auditor's certification with date. Handwritten on printed forms. 24 x 12. Commissioners' office, on wall.

Miscellaneous

13. COUNTY DOG WARDEN REPORTS
1928—. 3 file boxes.
Reports of the dog warden to county commissioners on investigation of claims for damage to livestock inflicted by dogs, showing date of report, name and address of claimant, number of animals injured, extent of injuries, value, and amount claimed. Arranged chronologically by dates or reports. No index. Handwritten on printed forms. 10 x 8 x 13. Auditor's office room 1.

14. ANNUAL INVOICE
1893-1905. 4 volumes. (three unlabeled; 1900-1905, A).
Record of appraisal of lands, buildings, stock, and equipment at the county infirmary at the beginning of each fiscal year, showing date of inventory, itemized list, and appraised value; also includes a record of receipts from all sources and disbursements for maintenance, showing date, amount, and purpose. Arranged chronologically by dates of inventories or entries. No index. Handwritten. Average 350 pages. 14 x 9 x 2. Auditor's record room E.

Sanitary Department

15. COMMISSIONERS' JOURNAL [Sanitary Department]
1925-1934. 6 volumes. 1935—, in Commissioners' Journal, entry 1.
Minutes of the county commissioners dealing with sanitary department, showing date of meeting, description of the improvement, whether water or sanitary,

location, and lot numbers of area of improvement. Arranged chronologically by dates of meetings. Indexed alphabetically by subjects or names of principles. Typed. Average 250 pages. 18 x 12 x 2. Sanitary department.

16. CONSTRUCTION JOURNAL [Sewer and Water]
1924—. 2 volumes. (1, 2).
Record of disbursements for construction of sewer and water lines, showing date of entry, voucher number, name of payee, and total amount for engineering inspections, commissioners' fees, overhead, and miscellaneous costs. Also includes a record of money appropriated by the county commissioners and amount paid into the treasurer's office as a deposit for payment of materials used in construction work, showing date received and amount. Arranged chronologically by dates of entries. No index. Handwritten on printed forms. Average 300 pages. 26 x 15 x 3. Sanitary department.

17. MAINTENANCE JOURNAL AND DEPARTMENT OVERHEAD
1924—. 2 volumes. (1, 2).
Record of receipts and disbursements of the sanitary department fund, showing for receipts, number of individual or company, date, name of sanitary district, amount paid into sanitary department, and amount paid into treasurer's office. Arranged alphabetically by names of districts and chronologically thereunder by dates of entries. No index. Handwritten. Average 300 pages. 25 x 12 x 3.5. Sanitary department.

18. CONTRACTORS BIDS AND ESTIMATES
1924—. 10 file boxes.
Original bids and estimates submitted by contractors for furnishing material and labor in construction and repair of county water lines and sewers, showing date of bid or estimate, what sewer or water line, location of same, specifications of material and work to be performed, amount of estimate or bid, name of contractor, amount of bond filed by contractor, conditions of bond, estimate, and date filed. Arranged chronologically by dates of filing. No index. Handwritten and typed. 11 x 12 x 28. Sanitary department.

19. SANITARY SEWER DISTRICTS
1923—. 41 volumes.
Record of assessments for county sewer and water lines, showing name of property owner, lot number, description of property, acreage, foot frontage, cash assessment, installment assessments and dates due. Arranged numerically by lot numbers. No index. Handwritten and typed on printed forms. Average 200 pages. 18 x 12 x 2. Sanitary department.

20. SEWER AND WATER PERMITS
1922—. 11 Volumes.
Duplicate copies of permits issued for use of sewer and water, showing date, consumers name and address, and permit number. Arranged numerically by permit numbers. No index. Handwritten. Average 500 pages. 6 x 4 x 4. Sanitary department.

21. LEDGER [Department of Water]
1926—. 10 volumes. (1-10).
Ledger accounts of water consumers living outside of Dayton, showing date of entry, name and address of consumer, lot number, amount paid, amount of water consumed and name of water district. Arranged chronologically by dates of entries. Indexed alphabetically by names of water districts. Handwritten on printed forms. Average 250 pages. 24 x 18 x 2. Sanitary department.

22. SANITARY SEWER AND WATER SYSTEM
No date. 18 volumes.
District and sectional maps of water and sewer systems of the county, showing name of sewer or water district, and kind of improvement. Prepared by various engineers. Arranged alphabetically under tabs by names of sewer or water districts. No index. Hand drawn and blueprint. Scale, district maps, 1 inch equals 200 feet; sectional maps, 1 inch equals 500 feet. Average 100 pages. 36 x 18 x 1.5. Sanitary department.

23. VALVE LOCATION BOOK
No date. 28 volumes. Subtitled by names of sewer districts.
Maps of valve locations, showing street intersections, name of street, date of map, depth, and interference. Prepared by various engineers. Arranged alphabetically by names of sewer districts, and chronologically thereunder by dates of maps and

alphabetically thereunder by names of streets. No index. Hand drawn. Average 150 pages. 5 x 4 x .5. Sanitary department.

Aid for the Blind

24. BLIND RELIEF APPLICATIONS
1913—. 2 file boxes.

Original applications for blind relief, showing name and address of applicant, case number, number of dependents, extent of blindness (whether total or partial), date and place of birth, date loss of eyesight occurred, marital status, sex, names and addresses of living relatives, names of attending physician, and their reports on the true condition of applicants eyes, names of witnesses and reports of investigators case; also includes complete history case of each applicant and for applications allowed, shows date and amount; also includes applications pending additional information needed for certification and applications rejected giving the cause of ineligibility. Arranged alphabetically by names of applicants or clients. No index. Handwritten on printed forms. 12 x 15.5 x 25.5. Commissioners' office.

25. RESOLUTIONS–BLIND RELIEF
1913—. 1 file box.

Transcripts of county commissioners' resolutions certifying eligibility of applicants for blind relief, showing date of resolution, name and address of applicant, amount allowed, and date payable; also shows the total amount necessary for blind aid for the month, signatures of the county commissioners, and remarks. Arranged chronologically by dates of resolutions. No index. Handwritten and typed on printed forms. 12 x 15.5 x 25.5. Commissioners' office.

Relief Administration

Case Records

26. MASTER FILES
1933—. 60 file boxes (labeled by contained letters of alphabet).

Card record of relief clients in county and city of Dayton, showing name of client, names of dependents, case number, date case was open, and date closed or transferred. Serves as a guide to information pertaining to case histories and other information of the case. Arranged alphabetically by names of clients. No index.

Handwritten. 6 x 6 x 17. Relief bureau, Barrar Building, 206 East Fifth Street, Dayton Ohio.

27. ACTIVE FILES
1933—. 20 file boxes (labeled by contained letters of alphabet).
Card record of active cases, showing name and address of applicant for relief, case number, age, nativity, marital status, number of dependents, report on application by investigator, and record of aid furnished. Arranged alphabetically by names of applicants. No index. Handwritten and typed on printed forms. 14 x 11.5 x 28. Relief bureau, Barrar Building, 206 East Fifth Street, Dayton Ohio.

28. CASE PAPERS
1933—. 48 file boxes (labeled by contained letters of alphabet).
Complete case histories of direct relief cases, showing name and address of relief applicant, case number, nativity, age, marital status, number of dependents, investigator's report on the application, and itemized record of aid furnished each applicant. All papers of each case are filed together in a separate folder, showing name, address, and case number of applicant. Arranged alphabetically by names of applicants. No index. Handwritten and typed on printed forms. 14 x 11.5 x 28. Relief bureau, Barrar Building, 206 East Fifth Street, Dayton Ohio.

29. PERMANENT RECORD FILES
1933—. 18 file boxes (labeled by contained letters of alphabet).
Card record of active and inactive relief cases, showing name and address of client, case number, marital status, date of birth, and date case closed or client given employment. Arranged alphabetically by names of clients. No index. Handwritten and typed. 5 x 6 x 11.5. Relief bureau, Barrar Building, 206 East Fifth Street, Dayton Ohio.

30. RELIEF CLIENTS
1933—. 3 volumes (labeled by contained case numbers).
Register of case numbers of active and closed relief cases, showing name of client, address, and case number. Arranged numerically by case numbers. No index. Typed. Average 300 pages. 15 x 10.5 x 3. Relief bureau, Barrar Building, 206 East Fifth Street, Dayton Ohio.

31. DUPLICATE ORDERS
1933—. 25 file boxes.
Copies of orders issued to relief clients, showing order number, name of client, kind of relief, name of dealer, amount, period covered, and date issued. Arranged alphabetically by names of clients and chronologically thereunder by dates of issue. No index. Handwritten on printed forms. 14 x 14 x 24. Relief bureau, Barrar Building, 206 East Fifth Street, Dayton Ohio.

32. VOIDS
1933—. 3 file boxes. Two subtitled county; one, Dayton.
Original orders which have been voided for various reasons, showing information as in Duplicate Order, entry 31. Arranged chronologically by dates of issue. No index. Handwritten on printed forms. 14 x 14 x 24. Relief bureau, Barrar Building, 206 East Fifth Street, Dayton Ohio.

33. COMBINED CARDS
1933—. 27 file boxes (labeled by contained letters of alphabet).
Record of individual case costs for relief granted in active cases, showing name of client, address, date granted, amount of order, period covered, description of kind of aid given, and remarks. Arranged alphabetically by names of clients. No index. Handwritten on printed forms. 14 x 14 x 24. Relief bureau, Barrar Building, 206 East Fifth Street, Dayton Ohio.

34. CLOSED CLIENTS CARDS
1933—. 3 file boxes (labeled by contained letters of alphabet).
Record of case cost for relief granted in cases closed, showing date granted, amount received, period covered, kind of aid, and name and address of client. Arranged alphabetically by names of clients. No index. Handwritten on printed forms. 14 x 14 x 24. Relief bureau, Barrar Building, 206 East Fifth Street, Dayton Ohio.

35. CORRESPONDENCE
1933—. 2 bundles, 6 file boxes.
Correspondence received and duplicate copies of out-going letters pertaining to investigations of clients and inquiries between Montgomery County relief director and other existing welfare agencies or associations, showing date filed, name of correspondent, and text of letter. Arranged chronologically by dates of filing. No

index. Handwritten and typed. Bundles, 16 x 12 x 2; file boxes, 14 x 14 x 28. Relief bureau, Barrar Building, 206 East Fifth Street, Dayton Ohio.

WPA and CCC Records

36. WPA CERTIFICATION FILE
1935—. 25 file boxes (labeled by contained letters of alphabet).
Record of WPA certifications of eligibility, showing case name, address, total number of persons in case, case number, telephone number, race, date of certification, agency, relief district, county, primary classification, secondary classification, veteran, sex, marital status, name of employee, identification number, relation to head of family, date and place of birth, citizen by birth or naturalized, if alien (declared intention, date, place), other employable persons (WPA or NYA) name, relation to head of family, sex, marital status, date of birth, veteran, citizen, alien (declared intention), primary and secondary classification. Also NYA certifications, showing same information as WPA certifications. Also includes record of cancellations certification of eligibility, showing name, address, date, case number, identification number, reason for cancellation, signature and title, agency, copy of form 402 (notice to report for work), and form 403 (notice of termination of employment). All papers of each case are filed together in a separate jacket. Arranged alphabetically by names of employees. No index. Handwritten and typed on printed forms. 6 x 17 x 28. Relief bureau, Barrar Building, 206 East Fifth Street, Dayton Ohio.

37. CCC RECORDS
1933—. 2 file boxes.
Case records of CCC and enrollees, including applications, showing case number, date of application, name of applicant, address, age, number and names of dependents, and name of allottee; reports on investigations, and medical certificates. Arranged numerically by case numbers. No index. Typed on printed forms. 6 x 4 x 14. Relief bureau, Barrar Building, 206 East Fifth Street, Dayton Ohio.

NYA Records

38. CERTIFICATION ON ELIGIBILITY
1933—. 1 file drawer.

Certificates of eligibility for NYA work, showing name of youth, identification number, address, sex, race, marital status, place and date of birth, citizenship affidavit, name and address of case head, case number, number in family employed, in school, income of family, signature of certifying agent and his title. Arranged alphabetically by names of youths. No index. Typed and handwritten on printed forms. 6 x 9 x 18. NYA office, Beckel Building, Dayton.

39. ELIGIBILITY CONTROL CARD
1933—. 1 file box.

Card record of eligibility, showing name of youth, address, identification number, date of birth, date of original certification, date of recertification, and initials of person making recertification. Arranged alphabetically by names of youths. No index. Typed and handwritten on printed forms. 4 x 6 x 14. NYA office, Beckel Building, Dayton.

40. CANCELLATION OF ELIGIBILITY
1933—. 1 file drawer.

Record of cancellation of eligibility, showing name and address of youth, effective dates, case number, identification number, reason for cancellation, date signed, and signature and title of NYA representative. Arranged alphabetically by names of youths. No index. Handwritten and typed on printed forms. 6 x 9 x 12. NYA office, Beckel Building, Dayton.

41. NOTICE TO REPORT TO WORK
1933—. 1 file drawer.

Copies of notices to report for work, showing name and address of worker, identification number, sex, race, time to report for work, occupation, project number, code, wages per day, per month, type of assignment, transfer, signature of employment officer, also youth's and supervisor's signatures. Arranged alphabetically by names of workers. No index. Handwritten and typed on printed forms. 5 x 7 x 12. NYA office, Beckel Building, Dayton.

42. CITIZENSHIP AFFIDAVIT
1933—. 1 file drawer.
Affidavits of citizenship, showing name and address of the youth, identification and case numbers, whether citizen of United States, witness to signature, signature of employee, and official seal of person administering oath. Arranged alphabetically by names of youths. No index. Handwritten and typed on printed forms. 6 x 9 x 12. NYA office, Beckel Building, Dayton.

43. FIELD TRANSFER
1933—. 1 file drawer.
Copies of transfers showing transferring project number, date prepared, effective date of separation, pay period ending, signature of supervisor, receiving project number, date to report, location of project, name and address of worker, identification number, type of work, wages per month, explanation, and signature of employment officer. Arranged alphabetically by names of workers. No index. Handwritten and typed on printed forms. 12 x 9 x 18. NYA office, Beckel Building, Dayton.

44. TRANSFER OF WORKER
1933—. 2 file drawers.
Card record of transfers, showing name and address of worker, identification number, sex, race, project number, time of day of transfer, occupation, wage per day, per month, hours per month, comments, date, and signatures of employment officer or supervisor. Arranged alphabetically by names of workers. No index. Handwritten and typed on printed forms. 5 x 7 x 12. NYA office, Beckel Building, Dayton.

45. RECOMMENDATIONS FOR CHANGE IN STATUS
1933—. 1 file drawer.
Copies of recommendations for changes in status, showing name and address of worker, classification, age, division, number of days effective, annual salary, allowable travel expense, names of functional supervisor or division director, area work project and official project numbers, findings, date and by whom requested, date recommended, and date approved. Arranged alphabetically by names of workers. No index. Handwritten and typed on printed forms. 12 x 9 x 18. NYA office, Beckel Building, Dayton.

46. MONTHLY ATTENDANCE RECORD
1933—. 2 file drawers.

Card record of attendance showing identification number, name and address of worker, official district, work project number, occupation, class, number of hours worked each day, date, payroll number, and signatures of supervisor and worker. Arranged alphabetically by names of workers. No index. Handwritten and typed on printed forms. 5 x 7 x 12. NYA office, Beckel Building, Dayton.

47. YOUTH RECORD
1933—. 2 file drawers.

Record of NYA workers, showing name and address of youth, date, social security and identification numbers, date of birth, age, race, sex, nationality, religion, health record, height and weight, financial status, names of father and mother, occupation and education, previous employment, test, NYA employment record, and follow -up record to date. Arranged alphabetically by names of youths. No index. Handwritten on printed forms. 10 x 14 x 25. NYA office, Beckel Building, Dayton.

48. RECEPTIONISTS RECORD
1933—. 1 file drawer.

Receptionist's record, showing name of receptionist, date of service, service completed, without service, ineligibility, information, record quest, certifying agent, Ohio State Employment Service, social security, and name of interviewer or supervisor. Arranged alphabetically by names of receptionists. No index. Typed of printed forms. 12 x 9 x 18. NYA office, Beckel Building, Dayton.

49. WORK PROJECT APPLICATION
1933—. 1 file drawer.

Original applications for project work, showing state file number, area, work project number, symbol, official number, name and location of the project, co-operating agency, status of property or agency, starting date, estimated duration, number of youths to be assigned, sex, cost, objectives, experience, operation schedule, co-sponsors, certificate and agreement, and signatures of sponsor, supervisor, and administrator. Arranged alphabetically by names of projects. No index. Typed on printed forms. 12 x 9 x 18. NYA office, Beckel Building, Dayton.

50. NOTICE OF TERMINATION OF UNIT OF OPERATION
1933—. 1 file drawer.

Notice to state NYA director of termination of an activity or unit of operation, showing date, name of sponsor, location, official and work project numbers, work symbol, NYA district number, date activity began, completion of unit of operation to co-sponsor and NYA, signatures and sponsor and supervisor and by whom approved. Arranged alphabetically by names of operation units. No index. Typed on printed forms. 12 x 9 x 18. NYA office, Beckel Building, Dayton.

51. VOUCHERS FOR OFFICIAL TRAVEL
1933—. 1 file drawer.

Travel vouchers, showing voucher number, bureau number, name and address of payee, department, amount certified, by whom paid, description of travel and other expenses, kind of carrier, date of travel, class or mileage, and speedometer reading. Arranged alphabetically by names of payees. No index. Typed and handwritten on printed forms. 12 x 9 x 18. NYA office, Beckel Building, Dayton.

52. CLASSIFICATION SHEET
1933—. 1 file drawer.

Work classifications, showing name of employee, office title, classification title, area number, monthly salary, rate, travel, and total; business and residence address, annual and sick leave, name of reviewer, recommendations, description of work performed, and signatures of functional and area supervisor, director, and administrative assistant. Arranged alphabetically by classification titles and alphabetically thereunder by names of employees. No index. Handwritten and typed on printed forms. 12 x 9 x 18. NYA office, Beckel Building, Dayton.

53. REPORT OF INVENTORY AND MOVEMENT OF PROPERTY
1933—. 1 file drawer.

Report of inventory and movement of property, showing name of state, area, official and work project numbers, date period ending, owned by whom, item number, item description, unit of measure, transfers, approved survey and surplus, and total to account for. Arranged alphabetically by names of areas. No index. Typed on printed forms. 12 x 9 x 18. NYA office, Beckel Building, Dayton.

54. MONTHLY SUMMARY OF TELEPHONE TOLL CALLS

1933—. 1 file drawer.

Monthly summary of long distance telephone calls, showing telephone exchange number, period covered, name of city, district and project number, date, station number, division, name of person making call, duration of call, name of person and place called, and signature of district director. Arranged alphabetically by names of cities called. No index. Typed on printed forms. 12 x 9 x 18. NYA office, Beckel Building, Dayton.

55. PROPERTY TRANSFER ORDER AND RECEIPT

1933—. 1 file drawer.

Orders and receipts for transfer of property, showing document number, name of state, area, date, property owned by, appropriation symbol, project number, total value, item number and description, units shipped and received, unit value, total value, where shipped, signatures of division certification sending officer, and names of carrier and receiving officer. Arranged chronologically by dates of transfers. No index. Handwritten and typed on printed forms. 12 x 9 x 18. NYA office, Beckel Building, Dayton.

The office of county recorder, although not unknown as an early English institution for the registration of land titles, developed in colonial America, where, because of the mobility of the restless pioneers, changes in land titles were frequent and some system was needed to protect purchasers against previous encumbrances. Public land registers, established in most other colonies during the colonial period and continued by the states following independence, served as a model of land registration for the territory at which the present state of Ohio was then a part. Thus the office of county recorder was established by an act of the Northwest Territory, effective August 1, 1795. This act, adopted from the Pennsylvania Code, provided for the appointment by the governor of a recorder in each county whose principal duty was the recording of the deeds.[1]

When Ohio entered the Union in 1803 no constitutional provision was made for the continuance of the office, but the legislature during its first session passed an act providing for a recorder in each county to be appointed by the judges of the court of common pleas for a seven-year term.[2] The recorder continued to be an appointive officer until 1829, when, by an act of the legislature, the office became elective for three-year term.[3] The tenure of office remained at three years until the constitutional amendment on November 7, 1905, which provided for the election of all county officers in the even-numbered years.[4] The term of office was fixed at two years, and so continued until the amendment of 1933, which extended the tenure of the incumbent until January 1937, at which time the recorder, elected at regular election in November 1936, began to serve a four-year term.[5]

The first county recorder was directed by statute to record "all deeds, mortgages and conveyances of lands and tenements," lying within his county, and also all instruments and writings required by law to be recorded.[6] In 1805 he was directed to record all plats and maps of newly laid out villages.[7]

---

1. Theodore Calvin Pease, comp., *The Laws of the Northwest Territory, 1788-1800* (Illinois State Bar Association *Law Series,* Springfield, 1925, I), 197-199.
2. *Laws of Ohio,* I, 136.
3. *Ibid.,* XXVII, 65.
4. *Ohio Const. 1851* (Amendment, 1905), Art. XVII, secs. 1, 2; *Laws of Ohio,* XCVIII, 271.
5. *Laws of Ohio,* CXV, 191.
6. *Ibid.,* I, 137.
7. *Ibid.,* III, 213-215.

In 1835 he was permitted, when authorized by the county commissioners, to transcribe from the records of other counties all deeds, mortgages, and other instruments of writing for the sale or conveyance of lands, tenements, or hereditaments affecting land titles in his county.[8]

Since the establishment of the office many duties besides those of recording land titles have been added. The present practice of recording powers of attorney had its beginning in 1818.[9] Although the mechanics of Cincinnati were authorized to file mechanics' liens with the recorder as early as 1823, it was not until 1840 that the privilege was extended to the laborers of Montgomery County.[10] Successive acts in 1865, 1872, 1881, 1884, 1888, 1904, and 1923 added new duties to the office in the recording of soldiers' discharges,[11] copies of certificates of compliance authorizing insurance companies not incorporated under the laws of Ohio to transact business in the state, and certified copies of renewal as granted by such companies to their agents[12] limited partnership agreements,[13] stallion keepers' liens,[14] oil and gas leases,[15] partition fence records,[16] and federal tax liens.[17] The recording of chattel mortgages and conditional sales began in 1846. Such instruments were to be deposited with the township clerk where the mortgagor was a resident. In all other townships, however, in which the recorder maintained his office such instruments were to be deposited with him.[18] Since 1906 chattel mortgages have been filed with the county recorder exclusively.[19] It is provided that in order to be valid against subsequent mortgages, the chattel mortgage must be deposited with the county recorder of the county where the mortgagor resides at the time of its execution, and to retain its validity the mortgage must be renewed every three years.[20]

---

8. *Ibid.,* XXXIII, 8; XXXV, 10-11.
9. *Laws of Ohio,* XVI, 155-156.
10. *Ibid.,* 8-10; XXXVIII, 115-116; XLI, 66. In 1843 the provisions of the act were extended to include all counties of the state.
11. *Ibid.,* LXII, 59.
12. *Ibid.,* LXIX, 32, 148, XCVII, 405.
13. *Ibid.,* LXXVIII, 248.
14. *Ibid.,* LXXI, 43.
15. *Ibid.,* LXXXV, 179.
16. *Ibid.,* XCVII, 140.
17. *Ibid.,* CX, 252.
18. *Ibid.,* XLIV, 61.
19. G. C. sec. 8561.
20. G. C. Sec. 8565.

In 1936 the legislature passed an act authorizing the recorder to destroy such instruments six years after the time of refiling has expired.[21]

An important extension of method of recording land titles known as the "Torrens System," was provided by an act of the general assembly in 1896.[22] In 1897 this act was declared unconstitutional by the supreme court of Ohio as being contrary to section 16 of the bill of rights of the state constitution.[23] The act of 1913, amended in 1913 and 1915, provides for the examination of land title by the recorder and the issuance, if the title proved to be held in fee simple, of a certificate of title by the court of common pleas or probate court. The official certificate becomes the title of ownership and is indefeasible. However, in the event an interest is found in the land, after the issuance of the certificate, a claim is allowed to the legal claimant from a fund created for that purpose at the time of registration.[24] This system, although adopted by a few counties, including Montgomery County, is not used as widely as it might be because of the difficulty of replacing the traditional complicated system.

The recorder, like other county officials, had been required in earlier years to keep records of the business of his office, but it was not until the middle of the nineteenth century that the legislature looking forward to some uniformity in land registration, enacted measures prescribing the form and contents of such records. Since 1850 the recorder has been required to keep a record of deeds in which is recorded all deeds, powers of attorney, and other instruments of writing for the unconditional sale of land, tenements, or hereditaments.[25] The same year saw the beginning of a record of mortgages in which was recorded all mortgages, powers of attorney, and other instruments of writing by which land, tenements, or hereditaments "shall or may be mortgaged" or otherwise conditionally sold; and a record of plats in which was to be recorded all plats and maps of town lots and of subdivisions thereof, and of other divisions of surveying lands, in like regular succession according to the priority other presentation.[26]

---

21. *Laws of Ohio,* CXVI, 324.
22. *Ibid.,* XCII, 220.
23. *Ohio State Reports* (Cincinnati, 1852—), LVI, 575.
24. G. C. secs. 8572-34—8572-56; *Laws of Ohio,* CIII, 914-960; CVI, 443.
25. *Laws of Ohio,* XLVIII, 64.
26. *Ibid.,* XLVIII, 64.

Since 1851 the recorder has been required to keep in a separate record of deeds and mortgages denominated respectfully as "Record of Deeds" and "Record of mortgages."[27] Since 1865 the recorder has been required to keep a separate record of leases.[28] The present practice of keeping a daily register of deeds and a daily register of mortgages had its beginning in Montgomery County in 1890 although not required by statute until 1896.[29]

Although indexes had been prepared in earlier years, the present system of indexing had its beginning in 1851 and took practically its present form in 1896.[30] At present the recorder, at the beginning of each day's business, is required to make and maintain a general alphabetical index, direct and reverse, of all names of both parties of all instruments recorded by him. The indexes show the kind of instruments, the date, the range, the township and section, the survey number and the number of acres or the lot and sublot numbers and the part thereof, of each tract or lots of land described in any such instrument of writing; the name of each grantor is entered in a direct index under the appropriate letter and followed on the same line by the name of the grantee; the name of each grantee is entered in a reverse index under the appropriate letter and followed on the same line by the name of the grantor.[31] Since 1867 the recorder has been required to maintain sectional or geographical indexes to records of all real estate in the county when so directed by the board of county commissioners.[32] Sectional or geographical indexes were not located in Montgomery County recorder's office.

Fees for filing and recording of the various instruments and for searches and other services have been set by the general assembly. However, since 1907, the recorder has been required to keep an account of the fees collected and to pay them into the general funds of the county treasury.[33] Fees earned by Montgomery County recorder's office in 1939 amounted to $33,923.49.[34]

---

27. *Ibid.,* XLIX, 103.
28. *Ibid.,* LXII, 170.
29. *Ibid.,* XCII, 268.
30. *Ibid.,* XLIX, 103; XCII, 268; CII, 288.
31. G. C. sec. 2764.
32. *Laws of Ohio,* LXIV, 256; LXXXI, 49; CII, 289; G. C. sec. 2766.
33. *Laws of Ohio,* XCVIII, 90-91; G. C. sec. 2983.
34. Ohio Auditor of State, *Annual report, 1939,* 374.

The present duties of the recorder do not differ, in the main, from those prescribed in the middle of the nineteenth century. His annual salary is $4,065 and is bonded for $2,000.[35] The recorder's records, bound in large bulky volumes, are open to the inspection and use of the public and are transferred to his successor.[36]

---

35. *Ibid., ;* G. C. sec. 2751.
36. G. C. sec. 2756.

Real Property Transfers

Deeds and Registers

56. DEEDS
1803—. 864 volumes (1803-1938, B-Z; 1838-1855, A2-12, K2-22; 1856-1866, A3-I3, K3-Z3; 1867-1873, A4-H4, J4-Z4; 1874—, 101-864).
Copies of deeds recorded conveying title to real estate in Montgomery County, showing names of grantor and grantee, kind of instrument, date filed, date recorded, description of property, and amount of consideration. Also contains; Lease Record, 1833-1864, entry 62 and Mortgage Record, 1805-1838, entry 64. Arranged chronologically by dates of filing. Indexed alphabetically by names of grantors, showing names of grantees; also separate indexes, 1805—, entries 57 and 58, and to leases, 1839-1864, entry 65. 1803-1903, handwritten; 1909-1930, typed; 1931—, photostat. Average 500 pages. 18 x 12 x 3.5. Recorder's office.

57. INDEX TO DEEDS [Direct]
1805—. 43 volumes (1-43).
Direct index to Deeds, entry 56, showing names of grantor and grantee, brief description of property, location of property, dates of filing and recording, and volume letter and page number of record. Arranged alphabetically by names the grantors. Handwritten. Average 250 pages. 18 x 12 x 2. Recorder's office.

58. INDEX TO DEEDS [Reverse]
1805—. 43 volumes (1-43).
Reverse index to Deeds, entry 56, showing names of grantee and grantor, brief description of property, location of property, dates of filing and recording, and volume letter and page number of record. Arranged alphabetically by grantees.

Handwritten. Average 250 pages. 18 x 12 x 2. Recorder's office.

59. INLOTS AND OUTLOTS [Abstract Book]
1803—. 110 volumes (70 volumes inlots, 1-70 and contained by lot numbers; 40 volumes outlots, 1.5-40.5).

Abstracts of titles to inlots and outlots, showing range, township, section and lot numbers, description, named of grantor and grantee, kind of estimate, volume and page numbers of Mortgage Record, entry 64 or Deeds, entry 56, and volume letter and page numbers of Plat Books, entry 75. Arranged numerically by lot numbers. No index. Handwritten. Average 500 pages. 18 x 12 x 4. Recorder's office.

60. DEEDS
1805—. 46 file boxes (labeled by contained letters of alphabet).

Original deeds to real estate which have been filed for recording and are uncalled for by owners, showing information as in Deeds, entry 56. Arranged alphabetically by names of grantors. No index. 1805-1903 handwritten; 1904—, typed on printed forms. 11 x 5 x 13.5 Recorder's office.

61. DAILY REGISTER OF INSTRUMENTS
1890—. 30 volumes. (dated). Title varies; Instruments Received for Recording, 1890-1912, 5 volumes.

Daily register of deeds and other instruments filed for recording, showing date filed, kind of instrument, instrument number, names of grantor and grantee, fee paid, time of day filed, number of acres, lot number, and amount of consideration. Arranged chronologically by dates of filing and numerically thereunder by instrument numbers. No index. Handwritten on printed forms. Average 300 pages. 24 x 14 x 3. 14 volumes, 1895-1923, Recorder's record room; 16 volumes, 1924—, Recorder's office.

Leases (See also entry 61)

62. LEASE RECORD
1865—. 35 volumes (1-35). 1833-1864 in Deeds, entry 56.

Copies of leases filed for record, showing name of lessor and lessee, date of lease, terms, description of property, location of property, date filed, and date recorded. Also includes copies of oil and gas leases, 1884—, showing information as in the lease record. Arranged chronologically by dates of filing. Indexed alphabetically by names of lessees showing names of lessors; also separate index, entry 65. 1865-1903, handwritten; 1904-1929, typed; 1930—, photostat. Average 300 pages. 18 x 12 x 3. Recorder's office.

63. LEASES
1865—. 4 file boxes (labeled by contained letters of alphabet).
Original leases filed for recording and not called for by owners, showing date filed, name of lessor and lessee, description of property, and terms of lease. Also includes oil and gas leases, 1884—. Arranged alphabetically by names of lessees. No index. 1865-1903, handwritten; 1904—, typed. 11 x 5 x 14. Recorder's office.

Mortgages (See also entry 61)

64. MORTGAGE RECORD
1839—. 798 volumes (1839-1866, A5-Z5; 1867-1874, A6-Z6; 1875—, 51-796). 1805-1838 in Deeds, entry 56.
Copies of mortgage deeds conveying conditional title to real estate as security for value received, showing names of grantor and grantee, mortgage number, date of mortgage, condition, amount secured, description of real estate covered by mortgage deeds, names of witnesses, copy of notarization, date filed, and date recorded. Date of cancellation written on margin, 1839-1891. Also includes copies of notices issued by state tax commission of payment of franchise or excise tax lien and discharge of lien. 1930—, showing date paid, name of firm, amount of tax, penalty, total tax paid, date and time received in recorder's office, date recorded, and amount of fee. Arranged chronologically by dates of recording. For index, see entry 65. 1839-1904, handwritten; 1905-1931 typed; 1932—, photostat. Average 650 pages. 18 x 14 x 4. Recorder's office.

65. INDEX TO MORTGAGE RECORD, LEASES AND LIENS
1839—. 59 volumes (1839-1923, 1-27; 1924—, 2 series: 28-43 direct; 28-43 reverse).
Index to Mortgage Record, entry 64, Lease Record, 1865—, entry 62, Lease Record in Deeds, 1839-1864, entry 56, Mechanics Liens, 1842—, entry 68, Subcontractors Liens, 1914—, entry 69, Showing name of grantor and grantee or principals, amount involved, date of instrument, date of filing, and volume and page numbers of record. Arranged alphabetically by names of grantors and grantees or other principles. Handwritten. Average 600 pages. 18 x 12 x 4. Recorder's office.

66. MORTGAGES

1839—. 10 file boxes (1839-1936, labeled by contained letters of alphabet; 1937—, by contained mortgage numbers).

Original mortgage deeds which have been filed for recording and are uncalled for by owners, showing information as in Mortgage Record, entry 64. Arranged chronologically by years; 1839-1936, alphabetically thereunder by names of mortgagees; 1937—, numerically thereunder by mortgage numbers. No index. 1839-1904, handwritten; 1905—, typed on printed forms. 11 x 5 x 13.5 Recorder's office.

67. MORTGAGE RELEASES

1891—. 20 volumes (1-20).

Record of mortgage releases, showing date of release, name of mortgagor, and mortgagee, town lots, acreage, total amount of mortgage, and signature of mortgagor releasing the same. Arranged chronologically by dates of releases. Indexed alphabetically by names of mortgagors. Handwritten. Average 400 pages. 18 x 12 x 2. 9 volumes, 1891-1922 Recorder's record room; 11 volumes, 1933—, Recorder's office.

Liens (See also entry 61)

68. MECHANICS LIENS

1842—. 22 volumes (A-I, K-W). Title varies: Liens, 1 volume.

Copies of mechanics' affidavits for liens, showing names of creditor and debtor, itemized statement of wages and material, location and description of property, amount of lien, date of filing, and date of recording. Also contains Sub-Contractors Liens, 1842-1913, entry 69. Arranged chronologically by dates of recording. Indexed alphabetically by names of creditors showing names of debtors; also separate index, entry 65. 1842-1908, handwritten; 1909-1930, typed; 1931—, photostat. Average 300 pages. 15 x 12 x 3. Recorder's office.

69. SUB-CONTRACTORS LIENS

1914—. 8 volumes (1-8). 1842-1913 in Mechanics Liens, entry 68.

Copies of affidavits for work performed, showing names of creditor and debtor, location of property, amount of lien, date of filing, and date of recording. Indexed alphabetically by names of creditors showing names of debtors; also separate index, entry 65. 1914, handwritten; 1915-1936, typed; 1937—, photostat. Average 300 pages. 18 x 12 x 3. Recorder's office.

70. MECHANICS LIENS [Affidavits]

1842—. 5 file boxes (4, labeled by contained letter of alphabet; 1, dated). Original affidavits which have been recorded and are uncalled for, showing information as in Mechanics Liens entry 68. Arranged alphabetically by names of creditors. No index. 1842-1908, handwritten; 1909—, typed. 11 x 5 x 14. Recorder's office.

71. FEDERAL TAX LIEN

1923—. 1 volume.

Record of federal tax liens filed, showing recorder's file number, name and address of person assessed, collector's serial number, date of filing, amount of taxes, penalty, and date and amount paid. Arranged alphabetically by names of persons assessed and chronologically thereunder by dates of filing. No index. Handwritten on printed forms. 300 pages. 18 x 12 x 3. Recorder's office.

72. CORPORATION RECORD

1930—. 1 volume.

Record of excise and franchise tax liens, showing recorder's file number of notice of lien, name of firm, date and time of filing, and amount of lien; also a record of releases, showing recorder's file number, dates released, and volume and page numbers of Mortgage Record, entry 64. Arranged alphabetically by names of firms and chronologically thereunder by dates of filing. No index. Handwritten on printed forms. 300 pages. 18 x 14 x 2. Recorder's office.

73. EXCISE AND FRANCHISE TAX LIEN

1931—. 5 file boxes. (dated).

Notice of liens for excise and franchise taxes, showing date of lien, name of corporation, year tax due, amount of tax and penalty, total amount, and date and hour filed, and recorder's file number. Arranged alphabetically by names of corporations and chronologically thereunder by dates of filing. No index. Handwritten on printed forms. 15 x 5 x 10. Recorder's office.

Registered Lands

74. REGISTERED LANDS
1913——. 3 volumes. (1-3).

Original certificates of title to registered lands, entered pursuant to decree of registration, showing name of court, date and registration, time of registration, diagram of registered lands, name of land owner, description of street where land is located, number of feet from street to street by parallel lines, and names of clerk, deputy, judge, and recorder. Arranged chronologically by dates of registration. Indexed alphabetically by names of owners of land. Handwritten and typed on printed forms. Average 500 pages. 20 x 17 x 4. Recorder's office.

Plats and Surveys

75. PLAT BOOKS
1803——. 37 volumes (1803-1848, 1-10; -1849-1873, 4 volumes, A; 1874-1899, 4 volumes. BO; 1890——, C-U).

Plat maps, surveyors' description, and survey data of all additions and subdivisions platted in Montgomery County, showing name of plat, boundary lines, lot lines, streets and alleys, streams and railroads, lot number, lot dimensions, name of lot owner, date surveyed and platted, date recorded, and name of surveyor. Arranged chronologically by dates of recording. For index, see entry 76. 1803-1930, handwritten and hand drawn; 1931——, handwritten and photostat. Average 98 pages. 24 x 18 x 2. Recorder's office.

76. INDEX TO PLATS
1803——. 1 volume.

Index to Plat Books, entry 75, showing name of plat, location of property, volume letter and page number of record and of Deeds, entry 56, and Inlots and Outlots [Abstract book], entry 59. Arranged alphabetically by names of plats. Typed. 500 pages. 27 x 18 x 4. Recorder's office.

77. PARTITION FENCE RECORD
1905—. 1 volume.

Record of petitions from landowners to township trustees to survey and establish line fences, showing date of petition, name of complainant, location of property, and dates of recording. Includes submissions of bids by contractors, records of bonds presented by bidders, acceptance of bids, specifications for work to be done, and amount of cost to each landowner. Arranged chronologically by dates of recording. Indexed alphabetically by names of complainants. Typed. 300 pages. 18 x 12 x 3. Recorder's office.

Personal Property Transfers

78. CHATTEL MORTGAGE RECORD
1877—. 6 volumes (1-6).

Copies of chattel mortgages and conditional bills of sale, showing name of grantor and grantee, amount of mortgage, itemized list of property mortgaged, condition of mortgage, copy of notarization, date filed for record, date recorded, and copy of cancellation of mortgage. Arranged chronologically by dates of recording. Indexed alphabetically by names of grantors showing names of grantees. Typed. Average 300 pages. 18 x 12 x 2. Recorder's office.

79. CHATTEL MORTGAGES
1926—. 99 file boxes (labeled by contained mortgage numbers). Prior records destroyed.

Original chattel mortgages, showing names of mortgagor and mortgagee, amount and date of mortgage, execution date, mortgage number, description and statement of claim, and dates of filing, renewal, release, or cancellation. Arranged numerically by mortgage numbers. For indexes, see entries 81, 82. Typed on printed forms. 44 file boxes, 12 x 4 x 16; 55 file boxes, 12 x 18 x 24. 44 file boxes, 1926-1934, Recorder's record room; 55 file boxes, 1938—, Recorder's office.

80. CHATTEL MORTGAGE INDEX
1910-1921. 11 volumes (dated; 1 unlabeled, 24-33).

Index to chattel mortgages which have been destroyed as provided by law, showing name of mortgagor and mortgagee, date of mortgage, amount, and dates of filing, refiling and cancellation. Arranged by names of mortgagors and mortgagees. Handwritten on printed forms.

Average 700 pages. 24 x 14.5 x 2. Recorder's record room.

81. CHATTEL MORTGAGE INDEX [Direct]
1922—. 32 volumes (34-51, 2 volumes for some years; all dated).
Direct index to Chattel Mortgages, entry 79, showing information as in Chattel Mortgage Index, entry 80. Arranged alphabetically by names of mortgagors. Handwritten on printed forms. Average 700 pages. 22 x 14.5 x 3. 20 volumes, 1922-1933, Recorder's record room; 12 volumes, 1934—, Recorder's office.

82. CHATTEL MORTGAGE INDEX [Reverse]
1922—. 32 volumes (34-51, two volumes for some years; all dated).
Reverse index to Chattel Mortgages, entry 79, showing information as in Chattel Mortgage Index, entry 80. Arranged alphabetically by mortgagees. Handwritten on printed forms. Average 700 pages. 22 x 14.5 x 3. 20 volumes, 1922-1933, Recorder's record room; 12 volumes, 1934—, Recorder's office.

83. DAILY RECEIPTS OF CHATTEL MORTGAGES
1923-1934. 12 volumes. (dated).
Daily register of chattel mortgages received for filing, showing names of grantor and grantee, description of property, value of property, amount of fee, and date of filing. Arranged alphabetically by names of grantors. No index. Handwritten. Average 300 pages. 18 x 8 x 1.5. Recorder's office.

Incorporations and Partnerships

84. INCORPORATED RECORDS
1846—. 3 volumes (A, B, 2).
Copies of incorporated agreements showing names of principals, name of company, location of business, whether old or new, statement of assets and liabilities, terms of agreement, names the stockholders, and date recorded. Also 1881—, record of limited partnership agreements, showing name of each partner, kind of business, location, amount involved, terms of agreement, and date recorded. Also includes record of partners and traders, 1884-1886, showing name of each partner, terms of agreement, and date recorded. Indexed alphabetically by names of principals. Incorporation records, 1846-1911, handwritten; 1921-1935, typed; 1936—, photostat; partnerships, 1881-1924, handwritten; 1921-1925, typed; 1935—, photostat. Average 300 pages. 18 x 12 x 3. Recorder's office.

Grants of Authority

85. POWER OF ATTORNEY
1893—. 3 volumes (1-3).
Copies of power of attorney agreements, showing name and address of principal and agent, extent of power, reason for granting of privilege, date recorded, and signature of certifying official. Arranged chronologically by dates of recording. Indexed alphabetically by names of agents. 1893-1906, handwritten; 1906-1933, typed; 1933—, photostat. Average 600 pages. 18 x 12 x 3. Recorder's office.

86. GENERAL FUND [Insurance Compliance]
1932—. 1 roll, 6 folders in 1 file box.
Compliances of insurance companies as submitted annually, showing date of statement, name of company, names of officers of company, statement of assets and liabilities, and date of filing. Arranged chronologically by dates of filing and alphabetically thereunder by names of companies. No index. Typed on printed forms. Roll, 12.5 x 9 x 1; file box, 12 x 15 x 25.5; folders, 9 x 12.5 x 1. Recorder's office.

87. INSURANCE CERTIFICATES
1903—. 13 volumes (1-13).
Copies of licenses issued to insurance agents by state department of insurance and filed with county recorder, showing name of company, name of agent, address, date license issued, and date filed. Arranged alphabetically by names of agents and chronologically thereunder by dates of filing. No index. Handwritten on printed forms. Average 200 pages. 14 x 12 x 1. 11 volumes, 1903-1933, Recorder's record room; 2 volumes, 1934—, Recorder's office.

Miscellaneous

88. DAILY RECEIPTS
1907—. 8 volumes.
Daily record of fees paid into recorder's office for the filing of instruments, showing kind of instrument, instrument number, by whom paid, amount, and date of receipt. Arranged chronologically by dates of receipts. No index. Handwritten on printed forms. Average 300 pages. 15 x 9 x 2. Recorder's office.

89. DISCHARGE RECORDS [Soldiers]
1865—. 6 volumes (1-6).

Record of military discharges recorded, showing name of soldier, place of birth, age, personal description, training, promotions, citations, names of superior officer, dates enlisted, discharged, or transferred, signature of soldier, and date recorded. Volumes 2-6, 1919—,contain discharges for soldiers of World War. Arranged chronologically by dates of recording. Indexed alphabetically by names of soldiers. 1865-1913, handwritten; 1919—, typed. Average 600 pages. 18 x 12 x 3. Recorder's office.

The office of clerk of courts, and ancient English Institution originating before the time of Edward I[1] was transplanted to America during the colonial period. The American Revolution made no radical change in the political heritage derived from England, and the office was continued by the states. The duties of the office were modified in the newer states, however, because of a separation of administrative and judicial functions, which under the English system had been combined.

The sections of the Ohio Constitution of 1802 creating the judicial system for the state provided for the appointment of a clerk of courts by the judges of the court of common pleas. He was to serve a seven-year term, but was subject to removal by the appointing power for breach of good behavior.[2] The constitution of 1851 made the office of clerk elective with a three-year term.[3] A constitutional amendment in 1905 provided that the term of all elective offices should be for an even number of years not exceeding four. In compliance with this amendment, the general assembly passed an act fixing the term of office of the clerk at two years.[4] The term remained at two years until 1936 when it was extended to 4 years.[5] The remuneration of the office was by salary and fees until 1906 when the legislature prescribed a definite salary based on the population of his county.[6]

The duties of the clerk of courts, like those of other county officers, are prescribed by statute. In 1853 a code of civil procedure was adopted summarizing the earlier duties and forming the bases for the present ones which are in most respects similar to those prescribed during the early years of the office. The clerk of courts was directed to issue all writs and orders for provisional remedies; endorse the date upon all papers filed in his office; keep the journal, record books, and papers appertaining to the court of common pleas and record its proceedings, and keep five books to be called the appearance docket, the trial docket, and a printed duplicate of the trial docket, the journal, the record, and the execution docket.[7]

---

1. Sir Frederick Pollock and Frederic William Maitland, *The History of English Law Before the tTme of Edward I* (Cambridge, 1895), I, 184.
2. *Ohio Const., 1802,* Art. III, sec. 9.
3. *Ohio Const., 1851,* Art, IV, sec. 16.
4. *Laws of Ohio,* XCVIII, 273.
5. *Ibid.,* CXVI, pt. ii, 184.
6. *Ibid.,* XCVIII, 94, 117. The salary in Montgomery County for 1939 was $5,190. Ohio Auditor of State, *Annual Report, 1939,* 372.
7. *Laws of Ohio,* LI, 107, 158-159; LXXVIII, 108; LXXXIX, 115; LXXXVI, 174.

The present practice of keeping an index, direct and reverse, to judgments began in 1866.[8] In 1871 the clerk was made official custodian of the law reports and books furnished by the state for the use of the court and bar, and was made liable in the event of their destruction.[9]

Some of the duties of the clerk as defined by the civil code of 1853 are still effective, others have been added by subsequent legislation. Thus, for example, in 1858 the clerk was directed to receive notary commissions for record.[10] He was required, also, to receive for record special police commissions (1867), timber trade-marks (1893), partnership agreements (1894), copies of judgments of federal courts (1898), marks of ownership [trade-marks] (1911), motor vehicle bills of sale (1921), and certificates of judgments to operate as a lien (1935).[11] Since January 1, 1938 he has issued certificates of title to motor vehicles.[12] On the other hand, many of the earlier duties of the clerk have been transferred to other departments of local government or have been abolished. The clerk issued marriage licenses and recorded ministers' licenses until 1852, after that date they have been issued by the probate court,[13] to which court the records have been transferred. Moreover, the clerk issued peddler' licenses until the decade of the sixties, since that time they have been issued by the auditor.[14] The clerk has been authorized to act as an agent of the state in the sale of hunting and trapping licenses to nonresidents of the state since 1904 and to residents since 1919.[15] He has been authorized also to serve as an agent in the sale of fishing licenses to nonresidents since 1919 and to residents since 1925.[16] The practice of recording in the office of the clerk, the name of black or mulatto persons to be used as certificates of freedom was, of course, discontinued after the close of the War between the States and 1865. In 1865 the clerk was directed by the legislature to preserve a list of births, marriages, and deaths as returned to his office by the assessors, and to transmitted annually, on or before the first day of June, a copy of such statistics to the secretary of state.

---

8. *Ibid.,* LXIII, 10; LXXV, 103; LXXVIII, 88; LXXXII, 33; LXXXVI, 26.
9. *Ibid.,* LXVIII, 109.
10. *Laws of Ohio,* LU, 13; XCIII, 406.
11. *Ibid.,* LXIV, 60; LXXX, 195; XCI, 357; XCII, 25; XCIII, 285; CII, 513-514; CIX, 3331 CXVI, 274.
12. G. C. sec. 6290-6. See also p. LX
13. *Laws of Ohio,* I, 31; XXIX, 429; L, 84; *Ohio Const. 1851,* Art. IV, sec, 8.
14. *Laws of Ohio,* LIX, 67.
15. *Ibid.,* XCVII, 474; CVIII, pt. i, 595. For additional licenses, see pp. XLIV, 62.
16. *Laws of Ohio,* CVIII, 923; CXI, 276.

These lists are no longer preserved. From these county lists, the secretary of state prepared tabular statements showing the vital statistics in each county. The clerk received ten copies of the report, one of which he was required to preserve in his office.[17] The clerk was relieved of the task of collecting and preserving vital statistics, when, in 1867, such powers and duties were vested in the probate judge.[18]

The clerk of courts was given other duties in addition to those of serving the court of common pleas and receiving documents for record. Since 1850 he has been required to report each year to the county commissioners all fines assessed by the courts in criminal cases, together with the names of parties to each case, and the amount of money he has paid to the county treasurer.[19] Duplicate copies of these reports have been preserved in the clerk's office and are recorded in the Commissioners' Journal, entry 1. Moreover, since 1867 he has been required to report annually to the secretary of state the number of crimes committed in his county, the number of pending cases, and the amount of fines collected.[20] An act of 1927, amending the act of 1867, directed the clerk to report on any matters which the secretary of state might require, and to forward a duplicate copy of his report on crime in his county to the state board of clemency [board of pardons and parole].[21] The state board of clemency was abolished in 1921 and its duties were assigned to a board of pardons and parole within the department of public welfare.[22] The clerk is also directed to receive the report of the coroner on his findings of facts and inquest and autopsies and his account of fees received for each service.[23]

Since 1907 the clerk has been required to keep an accurate account of fees collected for recording licenses and commissions, issuing certificates of title to motor vehicles, court costs, and fines, and report monthly to the county treasurer.[24]

The county clerk of courts, like the county prosecuting attorney, is one of the most important persons in the judicial system. His significance and influence, however, was not recognized until recent years.

---

17. *Ibid.,* LIII, 73-75.
18. *Ibid.,* LXIV, 63-64.
19. *Ibid.,* XLVIII, 66; LVIII, 69; LXXXVI, 239.
20. *Ibid.,* LXIV, 17.
21. *Ibid.,* CXII, 203.
22. *Ibid.,* CIX, 111, 124.
23. G. C. sec. 2859. See p. 140.
24. G. C. sec. 2983.

90. CALENDAR OF GENERAL DOCKET
1900-1909. 9 volumes. Discontinued.

Docket of court cases, showing names of litigants and attorneys, case number, date set for hearing, and kind of case. Arranged chronologically by dates of hearings. No index. Typed. Average 75 pages. 14 x 6 x .5. Clerk of courts' record room 1.

91. PRAECIPE DOCKET
1874—. 28 volumes (3-30). Prior records missing.

Docket of writs issued by the clerk of courts, showing names of plaintiff and defendant, date issued, kind of writ, date returnable, names of attorney, and volume and page numbers of dockets where entered. Arranged chronologically by dates issued. No index. Handwritten on printed forms. Average 500 pages. 14 x 8 x 2.5. 25 volumes, 1874-1935, clerk of courts' record room 1; 3 volumes, 1936—, Clerk of courts' office.

92. CASE RECORDS [Civil]
1803—. 506 file boxes. (thirty-two unlabeled: four hundred and seventy-four labeled by contained case numbers.

Original papers in civil causes filed in court of common pleas and court of appeals, including declaration of particulars, all writs, court orders, general entries, sheriff's returns on writs, itemized cost bills, and 1874—, *praecipes*. All papers of each case are filed together in a jacket, showing title of case, names of litigants, court term, case number, and volume and page numbers of dockets and record were entered. Also contains: Case Records [Criminal], 1803-1847, entry 93; Original Papers, [Divorce], [1843]-1920, entry 166; [Original papers, Court of Appeals], 1913—, entry 222. Arranged numerically by case numbers. 1803-1841, no index; for index, 1842—, see entry 144. 1803-1840, handwritten; 1840-1902, handwritten on printed forms; 1903—, typed on printed forms. 32 file boxes, 10 x 10 x 25; 474 file boxes, 11.5 x 15.5 x 27. 302 file boxes, 1803-1936, clerk of courts' record room 3; 204 file boxes, 1937—, Clerk of courts' office.

93. CASE RECORDS [Criminal]
1848—. 20 file boxes (labeled by contained case numbers). 1803-1847 in Case Records [Civil], entry 92.

Original papers in criminal causes heard in court of common pleas and court of appeals, including summonses, warrants to arrest, affidavits of information, transcripts, subpoenas, writs, pleas, executions for cost, certificate of sentence to penal institutions, and itemized cost bills. All papers of each case are filed together in a jacket, showing name of defendant, court term, case number, charge, and volume and page numbers of dockets and records where entered. Also contains [Original Papers, Court of Appeals], 1913—, entry 222. Arranged numerically by case numbers. No index. Handwritten on printed forms. 10.5 x 16 x 34. 11 file boxes, 1848-1938, clerk of courts' record room 2; 9 file boxes, 1939—, Clerk of courts' office.

94. BILL OF EXCEPTIONS
1917—. 820 bills.

Bills of exceptions filed on appeal from decision or verdict asking for a review of the case on error or other grounds, showing name of plaintiff and defendant, date case filed, from what court, to what court appealed, name of person filing exception, transcripts of testimony and dispositions, volume and page numbers of docket and records where entered, and date motion overruled. No obvious arrangement; each bill bound separately. No index. Typed. Average 50 pages. 15 x 8 x 1.5. 520 bills, 1917-1934, clerk of courts' record room 2; 300 bills, 1935—, Clerk of courts' office.

95. RECEIVERSHIPS
1935—. 1 volume.

Record of receivership cases, showing case number, names of persons involved, date petition filed, date of answer, date receiver appointed, name of receiver, date bond filed, date of inventory and appraisal, dates of first and second reports of receiver, and names of judge and attorneys for each party. Arranged chronologically by dates petitions filed. No index. Typed. 100 pages. 12 x 8 x 1. Assignment commissioner's office.

Judgments and Executions

96. JUDGMENT DOCKET
1935—. 3 volumes. (1-3).

Certificates of judgments rendered to act as a lien, showing name of court, case number, certificate number, title of case, names of judgment creditor and debtor, amount of judgment and rate of interest, date decree rendered, volume and page numbers of Minutes, entry 146, date filed, filing fee, names of attorneys, date judgment satisfied, and date lien cancelled. Arranged numerically by certificate numbers. For indexes, see entries 97 and 98. Handwritten on printed forms. Average 600 pages. 18 x 12 x 3. Clerk of courts' office.

97. GENERAL INDEX TO JUDGMENT DOCKET, DIRECT
1935—. 2 volumes. (labeled by contained letters of alphabet).
Direct index to Judgment Docket, entry 96, showing certificate number, names of judgment creditor and debtor, date certificate filed, volume and page numbers of docket, and date cancelled. Arranged alphabetically by names of judgment creditors. Handwritten on printed forms. Average 400 pages. 17 x 14 x 2. Clerk of courts' office.

98. GENERAL INDEX TO JUDGMENT DOCKET, REVERSE
1935—. 2 volumes. (labeled by contained letters of alphabet).
Reverse index to Judgment Docket, entry 96, showing certificate number, names of judgment debtor and creditor, date certificate filed, volume and page numbers of docket, and date cancelled. Arranged alphabetically by names of judgment debtors. Handwritten on printed forms. Average 400 pages. 17 x 14 x 2. Clerk of courts' office.

99. JUDGMENT INDEX, DIRECT
1803-1920. 11 volumes (1-11). 1920—, in Judgment Index, Direct and Reverse, entry 101.
Direct index record of judgments rendered, showing date of case filed, names of judgment creditor and debtor, court term, date judgment satisfied, volume and page numbers of Minutes, entry 146, amount of judgment, amount of costs, and volume number or letter and page number of Common Pleas Record, entry 150. Arranged alphabetically by judgment creditors. Handwritten on printed forms. Average 600 pages. 18 x 12 x 3.25. Clerk of courts' record room 1.

100. JUDGMENT INDEX, REVERSE
1803-1920. 11 volumes (1-11). 1920—, in Judgment Index, Direct and Reverse, entry 101.
Reverse index record of judgments rendered, showing date case filed, names of judgment creditor and debtor, court term, date judgment satisfied, volume and page numbers of Minutes, entry 146, amount of judgment, amount of cost, and volume number or letter and page number of Common Pleas Record, entry 150.

Arranged alphabetically by names the judgment debtors. Handwritten on printed forms.

101. JUDGMENT INDEX, DIRECT AND REVERSE
1920—. 7 volumes (12-18).

Direct and reverse index record of judgment decrees, showing names of judgment creditor and debtor, term of court in which judgment rendered, case number, volume and page numbers of Minutes, entry 146, and Common Pleas Record, entry 150, nature of suit, nature and amount of judgment, and date satisfied. Also contains: Judgment Index, Direct, entry 99; Judgment Index, Reverse, entry 100. Arranged alphabetically by names of judgment creditors and debtors. Handwritten on printed forms. Average 500 pages. 18 x 12 x 3. 2 volumes, 1920-1926, Clerk of courts' record room 1; 5 volumes, 1927—, Clerk of courts' office.

102. EXECUTION INDEX, NOT DORMANT
1878. 1 volume.

Record of living executions, showing name of judgment debtor, case number, and execution number. Arranged alphabetically by names of judgment debtors. No index. Handwritten on printed forms. 250 pages. 16 x 11 x 1.5. Clerk of courts' office.

103. GENERAL INDEX [Index to Pending Suits and Living Judgments]
1876—. 26 volumes (1-26 and by contained case numbers).

Index record of pending suits, living judgments, and living executions, showing name of each litigant but not designated as plaintiff or defendant, case number, living judgment number, living execution number, volume and page numbers of Execution Docket, entry 104, Civil Docket, entry 143, and of Criminal Dockets, entry 153-156. Arranged alphabetically by names of litigants. Handwritten on printed forms. Average 550 pages. 18 x 12 x 3. Clerk of courts' office.

104. EXECUTION DOCKET
1804—. 65 volumes (1804-1858, A1-M1, N-T; 1859-1876, by contained case numbers; 1876—, 5-46).

Docket of executions ordered to satisfy judgments rendered by Montgomery County courts, showing execution number, name of person in whose favorite judgment rendered, what court, names of plaintiff and defendant, case number, names of judgment creditor and debtor, date execution issued, itemized account of fees, dates of issuing a various writs and receipts for fees paid. Arranged chronologically by dates executions issued. Indexed alphabetically by names of plaintiffs showing names of defendants and case number. Handwritten. Average 500 pages. 18 x 12 x 3. 43 volumes, 1804-1926, clerk of courts' record room 1; 22 volumes, 1927—, Clerk of courts' office.

105. CRIMINAL EXECUTION DOCKET
1895—. 2 volumes (1, 2).

Docket of defendants unable to pay costs in criminal cases, showing execution number, name of defendant, date issued, case number, amount of cost, name of sheriff, name of deputy, and fee charged. Arranged numerically by execution numbers. Indexed alphabetically by names of defendants. Handwritten on printed forms. Average 300 pages. 24 x 12 x 1.5. 1 volume, 1895-1919,clerk of courts' record room 1; 1 volume, 1920—, Clerk of courts' office.

106. EXECUTIONS
1804—. 38 file boxes (labeled by contained case numbers).

Original execution orders to satisfy judgments rendered, showing date issued, case number, execution number, names of litigants, kind of action, amount of judgment, date of sheriff's returns, cost bill of execution, and date of filing. Arranged chronologically by dates issued. 1804-1940, handwritten; 1841-1904, handwritten on printed forms; 1903—, typed on printed forms. 2 file boxes, 14 x 12.5 x 16.5; 12 file boxes, 11.5 x 15.5 x 27. 24 file boxes, 5 x 4 x 10.5. 14 file boxes, 1804-1937, clerk of courts' record room 3; 24 file boxes, 1937—, Clerk of courts' office.

107. LEVY RECORD
1851-1908. 4 volumes (1-4).

Record of levies on chattels and real estate to satisfy judgments rendered, showing complete description of property upon which levy is made, case number, date of judgment, name of plaintiffs and defendant, and dates writs returned by sheriff. Arranged chronologically by dates of entries. Indexed alphabetically by names of plaintiffs and defendants. Handwritten. Average 750 pages. 16 x 11 x 3.5. Clerk of courts' room 1.

Jury and Witness Records

108. CIVIL JURY DOCKET
1865—. 12 volumes.

Record of jurors called in civil cases, showing court term, names of plaintiff and defendant, case number, names of attorneys, names of jurors, date and number of days served, amount of fees, and date paid. Arranged chronologically by court terms. No index. Handwritten. Average 600 pages. 18 x 8 x 3. Clerk of courts' office.

109. JURY RECORD
1885—. 10 volumes (1-10). Title varies Jury Docket, 1885-1890; Tales Jury, 1881-1912.

Record of jury venues; grand jury, showing court term, date jury subpoenaed, name and address, date reported, number of days served, mileage, fee, and date certificate for fees issued; petit jury, showing term of court, nature of case, trial date, date subpoenaed, name and address, date reported, number of days served, mileage, fee, and date certificate for fees issued. Arranged chronologically by court terms. No index. Handwritten on printed forms. Average 450 pages. 18 x 12 x 3. 7 volumes, 1885-1930, clerk of courts' record room 2; 3 volumes, 1931—, Clerk of courts' office.

110. WITNESS DOCKET
1864—. 16 volumes (1-13).

Record of witnesses for plaintiff and defendant subpoenaed in common pleas court cases, showing court term, names of plaintiff and defendant, case number, names of witnesses, dates and days served, and amount of fees. Arranged chronologically by court terms. Indexed alphabetically by names of plaintiffs showing names of defendants. Handwritten on printed forms. Average 350 pages. 14 x 7 x 2. 10 volumes, 1864-1918, clerk of courts' record room 2; 6 volumes, 1919—, Clerk of courts' office.

111. WITNESS DOCKET [Grand Jury]
1895—. 27 volumes (1-27).

Record witnesses appearing before grand jury, showing court term, case number, name of defendant, names of witnesses, days served, and amount of fees. Arranged chronologically by court terms. Indexed alphabetically by names of defendants.

Handwritten on printed forms. Average 350 pages. 14 x 7 x 2. Clerk of courts' office.

Motor Vehicles

112. MOTOR VEHICLE BILLS OF SALE AND SWORN STATEMENTS OF OWNERSHIP

1921—. 36 file drawers (labeled by contained instrument numbers). Discontinued; law revised.

Copies of motor vehicle bills of sale and sworn statements of ownership, showing consecutive instrument number, date of transfer, names of grantor and grantee, name of manufacturer, factory and motor numbers, year, horsepower, type of vehicle, name of original purchaser, names of subsequent owners, and fees. Arranged numerically by consecutive instrument numbers. For indexes, see entry 113 and 114. Typed on printed forms. 11 x 11 x 25. Clerk of courts' record room 2.

113. INDEX, MOTOR VEHICLE BILLS SALE AND SWORN STATEMENT OF OWNERSHIP, DIRECT

1921-1937. 31 volumes (1-31).

Index to Motor Vehicle Bills of Sale and Sworn Statements of Ownership, entry 112, showing name of grantor and grantee, date filed, instrument number, make of vehicle, horsepower, type, model, motor and manufacturer's numbers, and if new or used vehicle. Arranged alphabetically by names of grantors and chronologically thereunder by dates of filing. Handwritten on printed forms. Average 540 pages. 16 x 15 x 3. Clerk of courts' record room 2.

114. INDEX, MOTOR VEHICLE BILLS OF SALE AND SWORN STATEMENTS OF OWNERSHIP, REVERSE

1921-1937. 31 volumes (1-31),

Reverse index to Motor Vehicle Bills of Sale and Sworn Statements of Ownership entry 112, showing name of grantee and grant her, date filed, instrument number, make of vehicle, horsepower, type, model, motor and manufacturer's number, and if new or used vehicle. Arranged alphabetically by names of grantees and chronologically thereunder by dates of filing. Handwritten on printed forms. Average 550 pages. 16 x 14 x 3. Clerk of courts' record room 2.

115. CERTIFICATE OF TITLE, MOTOR VEHICLE
1938—. 110 file boxes (labeled by contained certificate numbers).
Duplicate certificates of title to motor vehicles, showing consecutive certificate number, date of certificate, name of purchaser and vendor, if new or used vehicle, make, type, model, motor number, date purchase, amount of lien and filing fee, and date and amount of fee for cancellation of lien. Arranged numerically by certificate numbers and chronologically by dates of certificates. For index, see entry 116. Typed on printed forms. 7 x 10 x 22. Clerk of courts' office.

116. INDEX TO CERTIFICATE OF TITLE, MOTOR VEHICLE
1938—. 12 file drawers (Labeled by contained letters of alphabet).
Card index to certificate of Title, Motor Vehicle, entry 115, showing name of owner, address, make of car, description, motor number, and certificate number. Arranged alphabetically by names of owners. Typed. 4 x 14 x 26.5. Clerk of courts' office.

Commissions and Licenses

117. RECORD OF APPOINTMENTS RAILWAY POLICE
1867—. 2 volumes (1, 2). Title varies: Special Police Commission, 1867-1933, 1 volume.
Record of commissions issued by the governor of Ohio to individuals appointed to act as special police for railroad and other property, showing name of appointee, date of appointment, names of owners of property, location of same, and signature of governor and secretary of state; also shows copy of oath of appointee and date recorded. Arranged chronologically by dates of appointments. Indexed alphabetically by names of appointees. Handwritten on printed forms. Average 200 pages. 15 x 9 x 2. Clerk of courts' office.

118. RECORD BY JUSTICES' OATHS AND MAYORS' COMMISSION
1902—. 1 volume.
Copies of certificates commissioning individuals elected to offices of mayor and justice of the peace as issued by the governor and certified by the secretary of state, showing date of entry, name and address of official, township, name of city or village over which jurisdiction is held, dates of term of office, amount of bond, names of sureties to bond, date filed, and signature of clerk of courts; also shows oath of office with sworn statements and signature of deputy attesting same.

Arranged chronologically by dates of commission. Indexed alphabetically by names of officials. Handwritten on printed forms. 500 pages. 21 x 10 x 3. Clerk of courts' office.

119. NOTARIES COMMISSION RECORD
1916—. 12 volumes (7-18). Prior records missing.
Copies of commissions granted by governor of Ohio to perform the duties of notary public, showing name of appointee, date of appointment, term of appointment, names of governor and secretary of state, copy of oath of office of notary, and date recorded. Arranged chronologically by dates of appointments. Indexed alphabetically by names of appointees. Handwritten on printed forms. Average 400 pages. 14 x 6 x 2.5. e volumes, 1916-1923, clerk of courts' record room 1; 9 volumes, 1924—, Clerk of courts' office.

120. HUNTER'S LICENSES
1913-1935. 1 volume. Discontinued.
Record of hunters' licenses issued, showing license number, date issued, name of applicant, age, occupation, citizenship, personal description of licensee, and amount of fee. Arranged chronologically by dates of issue. No index. Handwritten. 120 pages. 15 x 11 x .5. Clerk of courts' record room 1.

121. FISHERS LICENSES
1936—. 32 sheets.
Record of fishing licenses issued, showing date issued, name of licensee, age, occupation, citizenship, personal description of licensee, total fee, and date license expires. Arranged chronologically by dates of issue. No index. Typed on printed forms. 18 x 8. Clerk of courts' office.

122. AUCTIONEERS' LICENSES
1925—. 25 sheets and 1 folder.
Record of licenses issued to sell merchandise at public auction, showing name of licensee, license number, date issued, names of sureties on bond, amount of bond, term of license, and amount of fee. Arranged chronologically by dates of issue. Handwritten on printed forms. 13.25 8.25 .25. Clerk of courts' office.

123. [LICENSES]
1803-1861. In Minutes, entry 146.
Record of licenses issued for peddlers, showing name of peddler, date issued, amount of fee, and mode of travel; also includes tavern and ferry licenses, 1803-1821, showing date of issue, name of license, term of license, and fee.

124. EMBALMER'S RECORD
1902-1910. 1 volume (1).
Copies of certificates issued to applicants by state board of embalming examiners granting license to embalm and prepare for burial, transport, or cremate dead human bodies, showing license number, name of licensee, date issued, and date recorded. Arranged chronologically by dates of issue. Indexed alphabetically by names of licensees. Handwritten on printed forms. 120 pages. 14 x 9 x 1. Clerk of courts' record room 1.

125. OPTOMETRISTS LICENSES
1920—. 2 volumes.
Copies of certificates issued by the state board of optometry permitting licensees to practice optometry in the county of Montgomery, showing license number, name of licensee, date of issue, and signature of president and secretary of board of optometry. Arranged chronologically by dates issued. Indexed alphabetically by names of licensees. Handwritten on printed forms. Average 300 pages. 14 x 10 x 2. Clerk of courts' office.

126. REAL ESTATE BROKERS LICENSES
1936—. 1 volume.
Record licenses issued to real estate brokers and salesmen, showing licensed number, name of business and address, name of salesman, name of broker, and date of issue. Arranged alphabetically under tabs by names of brokers showing license number. No index. Handwritten on printed forms. 100 pages. 24 x 18 x 2. Clerk of courts' office.

Partnerships

127. REGISTER OF PARTNERSHIPS
1894—. 1 volume.
Record of partnerships agreements, showing name and address of partnership, date

of filing, names of partners, and certificate number. Arranged alphabetically by names of partners. No index. Handwritten on printed forms. 400 pages. 14 x 9 x 3. Clerk of courts' office.

Elections

128. [ABSTRACT OF VOTES]
1803-1824. In blotter, entry 142.
Abstracts of votes cast for candidates of various state, county, and township offices, showing date of election, names of candidates, and total number of votes received by each.

Financial Records

129. CASH BOOK
1874—. 65 volumes (1-15, 1-50).
Record of cash receipts, fees, and disbursements. Receipts and fees, showing date, by whom paid, to whom due, source, and total amount due county clerk, sheriff, witnesses, jury, and sundry fund; disbursements, 1907—, showing date paid out, to whom paid, purpose, case number, and amount. Arranged chronologically by dates received. No index. Handwritten on printed forms. Average 450 pages. 18 x 18 x 2.5. 48 volumes, 1874-1932, Clerk of courts' record room 2; 17 volumes, 1933—, Clerk of courts' office.

130. ACCRUED COST BOOK
1906—. 4 volumes. (1-4).
Record of accrued fees, showing names of plaintiff and defendant, date accrued, case number, to whom due, from whom due, total amount of clerk's and sheriff's fees, date of payment, and remarks. Arranged chronologically by dates of accrual. No index. Handwritten on printed forms. 1 volume 100 pages 16 x 11.5 x 1.5. 3 volumes average 350 pages 16 x 11.5 x 3. 1 volume, 1906-1920, Clerk of courts' record room 1; 3 volumes, 1921—, Clerk of courts' office.

131. WITNESS FEES
1907-1917. 1 volume. Discontinued.
Record of fees for trial witnesses and court cases, showing name of court, name of witnesses, date of trial, length of service, title of case, and amount of fees paid.

Arranged chronologically by dates of trials. No index. Handwritten. 75 pages. 14 x 8 x .5. Clerk of courts' record room 1.

132. FEE BOOK
1803-1874. 28 volumes (A-Z, A1, B1).

Record of fees collected by the clerk of courts in court cases, showing date of entry, name of plaintiff and defendant, title of case, kind of action, amount of cost, date of receipt of payment, and amount of fees to court and attorneys. Arranged chronologically by dates of entries. No index. Handwritten. Average 250 pages. 12 x 8 x 1.5. Clerk of courts' record room 1.

133. COST BOOK
1803-1853. 50 volume (two each A-W, Y-z).

Record of cost in common pleas court cases, showing date of entry, term of court, names of plaintiff and defendant, amount of judgment and cost, and volume and page numbers of dockets and records where entered. Arranged chronologically by dates of entries. For index, see entry 134. Handwritten. Average 50 pages. 13 x 8 x .5. Clerk of courts' record room 1.

134. INDEX TO COST BOOK
1803-1853. 4 volumes.

Index to cost book, entry 133, showing court term, names of plaintiff and defendant, amount of cost, and volume letter and page number of records. Arranged alphabetically by names of plaintiff showing names of defendants. Handwritten. Average 100 pages. 13 x 8 x .5. Clerk of courts' office.

135. RECORD OF UNCLAIMED COSTS
1889-1916. 8 volumes.

Copies of clerk of courts annual reports of unclaimed costs as certified to the auditor, showing to whom due, amount, case number, and names of plaintiff and defendant. Arranged chronologically by years and alphabetically thereunder by names of persons to whom due. No index. Handwritten on printed forms. Average 400 pages. 14 x 9 x 2. Clerk of courts' record room 1.

136. REPORT OF FINES
1851—. 1 carton, 2 file boxes.

Copies of clerk of courts' reports to county commissioners of fines collected in criminal cases, showing date of report, number of cases, total amount of fines, type or class of offense, amount of fines collected, and amount of cost collected. Arranged chronologically by years. No index. Handwritten. Carton, 7.5 x 15 x 17; file drawer, 11.5 x 15.5 x 27. 1 carton, 1 file drawer, 1851-1937, Clerk of courts' record room 2; 1 file drawer, 1938—, Clerk of courts' office.

Coroners' Inquests

137. CORONER'S VERDICTS
1893-1903, 1908-1912, 1919—. 4 volumes.

Copies of coroner's reports to the clerk of courts relative to deaths of a violent or accidental nature, showing date of report, name of decedent, color, sex, nativity, age, name of coroner, and date transcript filed. Arranged chronologically by dates of filing. Indexed alphabetically by names of descendants. Handwritten on printed forms. Average 500 pages. 15 x 12 x 3. 2 volumes, 1893-1903, 1908-1912, Clerk of courts' record room 1; 2 volumes, 1919—, Clerk of courts' office.

138. CORONER'S RECORD
1868-1902. 22 volumes. Title varies: Corner's Inquest, 1868-1879, 1 volume.

Coroners' records of accidental or violent deaths, showing date of death, name of decedent, late address, cause of death, age, place of death, name of coroner, names of witnesses or other principles, findings, and date of inquest. Arranged chronologically by dates of deaths. Indexed alphabetically by names of decedents. Handwritten. Average 500 pages. 15 x 12 x 3. Clerk of courts' record room 1.

139. REPORTS OF INQUESTS
1903—. 65 bundles, 2 file drawers.

Original reports of the coroner to the clerk of courts relative to all deaths of accidental or violent nature, showing name of decedent, late address, cause of death, age, place of death, name of coroner, names of witnesses or other , persons, either related to decedent or responsible for the demise or both, findings at inquest, and date of filing. Arranged chronologically by dates are filing. No index. Handwritten on printed forms.

Bundles, 5 x 8 x 15; file drawers, 12 x 15 x 26. 65 bundles, 1903-1931, Clerk of courts' record room 1: 2 file drawers, 1932—, Clerk of courts' office.

Miscellaneous

140. RECORD OF STRAYS
1852- April 1919, 2 volumes (C1, 2). Title varies: Estray Book, 1852-1882, 1 volume.

Report of stray property, both livestock and conveyances, found and held for redemption, showing date of finding, description of property found, place found, place held, name of finder and address, notice to clerk of courts, certification of various township officials, and date filed. Arranged chronologically by dates of filing. No index. Handwritten. 1 volume, 50 pages. 14 x 9 x .5. 1 volume 200 pages. 14 x 10 x 2. Clerk of courts' record room 1.

141. ATTORNEY'S RECEIPT BOOK
1901-1914. 3 volumes.

Attorneys receipts for papers taken from court files, showing case number, names of plaintiff and defendant, date taken out, signature of attorney, and date returned. Arranged chronologically by dates taken out. No index. Handwritten on printed forms. Average 600 pages. 16 x 6 x 2.5. Clerk of courts' record room 1.

The court of common pleas, like many other county institutions, originated in England during the reign of Henry II.[1] Established in America during the colonial period, the office was continued by the states following the War of American Independence.

The Northwest Ordinance of 1787 established a government consisting of a governor, a secretary, and three judges all appointed by Congress. The judges were to form a court, known as a general court, which had common law jurisdiction and together with the governor was authorized to draw up a code of civil and criminal law. The territorial act of 1788, establishing the American colonial policy in the newer west in respect to the judiciary, contained sections authorizing the establishment in each county of a common pleas court to be composed of not less than three nor more than five members. These members appointed and commissioned by the territorial governor, were given jurisdiction in all civil matters.[2] The same act established in each county a primary court called the court of general quarter sessions of the peace to be composed of not more than five nor less than three justices of the peace, appointed and commissioned by the governor.[3] This court, which had limited jurisdiction in criminal matters, was not re-established by the constitution of 1802 and the jurisdiction which had been exercised by this court was conferred upon the justices of the peace and the court of common pleas.[4]

When a constitution was drafted for Ohio in 1802, preparatory to the entrance of the state into the Union, provision was made for a continuation of the territorial court of common pleas.[5] The articles of the Ohio Constitution, regarding judiciary, provided for a court of common pleas in each county to be composed of a president and associate judges. For each county[6] not more than three nor less than two associate judges were to be appointed, with one president for each of the three judicial districts into which the counties were grouped. The associate judges were not as a rule men who had a legal education. [7]

---

1. George Burton Adams, *Constitutional History of England* (New York, 1921), 109, 134.

2. Pease, *op, cit.,* 7.

3. Pease, *op, cit.,* 4.

4. Pease, *op, cit.,* 5; *Laws of Ohio,* I, 40; II, 235.

5. *Ohio Const, 1802,* Art. III, sec. 1.

6. At this time there were nine counties in the state.

7. Francis J. Amer, *Development of the Judicial System in Ohio from 1787 to 1932* (John Hopkins University, Baltimore, 1932. *Institute of Law Bulletin No. 8),* 17.

The members of the court, appointed by joint ballot of both houses of the general assembly, where to hold court in three judicial districts into which the state was to be divided by legislative action. The term of office was seven years; if so long they behaved well."[8]

It was almost half a century before any significant changes were made in the structure of the court. The constitution of 1851 provided that judges of the common pleas court were to be elected for a five-year term. For the purposes of their election the state was divided into nine districts composed of three or more counties. Each district, in turn, was to be subdivided into three parts, in each of which one common pleas judge was to be elected. The court of common pleas was to be held by one or more of these judges in each county in the district.[9] Power was given to the general assembly to increase or diminish the number of districts of the court of common pleas or the number of judges in any district and to change the district or the subdivisions thereof, whenever two thirds of the legislature concurred therein.[10] Provision was also made for the removal of judges by a concurrent resolution of two thirds of the members elected to each house of the legislature.[11] An appellate court known as a district court was created, which was to be composed of one supreme court judge and the several common pleas judges of the district. This court was to be held in each county of the district at least once in each year or at least three annual sessions in not less than three places.[12] The district courts were not a success, and after many attempts at revision the circuit courts, staffed by a separate group of elected judges, were adopted by vote of the people in 1883, thus relieving the common pleas judge of this appellate work.[13]

The juvenile court was created in 1904 with jurisdiction in special matters related to minors and was to be held by a judge of the court of common pleas, court of insolvency, or probate court who should be designated by the judges to hold such courts.[14]

At the opening of the twentieth century sweeping changes in the organization of the courts were made.

---

8. *Ohio Const. 1802,* Art. III sec. 8.
9. *Ohio Const. 1851,* Art. IV, secs. 3, 4
10. *Ibid.,* Art. IV, sec. 15.
11. *Ibid.,* Art. IV, sec. 17.
12. *Ibid.,* Art. IV, secs. 5, 6.
13. Amer, *op. cit.,* 31-33; *Laws of Ohio,* LXXXI, 168.
14. *Laws of Ohio,* XCVII, 562. See also p. 78.

Constitutional amendments adopted in 1912 abolished the divisions and subdivisions of the common pleas provided by the constitution of 1851, and authorized the election of one or more common pleas judges in each county.[15] The chief justice of the supreme court was given authority to determine the disability or disqualification of any judge of the court of common pleas and also to assign any judge to hold court in any county.[16] Under an act of March 13, 1913, selection of a chief justice of the court of common pleas by vote of the judges was authorized in counties having two or more common pleas judges. The justice so designated was to serve in such capacity until the expiration of his term, after which time the office was to be an elective one.[17] The elective section of the act was nullified in effect in 1924 by the supreme court on the grounds that the creation of a new elective office was unconstitutional. Accordingly, in 1927 an amendment was passed eliminating the elective provision of the act.[18]

In recent years attempts have been made to improve the efficiency of the court by imposing stricter qualifications upon those who seek election to the bench. In 1917 an act was passed providing that a common pleas judge shall have been admitted to practice as an attorney at law for a period of six years preceding his election.[19] The salary of the office was also increased to $3,000 per year plus an amount based on the population of the county[20] – thus making the position financially attractive, especially as the term of office is six years.[21] In addition to the regular salaries, common pleas judges maybe be paid a per diem and expenses when assigned to special duty by the chief justice of the supreme court in a district not their own. When dockets become crowded or judges are incapacitated or disqualified, such assignments may be made.[22] In Montgomery County, as in a few other large counties, judicial efficiency is promoted by assigning to certain common pleas judges specialized duties such as a hearing of domestic relations and juvenile court cases.

---

15. *Ohio Const. 1851,* Art. IV, sec. 3.
16. *Ibid.,* Art. IV, secs. 3, 6.
17. *Laws of Ohio,* CX, 52.
18. *State ex rel.,* v. *Powell, Ohio State Reports,* CIX, 383; *Laws of Ohio* ,CXII, 5.
19. *Laws of Ohio,* CVII, 164.
20. G. C. secs. 2251, 2252.
21. G. C. sec. 1532.
22. *Ohio Const. 1851,* (Amendment, 1912). Art. IV, sec. 3; G. C. secs. 1469, 1687, 2253.

The jurisdiction of the court of common pleas has also been the product of a long period of historical development. The territorial law of 1788 which created the court provided that "the judges so appointed and commissioned . . . shall hold pleas of *assizes, scire facias, replevins,* and hear and determine all matter of pleas, action, suits, and causes of a civil nature, real, personal, and mixed, according to the constitution and laws of the territory."[23] Individually, each judge of the common pleas was given jurisdiction over contract actions not exceeding five dollars.[24] The probate court was established by the an act adopted August 30, 1788, and two of the judges of the court of common pleas sat with this judge in ruling on contested points, definitive sentences, and final judgments. Under the laws of 1788 the common pleas had no criminal jurisdiction, and the court of quarter sessions of the peace had no civil jurisdiction. There was no provision for an appeal from one court to another except from the probate court to the general court of the territory.[25]

In 1795 the judicial system underwent the first general revision and this increased the duties of the court of common pleas. A single justice of the peace or judge of the common pleas was given jurisdiction to hear certain civil actions up to $12. Actions under $5 were exclusive with the judges or justices and there was no appeal from their judgment. Actions between $5 and $12 could be appealed to the court a common pleas. In 1799 this jurisdiction was raised to $20, and appeals could be taken to the common pleas if the judgment was over $2. If the judgment was for plaintiff, he could appeal only if the original demand was $4 more than the sum recovered.[26] Appeal from the common pleas to the general court was provided for in 1795, and could not be taken unless the title to land was in question or when the amount in controversy exceeded $50.[27]

The constitution of 1802 gave the court of common pleas jurisdiction in such common law and chancery cases as should be directed by law. In addition it was given jurisdiction of all probate and testamentary matters, and the appointment and supervision of guardians.[28]

---

23. Salmon P. Chase, comp., *The Statutes of Ohio and of the Northwestern Territory, 1788-1833* (Cincinnati, 1833), I, 94.
24. Pease, *op. cit.,* 8.
25. Pease, *op. cit.,* I, 96.
26. Chase, *op. cit.,* I, 143, 233, 307.
27. Chase, *op. cit., I, 306.*
28. *Ohio Const. 1802,* Art. III, secs. 3, 5.

Moreover the court of common pleas and supreme court were assigned original cognizance of criminal cases as might be provided by law.[29] By statutory provision in 1804 appeals in civil cases might be made to the court of common pleas from the county commissioners, justices of the peace and other inferior courts.[30]

An act of the first general assembly in 1803 provided for the organization of the courts and defined their jurisdiction. The court of common pleas was given original jurisdiction in all cases, both in law and in equity, when the matter in dispute exceeded the jurisdiction of the justices of peace; of all probate, testamentary, and guardianship matters; and of all criminal matters exceeding the jurisdiction of the justices of peace, except when the punishment of the crime was capital. It was allowed to review certain cases from the justices of peace and also to review the decisions of the county commissioners in highway matters. In addition, the court had the same power to issue remedial and other process, writs of error and *mandamus* excepted, as had the supreme court.[31] In 1804 the court's jurisdiction in chancery cases was limited to cases involving less than $500,[32] and in 1805 it was given appellate jurisdiction from the justices of peace in all cases regardless of the amount involved.[33] In 1806 crimes wherein the punishment was capital could be tried in the common pleas court if the accused so elected.[34] In 1807 it was given jurisdiction in all chancery cases and concurrent jurisdiction with the supreme court in such cases involving over $500.[35] In 1810 all cases in which the common pleas had original jurisdiction were permitted to be appealed to the supreme court.[36] By this act the right to appeal was established in Ohio in all civil cases. However the business of the supreme court increased so rapidly that in 1845 the right to appeal from a judgment of the common pleas court to the supreme court in actions at law was abolished. Instead, new trials were allowed "when law and justice required it."[37] Even earlier, appeals to the common pleas from inferior courts had been limited.[38]

---

29. *Ibid.,* Art. III, sec. 4.
30. Chase, *op. cit.,* I, 421, 425.
31. Chase, *op. cit.,* I, 355.
32. *Laws of Ohio,* II, 261.
33. *Ibid.,* III, 14.
34. *Ibid.,* IV, 57.
35. *Ibid.,* V, 117.
36. *Ibid.,* VIII, 259.
37. *Ibid.,* XLIII, 80.
38. *Ibid.,* XXXVIII, 27.

The chancery act, adopted in 1824, conferred general chancery powers on the court,[39] and in 1843 it was given concurrent jurisdiction with the supreme court in cases of divorce and alimony.[40]

The constitution of 1851 left the jurisdiction of the common pleas court to be fixed by law.[41] The jurisdiction conferred on this court by subsequent legislation was essentially the same as that exercised since 1810, with the exception of the jurisdiction which is transferred to the probate court,[42] and the addition, in 1853, of exclusive jurisdiction in divorce and alimony cases.[43] The court of common pleas was denied jurisdiction in cases of probate, testamentary, and guardianship matters, but final orders, judgments, and decrees of the probate court could be reviewed in common pleas on appeal or by writ or *certiorari*.[44] In 1853 the court of common pleas was given original jurisdiction of all crimes and offenses except minor criminal cases, the exclusive jurisdiction of which was vested in the justice of peace or other minor courts.[45]

The creation of criminal, mayors', and police courts also made certain changes in the powers and duties of the common pleas court.[46] The right to appeal from common pleas to the district court was restored in all civil actions in which the common pleas had original jurisdiction,[47] but by an act of 1858 appeals were allowed to the immediate court only in nonjury cases. However, the same act provided for a second jury trial in common pleas as a matter of right in jury cases. This was granted upon demand made by either party at the close of the first trial on condition of his giving bond.[48] The abuse of this privilege led to its abolition in 1875.[49]

---

39. *Ibid.*, XXIX, 75.
40. *Ibid.*, XLI, 94.
41. *Ohio Const. 1851*, Art. IV, secs. 3, 4.
42. *Laws of Ohio*, L, 87. Records pertaining to probate matters were to be transferred to the probate court wherever it was possible to separate them from common pleas records. *Ibid.*, L, 88. See also p. 106.
43. *Ibid.*, LI, 377. See also p. 91.
44. *Laws of Ohio*, L, 84; LI, 145.
45. G. C. sec. 13422-5; *Laws of Ohio*, LI, 474; LII, 73.
46. *Laws of Ohio*, L, 90, 240, 246, 251, 253.
47. *Ibid.*, L, 93.
48. *Ibid.*, LV, 81.
49. *Ibid.*, LXXXII, 34.

This period witnessed the re-establishment of the superior courts in the state which were given the same jurisdiction as the courts of common pleas with certain exceptions.[50] At the same time as the superior court was established at Cincinnati, the legislature abolished the criminal court and transferred its jurisdiction to the common pleas court.[51] The criminal jurisdiction of the probate court was transferred to the common pleas court in 1857.[52] A limitation was placed on the right to appeal from probate court to common pleas in 1854.[53] This limitation was repealed, however, in 1856.[54]

For many years there were few changes in the powers of the court of common pleas except in the forms of appeal to higher courts,[55] and such added powers as resulted from the decline in the number of superior courts.[56] In 1906 the probate court was given concurrent jurisdiction with common pleas in all counties in the trial of misdemeanors and all proceedings to prevent crime.[57]

Since 1906 the court of common pleas has had jurisdiction in naturalization proceedings. In that year the federal statute was amended to limit jurisdiction in the granting of naturalization to the United States district courts and state courts having a clerk, a seal, and jurisdiction in matters of law and equity in which the amount of controversy is unlimited.[58]

Constitutional amendments adopted in 1912 had little effect upon the jurisdiction of the court of common pleas, this power being determined by law.[59] However the establishment of a municipal court of Dayton, in 1913, relieves the common pleas court of Montgomery County of certain civil jurisdiction.[60] In 1911 the juvenile courts were given jurisdiction of all misdemeanors against minors and certain other offenses.[61]

---

50. *Laws of Ohio,* LII, 34; LIII, 38; LIV, 37.
51. *Ibid.,* LI, 107.
52. *Ibid.,* LIV, 97.
53. *Ibid.,* LII, 104.
54. *Ibid.,* LIII, 8.
55. *Ibid.,* LXXIV, 359; LXXXII, 230.
56. *Ibid.,* LXII, 58; LXXII, 89, 105; LXXXII, 85.
57. VXCVIII, 49.
58. *United States Statutes at Large,* XXXIV, pt. i, 596.
59. *Ohio Const. 1851,* Art. IV, sec. 6.
60. *Laws of Ohio,* CIII, 345.
61. *Ibid.,* CIII, 875.

Provision was also made for error proceedings from juvenile court to the court of common pleas.[62] The jurisdiction of the common pleas court of today is essentially the same as that of 1913. The few changes that have been made in the judicial system are found in the local, special courts, particularly in the rapidly developing municipal courts.

The common pleas court has never possessed extensive appointing powers. The constitution of 1802 authorized each court to appoint a clerk,[63] and in 1805 it was directed to appoint a county prosecuting attorney.[64] In the first three decades of Ohio history, the movement for the extension of the popular election of public officers deprived the court of common pleas of the privilege of appointing the county recorder (1929), the county surveyor (1931), and the county prosecuting attorney (1838).[65] The court continued to appoint a clerk of court until 1851. In recent years, however, as new functions have been added to the county government, the court has again been given a limited appointive power. Successive acts in 1886, 1891, 1913, 1914, and 1925 authorized the court to appoint a soldiers' relief commission, a jury commission, an assignment commissioner, a conservancy district board, and a probation officer.[66] In 1882 the court was empowered to appoint a board of county visitors but this power was transferred to the probate court in 1913.[67] Other appointments authorized are those of court interpreter and criminal bailiff (1911),[68] inspectors of meetings of corporation stockholders, trustees for county memorial buildings, and boards of trustees for endowed libraries.[69]

The court may also appoint a court reporter (or reporters),[70] and may cooperate with the county commissioners for the establishment of a county department of probation, in which case the court appoints certain probation officers and supervisors their work.[71]

---

62. *Ibid.*, CIII, 875.
63. *Ohio Const, 1802,* Art. III, sec. 9.
64. *Laws of Ohio,* III, 47.
65. *Ibid.*, XXVII, 65; XXIX, 399; Chase, *op. cit.,* III, 1935.
66. *Laws of Ohio,* LXXXIII, 232; LXXXVIII, 200; CIII, 512; CIV, 13-64; CXI, 423.
67. *Ibid.*, LXXIX, 107; CIII, 173.
68. G. C. sec. 1541.
69. *Laws of Ohio,* LXXXIV, 115; XCV, 41; CVI, 485.
70. G. C. secs. 1546-1554.
71. G. C. secs. 1554-1--1554-6.

In case the sheriff is absent, disabled, or disqualified from serving the court's warrant, the judge may appoint temporarily an official for this service.[72] By and large, however, the patronage power of the court of common pleas is a negligible factor county in government. The court of common pleas has shared with other governmental agencies the function of issuing various licenses.[73] Since 1805 the court has been authorized to issue ferry licenses[74] and tavern keepers licenses.[75] Both ferry and tavern licenses may now be issued by municipal corporations also and the latter by the state fire marshal.[76] From 1803 to 1852 this court also issued licenses to ministers to solemnize marriages ceremonies; since the latter year this function has been exercised by the probate court.[77]

The keeping of the records of the common pleas court presented no particular difficulties for many decades. However, with the increased number of issues presented to the court in recent years the problem of judicial administration has become greater. This problem was solved in part by the creation of the office of chief justice of the court of common pleas who has been given the duties of superintending the business of the court, classifying it, and distributing it among the judges. Besides the duties enumerated, the chief justice annually makes a report to the clerk of courts showing the work performed by the court and by each judge in the proceeding calendar year. Moreover, he reports such other data as the chief justice of the supreme court may require.[78]

Judges of the common pleas court are also required to issue an annual order as to the exact time of sessions. The clerk of courts is required to make this information public and also send a copy to the secretary of state. The law sets certain requirements as to the sessions of the court and the power of the judge to call special sessions.[79] The records of the court are deposited for safekeeping with the clerk of courts. The clerk is custodian also of all law reports and books furnished by the state for the use of the court and the bar and is made liable in the event of their destruction.[80]

----

72. G. C. sec. 2828.
73. See pp. l, li, 46, 106, 157, 158.
74. *Laws of Ohio,* III, 96; G. C. secs. 5947, 5949.
75. *Laws of Ohio,* III, 96; XXIX, 310.
76. G. C. secs. 3641-3642, 843-3.
77. *Laws of Ohio,* I, 31; L, 84.
78. G. C. sec. 1558. See p. 63.
79. G. C. secs. 1533-1539.
80. *Laws of Ohio,* LXVIII, 109.

Civil Cases

142. BLOTTER
1803-1853. 26 volumes (A1, B1, E1-I1, W1-Z1, A2-E2).
Register of civil cases filed for appearance in common pleas court, showing court term, names of attorneys, names of plaintiff and defendant, title of case, case number, date of filing case, dates of filing of various writs, dates of returns on writs, amount of judgment rendered or sentence imposed, names of witnesses, names of jurors, dates and time served by jurors and witnesses, and amounts of sheriff's and clerk's costs itemized. Also contains [Abstracts of Votes], 1803-1824, entry 128. Arranged chronologically by dates of filing of cases. 1803-1824, no index; 1824-1853, indexed alphabetically by names of plaintiffs showing names of defendants. Handwritten. Average 460 pages. 13 x 9 x 2.5. Clerk of courts' record room 1.

143. CIVIL DOCKET
1854—. 255 volumes. (45 unlabeled; 1901—, 1-210). Title varies: Justices Docket, 1854-1900, 45 volumes.
Docket and record of cases appealed from justices' of the peace courts to the court of common pleas, showing court term, names of plaintiff and defendant, case number, title of case, cause of action, names of attorneys, date transcript and justice of peace court was filed, amount of cost, dates and briefs of court orders and decrees, amount of cost, and final disposition of the case. Arranged numerically by case numbers. Indexed alphabetically by names of plaintiffs showing names of defendants. Handwritten. Average 570 pages. 20.5 x 10.5 x 2.5. 45 volumes, 1854-1900, Clerk of courts' record room 1; 210 volumes, 1901—, Clerk of courts' office.

144. APPEARANCE DOCKET
1842—. 209 volumes (1-209 and labeled by contained case numbers).
Docket of appearance and record of civil cases filed and heard in common pleas court, showing court term, date case filed, names of plaintiff and defendant, case number, names of attorneys for each party to suit, title of case, kind of case, date and brief a journal entries, writs and court orders, amount of clerk's and sheriff's fees, date of sheriff's returns, total amount of costs, date cost paid, and volume letter and page number of minutes, entry 146 and volume number or letter and page number of Common Pleas Record, entry 150. Also serves as an index to Case Records [Civil], entry 92 by showing case number. Arranged numerically by case numbers and chronologically by dates of filing of cases. Indexed alphabetically by

names of plaintiffs showing names of defendants. Handwritten on printed forms. Average 550 pages. 16.5 x 12 x 3.5. 43 volumes, 1842-1926, Clerk of courts' record room 2; 166 volumes, 1927—, Clerk of courts' office.

145. COURT DOCKET

1805—. 200 volumes (labeled by court terms).

Docket of civil causes filed and heard in common pleas court, showing court term, case number, title of case, kind of case, names of plaintiff and defendant, dates of hearings and motions, names of attorneys for each party to suit, and disposition of case. Arranged chronologically by court terms. No index. Handwritten. Average 300 pages. 14.5 x 9.5 x 2.5. 189 volumes, 1805-1907, Clerk of courts' record room 1; 11 volumes, 1908—, Clerk of courts' office.

146. MINUTES

1803—. 178 volumes. (A1-Z1, 1-152).

Proceedings in cases filed and heard in common pleas court, showing court term, names of plaintiff and defendant, or other principal, title of the case, case number, kind of action, date case filed, and date and copies of journal entries. Entries include petitions, bills of particulars, court orders, demurrers, and court decrees; 1853—, journal entries in divorce and alimony matters. Also contains [Licenses], 1803-1861, entry 123. 1803-1861, arranged alphabetically by names of plaintiffs or other principles; 1862—, arranged chronologically by dates of journal entries. For index to judgments, see entries 99-101; otherwise no index. 1803-1914, handwritten; 1915—, typed. Average 750 pages. 18.5 x 12.5 x 3.5. 26 volumes, 1803-1861, Clerk of courts' record room 1; 91 volumes, 1862-1924, Clerk of courts' record room 2; 61 volumes, 1925—, Clerk of courts' office.

147. COMMON PLEAS CHANCERY RECORD

1824-1855. 13 volumes. (A-K, M, N).

Complete record of chancery cases filed and heard in common pleas court, including copies of petitions, bills of particulars, affidavits, motions, pleas and answers, court orders, and decrees, all showing court term, names of plaintiff and defendant, title of case, case number, names of attorneys, and date case filed. Arranged chronologically by court terms. Indexed alphabetically by names of plaintiffs showing names of defendants; also separate index, 1839-1855, entries 148, 149, and 1826-1836, 1843-1853, entry 151. Handwritten. Average 700 pages. 18 x 12 x 3.5. Clerk of courts' record room 2.

148. CHANCERY INDEX, FORWARD
1839-1855. 1 volume.

Index to common pleas Chancery Record, entry 147, showing year filed, term of appearance, names of plaintiff and defendant, title of case, case number, term in which disposed of, volume and page numbers of Minutes, entry 146, amount of judgment cost, and volume letter and page number of record. Arranged alphabetically by names of plaintiffs. Handwritten on printed forms. 460 pages. 16.5 x 11.5 x 2. Clerk of courts' record room 2.

149. CHANCERY INDEX, REVERSE
1839-1855. 1 volume.

Index to common pleas Chancery Record, entry 147, showing year filed, term of appearance, names of defendant and plaintiff, title of case, case number, term in which disposed of, volume and page numbers of Minutes, entry 146, amount of judgment cost, and volume letter and page number of record. Arranged alphabetically by names of defendants. Handwritten on printed forms. 460 pages. 16.5 x 11.5 x 2. Clerk of courts' record room 2.

150. COMMON PLEAS RECORD
1803—. 328 volumes. (A1-Y1, SA, 1, 1-301).

Complete record of cases filed and heard in common pleas court, showing date case filed, case number, court term, names of plaintiff and defendant, title of case, kind of case, and date and brief of testimony, evidence, and court orders. Also contains; [Circuit Court Record], 1884-1912, entry 218; [Court of Appeals Record], 1913—, entry 221. Arranged chronologically by dates of filing of case. Indexed alphabetically by names of plaintiffs showing names of defendants; also separate index, 1803-1836, 1843-1853, entry 151. 1803-1898, Handwritten; 1899—, typed. Average 600 pages. 18 x 12 x 3. 63 volumes, 1803-1893, Clerk of courts' record room 2; 265 volumes, 1894—, Clerk of courts' office.

151. LAW INDEX
1803-1836, 1843-1853. 1 volume.

Index to Common Pleas Record, entry 150, and 1824-1836, 1843-1853 to Common Pleas Chancery Record, entry 147, showing names of plaintiff and defendant, and volume number or page letter and page number of record. Arranged alphabetically by names of plaintiffs and defendants.

1803-1836, handwritten; 1843-1853, handwritten on printed forms. Average 200 pages. 12 x 7 x 1.25. Clerk of courts' office.

Criminal Cases

152. BLOTTER, STATE ACTIONS
1836-1863. 4 volumes. (A-D).

Register of criminal cases in common pleas court, showing court term, name of defendant, charge, case number, return of grand jury, amount of cost, and verdict. Arranged chronologically by court terms. Indexed alphabetically by names of defendants. Handwritten. Average 450 pages. 12.5 x 9 x 2. Clerk of courts' record room 1.

153. CRIMINAL DOCKET
1853-1929. 116 volumes (thirty-six unlabeled; 1-80).

Docket of criminal cases filed and heard in common pleas court, showing name of defendant, case number, charge, action, arrangement, amount of costs, and findings. Arranged numerically by case numbers. 1853-1896, no index; 1897-1929, indexed alphabetically by names of defendants. 1853-1917, handwritten; 1918-1929, typed. 36 volumes average 52 pages. 18 x 8 x .25. 80 volumes average 475 pages. 16 x 12 x 2.5. Clerk of courts' office.

154. CRIMINAL DOCKET, FELONY
1929—. 35 volumes (1-35).

Docket of felonies in common pleas court cases, showing name of defendant, case number, charge, action, arrangement, amount of cost, and findings. Arranged numerically by case numbers. Indexed alphabetically by names of defendants. Handwritten on printed forms. Average 475 pages. 16 x 12 x 2.5. Clerk of courts' office.

155. CRIMINAL DOCKET, MISDEMEANORS
1929—. 2 volumes.

Docket of misdemeanors in common pleas court cases, showing name of defendant, case number, charge, action, arrangement, amount of cost, and findings. Arranged numerically by case numbers. Indexed alphabetically by names of defendants. Handwritten on printed forms. Average 475 pages. 16 x 12 x 2.5. Clerk of courts' office.

156. PRELIMINARY DOCKET
1935—. 3 volumes (1-3).
Docket of preliminary hearings in criminal cases, showing date of hearing, title of case, name of defendant, charge, pleading, dates of writs issued, returns, and amount of cost. Arranged chronologically by dates of hearings. Indexed alphabetically by names of defendants. Handwritten on printed forms. Average 475 pages. 16 x 12 x 2.5. Clerk of courts' office.

157. APPEARANCE DOCKET AND FEE BOOK
1857—. 30 volumes (1-30 and labeled by contained case numbers).
Docket of criminal cases filed in common pleas court, showing name of defendant, case number, date case filed, charge, dates of writs and returns, amount of cost, and verdict. Arranged numerically by case numbers. Indexed alphabetically by names of defendants. Handwritten on printed forms. Average 600 pages. 18 x 12 x 3. 25 volumes, 1857-1930, Clerk of courts' record room 1; 5 volumes, 1931—, Clerk of courts' office.

158. CRIMINAL RECORD
1853-1904. 9 volumes (1-9).
Record of criminal cases filed and heard in common pleas court, showing date of case filed, name of defendant, case number, charge, dates of affidavits, indictment, warrants, and sheriff's returns. Arranged numerically by case numbers. Indexed alphabetically by names of defendants. Handwritten. Average 600 pages. 18 x 12 x 3. Clerk of courts' room 1.

159. STATE ACTION RECORD
1813—. 22 volumes (A1-V1).
Complete record of criminal trials for violation of state laws, showing court term, name of defendant, case number, charge, and verdict. Arranged chronologically by court terms. Indexed alphabetically by names of defendants. 1813-1895, handwritten; 1896—, typed. Average 500 pages. 18 x 12 x 3. 19 volumes, 1813-1930, Clerk of courts' record room 2; 3 volumes, 1931—, Clerk of courts' office.

Naturalization

160. NATURALIZATION INDEX BOOK
1852-1891. 2 volumes (1, 2).

Index to Naturalization Record, First, entry 161 and Naturalization Record, Second, entry 162, showing date of proceeding, name of alien, and volume and page numbers of record. Arranged alphabetically by names of aliens. Handwritten. Average 250 pages. 14 x 10 x 1.5. Clerk of courts' office.

161. NATURALIZATION RECORD, FIRST
1843-1915. 9 volumes (1A, 1-5; 4 unlabeled). Title varies: Naturalization
Docket, 1834-1952, 1 volume,

Record of first papers for citizenship, showing name of alien, nativity, personal description, and date of issue; 1852-1854, also includes some second papers, showing information as in Naturalization Record, Second, entry 162. Arranged chronologically by dates of issues. 1834-1852, no index; 1852-1915, indexed alphabetically by names of aliens, also separate index, 1852-1891, entry 160. Handwritten. Average 250 pages. 14 x 7 x 2. Clerk of courts' office.

162. NATURALIZATION RECORD, SECOND
1852-1891. 7 volumes (1 unlabeled, 1, 2, 2; 3, 3, 4).

Record of second papers issued to aliens for citizenship, showing name of alien, record of first papers, past and present personal history of alien, and dates of issues of various papers. Arranged chronologically by dates of issues. For index, see entry 160. Handwritten. Average 350 pages. 14 x 6 x 3. Clerk of courts' office.

163. PETITION AND RECORD
1907-1916. 6 volumes (1-6). Discontinued; jurisdiction transferred to
federal courts.

Petitions of aliens for citizenship in the United States, showing name of alien, date of application, occupation, date and place of birth, date and place of debarkation and arrival, length of residence in the United States, list of dependents, personal description of applicant, and action taken on first papers; record of aliens naturalized, showing date of first, second, and final papers, and copies of oath of allegiance to the United States. Arranged chronologically by dates of applications. Indexed alphabetically by names of applicants. Handwritten. Average 75 pages. 20 x 10 x 1. Clerk of courts' office.

A. DIVISION OF DOMESTIC RELATIONS

Prior to 1915 family matters in Montgomery County have been handled in several courts. Jurisdiction in divorce and alimony cases had been exercised by the supreme court (1803-1853) and by the court of common pleas (1843-1914); while the probate judge, following the juvenile court law of 1904, had original jurisdiction in children's cases.[1] The realization that such a system was unsatisfactory led to the enactment in 1915 of a law (effective in 1917) providing for a court of domestic relations in Montgomery County. This act simply provided for the election of an additional judge to be designated as judge of the court of common pleas, division of domestic relations.[2] Similar legislation was enacted for Hamilton (1914), Summit (1917), Mahoning (1917), Lucas (1917), Stark (1927), and Franklin (1927) Counties.[3]

The Montgomery County division of domestic relations has exclusive original cognizance in divorce and alimony cases and those concerning delinquent, neglected, and dependent children as defined by the Ohio juvenile court laws. Moreover the division has original jurisdiction in determining the paternity of illegitimate children, in charging adults with contributing to the delinquency of minors, and in cases of desertion or failure to provide for minor children.[4]

In order to carry on the work of the court, the domestic relations judge is authorized to appoint a referee in juvenile matters and to fix his salary. The referee, having the usual powers of masters in chancery, hears all cases and certifies to the judge of the domestic relations court his findings, together with his recommendations. The court may accept or reject the findings of the referee.[5]

The court is authorized, also, to appoint a probation officer. This official, like the referee, receives such compensation as is designated by the court, not to exceed the amount appropriated by the county commissioners.[6] It is the duty of the probation officer or his assistance, after complaint has been filed against a minor,

---

1. See P. 106.
2. *Laws of Ohio,* CVI, 424.
3. G. C. secs. 1639, 1532-1, 1532-2, 1535-4, 1532-6, 1532-3, 1532-7.
4. G. C. secs. 13008, 1654, 1655. For additional jurisdiction of the court, see G. C. secs. 6344, 12787, 13041.
5. G. C. sec. 1662-1.
6. G. C. sec. 1552.

neglect, or dependency. It is the duty of this official or his assistance to investigate to investigate the facts and circumstances surrounding the alleged delinquency, the habits of the child, his school record, and other facts which might tend to throw light on his life and character. The probation officer represents the interest of the child in court, furnishes information to the judge during the proceedings, and takes charge of the child before, during, and after the trial. He has the same powers and authority as a county sheriff to serve warrants within or outside the county.[7] The probation department enables the court to carry into execution its decisions and to discover what provisions should be made for the welfare of each child coming before the court.

Realizing the need of special treatment of children's cases, the members of the Ohio legislature made provision for the segregation of juvenile from adult offenders. To make this segregation as complete as possible, the judge is directed, by statute, to hear the trial cases of juvenile and adults offenders in separate rooms.[8] Then, too, upon the recommendation of the judge exercising jurisdiction, the county commissioners are required to provide by purchase or lease of a place to be known as the "detention home," to be located a convenient distance from the courthouse.[9] Here a delinquent, dependent, or neglected child may be detained until after the final disposition of his case. Here, too, dependent children may be separated from delinquents, and first offenders from recidivists. The judge is authorized to appoint a matron to manage such a detention home.[10]

Besides empowering the judge to classify juvenile offenders, the legislature has made provision whereby children coming before the court may be subjected to physical and mental tests.[11] The results of these tests, which are made by experienced physicians and psychiatrists, enables the court and its attaches to determine the disposition of each offender. Conflicts in the home or in the school may be the result of placing a superior or inferior child in the improper mental group.

Another statutory function of the court of domestic relations is the administration of aid to dependent children. This form of aid supersedes mothers'

---

7. G. C. sec. 1663.
8. G. C. sec. 1649.
9. G. C. sec. 1670.
10. G. C. sec. 1670. A detention home was established in Montgomery County, September 1911. Commissioners' Journal, volume 20 [1911], p. 468, see entry 1.
11. G. C. sec. 1652-1.

pensions which were abolished in April 1936 with the acceptance by the Ohio legislature other provisions of title IV of the Federal Social Security Act. The administration of the act in the state is delegated to the department of public welfare, through the division of charities, and in the counties to the juvenile judge or the judge of the court of domestic relations, excepting in counties in which by charter or by law the powers were vested in or imposed upon "a county department, board, commission, or officer other than the juvenile judge." In Montgomery County the judge of the court of domestic relations performs this function. When he serves in the capacity of county administrator, the judge is directed to utilize the services of the employees of the court exercising juvenile jurisdiction. In the performance of his duties the judge is authorized to compel the attendance of witnesses and the production of books, and may institute contempt proceedings against persons refusing to testify. Except for this, power is conferred upon a judge are administrative powers only.

Those entitled to aid under the act include, among others, a child less than sixteen years of age residing in the state who has been deprived of parental support or care by reason of death, continued absence of a parent, or metal or physical incapacity of a parent. However, a child more than sixteen but less than eighteen years of age may receive aid at the discretion of the county administrator.

Application for aid is made to the court by the parent or a relative, with whom the child must be living. Before aid is granted, a careful examination of the home is made by the employees of the court. If the child is found to be eligible, the court may grant such amount as is deemed proper. The amount of aid payable to any child is determined on the basis of actual needs "and shall be sufficient to provide support and care requisite for health and decency." In the event aid is granted, the home of such a child must be visited four times during each year. Each month the county auditor issues warrants upon the county treasurer for the payment of the warrants certified by the court. The decisions of the juvenile judge are subject to the abrogation or modification by the department of public welfare. Any person attempting to receive aid on behalf of any child not entitled to such aid is deemed guilty of a misdemeanor and upon conviction may be punished by fine or imprisonment or both.[12]

The clerk of the court of common pleas serves at the clerk of the division of domestic relations. The prescribed records of the court include, among others,

---

12. G. C. secs. 1683-2--1683-10; 1359-31–1359-45.

an appearance docket, a journal, case cards, case studies, and juvenile court cash book.[13] Although it returns statistical reports to the secretary of state and to the United States Children's Bureau, the court publishes no annual report.

The court of domestic relations, aside from administering justice and adjudicating controversies, attempt to solve social problems which have steadily increased in the postwar years. An immense amount of work, the object of which is crime prevention and placing the maladjusted child in normal society, is done by nonlegal agencies and co-operation with the court. Thousands of cases are dealt with informally by the Humane Society, the Council of Social Agencies, and municipal and county clinics. Protestant, Roman Catholic, and Jewish institutions throughout the county assist the court in its effort to make social readjustments.

---

13. G. C. secs. 1639-13, 1639-17.

Divorce Records
(See also entries 146, 150)

164. APPEARANCE DOCKET
1921—. 33 volumes (1-33).
Docket of cases filed and heard in the court of common pleas, division of domestic relations, showing names of plaintiff and defendant, case number, brief of proceedings, record of witnesses, and amount of cost of case. Arranged numerically by case numbers. Indexed alphabetically by names of plaintiffs. Handwritten. Average 600 pages. 24 x 20 x 3. Clerk of courts' office.

165. MOTION DOCKET
1916—. 10 volumes (1-10).
Docket of motions in cases before the court of common pleas, division of domestic relations including alimony hearings and rehearings, and awarding custody of children. All motions show names of plaintiff and defendant, case number, date of filing of case, date of motion, names of attorneys, and final disposition of case. Arranged chronologically by dates of filing. No index. Handwritten on printed forms. Average 500 pages. 14 x 8.5 x 2. 7 volumes, 1916-1930, Clerk of courts' record room 1; 3 volumes, 1931—, Clerk of courts' office.

166. ORIGINAL PAPERS [Divorce]
1921—. 37 file drawers (labeled by contained case numbers). [1843]-1920
in Case Records [Civil], Entry 92.

Original papers issued in divorce cases in court of common pleas, division of
domestic relations, showing case number, names of plaintiff and defendant, names
of attorneys, volume and page numbers of Minutes, entry 146, and Common Pleas
Record, entry 150. All papers of each case are filed together in a folder. Arranged
numerically by case numbers. No index. Handwritten and typed on printed forms.
11.5 x 15.5 x 27. 36 File drawers, 1921-1939, Clerk of courts' record room 2; 1 file
drawer, 1939—, Clerk of courts' office.

Juvenile Court

Delinquents

167. JUVENILE COURT BLOTTER
1917-1936. 3 volumes (1-3).

Register of cases filed for hearing in juvenile court, showing date case filed, case
number, names and addresses of juvenile and complainant, charge, name of
investigator, report, date of hearing, disposition of case, and volume and page
numbers of dockets and records where entered. Arranged numerically by case
numbers. Indexed alphabetically by names of juveniles. Handwritten. Average 350
pages. 17.5 x 14.5 x 1.5. Clerk of courts' record room 1.

168. JUVENILE INDEX
1908—. 2 volumes (1, 2).

General index to juvenile court records, showing name of plaintiff and defendant,
whether minor or adult, case number, and volume and page numbers of dockets and
records where entered. Arranged alphabetically by names of plaintiffs and
defendants. Handwritten. Average 350 pages. 16 x 10 x 2. Clerk of courts' office.

169. JUVENILE APPEARANCE DOCKET
1909—. 41 volumes (1-7; 1-34). Seven, 1901-1931, subtitled Adults; 22,
1909-1931, Minors; 12 1932—, Adults and Minors.

Docket of cases appearing before the court pertaining to juvenile delinquencies,
showing case number, name of juvenile, offense charged, date and time of filing of
case, and disposition of same; in cases of minors, also shows names and address of

parents or guardians. Arranged chronologically by dates of filing. Indexed alphabetically by names of juveniles. Handwritten. Average 600 pages. 30 x 24 x 3. Clerk of courts' office.

170. JUVENILE JOURNAL
1908—. 21 volumes (1-21).

Entries of daily proceedings before juvenile court including delinquencies, non-support, and dependency, showing date, names of plaintiff and defendant, case number, and findings. Arranged chronologically by dates of entries. No index. 1908-1912, handwritten; 1913—, typed. Average 600 pages. 16.5 x 12 x 3. 17 volumes, 1908- September 1930, Clerk of courts' record room 1; 4 volumes, October 1930—, Clerk of courts' office.

171. ORIGINAL PAPERS [Juvenile Cases]
1915—. 46 file boxes (labeled by contained case numbers).

Original papers in cases filed in juvenile court, division of domestic relations, showing name of juvenile, case number, history of case, charge, disposition of case, and volume and page numbers where entered. All papers of each case are filed together in a folder. Arranged numerically by case numbers. No index. Handwritten and typed on printed forms. 30 file boxes, 11.5 x 15.5 x 16; 16 file boxes, 5.5 x 19 x 25. 36 file boxes, 1915-1930, Clerk of courts' record room 3; 10 file boxes, 1939—, Clerk of courts' office.

Aid to Dependent Children (See also entry 170).

172. MOTHERS' PENSION DOCKET
1915- June 1936. 5 volumes (1-5). Discontinued; superseded by aid to dependent children.

Docket of mothers' pensions, showing name and address of applicant, case number, color, names and ages of children, status of husband, date application filed, and volume and page numbers of Juvenile Journal, entry 170. Arranged chronologically by dates of filing of applications and numerically by case numbers. Indexed alphabetically by names of applicants. Handwritten on printed forms. Average 500 pages. 17 x 10.5 x 3. Clerk of courts' office.

173. REGISTER OF APPLICATIONS RECEIVED
1936—. 1 volume.

Register of applications received for aid to dependent children, showing date of application, name and address of applicant, name of caseworker, names and ages of dependent children, and for approved cases, the amount of aid granted; also shows dates for cases denied, pending further information or approval, and cases closed. Arranged by statutes of cases in four divisions (pending, active, denied, and closed), and chronologically thereunder by dates of applications. No index. Handwritten on printed forms. 50 pages. 17 x 12 x 1. ADC office.

174. APPLICATIONS PENDING
March 1937—. 1 file drawer (labeled by contained letters of alphabet).

Applications for aid pending investigation and approval, showing name of applicant, address, relationship to children, surnames of children, surnames and birth dates of parents, birthplace, color, nationality, marital status, full case history of children, financial status of children over 18 years of age, assistance from relatives, sworn statement of applicant, case number, and date of filing. Arranged alphabetically by names of applicants. No index. Handwritten on printed forms. 15 x 15 x 25.5. ADC office.

175. ACTIVE CASES
1915—. 4 file drawers (labeled by contained letters of alphabet).

Case records of all active cases, showing name of child, address, case history, reports of worker and investigator, itemized account of medical attention received, school report, mental test, amount of grant, and remarks concerning all data. Arranged alphabetically by names of children. No index. Handwritten and typed on printed forms. 15 x 15 x 25.5 ADC office.

176. INDEX TO ACTIVE CASES
1915—. 1 file box. (Labeled by contained letters of alphabet).

Case record of active cases, showing name of client, names of parents or guardians, address, names of children in grant, date of grant, and amount. Arranged alphabetically by names of children. Typed on printed forms. 11.5 x 6.5 x 24. ADC office.

177. INACTIVE CASES

1915—. 12 file drawers (labeled by contained letters of alphabet).

Case papers of closed and rejected cases, showing information as in Active Cases, entry 175, and explanation of present status. Arranged alphabetically by names of children. No index. Handwritten and typed on printed forms. 15 x 15 x 25.5. ADC office.

178. INDEX TO ACTIVE CASES

1915—. 4 file boxes. (2unlabeled; two, by contain letters of alphabet). 2 subtitled Rejected; 2, Closed.

Card record of closed and rejected cases, showing information as an Index to Active Cases, entry 176, remarks pertaining to closing or rejection, and date closed or rejected. Arranged alphabetically by names of clients. Typed on printed forms. 11.5 x 6.5 x 24. ADC office.

179. MEDICAL

March 1937—. 1 file box.

Records of dependent children having received medical attention, showing name of child, date and cause of illness, case number, and reference to itemized account of service extended which is filed in Active Cases, entry 175. Arranged alphabetically by names of children. No index. Typed on printed forms. 6 x 9 x 12. ADC office.

180. DISTRICT SPOT MAP

1936—. 1 map.

Map of districts assigned to case workers, showing each district outline on a regular city and county map by use of colored pins, each color representing the district of a worker. Basic map prepared and painted by F. J. Cellarious and Company, Engineers, Dayton, Ohio. Scale, 1 inch equals 1500 feet. 24 x 36. ADC office.

181. MISCELLANEOUS [Correspondence]

1936—. 4 file drawers (labeled by contained letters of alphabet).

Interoffice communications, correspondence pertaining to clients receiving or applying for aid, and inquiries from other children's relief bureaus regarding aid for dependent children cases, showing names and addresses of correspondent and addresses, date filed, and text of letter. Arranged alphabetically by names of correspondence or addresses and chronologically thereunder by dates of filing. No index. Handwritten and typed, some on printed forms. 15 x 15 x 25.5. ADC office.

B. ASSIGNMENT COMMISSIONERS

In order to secure an even distribution of work among judges the legislature, in 1913, authorized the court of common pleas to designate the members of the jury commission to serve in the capacity of assignment commissioners. It was their duty, when serving in this capacity, to assign cases for trial and to perform such other duties as the court might require.[1] Eight years later, in 1921, the court of common pleas in any county having not more than one common pleas judge and having a population of 80,000 or more, with the consent of the county commissioners, was authorized to appoint such assignment commissioners.[2]

In 1931 the legislature passed an act relieving the jury commissioners of such task by making provision for a separate and distinct body of assignment commissioners. Under this act, the provisions of which are still in force, the judges of the court of common pleas in any county, where two or more judges held court at the same time, were authorized to appoint assignment commissioners. These officials, serving at the pleasure of the court were to receive such compensation as the court might direct, not to exceed $4,900 for each commissioner per year. In the event such appointments were made the names of the appointees, together with there salaries, were to be recorded in the court journal.[3] At the same time, the court of common pleas in any county having not more than one common pleas judge was authorized, when the business of the court required it, to appoint an assignment commissioner. The maximum annual salary of the assignment commissioner in such counties was set at $1,800.[4] This official, serving at the pleasure of the court, could also be appointed court constable.[5]

---

1. *Laws of Ohio,* CIII, 512; CVI, 534; CVIII, pt. ii, 1114; CIX, 281.
2. *Ibid.,* CIX, 152. Under this law Montgomery County appointed an assignment commissioner.
3. G. C. sec. 3007; *Laws of Ohio,* CXIV, 212.
4. *Laws of Ohio,* CXIV, 213; G. C. sec. 3007-1.
5. G. C. sec. 1692-3.

182. TRIAL DOCKET

1935—. 2 volumes. Records are destroyed after case is tried, settled, or dismissed.

Record of cases before the county courts, showing case number, names of plaintiff, defendant, and attorneys, nature of case, date petition filed, and dates of amended petitions, answers, releases, and assignment. One volume includes only non-injury cases. Arranged chronologically by dates petitions filed. No index. Handwritten on printed forms. Average 300 pages. 10 x 6 x 2. Assignment commissioner's office.

183. DIARY
1933—. 7 volumes. (dated).

List of cases before the county courts, showing case number, names of plaintiff, defendant, and attorneys, and date of trial. Arranged chronologically by dates of trials. No index. Handwritten. Average 200 pages. 12 8 x 1. Assignment commissioner's office.

184. SICK LIST
1939. 1 volume.

Record of cases running for one year on which no action has been taken, showing case number, names of plaintiff and defendant, and names of attorneys for plaintiff. Arranged numerically by case numbers. No index. Typed. 25 pages (loose-leaf), 12 x 8 x .5. Assignment commissioner's office.

C. PROBATION DEPARTMENT

Although the probation of offenders had met with success in some eastern states in the latter part of the nineteenth century, it was not until 1908 that the first statute was passed in Ohio providing for the probation of convicted offenders.[1] The act authorized the courts to place on probation convicted offenders who, in the opinion of the judge, were not likely to again engage in crime or offensive conduct. This did not include, however, persons convicted of murder, arson, burglary, incest, sodomy, rape without consent, or the administration of poison.[2]

The plan met with immediate success. As a result of this success the legislature, in 1925, passed an act extending the system of probation. The act provides that the judge of the court of common pleas of a county or judges of such court in joint session, if they deem it advisable, may, with the concurrence of the county commissioners, establish a county department of probation. The department consists of a chief probation officer, and such other employees, clerks, and

---

1. For an interesting discussion of the development of probation, see Louis N, Robinson, *Penology in the United States* (Philadelphia, 1922), 194-217.
2. *Laws of Ohio,* XCII, 339.

stenographers as may be fixed by the judges. The judge or judges of the court of common pleas appoint all officers in the department, fix the salaries of the appointees, and supervise their work. The person appointed as probation officer must possess such training, experience, and qualifications as may be prescribed by the department of public welfare. All positions within the department are in the classified service of the civil service of the county.[3]

The department has legal control and supervision of persons placed on probation in the county wherein the department is located and of any person resident within the county who may have been placed upon probation by any other court exercising criminal jurisdiction in the state whether within or outside the county. Moreover, upon the request of the court, the probation department receives into legal custody any person remaining or residing in the county who has been paroled or conditionally pardoned from a penal, reformatory, or correctional institution. The period of probation is determined by the court and may be extended, but not beyond a period of five years.[4]

The department is required to furnish to each person on probation or parole under its supervision or custody, a written statement of the conditions of probation and parole and instruct him in his obligation to society. Moreover, the department is directed by law "to use all suitable methods, not inconsistent with the conditions of probation or parole, to aid and encourage such persons and bring about improvements in their conduct and condition."[5] The department is required, also, to keep informed concerning the conduct and conditions of each person in its custody. Persons on parole must report periodically to the county department and are visited regularly by members of the division.

Besides supervising and instructing probationers, the county department has the duty of keeping a detailed record of its work, an accurate and complete account of all moneys collected from persons under its supervision or in its custody; and to make such reports to the state department of public welfare as it may require.

In the counties where no county probation department has been established or where the trial court has no regular probation officer, the trial judge may designate some suitable person to act as a probation officer.

---

3. *Ibid.,* CXI, 423.
4. G. C. sec. 13452-5; *Laws of Ohio,* CXIII, 201.
5. *Laws of Ohio,* CXI, 425.

This probation officer is required to make reports at designated periods not less than once a month, concerning the conduct of the probationers in his charge. This officer is given the same power and is subject to the same rules as provided for regularly constituted officers.[6]

In the event the probationer absconds during the period of his probation or is confined in any institution, the period of probation ceases until he is returned before the court.[7] During the period of probation, any field officer or probation officer may arrest the defendant without warrant and bring him before the judge before whom the case is pending.[8] This judge or magistrate may inquire into the conduct of the defendant, and approve the sentence originally imposed, or continue the probation. At the end of the probation period, the jurisdiction of the judge or magistrate ceases, the defendant is discharged, and the judge may restore his citizenship.

Since the probation department is relatively new, there is, to be sure, some inefficiencies in its administration. The argument has been advanced, that the probationers need no supervision. But authorities on criminal administration generally agree that suspension of sentences without supervision is not probation. Since modification of the offender's behavior, rather than punishment, is the logic of probation, it is important that trained men be employed to supervise the activities of the probationer–preferably not former policemen, who, because of their earlier training, are not always careful to make a distinction between the principles of supervision and discipline. There is likewise a need for scientific diagnosis by specialists in order to determine not only which individuals should be placed on probation, but also the policies that should be used by the department in dealing with various classes of offenders. Finally, organization and centralization of records is becoming increasingly important. The entire record of previous crimes of each probationer, as well as an educational and home record, should be carefully compiled, filed, and preserved for future reference.

In spite of its few defects, probation offers a solution for stamping out crime. Through such a system society learns what is needed to prevent men and women from becoming criminals and his steps necessary to lead them back into normal society, after they had started a criminal career.

---

6. G. C. sec. 13452-8.
7. G. C. sec. 13452-11.
8. G. C. sec. 13452-6.
9. Robinson, *op. cit.,* 216.

185. RECORD OF PROBATION
1930—. 3 volumes.
Record of probationers, showing name and address, case number, term served, name of sentencing judge, date of release, terms of probation. Arranged alphabetically by names of probationers. No index. Handwritten. Average 200 pages. 14 x 8.5 x 2. Probation department office.

186. ADULT CASE RECORD
1928—. 8 file boxes (labeled by contained letters of alphabet).
Papers of probation department, with correspondence relative to failure to report as ordered, investigations, case record, complete cases, and records of paroles revoked and probationers returned to penal institutions. Papers show date, name of probationer or other principal, and subject covered. Arranged alphabetically by names of probationers. No index. Handwritten and typed. 18 x 6 x 24. Probation department office.

187. RECORD BOOK
1930—. 2 volumes. Title varies slightly.
Record of persons on probation, showing name and address, charge, expiration date of probation, and dates reported to probation officer. Arranged alphabetically by names of probationers. No index. Handwritten on printed forms. Average 300 pages. 14 x 8.5 x 2. Probation department office.

188. CASH BOOK
1935—. 3 volumes (1-3). Title varies: Old Cash Book 1935-1936, 1 volume; Receipts and Disbursements, 1937-1938. 1 volume.
Record of receipts of probation department, showing name of payer, receipt number, date, and total amount received; disbursements, showing name of payee, check number, date, case number, and amount. Arranged chronologically by dates of entries. No index. Handwritten on printed forms. Average 200 pages. 16 x 10 x 1.5. Probationers Department office.

189. LEDGER
1930—. 3 volumes. (dated).
Cash accounts of each probationer, showing name, amount due, for what, date and amount paid, and date account closed. Arranged alphabetically by names of probationers. No index. Handwritten. 14 x 8.5 x 2. Probation department office.

The first constitution of Ohio provided for a supreme court consisting of three judges appointed by a joint ballot of the legislature for a seven-year term. This court was required to hold sessions at least once a year in each county.[1] The number of judges, according to constitutional provisions, might be increased to four after a period of five years, in which case the judges were permitted to divide the state into two circuits. Accordingly, in 1808, the membership of the court was increased to four and the state was divided into the requisite number of circuits.[2] Two years later, in 1810, the membership of the court was reduced to three;[3] in 1824 it was again increased to four.[4]

By constitutional provision, this court was given original and appellate jurisdiction "both in common law and chancery," and such cases as should be provided by law.[5] Accordingly, by a statutory provision of 1803, the supreme court was given original jurisdiction of all cases both in law and equity where the title of land was in question or the sum or matter in dispute did not exceed the value of one thousand dollars and appellate jurisdiction from the courts of common pleas in all cases respecting the title of lands, or where the matter in controversy exceeded the value of one hundred dollars and in all cases where the proof of validity of wills or right of administration was in question. It was further enacted that the court had exclusive jurisdiction of all cases of divorce and alimony, and of criminal cases where the punishment was capital and concurrent jurisdiction with the courts of common pleas in other cases and offenses not cognizable by a justice of peace.[6]

An act passed in 1815, amending the act of 1803, the courts of common pleas were given concurrent jurisdiction with the supreme court in all cases in law and equity, where the cause or matter in dispute exceeded one thousand dollars. The supreme court was given appellate jurisdiction from the courts of common pleas in all cases in which the latter courts had original jurisdiction. All cases in which the title of land or freehold was in question were to be tried in the county in which the land was situated.[7]

---

1. *Ohio Const. 1802,* Art. III, secs. 2, 8, 10.
2. *Laws of Ohio,* VI, 32.
3. *Ibid.,* VIII, 259.
4. *Ibid.,* XXII, 50.
5. *Ohio Const. 1802,* Art. III, sec. 2.
6. *Laws of Ohio,* I, 36-37, 42.
7. *Ibid.,* XIV, 310-354.

The court retained original, exclusive cognizance in divorce and alimony until 1843,[8] and had concurrent jurisdiction with the courts of common pleas in such cases from 1843 to 1853 when the latter court was granted exclusive jurisdiction.[9] During the first half century of Ohio history the legislature also granted decrees in divorce. The constitution of 1802 did not prohibit the legislature from exercising such jurisdiction but the supreme court prohibited the practice in 1848, and the constitution of 1851, Article II, section 32, contained a prohibiting clause.[10]

In 1831 the supreme court was directed to meet annually in the town of Columbus for the final adjudication of all such questions of law as may have been reserved in any county for decision. This session of the court, known as the court in bank, was required to have its decisions in each case reduced to writing, and transmitted to the clerk of the supreme court in each county in which such question was reserved. The clerk was directed to enter such decisions "on the journal of the said court" and such proceedings were to be taken as if such decisions had been made in the county.[11] Six years later, in 1837, an act was passed providing that the final judgments in the supreme court, held within any county within the state, could be re-examined and reversed or affirmed in the court in bank upon a writ of error.[12]

This judicial arrangement continued until the adoption of the constitution of 1851, which provided a judicial system modeled upon the federal system existing at the time. The supreme court, as established in 1851, became for the first time in Ohio history, a reviewing court of last resort in the state. At the same time the jurisdiction of the supreme court was restricted. In 1853 the court of common pleas, rather than the supreme court, was given original cognizance of all crimes and offenses, except minor criminal cases, the exclusive jurisdiction of which was vested in the justices of the peace and other minor courts.[13]

The opinions of the supreme court on circuit and the decisions of the court in bank, as transmitted to the clerk of the supreme court in each county, are in the offices of the respective clerks of courts.

---

8. *Ibid.*, XLI, 94.
9. *Ibid.*, LI, 377.
10. *Bingham* V. *Miller, Ohio Reports* XVII, 445.
11. *Laws of Ohio*, XXIX, 93-94.
12. *Ibid.*, XXXV, 60-62.
13. *Ohio Const. 1851*, Art. IV, sec. 2.

190. BLOTTER [Supreme Court]
1825-1951. 2 volumes (B1, C1).
Register of cases filed for appearance in supreme court, showing term of court, names of attorneys, names of plaintiff and defendant, title of case, dates of filing various writs, dates of returns on writs, amount of judgment rendered, names of witnesses, names of jurors when used, and amount of clerks and sheriff's cost itemized. Arranged chronologically by dates filed. Indexed alphabetically by names of plaintiffs showing names of defendants. Handwritten. Average 470 pages. 13 x 9 x 2.5. Clerk of courts' record room 1.

191. MINUTES [Supreme Court]
1803-1852. 3 volumes (A1-C1).
Journal entries of court proceedings and court orders, showing case number, names of litigants, kind of action, and disposition of case. Arranged chronologically by dates of entries. No index. Handwritten. Average 500 pages. 13 x 8.5 x 2.5. Clerk of courts' record room 2.

192. SUPREME COURT RECORDS
1803-1851. 7 VOLUMES (A1-G1).
Complete record of proceedings, including copies of affidavits of information or complaints, petitions, answers, pleas, motions, demurrers, jury verdicts, decisions and opinions of the court, briefs of testimony and evidence submitted, and sentences, all showing court term, names of plaintiff and defendant, title of case, case number, date filed, and date case disposed of. Arranged chronologically by court terms. Indexed alphabetically by names of plaintiffs showing names of defendants. Handwritten. Average 600 pages. 18 x 12 x 3. Clerk of courts' record room 2.

193. ORIGINAL PAPERS
1803-1853. 1 file drawer.
Original papers in cases filed in supreme court, including divorce and alimony, judgments, declarations of particulars, injunctions, petitions, capias, summonses, and transcripts from lower courts, all showing case number, court term, names of litigants, kind of action, and date of filing. All papers of each case are banded together. Arranged chronologically by dates of filing. Handwritten. 5 x 15.5 x 25. Clerk of court' record room 2.

On March 29, 1856, the legislature made provision for a superior court in Montgomery County which was deemed and held a court of general jurisdiction and was presided over by one judge. This court was given the same power, authority, and original jurisdiction and civil actions and other proceedings as by the constitution and laws had been conferred upon the court of common pleas, except that the superior court was denied any jurisdiction in criminal or bastardy cases, divorce and alimony, or the relief of insolvent debtors. All laws for the courts of common pleas or the district courts, giving them power to hear and determine cases, preserve order, punish contempt, remove officers, enforce judgments, issue orders of decrees, and authorized the execution of the same, were extended to the superior court, unless these laws were inconsistent with the terms of the act or plainly inapplicable. The court also had the same power to vacate or modify its own judgments or orders doing or after the term, and to enter judgments by confession, as is, or may be, vested by law in the courts are common pleas.[1]

The supreme court was given appellate jurisdiction from the superior court by appeal, writ of error, or other processes in the same manner and under the same provisions as from the court of common pleas. Cases commenced and pending in the court of common pleas, in which the superior court has jurisdiction, could be transferred to the superior court by the clerk by removal from the court of common pleas docket to the docket of the superior court together with all papers of the case and a statement of cost.[2]

The term of court, held at the courthouse in Dayton, commenced on the first Monday of each month except the months of July, August, and September, and the court term could be dispensed with or adjourned at the pleasure of the judge.[3] However, the act of March 27, 1875, stipulated that the terms of the court commenced on the first Monday in October, January, March, and May.[4] The court had full power to classify and distribute the business therein as necessary; to make rules and regulations or practice therein; to appoint masters, receivers, and other officers to facilitate its business; to direct as to the mode of proceedings by or before said officers; and to tax costs.[5]

---

1. *Laws of Ohio,* LIII, 38.
2. *Ibid.,* 41.
3. *Ibid.,* 39.
4. *Ibid.,* LXXXII, 90.
5. *Ibid.,* LIII, 10.

The clerk of the court of common pleas was designated as clerk of the superior court and was required prior to give additional bond of not less than $10,000 nor more than $30,000 which would be acceptable to the county commissioners.[6] Sheriffs, coroners, and constables were bound to attend the superior court and to preserve order. They were also required to execute and return its processes.[7]

The judge of the superior court who was commissioned by the governor was elected for a five-year term and vacancies were to be filled by the governor pending the next election.[8] The salary of the judge was set at $1,500 annually payable at the state treasury and the county commissioners could provide an additional $1,000 annually payable from the county treasury.[9] An act of February 17, 1870, raises the amount paid by the state treasurer to $2,500.[10]

The jurisdiction of the court remained unchanged during the period of its existence, but on June 20, 1879, the legislature abolished the court[11] and unfinished cases were disposed of by the court of common pleas and the case records were completed in the volumes and papers of the abolished superior court.[12]

---

6. *Ibid.*, 38.
7. *Laws of Ohio*, LIII, 39.
8. *Ibid.*, 38.
9. *Ibid.*, 41.
10. *Ibid.*, LXVII, 16.
11. R. S., sec. 1746.
12. See p. 145-147.

General Court Proceedings

194. APPEARANCE DOCKET

1856-1886. 33 volumes (1-33 and labeled by contained case numbers) Docket of cases filed and heard in superior court, showing court term, names of attorneys, title of case, names of plaintiffs and defendant, case number, date case filed, copies of various journal entries, writs, and court orders, amount of clerk's and sheriff's fees, copies of sheriff's returns on writs, date cost paid, and volume and page numbers of docket and records where entered. Arranged chronologically by dates of filing of case. Indexed alphabetically by names of plaintiffs showing names of defendants. Handwritten. Average 500 pages. 16 x 12 x 3. Clerk of courts' record room 2.

195. COURT DOCKET
1857-1891. 113 volumes.
Docket of causes filed and heard in superior court, showing court term, names of attorneys, case number, kind of case, names of plaintiff and defendant, and disposition of case. Arranged chronologically by court terms. No index. Handwritten. Average 200 pages. 13.5 x 8.5 x 1. Clerk of courts' record room 1.

196. ENTRY DOCKET
1877-1890. 4 volumes (2-5).
Record of partition cases in superior court, showing names of plaintiff and defendant, case number, date of entry, volume and page numbers of dockets and records where entered, dates of order of sale, and name of purchaser, amount of sale, and amount of cash put down. Arranged chronologically by dates of sales. Indexed alphabetically by names of plaintiffs showing names of defendants. Handwritten on printed forms. Average 250 pages. 16 x 10 x 2. Clerk of courts' record room 1.

197. BAR DOCKET
1857-1885. 23 volumes.
Docket of causes in superior court, showing term of court, case number, trial date, names of litigants and attorneys, title of case, and disposition of case. Arranged chronologically by court terms and chronologically thereunder by trial dates. No index. Handwritten. Average 120 pages. 13 x 8.5 x 1. Clerk of courts' record room 1.

198. MINUTES
1856-1886. 17 volumes (1-17).
Record of daily proceedings in superior court, showing date of entry, names of plaintiff and defendant, case number, kind of action, and copy of journal entry. Arranged chronologically by dates of entries. Indexed alphabetically by names of plaintiffs showing names of defendants. Handwritten. Average 700 pages. 17.7 x 12 x 3. Clerk of courts' record room 1.

199. SUPERIOR COURT RECORDS
1856-1886. 49 volumes (1-49).
Complete record of proceedings in superior court, including copies of affidavits of information or complaints, petitions, answers, pleas, motions, demurrers, jury

verdicts, decisions, opinions of the court, and sentences, showing term of court, names of plaintiff and defendant, title of case, case number, date filed, brief of testimony and evidence submitted, and date case disposed of. Arranged chronologically by dates of entries. Indexed alphabetically by names of plaintiffs showing names of defendants; also separate index to judgments, entries 203, 204. Handwritten. Average 600 pages. 18 x 12 x 3. Clerk of courts' record room 2.

200. SUPERIOR COURT
1856-1887. 31 file boxes (labeled by contained case numbers).
Original papers of cases in superior court, including affidavits on appeals, appeal bonds, petitions, amended petitions, answers, demurrers, writs, sheriff's returns on writs, depositions, journal entries, and itemized cost bills. All papers show names of litigants, nature of case, case number, date issued, and volume and page numbers of Appearance Docket entry 194. All papers of each case are filed together in a jacket. Arranged numerically by case numbers. No index. Handwritten on printed forms. 11.5 x 15.5 x 25. Clerk of courts record' room 2.

Jury and Witness Records

201. JURORS
1865-1886. 2 volumes (1, 2).
Record of jury venires, showing court to term, names the litigants, volume and page numbers of Appearance Docket, entry 194, names of jurors, date subpoenaed, number of days, mileage, total fee, and date certificate for fees issued. Arranged chronologically by court terms. No index. Handwritten. Average 350 pages. 14 x 9 x 2. Clerk of courts' record room 1.

202. WITNESS DOCKET
1883-1886. 1 volume. (5).
Record of witnesses subpoenaed in superior court cases, showing court term, names of plaintiff and defendant, case number, names of plaintiffs and defendants witnesses, number of days served, mileage, and fees. Arranged chronologically by court terms. Indexed alphabetically by names of plaintiffs showing names of defendants. Handwritten on printed forms. 740 pages. 14 x 9.5 x 2.5. Clerk of courts' record room 1.

203. JUDGMENT INDEX, DIRECT
1856-1887. 3 volumes (1-3).

Direct index record of judgments rendered, showing date case filed, names of judgment creditor and debtor, case number, term in which disposed of, date judgment satisfied, volume and page numbers of Minutes, entry 198, amount of judgment, cost, volume and page numbers of Appearance Docket, entry 194 and Superior Court Records, entry 199. Arranged alphabetically by names of judgment creditors. Handwritten on printed forms. Average 350 pages. 16 x 12 x 3. Clerk of courts' record room 1.

204. JUDGMENT INDEX, REVERSE
1856-1887. 3 volumes (1-3).

Reverse index record of judgments rendered, showing date case filed, names of judgment debtor and creditor, case number, term in which disposed of, date judgment satisfied, volume and page numbers of Minutes, entry 198, amount of judgment, amount of cost, volume and page numbers of Appearance Docket, entry 194, and Superior Court Records, 199. Arranged alphabetically by names of judgment debtors. Handwritten on printed forms. Average 350 pages. 16 x 12 x 3. Clerk of courts' record room 1.

205. EXECUTION DOCKET
1856-1887. 4 volumes (1-4).

Docket of executions ordered to satisfy judgments rendered, showing execution number, names of judgment creditor and judgment debtor, date execution issued, itemized account of fees, dates of issuing various writs, and receipt for fees paid. Arranged numerically by execution numbers. Indexed alphabetically by names of judgment creditors showing names of judgment debtors. Handwritten. Average 700 pages. 18 x 12 x 2. Clerk of courts' record room 1.

206. INDEX TO EXECUTION DOCKET, NOT DORMANT [Superior Court]

1878, 1 volume.

Record of living executions issued in superior court cases, showing case number, execution number, names of judgment creditor and debtor, and amount of judgment. Arranged alphabetically by names of judgment debtors. No index. Handwritten on printed forms. 250 pages. 16.5 x 11 x 2. Clerk of courts' record room 1.

207. LEVY RECORD

1859-1886. 2 volumes (1, 2).

Record of levies on chattels and real estate to satisfy judgment rendered, showing complete description of property upon which levy is made, case number, names of plaintiff and defendant, and dates writs return by sheriff. Arranged alphabetically by names of plaintiffs showing names of defendants. No index. Handwritten. Average 500 pages. 15 x 13 x 3. Clerk of courts' record room 1.

Until 1851 the judicial power of the state of Ohio in matters of both law and equity was vested in the supreme court, the court of common pleas, and the justices' courts.[1] During the first fifty years of Ohio history the supreme court served as a court of appeals, holding court in each county annually.[2] When a new constitution was adopted in 1851 the judicial system was extended by the creation of district courts composed of one supreme court justice and several common pleas judges in the district. These courts were assigned original jurisdiction in the same matters as the supreme court, and such "appellate jurisdiction" as might be provided by law.[3] Thus by constitutional provision the courts were assigned original cognizance in *quo warranto, mandamus, habeas corpus,* and *procedendo.*[4] In addition to this, in 1852 the legislature authorized the courts to issue writs of error, *certiorari, supersedeas, ne ereat,* and all other writs not specifically provided by statute, whenever such writs were necessary for the exercise of its jurisdiction. The same act gave the courts appellate jurisdiction from the court of common pleas in civil cases wherein the latter court had original jurisdiction.[5]

For the purpose of the district courts the nine common pleas districts were apportioned into five judicial districts. A judge of the supreme court was designated to preside at the sessions of the district courts, in the event that no judge of the supreme court were present, as was often the case, the judge of the court common pleas in whose subdivision court was being held was directed to preside.[6]

The district courts failed to function properly. Evidence seems to indicate that the increasing number of cases coming before the supreme court made it difficult for the justices to attend the meetings of the district courts. Indeed, six years before the creation of the district courts, the supreme court docket was overcrowded. In 1845 the legislature found it necessary to afford temporary relief by prohibiting appeals from the courts of common pleas to the supreme court.[7]

---

1. *Ohio Const, 1802,* Art. III, sec. 1.
2. See p. 90.
3. *Ohio Const. 1851,* Art. IV, secs. 5, 6.
4. *Ibid.,* Art. IV, sec. 2.
5. *Laws of Ohio,* L, 69.
6. *Ibid.,* L. 69.
7. *Ibid.,* XLIII, 80.

A similar condition of overcrowding existed in the sixties; so that, in 1865, the supreme court justices were relieved of the duty of attending the meetings of the district courts for that particular year.[8] The judicial system had become slow and cumbersome. The courts declined rapidly after 1865 and were finally abolished.

Following the complete collapse of the district courts an amendment to the constitution, adopted in 1883, made provision for circuit courts. "The circuit courts," stated the amendment, "shall be successors of the district courts, and all cases, judgments, records, and proceedings pending in said district courts, in the several counties, of any district, shall be transferred to the circuit courts." The district courts, however, were to continue in existence until the election and qualification of the judges of the circuit court.[9] The circuit courts were assigned the same "original jurisdiction with the supreme court, and such appellate jurisdiction as may be provided by law." The composition of the courts and the number of circuits were left to the discretion of the legislature. Accordingly, in 1884, an act was passed dividing the state into seven circuits, and providing for the election of three judges in each circuit.[10]

The circuit courts, in addition to the jurisdiction conferred upon them by the constitution,[11] were authorized by the legislature to issue writs of *supersedeas* in any case, and all other writs not specifically provided by statute when they were necessary for the exercise of their jurisdiction.[12] Moreover, the courts were authorized to make and publish, as they deemed expedient, rules of procedure of their respective circuits, not in conflict with the law or rules of the supreme court. The legislature directed that all cases taken to the circuit courts were to be entered on the docket in the order in which they were commenced, received, or filed, and "to be taken up and disposed of in the same order." However, cases in which persons seeking relief were imprisoned or were convicted of a felony; cases involving the validity of any tax levy or assessment; cases involving the constitutionality of a statute; and cases involving public right and proceedings in *quo warranto, mandamus, procedendo,* or *habeas corpus,* could be taken up in advance of their assignment or order on the docket.[13]

---

8. *Ibid.,* LXII, 72.
9. *Ohio Const, 1851,* Art. IV, sec. 6.
10. *Laws of Ohio,* LXXXI, 168.
11. *Ohio Const. 1851,* Art. IV, sec. 6.
12. *Laws of Ohio,* LXXXI, 168.
13. *Ibid.,* LXXXI, 168.

The judicial system of Ohio was again slightly changed in 1912 when, by constitutional amendment, the circuit courts were renamed courts of appeal. "The court of appeals shall continue the work of the respective circuit courts and all pending cases and proceedings in the circuit courts shall proceed to judgment and be determined by the respective courts of appeals." The judges of the several circuit courts were designated as judges of the courts of appeals, and were directed to perform the duties thereof until the expiration of their terms of office. Vacancies caused by the expiration of terms of office of the judges were to be filled by the electors of the respective appellate district. The term of office was fixed at six years.[14]

The jurisdiction of the court of appeals remained much the same as that of the district court in 1851. However, the court was assigned original cognizance in writs of probation and appellate jurisdiction in the trial of chancery cases.[15] Certain restrictions were imposed upon the court: "No judgment of a court of common pleas, a superior court, or other court of record" shall be reversed except by "the concurrence of all judges of the court of appeals."[16]

At present the court consists of three judges in each of the nine districts into which the state is divided, each of whom shall have been admitted to practice as an attorney at law in the state for a period of six years immediately preceding his election. One court of appeals judge is chosen every two years, and he holds office for six years beginning on the ninth day of February next after his election. The salary of the court of appeals judge, fixed at $6,000 per year in 1913, was increased to $8,000 in 1920 and so continues.[17] The judges hold at least one session of court annually in each county in the district.[18]

---

14. *Ohio Const, 1851* (Amendment, 1912), Art. IV, sec. 6.
15. *Ohio Const, 1851* (Amendment, 1912), Art. IV, sec. 6.
16. *Ibid.,* Art. IV, sec. 6.
17. *Laws of Ohio,* CIII, 418; CVIII, pt. II, 1301.
18. G. C. sec. 1517.

District Court

208. BLOTTER [District Court]
1852-1885. 1 volume (A1).
Register of cases filed for appearance in district court, showing date filed, court term, name of plaintiff and defendant, title of case, case number, names of

attorneys, state of suit, and how disposed of. Arranged chronologically by dates of filing of cases. Indexed alphabetically by names of plaintiffs showing names of defendants. Handwritten. 300 pages. 11.5 x 8.5 x 2.5. Clerk of courts' record room 1.

209. APPEARANCE DOCKET [District Court]
1852-1885. 1 volume (1).

Docket of cases filed and heard in district court, showing names of plaintiff, defendant, and attorneys, case number, title of case, date appeal filed, dates petitions and answers filed, writs issued, notations of court orders and decisions in case, itemized cost bill, date costs paid, name of person paying cost, and amount. Arranged chronologically by dates of filing of appeals. Indexed alphabetically by names of plaintiffs showing names of defendants. Handwritten. 400 pages. 15.5 x 11.5 x 3. Clerk of courts' record room 2.

210. COURT DOCKET
1851-1885. 7 volumes.

Docket of cases appearing before district court, showing courts term, title of case, names of plaintiff, defendant, and attorneys, case number, and disposition of case. Arranged numerically by case numbers. Indexed alphabetically by names of plaintiffs showing names of defendants. Handwritten. Average 300 pages. 16 x 8 x .25. Clerk of courts' record room 1.

211. CASE RECORDS
1852-1885. 1 file drawer.

Original papers issued in district court cases, including appeal affidavits, appeal bonds, petitions, answers, demurrers, writs, sheriff's returns on writs, court orders, and itemized cost bills. All show names of litigants, nature of case, case number, date filed, and page numbers of Appearance Docket [District Court], entry 209. Arranged chronologically by dates of filing. No index. Handwritten on printed forms. 11.5 x 15.5 x 235. Clerk of courts' record room 2.

212. DISTRICT COURT RECORD
1852-1885. 2 volumes (A1, A2).

Complete record of proceedings in district court cases, including copies of affidavits of information or complaint, petitions, answers, pleas, motions, demurrers, jury verdicts, decisions and opinions of the court, briefs of testimony and evidence, and sentences, all showing court terms, names of plaintiff, and defendant, case number, date filed, and date disposed of. Arranged chronologically by court terms. Indexed alphabetically by names of plaintiffs showing names of defendants. Handwritten. Average 600 pages. 18 x 12 x 3. Clerk of courts' record room 2.

213. DISTRICT COURT CHANCERY RECORD
1852-1880. 1 volume. (A1).

Record of chancery cases, including copies of petitions, bills of particulars, affidavits, motions, pleas and answers, briefs of testimony and evidence, court orders, and decisions, showing court term, names of plaintiff and defendant, title of case, case number, and date of filing. Arranged chronologically by court terms. Indexed alphabetically by names of plaintiffs showing names of defendants. Handwritten. Average 700 pages. 18 x 12 x 3.5. Clerk of courts' record room 2.

214. APPEARANCE DOCKET
1885-1912. 4 volumes. (1-4 and labeled by contained letters of alphabet).

Record of cases filed and heard in circuit court, showing names of plaintiff and defendant, court term, date of trial, case number, copy of appeal, and copies of petitions, writs, court orders, and decrees. Arranged chronologically by court terms and chronologically thereunder by dates of trials. Indexed alphabetically by names of plaintiffs showing names of defendants. Handwritten. Average 500 pages. 15.5 x 11.5 x 3. Clerk of courts' record room 2.

215. COURT DOCKET
1891-1912. 24 volumes.

Docket of cases before the circuit court, showing case number, names of plaintiff and defendant, court term, names of attorneys, date case filed, and judges memorandum. Arranged numerically by case numbers. No index. Handwritten. Average 30 pages. 16 x 8 x .25. Clerk of courts' record room 1.

216. MINUTES
1885-1912. 4 volumes (1-4).

Copies of journal entries in circuit court cases, showing date of entry, court term, names of plaintiff and defendant, kind of action, and dates of hearings. Arranged chronologically by court terms and chronologically thereunder by dates of entries. Indexed alphabetically by names of plaintiffs showing names of defendants. Handwritten. Average 600 pages. 16.5 x 11.5 x 3. Clerk of courts' record room 2.

217. CASE RECORDS
1880-1912. 1 file drawer.

Original papers issued in circuit court cases, including itemized cost bills, appeal affidavits, petitions, answers, demurrers, writs, sheriff's return on writs, and court orders. All papers show names of litigants, nature of case, case number, date filed, and volume and page numbers of Appearance Docket, entry 214. Arranged chronologically by dates of filing. No index. Handwritten on printed forms. 11.5 x 15.5 x 25. Clerk of courts record room 2.

218. [CIRCUIT COURT RECORD]
1884-1912. In Common Pleas Record, entry 150.

Complete record of circuit court cases, showing information as in Common Pleas Record, entry 150.

Court Of Appeals

219. APPEARANCE DOCKET AND FEE BOOK
January 20, 1913——. 4 volumes (1-4).

Docket of cases before the court of appeals, showing names of plaintiff and defendant, case number, copies of transcripts of case, dates bills of exceptions and acknowledgments filed, and amount of cost. Arranged chronologically by dates of entries. Indexed alphabetically by names of plaintiffs showing names of defendants. Handwritten. Average 600 pages. 15 x 13 x 3. Clerk of courts' office.

220. MINUTES
1913——. 6 volumes (1-6).

Copies of journal entries in court of appeals cases, showing date of entry, kind of case, names of plaintiff, defendant, and judge, court term, and case number. Arranged chronologically by dates of entries. No index. Handwritten on printed forms. Average 500 pages. 15 x 13 x 3. Clerk of courts' office.

221. [COURTS OF APPEALS RECORD]
1913—. In Common Pleas Record, entry 150.
Complete record of court of appeals cases, showing copies of all court orders and decrees, term of court, names the litigants, title of case, case number, date case filed, and date disposed of.

222. [ORIGINAL PAPERS, COURT OF APPEALS]
1913—. In Case Records [Civil], entry 92, and Case Records [Criminal], entry 93.
Original papers in court of appeals cases, showing date of issue, names of litigants, title of case, case number, kind of action, and date case filed.

The probate court, established by an act of the Northwest Territory on August 30, 1788, consisted of a probate judge with jurisdiction in probate, testamentary, and guardianship matters, and two judges of the court of common pleas, who sat with him and ruled on contested points, definitive sentences, and final judgments.[1]

The judicial system established under the first constitution of Ohio in 1802 did not provide for a probate court but vested the court of common pleas with such powers as had been exercised by the court in the territorial period. The constitution of 1851 recreated the probate court and gave it original jurisdiction in "probate and testamentary matters, the appointment of administrators and guardians, the settlement of the accounts of executors, administrators and guardians, and such jurisdiction in *habeas corpus,* . . . and for the sale of land by executors, administrators and guardians, and such other jurisdiction, . . . as may be provided by law."[2] An amendment to the constitution adopted in 1912, authorized the common pleas judge, when petitioned by ten percent of the qualified voters in the counties having a population less than 60, 000 to submit to the voters at any general election the question of combining the probate court and court of common pleas.[3]

One of the primary functions of the court since its inception has been the settlement of estates. The civil code adopted in 1853 gave the court original jurisdiction in taking proof of wills, in granting letters testamentary and settling accounts of executors and administrators.[4] Until 1854 the court has had jurisdiction in enforcing the payment of debts and legacies of deceased persons. While the court retains the original jurisdiction regarding estates, new duties have been added in recent years. With the development of inheritance tax laws in 1919 as a new means of taxation the probate court has been required to determine and assess the tax after the county auditor has appraised the decedent's estate.[5]

By constitutional provision the probate court has original jurisdiction in granting marriage licenses.[6]

---

1. Pease, *op. cit.,* 9.
2. *Ohio Const. 1851,* Art. IV, secs, 7, 8.
3. *Ibid.,* sec. 7 (as amended, 1912). See also p. 64.
4. *Laws of Ohio,* LI, 167.
5. *Ibid.,* CVIII, pt. i, 561. See also p. xxxix.
6. *Ohio Const. 1851,* Art. IV, sec. 8.

The court also issues licenses to ministers to solemnize marriages.[7] The former provision was modified by an act adopted in 1931, which requires an elapse of at least five days between the time of application and that of the issuance of marriage licenses. However, power to suspend the operation of the act is vested in the probate judge.[8] Moreover, the probate courts in certain counties, exclusive of Montgomery, were given concurrent jurisdiction with the court of common pleas in "divorce, alimony, foreclosure, and partitions" cases. Thus, in 1894, the legislature conferred such jurisdiction upon the probate court in Butler, Allen, Richland, Perry, Defiance, and Wood Counties.[9] The original act, subject to amendments in 1896, 1900, and 1904, which granted and denied such jurisdiction to the probate courts in certain counties, was repealed in 1911.[10] In 1919 concurrent jurisdiction in such matters was re-established in Pickaway, Licking, Richland, Perry, Defiance, Henry, and Coshocton Counties, and established in Fayette County.[11] This jurisdiction was abolished in 1931.[12]

The jurisdiction of the court extends to the state's unfortunate. By the probate code of 1853, re-enacted in 1854, exclusive jurisdiction was granted to the court to make inquests respecting lunatics, insane persons, idiots, and deaf and dumb persons, subject by law to guardianships.[13] In 1856 the court was authorized to commit mentally incompetent persons to state institutions maintained for the care of such persons.[14] Two years later the court was given power to appoint and remove guardians over minors.[15] The act of 1859 authorized the court to render adoption decrees.[16] Since 1904 the court has been given jurisdiction in trial cases involving neglected, dependent, and delinquent children.[17]

Since the middle of the nineteenth century the probate judge has been required to keep a record of vital statistics.

---

7. *Laws of Ohio,* L, 84.
8. *Ibid.,* CXIV, 93.
9. *Laws of Ohio,* XCI, 791, 799-800.
10. *Ibid.,* XCII, 643; XCIV, 137-138; XCVII, 113-114; CII, 100.
11. *Ibid.,* CVIII, pt. i, 625.
12. *Ibid.,* CXIV, 320.
13. *Ibid.,* LI, 167; LII, 103.
14. *Ibid.,* LIII, 81-86.
15. *Ibid.,* LV, 54.
16. *Ibid.,* LVI, 82; LXVII, 14.
17. See p. 78.

In1867 the duty of keeping a permanent record of births and deaths, which, in 1856, had been conferred upon the clerk of courts, was transferred to the probate judge.[18] When, in 1908, a bureau of vital statistics under the direction of the secretary of state was created the probate judge was relieved temporarily of this task.[19] In 1921 the act of 1908 was amended so as to require the local registrars to transmit to the district health commissioners, who was directed to serve as a state deputy registrar of vital statistics, all certificates of births and deaths received during the preceding month, and a copy of all such certificates to the probate court. Although the General Code still requires the probate judge to keep a permanent record of births and deaths and an index to such records,[20] neither has been kept in Montgomery County since 1909.

Jurisdiction in naturalization proceedings was exercised by the probate court until 1906 when an amendment to the federal statute vested exclusive jurisdiction in naturalization matters in the United States district courts and all state courts of record having a seal, a clerk, and jurisdiction in actions at law and equity in which the amount in controversy was unlimited.[21] The General Code still requires the probate judge to keep a naturalization record and an index to the records,[22] but jurisdiction was transferred to the court of common pleas. No naturalization records have been kept since 1906.

During the early years of its existence the court was given limited criminal jurisdiction in cases in which the sentence did not impose capital punishment or punishment by imprisonment. By the code of civil procedure adopted in 1853 the judgments of final decrees of the probate court could be revived by the court of common pleas on error.[23] In 1857 the criminal jurisdiction of the probate court was transferred to the court of common pleas,[24] but later acts retained it in certain counties only. Thus, in 1858 the probate courts of certain counties, including Montgomery, were granted jurisdiction in all crimes in which sentence did not impose capital punishment or imprisonment in a penitentiary.[25]

---

18. *Laws of Ohio,* LXIV, 63-64.
19. *Ibid.,* XCIX, 296-307.
20. G. C. sec. 10501-15.
21. *United States Statutes at Large,* XXXIV, pt. i, 569; See also *State of Ohio* v, *George G. Metzger and Albert L. Irish,* 10 N. P., n. s., 97 *et seq.*
22. G. C. Secs. 10501-15, 10501-16.
23. *Laws of Ohio,* LI, 145.
24. *Ibid.,* LIV, 97.
25. *Ibid.,* LV, 186.

This act was repealed in 1878 and the probate courts of certain counties which included Montgomery were granted concurrent jurisdiction with the court of common pleas in all misdemeanors and proceedings to prevent crime and in 1880 such jurisdiction was extended to other counties.[26] The probate court continued to exercise such jurisdiction until 1931 when the last vestige of criminal jurisdiction disappeared with the adoption of the probate code.[27]

Miscellaneous duties, remotely related to probate and testamentary matters, have been added by legislative action. Since 1888 the court has been required to file a certified list of all unknown depositors as furnished by institutions or persons engaged in lending money for profit.[28] In 1896 the probate court was given concurrent jurisdiction with the court of common pleas in the matter of changing the names of persons who desired it,[29] a matter in which the court of common pleas had exclusive cognizance from 1842 to 1896.[30] Since 1896 the probate court has been required to record certificates of doctors and surgeons, and since 1916 the certificates of registered nurses which authorize them to practice their profession in the state.[31] Since 1913 the court has been vested with the power to grant injunctions,[32] and since 1915 has had concurrent jurisdiction with the court of common pleas in condemnation proceedings for roads.[33]

In like matter the appointive powers of the probate judge have been expanded. In addition to the authority to appoint administrators and guardians he was authorized by the act of 1891 to appoint the members of the county board of elections; however this appointive power was abrogated by the act of 1892.[34] Then, too, from 1908 to 1913 the probate judge was authorized to appoint a county blind relief commission,[35] comprised of three members of each who serve a three-year term.[36]

---

26. *Ibid.,* LXXV, 960.
27. *Ibid.,* CXIV, 475.
28. *Ibid.,* LXXXIV, 65; G. C. sec. 9864.
29. *Laws of Ohio,* XCII, 28.
30. *Ibid.,* XL, 28-29.
31. *Ibid.,* XCII, 46; XCIX, 499; CVI, 193, 202.
32. *Laws of Ohio,* CIII, 427.
33. *Ibid.,* CVI, 583.
34. *Ibid.,* LXXXVIII, 449; LXXXIX, 455.
35. See p. 243.
36. *Laws of Ohio,* XCIX, 56; CIII, 60.

Since 1906 he has been authorized to appoint members of the board of county visitors.[37]

The probate judge, like other county officials, have been required by statute to keep a record of the business of his office. The present system of records, originating for the most part in 1853 and continued by the probate code of 1931, includes a criminal record, an administrative docket, a guardians' docket, a marriage record, a record of bonds, a naturalization record, and a permanent record of birth and deaths.[38]

The probate judge has the care and custody of the files, papers, books, and records belonging to the probate office and is ex-officio clerk of the court. The probate court code, adopted in 1931, directed the probate judge to preserve for future reference and examination all pleadings, accounts, vouchers, and other papers in each estate, trust, assignment, guardianship, or other proceedings, and such papers to be properly jacketed and tied together; he is required also to make proper entries and indexes omitted by his predecessors. Certificates of marriages, reports of birth, and similar papers not a part of a case or proceeding are to be arranged and preserved separately in the order of dates in which they are filed.[39]

At present the probate judge is elected for a four-year term.[40] In recent years there has been an attempt to raise the qualifications of those seeking election to the office. Accordingly, an amendment to the probate code in 1935 restricted eligibility to the office to a practicing attorney or to a person who *"shall have previously served as probate judge immediately prior to his election."*[41]

---

37. *Ibid.,* XCVIII, 28; CIII, 173-174.
38. *Ibid.,* LI, 167; LII, 103; LXXV, 9; CXIV, 324.
39. *Ibid.,* CXIV, 321-322.
40. *Ibid.,* CXIV, 320.
41. *Ibid.,* CXVI, 481.

Civil Cases

223. COURT CALENDAR
1928-1932. 5 volumes. (dated).
Daily calendar of causes for hearing in probate court, showing date case filed, date and time of hearing, title of case, kind of case, names of attorneys, and dates set for any continuances. Arranged chronologically by dates of filing of case. No index. Handwritten on printed forms. Average 106 pages. 17.5 x 12 x 1. Probate record room 2.

224. CIVIL DOCKET
1803—. 44 volumes (1803-1851, 2 each A1-C1; 1852—, 1-38).
Docket of probate matters heard in court of common pleas, 1803-1852, and in probate court, 1852—, pertaining to probation of wills, administration of estates, guardianships and trusteeships, dependents, and other civil matters. All entries show date case filed, case number, title of case, kind of case, names of plaintiff, defendant, or other principles, and a record of court orders and writs; also 1852—, shows volume letter or number and page number of Journal, entry 243, and includes a record of adoptions. Arranged chronologically by dates of filing. Indexed alphabetically by names of plaintiff or other principles; also separate index, entry 225. Handwritten. Average 250 pages. 18 x 10 x 2.5. Probate office room 1.

225. CIVIL INDEX
1803—. 3 volumes (1-3).
Index to Civil Docket, entry 224 and Civil Record, entry 234, showing year, case number, kind of case, name of estate or names of plaintiff and defendant, and volume and page numbers of record. Serves as an index to case record [Civil], entry 235 by showing case number. 1803-1893, typed on printed forms (transcribed); 1893—, handwritten. Average 200 pages. 17 x 12 x 1.5. Probate office room 2.

226. DOCKET LAND TITLE REGISTRATION
1914-1915. 1 volume.
Docket of hearings relative to the disposition of registered lands, showing names of plaintiff and defendant, dates, motions, entries, orders filed, issued or returned relative to publication of notices, deeds to purchaser, confirmations, appraisements, and page number of Record of Land Title Registration, entry 227. Arranged chronologically by dates of entries. Indexed alphabetically by names of plaintiffs

showing names of defendants. Handwritten. 600 pages. 10 x 8 x 3. Probate record room 3.

227. RECORD OF LAND TITLE REGISTRATIONS
1914-1915. 1 volume (1).

Record of petitions in application by administrator or executor to settle and register title to, and to sell land and buildings belonging to decedent, as outlined in petition, showing names of decedent, administrator or executor, petitioner or other persons, if any, having any right, interest, or liens upon the land or any part thereof, as described; appointment and qualifications of administrator, dates and remarks, together with copies of instruments releasing claims on land for the purpose of dissolving same, showing names of holders of claims, names of administrator or executor releasing same, name of notary, and date of entry. Arranged chronologically by dates of entries. No index. 600 pages. 10 x 8 x 3. Probate record room 3.

228. EXECUTOR'S AND ADMINISTRATOR'S DOCKET
1861-1932. 70 Volumes (1-10). Title varies: Administrators, Executors, Guardians, Trustees, and Assignees Docket, 1865-1864. 8 volumes.

Docket of estate settlements, showing case number, dates case filed, names of decedent, administrator or executor, names of attorneys, volume and page numbers where entered, and 1865-1884, names of ward, assignor, guardian, and trustee. Also contains: Testamentary Docket, entry 229; Administrator's Docket, entry 230; Guardians and Trustees Docket, 1865-1884, entry 232. Arranged chronologically by dates of filing of case. Indexed alphabetically by names of decedents, wards, or assignors. Handwritten on printed forms. Average 550 pages. 18 x 12 x 3.25. Probate office room 1.

229. TESTAMENTARY DOCKET
1932—. 11 volumes (72, 74, 76, 78, 80, 82, 84, 86, 88, 90, 92). 1861-1932 in Executor's and Administrator's docket, entry 228.

Docket of estate settlements in accordance with terms of will, showing name of decedent, date of death, name of executor, case number, date case filed, dates of filing of various case papers, amount of bond, volume and page numbers of Will Record, entry 246, Executors', Administrators', and Guardians' Inventories and Sale Bills, entry 252, also of Journal, entry 243, and Civil Record entry 234.

Arranged chronologically by dates of filing a case. Indexed alphabetically by names of decedents. Handwritten on printed forms. Average 500 pages. 16 x 11 x 3. Probate office room 1.

230. ADMINISTRATOR'S DOCKET
1932—. 11 volumes (71, 73, 75, 77, 79, 81, 83, 85, 87, 89, 91). 1861-1932 in Executor's and Administrator's Docket, entry 238.

Docket of estate settlements without wills, showing name of decedent, date of death, case number, name of administrator, date case filed, dates of filing of various case papers, amount of bond, names of sureties to bond, names of appraisers, and volume and page numbers of Proof of Publication, entry 255, Executors', Administrators', and Guardians Inventories and Sale Bills, entry 255, and Journal, entry 243. Arranged chronologically by dates of filing of case. Indexed alphabetically by names of decedents. Handwritten on printed forms. Average 500 pages. 16 x 11 x 3. Probate office room 1.

231. ADMINISTRATORS AND EXECUTORS GENERAL INDEX
1803—. 9 volumes (1-9). Transcribed in 1938'

General index to administrators' and executors' dockets, showing name of decedent, name of administrator or executor, volume and page numbers of dockets where case is entered, and volume letter or number and page number of Will Record, entry 246; 1907—, also shows case number. Arranged alphabetically by names of decedents. Typed on printed forms. Average 400 pages. 18 x 12 x 2. Probate office room 2.

232. GUARDIANS AND TRUSTEES DOCKET
1884—. 17 volumes (15-31). 1865-1884 in Executor's and Administrator's Docket, entry 228.

Docket of guardianships and trusteeships, showing names of attorneys, case number, date case filed, names of estates and ward, name of guardian or trustee, dates and titles of various papers filed, and for journal entries, volume and page numbers of journal entry 243. Arranged chronologically by dates of filing of case. Indexed alphabetically the names of wards or estates; also separate index, entry 233. Handwritten on printed forms. Average 500 pages. 16.5 x 11.5 x 3. Probate office room 1.

233. INDEX TO GUARDIANS AND TRUSTEES DOCKET

1803—. 2 volumes (1, 2). Transcribed in 1938.

Index to Guardians and Trustees Docket, entry 232, showing names of ward and estate, name of guardian or trustee, case number, and volume and page numbers of docket. Arranged alphabetically by names of wards or estates. 1803-1938 typed; 1938—, handwritten. Average 300 pages. 17 x 12 x 1.5. Probate office room 2.

234. CIVIL RECORD

1803—. 245 volumes (A1, 1-244).

Complete record of probate matters before the court of common pleas, 1803-1851, and probate court, 1852—, showing names of plaintiff, defendant, and attorneys, date cases filed, type of case, case number, dates and brief of all court actions, and disposition of case. Arranged chronologically by dates of filing of case. For index, see entry 225. 1803-1896, handwritten; 1897—, typed. Average 250 pages. 18 x 12 x 3. 185 volumes, 1803-1934, Probate record room 4; 60 volumes, 1935—, Probate office room 1.

235. CASE RECORD [Civil]

1804—. 2999 file boxes (labeled by contained case numbers).

Original papers issued in estates, guardianships, trusteeships, and assignments, including applications for appointments, letters of authority, petitions, wills, bonds, inventory, appraisements, accounts, and cost bills. All papers of each case are filed together in a separate jacket, showing case number, name of decedent, title of case, name a probate judge, and volume and page numbers of dockets and records where entered. Arranged numerically by case numbers. For index, see entry 225. 1804-1857, handwritten; 1858-1911, handwritten on printed forms; 1912—, typed on printed forms. 12 x 4 x 16. 1852 file boxes, 1804-1925, Probate record room 4; 773 file boxes, 1926-1934, Probate record room 3; 374 file boxes, 1935—, Probate office room 2.

Criminal Cases

236. CRIMINAL CALENDAR
1927-1931. 10 volumes (1A-5A; 1-5). Discontinued; jurisdiction transferred to court of common pleas.

Calendar of criminal cases, showing case number, name of defendant, offense charged, plea, findings, costs dates of hearings, and remarks. Arranged numerically by case numbers. Indexed alphabetically by names of defendants. Handwritten. Average 100 pages. 26 x 24 x 1. Probate record room 2.

237. CRIMINAL APPEARANCE DOCKET
1867-1927. 5 volumes (1-5). 1927-1931 in Appearance Docket and Criminal Record, entry 238.

Docket of criminal cases in probate court, showing case number, name of defendant, title of case, date of filing of case, dates of journal entries, court orders, and decrees, cost bill, and volume and page numbers of Journal, entry 243 and Criminal Record, entry 240. Arranged numerically by case numbers. Indexed alphabetically by names of defendants. Handwritten on printed forms. Average 450 pages. 16 x 11 x 3. Probate record room 2.

238. APPEARANCE DOCKET AND CRIMINAL RECORD
March 1927-1931. 7 volumes (1-7).

Docket of criminal cases in probate court, showing case number, name of defendant, charge, dates of filing of case, and various court orders, disposition of case, amount of cost, and date cost paid. Also contains Criminal Appearance Docket 1927-1931, entry 237. Arranged numerically by case numbers. Indexed alphabetically by names of defendants; also separate index, entry 239. Handwritten on printed forms. Average 300 pages. 18 x 15 x 2. Record room 2.

239. INDEX TO APPEARANCE DOCKET AND CRIMINAL RECORD
1927-1931. 1 volume.

Index to Appearance Docket and Criminal Record, entry 238, showing name of defendant, and volume and page numbers of record; also shows volume letter or number and page number of Criminal Calendar, entry 236, and Criminal Record, entry 240. Arranged alphabetically by names of defendants. Handwritten on printed forms. 200 pages. 18 x 12 x 1.5. Probate record room 2.

240. CRIMINAL RECORD
1853-1931. 18 volumes (1-18).
Complete record of criminal cases in probate court, showing name of defendant, case number, date case filed, dates of various court orders issued and 1928-1931, records of violations of liquor laws. Arranged chronologically by dates of filing of case. Indexed alphabetically by names of defendants. 1853-1900, handwritten on printed forms; 1901-1931, typed on printed forms. Average 500 pages. 18 x 12 x 3. Probate record room 2.

241. CASE RECORDS [Criminal]
1853-1931. 45 bundles, 6 cartons.
Original papers issued in criminal cases in probate court, including affidavits of information, transcripts for magistrates' courts, warrants to arrest, bonds, warrants to commit to institution, and cost bills. All papers of each case are filed together in a jacket, showing case number, name of defendant, offense charged, date case filed, amount of bond, names of sureties to bond, and volume and page numbers of dockets and records where case is entered. Arranged chronologically by dates of filing of case. No index. Handwritten on printed forms. Bundles, 4 x 10 x 10; cartons, 3.5 x 8 x 12. Probate record room 3.

General Court Proceedings

242. CASE NUMBERING BOOK
1933—. 2 volumes.
Register of case numbers, showing case number, names of principals, title of case, nature of case, date case filed, and volume and page numbers of dockets and records where case is entered. Arranged numerically by case numbers. No index. Handwritten on printed forms. Average 200 pages. 15 x 8 x 1. Probate office room 2.

243. JOURNAL
1852—. 223 volumes (A-Z, 27-223).
Copies of journal entries relative to estates, guardianships, trusteeships, insanity, adoptions, and other matters of journal entry, showing date of entry, names of litigants or other principles, title of case, docket number of original entry, case number, and amount of costs. Arranged chronologically by dates of entries. No

index. 1852-1908, handwritten; 1909——, typed. Average 250 pages. 16.5 x 10.5 x 2. 191 volumes, 1852-1932, Probate record room 4; 12 volumes, 1933-1935, Probate record room 3; 20 volumes, 1936——, Probate office room 2.

244. PROCEEDINGS IN AID OF EXECUTION
1861——. 2 volumes (1, 2).
Record of proceedings in executions, showing names of plaintiff and defendant, date case filed, date of hearing, record of notices to sheriff, and dates of returns. Arranged chronologically by dates of hearings. Indexed alphabetically by names of plaintiffs showing names of defendants. Handwritten. Average 250 pages. 14.5 x 9 x 2.5. 1 volume, 1861-1930, Probate record room 1; 1 volume, 1931——, Probate office room 2.

245. WARRANTS AND AFFIDAVITS
1920-1930. 29 file boxes.
Original search warrants and affidavits for seizure of liquor, charges of intoxication, and violation of Crabbe Act, showing name of person accused, address, charge, and date of filing. Arranged chronologically by dates of filing. No index. Handwritten. 4 x 4 x 12. Probate record room 2.

Estates and Guardianships
(See also entry 235)

Wills

246. WILL RECORD
1803——. 106 volumes (A-Z, 27-106).
Copies of wills entered for probate showing date of will, name of testator, text of will, names of witnesses, date probated, and name of probate judge. Arranged chronologically by dates probated. Indexed alphabetically by names of testators. 1803-1903, handwritten; 1904——, typed. Average 600 pages. 18 x 12 x 3. Probate office room 2.

Appointments, Bonds, and Letters

247. EXECUTORS, ADMINISTRATORS AND GUARDIANS BONDS
1849-1858. 4 volumes (A1, B1, C, D).

Copies of surety bonds filed by administrators, executors, and guardians, showing name of estate or ward, name and title of principal, names of sureties to bond, amount of bond, and date filed. Arranged chronologically by dates of filing. Indexed alphabetically by names of principles. Handwritten. Average 550 pages. 15 x 12 x 2.5. Probate record room 3.

248. RECORD OF BONDS AND LETTERS OF ADMINISTRATION
1859—. 74 volumes (1-74). Title varies: Administrator Bonds, 1859-1886.

Copies of applications for appointments as administrators, showing name of decedent, date of death, date of application, names and degree of kinship of heirs-at-law, and estimated value of chattel and real property of decedent; copies of letters of administration, showing name of decedent, name of appointee, and date of appointment; copies of notices of appointments of administrators; and copies of bonds filed by administrator, showing name of administrator, names of sureties, amount of bond, name of decedent, and date filed. Arranged chronologically by dates of applications. Indexed alphabetically by names of decedents. Handwritten on printed forms. Average 500 pages. 18 x 12 x 3. 70 volumes, 1859-1933, Probate record room 3; 4 volumes, 1934—, Probate office room 2.

249. RECORD OF BONDS AND LETTERS OF EXECUTORS
1859—. 65 volumes (1-65). Title varies slightly.

Copies of applications for appointments as executors, showing date of application, name of testator, date of death, name and degree of kinship of legatees or devisees, and estimated amount of real and personal property; copies of notices of appointment as executor; copies of bonds filed by executors; showing name of executor, names of sureties to bond, date and amount of bond, name of decedent, and date filed; also includes copies of letters testamentary. Arranged chronologically by dates of applications. Indexed alphabetically by names of decedents. Handwritten on printed forms. Average 500 pages. 18 x 12 x 3. 63 volumes, 1859-1936, Probate record room 3; 2 volumes, 1937—, Probate office room 2.

250. RECORD OF BONDS AND LETTERS OF GUARDIANS
November 1858—. 45 volumes (E-H, 1-4, 4-7, 7-19, 19-38). Title varies: Guardians Bonds, 1858-1854.

Copies of applications for appointments as guardians of minors or incompetents, showing date of application, name of ward, name of applicant, age of ward, if minor, names of parents, estimated value of real and personal property, and names of proposed sureties to bond; copies of orders or appointments of guardians; copies of bonds filed by guardians, showing name of guardian, name of ward, names of sureties to bond, and amount of bond; also copies of letters of guardianship, showing name of appointee, name of ward, and date of appointment. Arranged chronologically by dates of applications. Indexed alphabetically by names of wards. Handwritten on printed forms. Average 500 pages. 18 x 12 x 3. 42 volumes, 1858-1933, Probate record room 3; 3 volumes, 1934—, Probate office room 1.

251. RECORD OF GUARDIANS' BONDS, SALE OF REAL ESTATE
1862-1900. 1 volume.

Record of bonds given by guardians appointed by the court for the faithful discharge of their duties in the sale of real estate, as an agent of their wards, showing names of appointee, name of ward, names of sureties to bond, amount of bond and date. Arranged chronologically by dates of bond. Indexed alphabetically by names of wards. Handwritten. 780 pages. 18 x 10 x 4. Probate record room 3.

Inventories, Sale Bills, and Claims

252. EXECUTORS' ADMINISTRATORS' AND GUARDIANS' INVENTORIES AND SALE BILLS
1829—. 384 volumes (A1-G1, H-Z, 27-384).

Copies of inventories of estates of decedents and wards, showing name of decedent or ward, names of administrator, executor, or guardian, date inventory ordered, names of appraisers, itemized appraisement list, date filed, date sale was ordered, copy of order, date of sale, itemized account of sale of chattels, and date sale account was filed. Records, 1829-1851, transferred from common pleas court. Arranged chronologically by dates of filing. Indexed alphabetically by names of decedents or wards. 1829-1908, handwritten; 1909—, typed on printed forms. Average 450 pages. 15 x 12 x 3. 339 volumes, 1829-1936, Probate record room 3; 45 volumes, 1937—, Probate office room 1.

253. SCHEDULE OF ALL KNOWN CLAIMS
1932—. 24 volumes (1-24). Initiated 1932.

Record of debts of estates, showing names and addresses of creditors and their attorneys, name of decedent or estate, amount of claim, amount allowed or rejected, oath of administrator or executor has to correctness of claim, complete schedule of all debts, and date filed. Arranged chronologically by dates of filing. Indexed alphabetically by names of decedents. Typed. Average 250 pages. 18 x 8 x 2. 17 volumes, 1932-1936, Probate record room 3; 7 volumes, 1937—, Probate office room 1.

Accounts and Settlements

254. EXECUTORS' ADMINISTRATORS' AND GUARDIANS' ACCOUNTS
239 volumes (1803-1866, A1-V1, W-Z; 1866—. 27-239).

Copies of accounts of estates and wards, showing case number, name of decedent, name of administrator, executor, or guardian, date account filed, itemized account of cash receipts, from whom received, date, and amount received; itemized list of disbursements, showing date paid, to whom, for what purpose, and amount. Arranged chronologically by dates of filing. Indexed alphabetically by names of decedents or wards. 1803-1912, handwritten; 1913—, typed. Average 450 pages. 14.5 x 9 x 2.5. 232 volumes, 1803-1938, Probate record room 3; 7 volumes, 1938—, Probate office room 1.

255. PROOF OF PUBLICATION
1882—. 32 volumes (1-32).

Record of affidavits newspapers regarding published notices in settlements of estates, showing name of estate, case number, name of administrator or executor, name of newspaper, dates for each publication, date of affidavit, fee charged, and signature of deputy clerk. Chronologically by dates of applications. No index. 1882-1935, handwritten; 1935—, typed on printed forms. Average 500 pages. 18 x 12 x 3. 31 volumes, 1882-1935, Probate record room 3; 1 volume, 1938—, Probate office room 1.

Inheritance Tax

256. INHERITANCE TAX RECORD
1919—. 8 volumes (1-8).

Record of inheritance tax findings, showing date filed, case number, name of decedent, late address, date of death, place of death, name and address of administrator or executor, estimated value of personal property, real property, total value, auditor's appraisal of value of real and personal property, value as fixed by probate judge on real and personal property, total indebtedness, cost of administration, net value of estate subject to tax, names and addresses and relationship of heirs-at-law, names and addresses of legatees and devisees, total value of each share of estate, legal exemption, net value subject to tax, amount of tax, name of taxing district, date tax accrued, date of payment, and volume and page numbers of docket where case is entered. Arranged chronologically by dates of filing. Indexed alphabetically by names of decedents. Typed on printed forms. Average 600 pages. 18 x 12 x 3. 6 volumes, 1919- 1935, Probate record room 2; 2 volumes, 1936—, Probate office room 2.

257. ESTATES NOT SUBJECT TO INHERITANCE TAX
1919-1920. 1 volume (1).

Register of estates on which no inheritance tax is due, showing case number, name of decedent, date of death, name and address of administrator or executor, volume and page number of Journal, entry 243, estimated value of property, inventory value, value as fixed by probate judge and total exemptions. No obvious arrangement. No index. Handwritten on printed forms. 500 pages. 18 x 12 x 3. Probate record room 2.

258. INHERITANCE TAX CIVIL RECORD
1925—. 62 volumes (A, A, B, B, C, C, D-Y, Y, Z, A1, A1, B1, B1, C1, D1, D1, E1, E1-H1, J1-L1, N1, P1, R1, T1, V1, X1, Z1, AA-JJ).

Record of proceedings and determination of inheritance tax, consisting of applications, itemized account of assets, schedules A, B, and C, determination of inheritance tax, journal entry, waiver by state tax commission, and treasurer's receipt of payment of tax, showing name of decedent, executor, or administrator, amount of assets, names of successor of heirs, relationship to decedent, degree of kinship, amount of exception, amount subject to tax, amount tax assessed, date of accrual, name of person to whom charged, name of taxing district, total amount of tax assessed, and date filed; also a record of estate not subject to inheritance tax, showing volume and page numbers of docket where entered, case number, name of decedent, date of death, name and address of administrator or executor, value of personal property, value of real estate, total assets, court costs, attorney's fees, administration fee, other debts, total liabilities, total assets, net value of estate, names and age of heirs, relationship to decedent, amount of interest in estate, names and addresses distributees or beneficiaries and date of filing. Arranged chronologically by dates of filing. No index. Typed on printed forms. Average 500 pages. 16 x 11 x 3. 42 volumes, 1925-1937, Probate record room 2; 20 volumes, 1937—, Probate office room 2.

Assignments
(See also entry 235)

259. ASSIGNMENT DOCKET
1859—. 18 volumes (1-18).

Record of assignments and transfers of real and personal property to satisfy creditors, showing an itemized list of property involved, description of same, appraised value, names of creditors and assignors, date and time filed, account of assignee, and case number. Arranged numerically by case numbers. Indexed alphabetically by names of assigners. Handwritten. Average 350 pages. 18 x 12 x 2.5. Probate office room 1.

Dependents

260. LUNACY RECORDS
1838—. 32 volumes (A-P, 1-16). Title varies: Lunacy, Epilepsy and Feeble-Minded, 1904-1905, 3 volumes; Lunacy and Epilepsy, 1913. 1 volume.

Record of inquest in lunacy and feeble-minded cases, showing date of affidavit, name of patient, names of nearest relatives, degree of kinship, case number, amount of fees, and copies of court orders, medical certificates, and sheriff's returns. Arranged numerically by case numbers. Indexed alphabetically by names of patients. Handwritten on printed forms. Average 250 pages. 16.5 x 11 x 2.5. 28 volumes, 1838-1938, marriage license bureau; 4 volumes, 1938—, Probate stenographer room.

261. CASE RECORDS [Lunacy and Epileptic]
1933—. 39 file boxes (labeled by contained case numbers).
Original papers issued in lunacy and epileptic cases including affidavits of complaint, medical certificates, applications for admission to institution, warrants to arrest, and warrants to convey. Arranged numerically by case numbers. No index. Typed on printed forms. 12 x 4 x 24. 16 file boxes, 1933-1936, Probate record room 3; 23 file boxes, 1936—, Probate stenographer room.

262. ADOPTION RECORD
September 1, 1939—. 1 volume (1).
Record of adoptions including petitions, recommendations, entries ordering hearings, appointments, and approvals and consents to adoptions by juvenile court, showing case number, name of child, name and address of petitioner, personal history of petitioner and child, names and history of parents of child, signatures of judge, petitioners, and witnesses, and volume and page number of Civil Docket entry 224. Arranged numerically by case numbers. Indexed alphabetically by names of children. Typed on printed forms. 500 pages. 15 x 9 x 2.5. Probate office room 2.

Naturalization

263. NATURALIZATION RECORD, FIRST PAPERS
1859-1906. 6 volumes (1-6). Discontinued; jurisdiction transferred to Federal courts.
Record of first papers or applications for citizenship, showing date of application, name of applicant, port of embarkation and debarkation, date of landing, and personal history of applicant. Arranged chronologically by dates of applications. Indexed alphabetically by names of applicants. Handwritten on printed forms. Average 250 pages. 18 x 12 x 2. Probate deputies' office.

264. NATURALIZATION RECORD, SECOND PAPERS
1859-1906. 15 volumes (1-15).
Record of second papers filed by applicants for citizenship, showing date of application, name of applicant, date of filing papers, length of residence in country, and date of order of judge to clerk to issue certificate. Arranged chronologically by dates of issues. Indexed alphabetically by names of applicants. Handwritten on printed forms. Average 350 pages. 18 x 12 x 3. Probate deputies' office.

265. NATURALIZATION OF SOLDIERS
1880-1906. 3 volumes (1-3).

Record of applications of enlisted men for citizenship papers, showing name of applicant, case number, date of application, and copies of compliance with requirements for naturalization, and signature of judge. Arranged numerically by case numbers. Indexed alphabetically by names of applicants. Handwritten on printed forms. Average 350 pages. 18 x 12 x 3. Probate deputies' office.

266. NATURALIZATION OF MINORS
1862-1906. 6 volumes (1-6).

Record of applications for citizenship for minors who have resided in the country five years, showing date of application, name of applicant, case number, and proof of age. Arranged chronologically by dates of applications. Indexed alphabetically by names of minors. Handwritten on printed forms. Average 250 pages. 18 x 12 x 2.5. Probate deputies' office.

Vital Statistics

Births and Deaths

267. BIRTH RECORD
1867-1909. 8 volumes (1-8). Discontinued; subsequent records kept by state registrar.

Record of births reported in county, showing name of child, date of birth, sex, place of birth, mother's maiden name, father's name and address, and date reported. Arranged alphabetically by names of children. No index. Handwritten on printed forms. Average 350 pages. 18 x 12 x 3. Probate deputies' office.

268. RECORD OF DEATHS
1886-1909. 6 volumes (1-6).

Record of deaths reported in the county, showing name of decedent, date and place of death, sex, address, cause the death, and date reported. Arranged alphabetically by names of decedents. No index. Handwritten on printed forms. Average 300 pages. 18 x 8 x 2.5. Probate deputies' office.

Marriages

269. MARRIAGE RECORD
1803—. 143 volumes (A-Z, 27-143).

Record of marriages, showing name and address of each applicant, age, date of application, occupation, and affidavit. Also includes consents of parents or guardians to marriages of minors and marriage returns, showing date of marriage, name and title of minister or official performing marriage, and date of filing of certificate. Arranged chronologically by dates of applications. For index, see entry 270. 1803-1852, handwritten; 1852—, handwritten on printed forms. Average 600 pages. 18 x 12 x 3. Marriage license bureau.

270. GENERAL INDEX TO MARRIAGES
1803—. 24 volumes (1-24).

Index to marriage record, entry 269, and Ban Marriage Record, April 1931—, entry 271, showing names of male and female applicants, date license issued, and volume letter or number and page number of records. Arranged alphabetically by names of males and females. Handwritten. Average 250 pages. 18 x 12 x 2. Marriage license bureau.

271. BAN MARRIAGE RECORD
April 1931—. 3 volumes (1-3).

Record of marriage bans, showing names and addresses of applicants, age, occupation, place of birth, name of father, maiden name of mother, record of previous marriages and divorces, date of marriage ban, and names of person solemnizing marriage. Arranged chronologically by dates of marriage bans. For index, see entry 270. Handwritten on printed forms. Average 300 pages. 12 x 10 x 1.5. Marriage license bureau.

Licenses and Certificates

272. MINISTERS' LICENSE TO SOLEMNIZE MARRIAGE
1845—. 4 volumes (1-3; 1 unnumbered).

Record of licenses issued to ministers to perform marriages in Montgomery County showing name of minister, denominational affiliation, date of license, and signature of probate judge. Arranged alphabetically by names of ministers. No index.

Handwritten on printed forms. Average 250 pages. 18 x 12 x 2. Marriage license bureau.

273. RECORD OF MINISTERS' LICENSE TO MARRY, GRANTED IN OTHER COUNTIES
1861—. 1 volume (1).

Records of licenses to perform marriages granted in other counties and recorded in Montgomery County, showing name of county in which issued, date filed, and information as in Ministers' License to Solemnize Marriages, entry 272. Arranged chronologically by dates of filing. Indexed alphabetically by names of ministers. Handwritten. 760 pages. 15 x 9 x 3.5. Marriage license bureau.

274. REGISTRATION OF PHYSICIANS
1896—. 2 volumes (1, 2).

Copies of certificates issued by the state board of medical examiners to applicants on examination, showing name of applicant, graduate of what medical school, date of graduation, date and results of examination, date certificate issued, and date recorded. Arranged chronologically by dates of recording. Indexed alphabetically by names of physicians. Handwritten on printed forms. Average 200 pages. 18 x 12 x 1.5. Probate office room 1.

275. REGISTRATION UNLIMITED PRACTITIONERS
1916—. 1 volume.

Copies of certificates issued by state board of medical examiners for practice of limited branches of medical service, showing name of practitioner, date of license, name of school from which graduated, date of graduation, for which branch issued, date recorded, and name of probate judge. Arranged chronologically by dates recorded. Indexed alphabetically by names of practitioners. Handwritten on printed forms. 400 pages. 15 x 12 x 2. Probate office room 1.

276. MIDWIFE CERTIFICATES
1896-1911. 1 volume.

Copies of certificates authorizing the practice of midwifery, showing name of midwife, date issued, result of examination, remarks, signatures of president of state board of medical examiners and probate judge, and date recorded. Arranged chronologically by dates of recording. Indexed by names of midwives. Handwritten on printed forms. 200 pages. 18 x 12 x 2. Probate office room 1.

277. RECORD OF REGISTERED NURSES
1916—. 2 volumes (1, 2).
Copies of licenses issued to graduate nurses by state board of medical examiners, showing certificate number, name of nurse, date of graduation, graduate of what training school for nurses, address, date of examination, name of chief examiner and secretary, date recorded, and name of probate judge. Arranged chronologically by dates of recording. Indexed alphabetically by names of nurses. Handwritten on printed forms. Average 400 pages. 14 x 12 x 2. Probate office room 1.

Financial Records

278. PROBATE JUDGE'S CASH BOOK
1856—. 48 volumes (1-48).
Record of cash received and disbursed; receipts show by whom paid, to whom due, case number, date, amount, county fund, sheriff's fees, witness fees, sundries, and publication fees; disbursements show to whom paid, date paid, check number, and for what purpose. Arranged chronologically by dates received or disbursed. No index. Handwritten on printed forms. Average 300 pages. 18 x 16 x 2. Probate office room 2.

279. RECORD OF UNCLAIMED COSTS
1917—. 1 volume.
Record of unclaimed cost, showing from whom received, to whom due, amount, case number, and date certificate for recovery was issued. Arranged chronologically by dates of certificates of recovery. No index. Handwritten. 200 pages. 18 x 10 x 2. Probate deputies' office.

280. RECORD OF UNCLAIMED DEPOSITS IN BANK
1889-1893. 1 volume.
Record of unclaimed deposits as reported to probate judge by bank officials, showing date of report, name of bank, name of bank official making report, name of depositor, amount deposited, accumulated interest or dividends, and total amount due. Arranged chronologically by dates of reports. No index. Handwritten on printed forms. 212 pages. 18 x 12 x 1. Probate record room 2.

Miscellaneous

281. INSPECTORS' REPORT OF COUNTY TREASURY
1860-1906. 2 volumes (1, 2). Title varies: Record of Reports of Condition
of Treasury, 1860-1896, 1 volume.

Copies of reports to the judge of probate court from inspectors regarding financial
standing of treasury, showing date of inspection, receipts and disbursements, and
cash on hand; also includes oath of inspector certifying correctness. Arranged
chronologically by dates of reports. No index. Handwritten. Average 300 pages. 18
x 12 x 3. Probate record room 2.

282. DOCKET OF CORONER'S INQUEST
1882-1925. 2 volumes, (1, 2).

Docket of itemized accounts of personal effects found on the bodies of deceased
persons, showing name of decedent, date of filing coroner's report, amount of
money returned by coroner, case number, name of person to whom money was
turned over, date and amount, remarks relative to effects found on the body, and
name of person to whom personal effects were turned over. Arranged
chronologically by dates of entries. Indexed alphabetically by names of decedents.
Handwritten on printed forms. Average 300 pages. 16 x 11 x 1.5. Probate record
room 3.

Jury commissioners were first authorized for Hamilton and Cuyahoga Counties in 1881.[1] In 1890 provision was made for the appointment of jury commissioners in counties having a city of the first class or of the first grade second class.[2] In 1891 the judges of the court of common pleas in counties having a city with a population of not less than 33,000 nor more than 50,000 were authorized to appoint four residents of the county to serve as a jury commission for a term of one year. The limitations of this act excluded Montgomery County. It was the duty of this commission to determine the qualifications and fitness of persons to be selected as jurors.[3] Three years later, in 1894, the provisions of the act were extended to all other counties in the state except Cuyahoga, Franklin, Hamilton, Lucas, Montgomery, and Mahoning.[4] In 1902 the statute was amended to include all counties.[5] In 1913 the number of jury commissioners in each county was reduced to two.[6]

The jury code, which became effective August 2, 1931, provided for a jury commission of the same number and same qualifications previously specified, to hold office at the pleasure of the court, and to meet and select prospective jurors, both grand and petit, for the ensuing year from a list provided by the board of elections.[7] At the beginning of each jury year the commissioners are required to make up a new and complete jury list, known as the annual jury list, arranged alphabetically by precincts, districts, and townships, recording the name, occupation, business address, and residence of each prospective juror, and to prepare an index to this list. A duplicate list is certified by the commissioners and filed in office of the clerk of the court of common pleas.[8]

The jury commissioners select prospective jurors for civil and criminal cases as well as for the grand jury. They also select jurors for the probate court, juvenile court, and other minor courts.

---

1. *Laws of Ohio,* LXXVIII, 95.
2. *Ibid.,* LXXXVII, 327.
3. *Laws of Ohio,* LXXXVIII, 200.
4. *Ibid.,* XCI, 176.
5. *Ibid.,* XCVI, 3.
6. *Ibid.,* CIII, 513; CVI, 106.
7. *Ibid.,* CXIV, 193-213.
8. *Ibid.,* CXIV, 205.

283. ANNUAL JURY LIST
1938—. 1 volume. List destroyed every two years.
List of eligible voters taken from poll books compiled by board of elections and submitted to the jury commission, showing year, name and address of voter, and precinct and ward number; also includes list of jurors drawn by the jury commission and results of examination of jurors drawn (whether accepted or excused). Arranged chronologically by years. No index. Typed. 3000 pages. 18 x 9 x 8. Assignment commissioners office.

284. ANNUAL JURY LISTS
1933—. 2 volumes.
Jury commissioners annual list of jurors called for jury duty, showing ward and precinct, township, name and address of juror, business address, occupation, age, date examined, term called, and date of list. Arranged alphabetically by names of jurors. Typed on printed forms. Average 300 pages. 20 x 12 x 1.5. Assignment commissioner's office.

285. RECORD [Names Drawn]
1935—. 1 volume.
Record of names drawn from jury wheel for jury service, showing name and address of person drawn, date of drawing, and name of judge. Arranged chronologically by dates of drawing. No index. Handwritten. 300 pages. 18 x 12 x 2. Assignment commissioner's office.

The grand jury, sometimes called the palladium of English liberty, has as its function the preliminary examination of persons charged with a capital or other infamous crime. The right, guaranteed by the federal constitution, to an examination by a grand jury, is recognized in the provision of the Ohio Constitutions of 1802 and 1851 and in the amendments of 1912.[1]

Under the present system, which does not differ in detail from that inaugurated in the early days of the state's history, the grand jury is composed of fifteen members, resident electors of the county having "the qualifications of jurors."[2] It is the duty of the grand jury "to inquire of and present all offenses committed in the county and for which it was empaneled and sworn."[3] The proceedings of the grand jury are secret and each juror is required to take an oath to preserve such secrecy. Moreover, no grand juror may be required to reveal the way he or other grand jurors voted.[4]

The grand jurors are aided in their investigations by the county prosecuting attorney, who, since 1869, has been authorized by statute to present evidence before this body and compel the attendance of witnesses against whom he may institute contempt proceedings if they refuse to testify.[5] The prosecuting attorney must leave the room before the jurors begin the expression of their views or before a poll is taken. The courts have decreed, however, that the mere presence of the prosecuting attorney in the room during the deliberation is "not sufficient to sustain a plea in abatement."[6] Since 1902 the official court stenographer of the county may take shorthand notes of the testimony and furnish a transcript to the prosecuting attorney at his request. This reporter, like the prosecuting attorney and his assistants, is required to retire from the jury room before the grand jury begins its deliberations.[7]

At least 12 of the 15 jurors must concur in finding an indictment.[8] Indictments found by the grand jury are presented by the foreman to the court and are filed with the clerk of courts.[9]

---

1. *Ohio Const. 1851,* Art. I, sec. 10.
2. G. C. sec. 13436-2.
3. G. C. sec.13436-5.
4. G. C. sec.13436-16.
5. See p. 134.
6. See *State of Ohio* v. *William Stichtenoth,* 8 N. P., n. s., 297-339.
7. G. C. sec. 13436-8.
8. G. C. sec. 13436-17.
9. G. C. sec.13436-21.

No grand juror or officer of the court is permitted to disclose that a person has been indicted, before such indictment is filed and the case is docketed.[10] Any incarcerated person charged with an indictable offense who has not been indicted during the term of court at which he is held to answer is discharged.[11]

Since 1869 it has been the duty of the grand jury to visit the county jail once at each term of court at which they may be in attendance, examine its state and condition and inquire into the discipline and treatment of prisoners, and return a written report to court.[12]

The majority of contemporary opinion holds that the grand jury, although still defended as a safeguard against oppressive prosecution, seems to be of little usefulness in the administration of modern criminal justice. It is argued that the grand jury not only delays the prosecution of criminal offenses but makes it impossible to place responsibility for neglect of duty, and is, in many instances a rubber stamp for the opinions of the county prosecuting attorney.

The grand jury keeps no separate records; for jury venires, see entry 109; for annual jury lists of jury commissioners, see entries' 283-285; and for prosecuting attorney's papers pertaining to grand jury cases, see entry 287.

---

10. G. C. sec. 13436-15.
11. G. C. sec. 13436-23.
12. G. C. sec. 13436-20.

PETIT JURY

The petit jury, like the grand jury, had its origin in England during the reign of Henry II.[1] The right of trial by jury, guaranteed by the federal constitution, was included in each of the Ohio constitutions. At any trial, in any court, for the violation of a statute of the state of Ohio, or any ordinance of any municipality, except in cases where the penalty involved does not exceed a fine of fifty dollars, the accused is entitled to a trial by jury.[2]

---

1. Adams, *op. cit.,* 116.
2. G. C. sec. 13443.

Except in the method of selecting prospective jurors, the petit jury has remained unchanged for over 134 years. At each session of the court the jury commissioners[3] select not less than 50 nor more than seventy-five names for jury service. A venire is issued to the county sheriff for persons who names are so drawn to appear on the day fixed for the trial.[4] From the persons so summoned a jury of twelve is empaneled. The county prosecuting attorney and the defense council may, in capital cases, peremptorily challenge six of the jurors. In other cases, four peremptory challenges are allowed.[5] Other challenges, alternately made, may be made for reasons prescribed by statute.[6]

When the case is submitted, the jury may decide the question before it in court, or retire to deliberate. Upon retiring, the jury members must be kept together at a convenient place by an officer of the court until they agree upon a verdict or are discharged by the court. The court may permit them to separate at night.[7] If the jurors disagree as to testimony, or desire to be further instructed on the law in the case, they may request the officer in charge to conduct them to the court for additional information.[8] In civil actions a jury renders a written verdict upon the concurrence of three-fourths or more of its members. This verdict is signed by each juror concurring therein.[9]

Under the criminal code adopted in 1929 the accused may waive his right to a jury trial in favor of a trial by a judge. This procedure, although criticized by some, is considered by others to be a logical step in the administration of criminal justice in a modern state.

No separate records are kept by the petit jury; for jury venires, see entries 108, 109; and for jury lists of the jury commissioners, see entries 283-285.

---

3. See p. 120.
4. G. C. sec. 13443-1.
5. G. C. secs. 13443-4, 13443-6.
6. G. C. sec. 13443-8.
7. G. C. sec. 11420-3.
8. G. C. sec. 11420-6.
9. G. C. sec. 11420-9.

The office of county prosecuting attorney, unlike those of the sheriff and the coroner, is one of the relatively newer agencies in the administration of criminal justice. Established in America by the English during the colonial period, it offers a striking difference in the development of American criminal procedure as contrasted with English procedure where criminal prosecutions were usually instituted by private persons. As developed in recent years, the office of the prosecuting attorney has become one of the state's most important agencies in its defense against modern crime.

The acts of Northwest Territory place the responsibility for criminal prosecutions upon the attorney general, who, in turn, appointed and commissioned persons to prosecute cases in their respective counties.[1]

While the acts of the Northwest Territory outlined the local institutions for the newer states, the constitution of Ohio contains no provision for a prosecutor, leaving the creation of the office to the discretion of the legislature. In 1803, during the first session of the legislature, an act was passed authorizing the supreme court to appoint in each county an attorney to prosecute cases on behalf of the state.[2] Two years later, the appointing power was vested in the court of common pleas.[3] The office remained an appointive one until 1833 when the electorate of the county was directed to choose a prosecuting attorney in each county for a two-year term.[4] The act of 1852 left the office elective and the term unchanged, but in 1881 the term of office was set at three years, and in 1906 it was reduced to two years, and in 1936 increased to four years.[5]

Under the present system the prosecuting attorney is elected for a four-year term.[6] He is required to give bond of not less than $1,000 conditioned for the faithful performance of the duties of his office. If the office becomes vacant the court of common pleas is authorized to appoint a successor.[7] The county prosecuting attorney is authorized to appoint clerks, assistants, and stenographers and to fix their salaries subject to the approval of the county commissioners. Since

---

1. Chase, *op, cit.,* I, 287, 348.
2. *Laws of Ohio,* I, 50.
3. *Ibid.,* III, 47.
4. *Ibid.,* XXXI, 13-14; Chase, *op. cit.,* III, 1935.
5. *Laws of Ohio,* LXXVIII, 260; XCVIII, 271-272; CXVI, pt. ii, 184.
6. G. C. sec. 2909.
7. G. C. secs. 2911, 2912.

1911 he has been authorized to appoint a secret service agent or officer whose duty it is to aid him in the collection of evidence to be used in the trial of criminal cases and in matters of a criminal nature. The compensation of such an officer is determined by the court of common pleas.[8]

Most important among the duties of the prosecuting attorney are those connected with criminal prosecutions. Differing little from those of the earlier days of the office, these duties include the prosecution on behalf of the state of all complaints, suits, and controversies in which the state is a party, and such other suits, matters, and controversies as he is directed by law to prosecute within or without his county, in the probate court, court of common pleas, and court of appeals. In conjunction with the attorney general, he prosecutes cases in the supreme court which originated in his county.[9]

In felony cases, when a complaint is made to the prosecuting attorney, he is required to examine the evidence and determine if it is sufficient for prosecution. If he decides in the affirmative, he prepares the evidence for presentation to the grand jury.[10] If this body returns an indictment the prosecuting attorney prepares to present the evidence in trial court. The court of common pleas may appoint an attorney to assist the prosecuting attorney in criminal cases.[11] In the case of conviction, the prosecuting attorney causes execution to be issued for the fines or costs and pays into the county treasury all moneys so received.[12] Without reference to the grand jury, the county prosecuting attorney may initiate prosecutions in misdemeanor cases in the court of common pleas by information.[13] After prosecution is inaugurated, he may eliminate the case without trial by means of the *nolle prosequi*. Although he is prohibited from enlisting the *nolle prosequi* without leave of the court on good cause shown, his requests are usually granted.[14] After prosecution has begun, it remains with the prosecuting attorney whether the case shall be pressed and steps taken that will lead to conviction.

Besides prosecution in criminal cases, the prosecuting attorney also acts in civil matters. He may bring suit in the name of the state when he is convinced that

8. G. C. secs. 2914, 2915-1.
9. G. C. sec. 2916.
10. See p. 131.
11. G. C. sec. 2918.
12. G. C. sec. 2916.
13. G. C. sec. 13437-34.
14. G. C. sec. 13437-32.

public money is being misapplied or is being illegally withheld or withdrawn from the county treasury. Moreover, he may bring suit against persons violating the obligations of contracts of which the county is a party, or when county property is being used or occupied illegally.[15]

In addition to these, other duties have been prescribed by statute. On the request of the judge having jurisdiction over juvenile cases, he must prosecute individuals for committing crimes against children.[16] Furthermore, when directed by the court of common pleas, he must prosecute persons for keeping a house of prostitution.[17] At the instance of the secretary of state, he must prosecute any officer who refuses to furnish gratuitously statistical information for the use of that office.[18]

The prosecuting attorney has also served in an advisory capacity since 1906.[19] He acts as an advisor to all county boards and officials and to township officers who may require his opinion in writing on matters connected with their official duties.[20] In addition to this, he prepares official bonds for all county officers.[21]

The prosecuting attorney is required to make an annual report to the county commissioners stating the number of criminal prosecutions completed, the name or names of the party or parties to each, and the amount collected in fines and costs, and the amount forfeited.[22] Moreover, on the demand of the attorney general he must make an annual report on forms provided by the state on all criminal actions prosecuted by indictments in his county.[23]

---

15. G. C. sec. 2921.
16. G. C. sec. 1939-42.
17. G. C. secs. 6212-5, 6212-7.
18. G. C. sec. 174.
19. *Laws of Ohio,* XCVIII, 160-161.
20. *Ibid.,* LXXVIII, 120; G. C. sec. 2917.
21. G. C. sec. 2920.
22. *Laws of Ohio,* LXXVIII, 120; G. C. sec. 2926.
23. G. C. sec. 2925; *Laws of Ohio,* XC, 225.

286. PENDING CASES

1933—. 4 file boxes.

Papers pertaining to pending cases, showing name and address of defendant, and case number. Arranged alphabetically by names of defendants. No index. Handwritten and typed. 3 x 4 x 10. Prosecuting attorney's office.

287. NEW GRAND JURY CASES

1933—. 7 file boxes, 7 file drawers.

Papers pertaining to grand jury cases, showing court term, case number, name of defendant, charge, name of attorney for defendant, amount of bond, amount of cost, and disposition of case. Arranged chronologically by court terms. No index. Typed. File boxes. 11 x 16.5 x 27; file drawers, 6 x 18 x 24. Prosecuting attorney's office.

288. TRIENNIAL LAND TAX CERTIFICATES OF DELINQUENT TRACTS OF LAND

1932—. 21 volumes (1932, 1; 1933-1934, 2 labeled by contained letters of alphabet; 1935, 3 by contained letters of alphabet A-T and 2 by letters A-P; 1935—, 1 by contained letters R-Z, U-Z; 1933—, 12, 1-12). Subtitled: City of Dayton and Townships, 1932, 1 volume; City of Dayton, 1933-1935 5 volumes; Dayton Corporation, 1935, 2 volumes; Dayton Corporation, City of Dayton, 1935—, 1 volume; Township and City of Oakwood, 1933—, 12 volumes.

Copies of delinquent land tax certificates as certified by the county auditor to the prosecuting attorney, showing date of certificate, name and address of property owners, appraised value of property, location, amount of general tax and special tax assessments, amount of penalties, and total. Arranged chronologically by dates for certificates. Indexed alphabetically by names of property owners. Typed on printed forms. Average 350 pages. 18 x 15 x 3. Prosecutor attorney's office.

For auditor's copies, see entry 348.

289. DELINQUENT TAX FORECLOSURES

1932—. 1 volume.

Record of foreclosures on delinquent tracts of land, showing name of property owner, location and description of land foreclosed, amount of appraisal, added general taxes and special assessments, interest on each to date of August settlement and penalties, and date of foreclosure. Arranged chronologically by dates of foreclosures. Indexed alphabetically by names of property owners. Typed on printed forms. 500 pages. 18 x 14 x 3. Prosecutor attorney's office.

290. ANNUAL REPORTS TO COMMISSIONERS

1936—. 1 envelope.

Copies of annual reports to the county commissioners summarizing activities of the prosecuting attorney's office, showing in condensed form all cases investigated, indictments returned, disposition of each case, and dates filed. Arranged chronologically by dates of filing. No index. Typed. 11 x 8 x .25. Prosecuting attorney's office.

The office of coroner, next to that of sheriff the oldest county office in America, had its inception in England during the latter part of the twelfth century when the coroner kept a record of the activities in the county, especially regarding the administration of criminal justice. At the end of the thirteenth century it was his duty to make inquests whenever there was a sudden death in the shire, and the results were recorded in the coroner's rolls and presented to the justices when they made their eyre.[1]

This office, transplanted to America during the colonial period, was continued by the states, and was adopted by the territory of which the state of Ohio was then a part. An ordinance of the Northwest Territory published in 1788 authorized the governor to appoint a coroner in each county within the territory. This act, together with a supplementary act of 1795 adopted from the Massachusetts Code, fixed the power and duties of the coroner. He was empowered to do any act which, by previous legislation had been delegated to the sheriff, and was given the ancient duty of English coroners in holding preliminary investigations over the bodies of all persons found within his county, who were believed to have died by violence or casualty.[2]

The Ohio Constitution of 1802 continued the historic office, making it elective for a two-year term.[3] A statute of 1805 defined the duties and authority of the coroner which, in the main were comparable with those prescribed in the territorial code, except that he was denied the privilege of concurrent jurisdiction with the sheriff.[4] The act further provided that the coroner should receive his remuneration from fees, and that if the office of sheriff were to become vacant the coroner was to execute temporarily the duties of the sheriff.[5] The latter provision remained active until its abrogation in 1887.[6]

The constitution of 1851 and the constitutional amendments of 1912 left the duties of the coroner unchanged and it was not until recent years when he became an aid in the scientific detection of crime that laws have been passed which materially affected his office.

---

1. Pollock and Maitland, *op. cit.,* I, 519, 571; II, 641.
2. Pease, *op. cit.,* 24-25, 272-275.
3. *Ohio Const. 1802,* Art, IV, sec. 1.
4. *Laws of Ohio,* III, 156-161.
5. *Ibid.,* III, 158-161.
6. *Ibid.,* LXXXIV, 208-210.

By the legislative act of 1921 the coroner was made official custodian of the morgue in counties where a morgue is maintained. The same act provided that only licensed physicians were eligible to the office in counties having a population of 100,000 or more,[7] and in 1937 such restriction was extended to all counties.[8]

The coroner is required to draw up and subscribe his findings of facts in inquest and autopsies and to report them to the clerk of courts. This record contains a detailed description of the body over which the inquest has been held and a statement of the coroner's findings as to the cause of death.[9] He is required also to return to the probate court any inventory of articles of property found on or about the body and to preserve such property until the proper distribution may be made.[10] All records are open to public inspection.[11]

In 1936 the tenure of office of the coroner was extended from two to four years.[12] He is required to give bond, which since 1927 has been required by statute to be not less than $5,000 nor more than $50,000.[13] The compensation of the office was based entirely on fees until 1927 when the legislature set the salary at $6,000 in counties having a population of 400,000 or more. In counties having a population of less than 400,000, the total compensation paid to the coroner as fees, under all sections of the General Code, shall in no case exceed $5,000 per annum nor be less than $150.[14] Fees as fixed by law in 1927 are $20 for an ordinary autopsy, $40 for an autopsy on infected or decomposed body, and $3 for an inquest.

---

7. *Ibid.,* CIX, 543-544.
8. *Ibid.,* CXVII, 43.
9. G. C. secs. 2856, 2857.
10. G. C. sec. 2859. See p. lxi.
11. G. C. sec. 2856-2.
12. G. C. sec. 2823.
13. *Laws of Ohio,* CXII, 111.
14. *Ibid.,* CXII, 204.

291. CORONER'S FINDINGS

1903—. 2 file drawers (labeled by contained letters of alphabet). Copies of reports of the coroner to the clerk of courts relative to accidental, homicidal, or violent deaths, showing date of report, name and last address of decedent, cause of death, age, place of death, name of coroner, names of witnesses, and report of findings at inquest. Arranged alphabetically by names of decedents. No index. Handwritten on printed forms. 12 x 15 x 26. Office of Dr. Robert D. Snyder, coroner, 1019 S. Brown Street, Dayton.

The office of sheriff antedates the Norman Conquest. This official was enjoying great power and importance centuries ago, and was probably brought into the English system after a model which existed in Roman law. The name comes from the Saxon "shie-reeve" softened to "shyrife," and finally to "sheriff." In ancient times he received his commission directly from the king and specifically represented the sovereign. Originally, the sheriff in England was a judicial as well as a ministerial officer. He once held court in the shire and exercised no inconsiderable jurisdiction. By the time Lord Cook (1560-1634), The functions of the English sheriff had become standardized under three general heads: (1) to serve process by which a suit was begun; (2) to execute the decree of the court; (3) to act as conservator of peace within the county.[1]

The office appeared in America in modified form among the earliest colonial institutions, being created in Virginia in 1634, and in Massachusetts in 1654. This ancient office was continued by the states created after independence.[2] The office assumed a new significance in the latter part of the eighteenth century when a flood of colonists swept across the ineffective Allegheny barrier to establish homes in the Northwest Territory organized by congress and 1787. In the remote west the pioneers, far removed from the orderly legal processes and courts of the east, were subjected to machinations of the lawless element prevalent in every new community.

In 1792 the governor and judges of the territory adopted an act providing for the appointment by the governor of a sheriff in each county and defining his duties.[3] This pioneer law clearly established three of the four major duties of the sheriff as they remain today, namely: attendance upon the court; execution of writs, warrants, and the like; and policing and the arrest of criminals.

When Ohio entered the Union as a state in 1803, the office of sheriff was continued by constitutional provision, and was made elective for two year term.[4] Since that time relatively few changes have been made in the structural organization of the office.

---

1. Adams, *op. cit.,* 17-19; William A. Morris, "The office of sheriff in the Anglo-Saxon Period," *English Historical Review,* XXXI (1916), 20-40;
2. For a comparative study of the sheriff in England and the Chesapeake colonies, see Cyrus Harreld Karraker, *The Seventeenth-Century Sheriff* . . . (Chapel hill, 1930).
3. Pease *op. cit.,* 8.
4. *Ohio Const. 1802,* Art. IV, sec. 1.

When a new county was erected the associate judges appointed a day on which the qualified voters met at the temporary seat of justice and elected a sheriff who served until the next general election.[5] Although the constitution of 1851 did not specifically provide for this office, it did declare that no person shall be eligible to the office for more than four in any period of six years.[6] No county officer was to have a longer term then three years,[7] but the matter of removal from office was left to the legislative action.[8] The limitations upon the consecutive term which a sheriff might serve remained in force until 1933, when it was repealed by an amendment authorizing any county to adopt a charter form of government. The term of office remained at two years until 1936 when it was extended to four years.[9] The sheriff received his remuneration from fees until 1906 when a definite salary was specified by the legislature.[10] The salary for each sheriff was based upon the population of the county according to the last federal census next proceeding is the election.[11] In 1831, due to the increasing complexity of the duties of the office, the sheriff was authorized to appoint, with the consent of the court of common pleas, one or more deputies. These men, like their superior, were required to give bond for the faithful performance of the duties of their office, and the sheriff was made responsible for their neglect of duty or misconduct in office.[12]

The present organization of the office may be briefly summarized: The sheriff is elected for a four-year term,[13] can hold no other elected office at the same time, and may not practice law while in office.[14] He is required to give bond, the cost of which is paid by the county commissioners[15] who are also required to provide an office for the sheriff at the county seat, equipment, supplies, and other essentials of the office.[16]

---

5. A. E. Gwynne, *A Practical Treatise on the :aw of sheriff and Coroner with Forms and References to the Statutes of Ohio, Indiana, and Kentucky* (Cincinnati, 1849). 3.
6. *Ohio Const. 1851,* Art. X, sec. 3.
7. *Ibid.,* Art, X, sec. 2.
8. *Ibid.,* Art. X, sec. 3.
9. *Laws of Ohio,* CXVI, pt. ii, 184.
10. *Ibid.,* III, 49-51; XXXIII, 18; LII, 86, XCVIII, 96.
11. *Ibid.,* XCVIII, 89.
12. *Ibid.,* XXIX, 410.
13. G. C. sec. 2823.
14. G. C. secs. 11, 1706, 2565, 2783, 2910.
15. G. C. sec. 2824.
16. G. C. sec. 2832.

The commissioners also appropriate funds for the expenses incurred by the sheriff in carrying out the various duties of his office.[17] The sheriff may appoint a deputy or deputies, but all appointees must be endorsed by the local judge of the common pleas court, be electors of the county, and are not permitted to be justice of peace or mayors.[18] Deputies are also forbidden to practice law while in office.[19] The sheriff fixes the salaries of the deputies, subject to the budget limitations of the county commissioners,[20] and shares with his deputies certain civil and criminal liabilities.[21] The salary of the sheriff, based on a graded scale according to population with a $6,000 per year maximum is $4,515.[22] The office may be vacated by failure to give proper bond, nonacceptance, or death.[23] Vacancies in the office are filled by the county commissioners.[24]

The sheriff may be removed for various financial defalcations,[25] for willfully refusing or neglecting his duty in criminal cases,[26] for malfeasance in office,[27] or for permitting the lynching of a person in his custody.[28] In the latter case the governor conducts the hearing and may remove the sheriff. If for some reason the sheriff is unable to serve a court order the judge of the common pleas court is authorized to make a temporary appointment for the post.[29] The retiring sheriff is required to deliver to his successor all money's, papers, books, and the like, as well as the custody of all prisoners.[30]

---

17. G. C. sec. 2997.
18. G. C. secs. 1706, 2830.
19. G. C. sec. 1706.
20. G. C. sec. 2981.
21. Willis A. Estrich, ed. *Ohio Jurisprudence* (Rochester, 1934), XXXVI, 660-672, 699-701.
22. G. C. secs. 2994, 2996, 2997; Estrich, *op. cit.,* XXXVI, 704-705; Ohio Auditor of State, *Annual Report, 1939,* p. 378.
23. G. C. secs. 2827, 12196.
24. G. C. sec. 2828.
25. G. C. secs. 3036, 3049.
26. G. C. secs. 12850, 12851.
27. *Ohio Const. 1851,* (Amendment, 1912). Art. II, sec. 38.
28. *Laws of Ohio,* CI, 109.
29. G. C. sec. 2828.
30. G. C. secs. 2842, 2843.

Aside from his power to appoint deputies, the sheriff has other special powers which are largely the products of historical development. From earliest years the sheriff has been empowered to call to his aid such persons as he deemed necessary to perform his lawful duty in the apprehension of criminals.[31] Thus the *posse comitatus* was at his disposal as it is today.[32]

The specific duties of the sheriff were and are prescribed by statute and may be classified under four main divisions: (1) attendance upon the courts; (2) executions of summonses, warrants, processes, and other writs; (3) control and responsibility in the care of the jail and courthouse; (4) policing and the arrest of criminals.

The territorial law of 1792 required the sheriff to attend upon the court of common pleas and the court of appeals during their sessions,[33] and this requirement has been carried over into the laws of Ohio;[34] the present duties of the sheriff in this respect are survivals from provisions of this act. He is required to attend the county court of common pleas,[35] the appellate court,[36] and the probate court if required by the judge of that division.[37] The sheriff may adjourn the court of common pleas from day to day upon failure of the judge to appear at regularly scheduled sessions.[38]

The duty of the sheriff to execute all warrants, writs, and processes directed to him by the proper and lawful authority has also been operating since the territorial period.[39] At present he executes every summons, order, or other process, and makes return thereof as required by law.[40] He executes processes from the probate, juvenile, common pleas, and appellate courts. Although the jury commission has supplanted the clerk of courts in the matter of selecting names of prospecting jurors from the jury wheel, the sheriff's duties in this respect remain much as they were in the earlier years of his office.

---

31. *Laws of Ohio,* III, 156-158; XXIX, 112-113.
32. G. C. sec. 2833.
33. Pease, *op. cit.,* 8.
34. *Laws of Ohio,* III, 156-158; XXIX, 112; LXXXII, 26.
35. G. C. sec. 2833.
36. G. C. secs. 1530, 2833.
37. G. C. sec., 2833.
38. G. C. sec., 2855.
39. Pease, *op. cit.,* 8; *Laws of Ohio,* III, 156-158; XXIX, 112; LXXXII, 26.
40. G. C. sec., 2834.

He also executes warrants issued by the governor of the state,[41] and serves writs and subpoenas issued by various state officers and boards.[42] In other words, the sheriff serves all the papers which concern the county as a unit of government and some for the state as well.

As early as 1805 the sheriff was made official custodian of the county jail.[43] Although the early statutes directed the county commissioners to provide dungeons for the incarceration of prisoners, the act of 1847 direct the sheriff to exercise reasonable care for the preservation of the life, health, and welfare of those committed to his care. He was and is authorized to transport prisoners to other counties for safekeeping.[44] Under the direction and control of the county commissioners the sheriff is also given charge of the courthouse.[45]

The sheriff has had extensive and important police powers since 1792 when the territorial act authorized him to keep and preserve the peace, and suppress affrays, routs, riots, unlawful assemblies, and insurrections; to apprehend, and confine fail all felons and traitors; and to return persons who have committed a crime in his county, had taken refuge in another.[46] During the legislative session of 1805 the general assembly passed an act defining the duties of the sheriff which were in all respects similar to the provisions inherited from the territorial code.[47] In the same year the sheriff was designated as the county's executioner, and was bound to carry out sentences of death by hanging when imposed by the courts upon those convicted of murder.[48] Public executions, the general rule during the earlier years, were abolished in 1844.[49] In 1886 the sheriff's duties in this respect were delegated to the warden of the Ohio penitentiary.[50]

---

41. G. C. sec., 118.
42. G. C. secs., 285, 346, 2709, *el al.*
43. *Laws of Ohio,* III, 157.
44. *Ibid.,* III, 157; XXIX, 112-113; XCIII, 131. For general provisions as to jail duties see G. C. sec. 2833.
45. G. C. sec. 2833.
46. Pease *op. cit.,* 8.
47. *Laws of Ohio,* III, 156-158.
48. Chase, *op. cit.,* I, 442.
49. *Laws of Ohio,* XLII, 71.
50. *Ibid.,* 145.

An act of 1831, repealing the act of 1905, redefined the duties of the sheriff as a conservator of the peace in his county,[51] and his present duties in this respect are survivals from the provisions of this act.[52] Although the sheriff is still regarded as a chief peace officer in the county, many of his earlier duties in this respect have been abolished by the development of other agencies of law enforcement, notably the state highway patrol. On the other hand, the power of the sheriff to suppress affrays, riots, and unlawful assemblies became especially important in times of strikes or threatened rights. On a properly issued warrant he may arrest any person charged with the probability of doing injury to another person or the property of another.[53] Moreover, since 1921 the sheriff has forwarded to the bureau of criminal identification all fingerprints of persons arrested for a felony,[54] and since 1913 has been authorized to arrest any person violating his parole.[55]

The present police powers of the sheriff are quite comprehensive. His jurisdiction is coextensive with the county, including all municipalities and townships, and he is the chief law enforcement officer of the county. In municipalities the sheriff and mayor stand on equality as law-enforcement officers so far as state laws are concerned, and neither is permitted to cast the burden of action upon the other.[56]

The sheriff has possessed and still possesses many powers and duties which are miscellaneous in nature. As in England the sheriff, during the earlier years of his office, was required to notify the electors of the county of the time and place of holding elections. He was enjoined to furnished ballot boxes at the expense of the county, hold special elections when so directed by the governor, and deliver the poll books to the secretary of state.[57] Since 1891 these duties have been taken over by the board of elections.[58] The sheriff also has many heterogeneous Brewers and duties regarding elections,[59]

---

51. *Ibid.,* XXIX, 112-113.
52. *Ibid.,* LXXXII, 26.
53. G. C. sec. 13428-1.
54. *Laws of Ohio,* CIX, 584; CX, 5.
55. *Ibid.,* CIII, 404.
56. Estrich, *op. cit.,* XXXVI, 645. For the most important police powers see G. C. secs. 2833, 3345, 4112, 12811.
57. *Laws of Ohio,* II, 88-90; III, 331-332. See also p. li.
58. See pp. 204-205.
59. G. C. secs. 4785-124, 4829.

Executive orders of the secretary of agriculture,[60] fish and game laws,[61] Probation officers,[62] military census,[63] traffic rules and regulations,[64] funds and deposits in court,[65] shanty boats,[66] and executive orders of the governor.[67]

The multiplicate duties of the sheriff have made it necessary to require many records of the business of the office to be kept. The present practice of keeping a foreign execution docket began in 1838.[68] Since 1842 the sheriff has kept a cashbook,[69] and since 1843 a jail register.[70] Indexes, direct and reverse to the foreign execution docket were prescribed by the legislature in 1925.[71] Since 1843 he has been required annually to transmit the jail register, in certified copies, to the clerk of courts, the county auditor, and the secretary of state.[72] Since 1850 he has been required, on the first Monday of September in each year, to submit to the county commissioners a certified statement of all fines and costs collected during the year, and the amount of fees collected and paid to the clerk of courts of common pleas.[73]

Thus modern sheriff keeps the following records: (1) a cashbook which is a record of all moneys handled; (2) a foreign summons docket which is a record of all summonses from counties other than his own; (3) a foreign execution docket which is a record of executions from counties other than his own; (4) a service record which includes all probate and divorce papers served; (5) an execution register which records all executions handled; (6) an accrued fee record which lists fees received; (7) a commission register which records the commission of all special deputies; (8) a jail register which records all prisoners brought in, the charge, how long detained, and when released.[74]

---

60. G. C. sec. 1110.
61. G. C. secs. 1434, 1441, 1444, 1451.
62. G. C. sec. 1639-19.
63. G. C. sec. 5188-5.
64. G. C. sec. 7251-1.
65. G. C. sec. 11900.
66. G. C. sec. 13403-1.
67. G. C. sec. 118.
68. *Laws of Ohio*, XXXVI, 18; LVII, 6; LXXXIV, 208-209.
69. *Ibid.*, XL, 25; LXV, 115; LXXXIV, 208; LXXXVI, 239.
70. *Ibid.*, XLI, 74.
71. *Ibid.*, CXI, 31.
72. *Ibid.*, XLI, 74.
73. G. C. sec. 2844; *Laws of Ohio*, XLVIII, 66.
74. G. C. secs. 2837, 2839, 2979, 3045, 3046, 3158.

By statute the sheriff is also required to make an annual financial report to the county commissioners.[75]

---

75. G. C. sec. 2844.

Court Orders

292. EXECUTION DOCKETS [Sheriff's]
1859—. 38 volumes (1-38).

Docket of executions to satisfy judgments rendered by Montgomery County courts, showing execution number, case number, names of plaintiff and defendant, date issued, date returned, amount of judgment, date of judgment, percent of interest, amount of plaintiff's and defendant's cost, cost of writs, accruing costs, sheriff's fees on writs, printer's and appraiser's fees, names of attorneys, and signature of sheriff. Arranged chronologically by dates of issues. Indexed alphabetically by names of plaintiffs showing names of defendants. Handwritten on printed forms. Average 500 pages. 18 x 12 x 3. 13 volumes, 1859-1928, Clerk of courts' record room 1; 25 volumes, 1929—, Sheriff's office.

293. FOREIGN EXECUTION DOCKET
1860—. 5 volumes (1-5).

Docket of executions to satisfy judgments issued by other than Montgomery County courts, on property located in Montgomery County, showing execution number, case number, names of plaintiff and defendant, date issued, date returned, amount of judgment, date received, from county received, percent of interest, plaintiff's and defendant's cost, cost of writs, accruing costs, sheriff's fees on writs, printer's and appraiser's fees, names of attorneys, and signature of sheriff. Arranged chronologically by dates of issues. Indexed alphabetically by names of plaintiffs and defendants; also separate index, 1925—, entry 294. Handwritten on printed forms. Average 480 pages. 16 x 11 x 2. 2 volumes, 1860-1892, Clerk of courts' record room 1; 3 volumes, 1893—. Sheriff's office.

294. INDEX FOREIGN EXECUTION DOCKET
1925—. 2 volumes. (1, 2).

Index to Foreign Execution Docket, entry 293, showing names of plaintiff and defendant, page number of record. Arranged alphabetically by names of plaintiffs and defendants. Handwritten. Average 150 pages. 18 x 12 x 1.5. Sheriff's office.

295. SHERIFF'S SUBPOENAS DOCKET
1882-1922. 2 volumes. (one unnumbered; 2).

Docket of fees received for serving subpoenas, showing name of court, case number, number of copies, number served, mileage, total fee, date received, and remarks. Arranged chronologically by dates received. No index. Handwritten. Average 300 pages. 15 x 10 x 2. Clerk of courts' record room 1.

296. SHERIFF'S ENTRY DOCKET
1877-1920. 15 volumes (1-15).

Sheriff's docket of orders of sale cases filed in common pleas and superior courts, showing name of court, page number of docket where entered, case number, volume and page numbers of Partition Record, entry 304, names of plaintiff and defendant, date entry filed, date premises sold, name of purchaser, amount of sale, page number of Cash Book, entry 302, dates payments are made, to whom, and amount. Arranged chronologically by dates of entries. Indexed alphabetically by names of plaintiff showing names of defendants. Handwritten on printed forms. Average 250 pages. 18 x 12 x 3. Clerk of courts' record room 1.

297. SHERIFF'S CIVIL DOCKET AND FEE BOOK
1877-1909/ 16 volumes.

Docket of writs received and served by the sheriff pertaining to civil cases and fees received for same, showing names of plaintiff and defendant, case number, page number of docket of original entry, names of attorneys, date of writ, kind of writ, date returnable, date served, date returned, and amount of fee. Arranged chronologically by dates of writs. Indexed alphabetically by names of plaintiffs and defendants. Handwritten on printed forms. Average 580 pages. 18 x 12 x 3. Clerk of courts' record room 1.

298. FOREIGN WRITS
1876—. 8 volumes (1-8).

Record of foreign writs received and served by the sheriff, showing names of plaintiff and defendant, kind of process, name of court, name of county from which received, dates received, date served, date returned, remarks, amount of sheriff's fees, and date paid. Arranged chronologically by dates of receipts of writs and alphabetically thereunder by names of counties. No index. Handwritten on printed forms. Average 250 pages. 16 x 12 x 2.5. Six volumes, 1876-1922, Clerk of courts' record room 1; 2 volumes, 1923—, Sheriff's office.

299. INQUEST OF LUNACY
1896-1900. 1 volume.

Record of lunacy warrants issued including warrants to arrest and warrants to convey to institutions, showing name of patient, date warrant issued; date served, amount of sheriff's fees, date paid, and remarks. Arranged chronologically by dates of issue. No index. Handwritten on printed forms. 475 pages. 17 x 15 x 2.5. Sheriff's office.

Jail Record

300. JAIL REGISTER
1881—. 16 volumes.

Record of prisoners confined in county jail, showing commitment number, name of prisoner, date a commitment, cause, nativity, color, sex, height, and complexion of prisoner, sickness and cause thereof, kind of labor performed and value thereof, habits of cleanliness, and diet; also shows date of discharge, by whose authority discharged, total amount of sheriff's fees, amount of board and laundry, total, and remarks. Arranged chronologically by dates of commitments. No index. Handwritten on printed forms. Average 200 pages. 20 x 15 x 2. 1 volume, 1881-1884, Clerk of courts' record room 1; 8 volumes, 1885-1930, County jail, sheriff's record room; 7 volumes, 1931—, Sheriff's office.

301. BOARDING DOCKET COUNTY JAIL
1884—. 9 volumes. (dated).

Record of prisoners confined in the county jail, showing commitment number, number of prisoners, age, nativity, charge, date committed, date discharge, by whose authority discharged, number of times before the judge, number of days in jail, amount of fees, and daily and total cost of board. Arranged numerically by commitment numbers. No index. Handwritten on printed forms. Average 200 pages. 18 x 12 x 1.5. 4 volumes, 1884-1908, County jail, attic; 5 volumes, 1908—, Sheriff's record room.

Financial Records

302. CASH BOOK
1869—. 17 volumes (1-17).

Record of cash receipts and disbursements of sheriff's office: receipts show date received, case number, name of payer, names of litigants, nature of suit, amount, and matter of payment; disbursements show to whom paid, date paid out, and amount. Arranged chronologically by dates of entries. No index. Handwritten on printed forms. Average 390 pages. 18 x 15 x 2. Sheriff's office.

303. RECORD OF ACCRUED FEES
1907—. 26 volumes (1-26).

Record of fees accrued, showing date of account or accrual, case number, in what matter, to whom charged, total amount for civil and criminal causes, amount due from county, amounts due for foreign writs, from probate and juvenile courts, and for sundries. Also shows date paid, amount of payment, and name of pair. Arranged chronologically by dates of payments. Indexed alphabetically by names of payers. Handwritten on printed forms. Average 250 pages. 18 x 15 x 3.5. 12 volumes, 1907-1923, Clerk of courts' record room 1; 14 volumes, 1924—, Sheriff's office, safe.

304. PARTITION RECORD
1869-1920. 6 volumes (1-6).

Sheriff's record of sales of real estate in partition proceedings, showing volume and page numbers of Executive Docket [Sheriff], entry 292, names of plaintiff and defendant, title of case, case number, date of sale, to whom sold, amount of sale, record of distribution of proceeds of sale to distributees, itemized amount of sheriff's and attorney's cost and fees, record of taxes, and volume and page numbers of Cash Book, entry 302. Arranged chronologically by dates of sales. Indexed alphabetically by names of plaintiffs showing names of defendants. Handwritten on printed forms. Average 300 pages. 16 x 10 x 2.5. Clerk of courts' record room 1.

305. COSTS COLLECTED BY PROBATE FOR SHERIFF
1915-1916. 1 volume.

Record of fees received by the sheriff from cost and fees in cases heard in probate court, showing case number, date received by the sheriff, and amount. Arranged chronologically by dates received. No index. Handwritten. 200 pages. 12 x 6 x 1. Clerk of courts' record room 1.

306. SHERIFF'S PROBATE DOCKET AND FEE BOOK
1904-1906. 1 volume.

Sheriff's docket of cases coming before the probate court, showing date case filed, names of plaintiff and defendant, title of case, case number, and kind of case; also an accounting of fees received from probate court cases, showing date received, amount, and in what matter. Arranged chronologically by dates of entries. Indexed alphabetically by names of defendants. Handwritten. 350 pages. 18 x 12 x 3. Clerk of courts' record room 1.

307. LIST OF UNCLAIMED MONEY
1906-1921. 1 volume.
Record of money collected and received by the sheriff which is unclaimed by owners. Showing dates collected or received, names of principles, by whom paid, to whom due, amount, volume and page numbers of Cash Book, entry 302, and amount of sheriff's fees; also shows date list filed, date payable to treasurer, and amount. Arranged chronologically by dates of filing. Indexed alphabetically by names of persons to whom due. Handwritten on printed forms. 244 pages. 16.5 x 11 x 1. Clerk of courts' record room 1.

308. JOURNAL AND DAILY ENTRY
1881-1928. 17 volumes.
Record of funds received daily by the sheriff from all sources showing date received, title of case, case number, kind of writs, name of court, volume and page numbers of execution docket [Sheriff'], entry 292, remarks, and amount of fees. Arranged chronologically by dates fees received. No index. Handwritten on printed forms. Average 200 pages. 18 x 12 x 2. Sheriff's office.

Miscellaneous

309. SALES NOTICE DOCKET
1842—. 11 volumes (1-11).
Record of newspaper clippings and sales of property sold by the sheriff, showing date of sale, case number, names of plaintiff and defendant, time of sale, name of court, description and location of property, appraised value, terms of sale, dates advertise, name of purchaser, amount of sale, signature of sheriff and remarks. Arranged chronologically by dates of sales. Indexed alphabetically by names of plaintiffs showing names of defendants. Clippings, printed; record, Handwritten. Average 400 pages. 16 x 11 x 3. 9 volumes, 1842-1937, Clerk of courts' record room 1; 2 volumes, 1938—, Sheriff's office.

The county dog warden, appointed by and responsible to the county commissioners, has as his duty the enforcement of the provisions of the General Code relative to licensing dogs, the impounding and destruction of unlicensed dogs, and the payment of compensation for damages to livestock inflicted by dogs. This officer, like other county officials, is required to give bond conditioned for the faithful performance of the duties of his office. This bond, in the sum of not less than $500 nor more than $2,000, is filed with the county auditor. His compensation and tenure, like that of his deputies, is determined by the county commissioners.[1]

In Montgomery County the duties of the dog warden were performed by the sheriff from 1917 to 1927 as provided by statute.[2] In 1927 and act authorized the county commissioners to appoint a county dog warden under which act the dog warden of Montgomery County was appointed on July 18, 1927.[3]

The dog warden is required to make a record of all dogs owned, kept, or harbored in his county; to patrol the county; and seize and impound dogs more than three months of age found not wearing a valid registration tag. The latter provisions do not apply, however, to dogs kept in a regularly licensed kennel. Moreover, he is required to make weekly written reports to the county commissioners of all dogs seized, impounded, redeemed, and destroyed. Then, too, he is required to report all claims for damages to livestock inflicted by dogs.

The dog warden and his deputies have, in the performance of their legal duties, the same "police powers" as are conferred by statute upon sheriff's and police. They may summon the assistance of bystanders in performing their duties, serve writs and other legal processes issued by any court in the county with reference to enforcing the provisions of the law relating to dogs.[4]

---

1. G. C. sec. 5652-7.
2. *Laws of Ohio,* CVII, 535.
3. *Ibid.,* CXII, 348; Commissioners' Journal, volume 33 [1927], p. 595, see entry 1.
4. G. C. sec. 5652-7.

310. DOG AND KETTLE REGISTER
1928—. 4 volumes. (dated).

Dog warden's record of dog and kennel licenses issued, showing name of owner, name of street and house number of owner, description of dog (sex, breed, age, and color of hair), amount of fee, tag number, date of issue, and signature of deputy issuing same. Arranged alphabetically by names of streets and numerically thereunder by house numbers. No index. Handwritten on printed forms. Average 300 pages. 11 x 8.5 x 2. Animal shelter, North Patterson Boulevard, Dayton.

311. NOTICE TO DOG WARDEN
1928—. 2 bundles.

Copies of notices to the dog warden from the county commissioners to investigate claims for animals killed or injured by dogs, showing date of filing of notice, name of claimant, date on damage claimed, and instructions. Also includes copies of reports on the investigation, showing name and address of claimant, date of investigation, number of animals killed or injured, extent of injuries, amount of dog warde,'s estimate of damage, and date report filed. No index. Handwritten on printed forms. 10 x 4 x 14. Animal shelter, North Patterson Boulevard, Dayton.

312. POUND KEEPERS RECORD
1928—. 4 volumes.

Copies of dog wardens report to the county commissioners of stray dogs place in the animal shelter, showing date of report; if dog sold, the amount of sale; if identified and claimed by owner, shows name of owner and amount of cost; and if destroyed, shows the date and manner of disposal. Arranged chronologically by dates disposed of. No index. Handwritten on printed forms. Average 200 pages. 18 x 10 x 1. Animal shelter, North Patterson Boulevard, Dayton.

AUDITOR 155

The first Ohio constitution, adopted in 1802, did not provide for the office of county auditor and it was not until 1820 that the general assembly by joint resolution appointed an auditor in each county for a one-year term.[1] In 1821 the office became elective and the term was fixed at one year.[2] In 1831 the term was set at two years, and 1877 at three years, and 1906 reduced to two years, and in 1919 extended to 4 years.[3]

The county auditor is required to take oath and give bond for faithful performance of the duties of the office; to preserve all copies of entries, surveys, extracts, and other documents transmitted to his office from the state auditor; and to transfer to his successor all books, records, maps, and other papers pertaining to his office.[4] With the approval of the county commissioners he is authorized to appoint deputies, for whose official acts he and his sureties are held liable; the record of these appointments which has been required to be filed with the county treasurer since 1869[5] have been filed in the office of Montgomery County auditor since 1913. If the office of county auditor falls vacant the county commissioners are authorized to appoint a successor.[6]

The first auditor in each county was required to list all lands in his county subject to taxation. From this list and one submitted to him by the county commissioners and one from the state auditor the county auditor was directed to make a tax duplicate to keep in a book for that purpose, and to give a copy of the list to the tax collector.[7] The auditor was also directed to compile from the treasurer's duplicate a list of lands on which taxes were delinquent, and if such lands were sold for taxes to grant a deed to the purchaser.[8]

Subsequent legislation expanded and itemized the duties of the auditor in regards to taxation; with modifications to meet modern requirements these duties had continued much as they were during the earlier years of his office.

---

1. *Laws of Ohio,* XVIII, 71.

2. *Ibid.,* XIX, 116.

3. *Ibid.,* XXIX, 250; LXXIV, 381; XCVIII, 271; CVIII, pt. ii, 1294.

4. *Ibid.,* XIX, 116; XLVII, 103; G. C. secs. 2559, 2582.

5. *Laws of Ohio,* LV, 20; LXVI, 35; G. C. sec. 2563.

6. G. C. secs. 2579, 2580, 2990, 2996.

7. *Laws of Ohio,* XVIII, 79.

8. *Ibid.,* XVIII, 82; XIX, 115.

During the 1840's the office of county assessor was abolished and provision was made for township assessors whose duty it was to list all taxable property and make a return to the auditor.[9] Since 1874 the auditor is required by statute to keep a book in which he lists additions to and deductions from the amount of tax assessment.[10] In 1915 he was made chief assessing officer of the county.[11]

The county auditor has served as a member and the secretary of the county budget commission since its beginning in 1911, his duties including keeping full and accurate records of the proceedings of that body. For the purpose of adjusting the tax rates and fixing the amount to be levied each year the commissioners are governed by the amount of taxable property as shown on the auditor's tax list for the current year. He submits to the commissioners the annual tax budget given him by each taxing authority of each subdivision, together with an estimate of any tax levy prepared by the state auditor, and such other information as a budget commission may request or the state tax commission require.[12]

Settlements have been made annually until 1858 when the auditor was required to make semiannual settlement with the treasurer to ascertain the amount of taxes the treasurer is to stand charged.[13] Since 1904 liquor, cigarette, and inheritance taxes have constituted separate funds. All other taxes are credited to the general funds.[14]

Since 1831 the county auditor has kept an account current with the county treasurer showing the payments of moneys into the treasury, listing the date, by whom paid, and to which fund. On receiving the treasurer's daily statement the auditor enters on his account current the amount shown as a charge to the treasurer.[15] Another important function of the county auditor is the approval before payment of bills and other claims against the county. Since 1831 he has been authorized to issue, on presentation of proper voucher, all warrants the county treasurer for moneys payable from the county treasury; and to preserve all warrants, showing the number, date of issue, amount for which drawn, in whose favor, and from which fund.[16]

---

9. *Ibid.,* XXXIX, 22-25. See also p. xlv.
10. *Laws of Ohio,* LXXI, 30.
11. *Ibid.,* CVI, 246.
12. G. C. sec. 5625-19; *Laws of Ohio,* CXII, 402.
13. G. C. sec. 2596; *Laws of Ohio,* LV, 62; LVI, 132; LXXVIII, 226.
14. *Laws of Ohio,* XCVII, 457.
15. *Ibid.,* XXIX, 280-291; LXVII, 103.
16. G. C. Sec. 2570; *Laws of Ohio,* XXIX, 280-291; LXVII, 103.

County money due the state is paid on warrant of the state auditor. Since 1904 a bill or voucher for payment from any fund controlled by the county commissioners or board of county infirmary directors is filed with the county auditor and entered in a book for that purpose at least five days before its approval for payment by the commissioners, and when approved the date is entered opposite the claim.[17]

Besides approving bills and claims against the county, the auditor in 1825 was given the duty of certifying all moneys, except collections on the tax duplicate, into the county treasury, specifying by whom paid and the fund to which such payment is credited. Such moneys he charges to the treasurer and keeps a duplicate copy of the statement in his office. Since 1835 all costs collected in penitentiary cases which have been or are to be paid to the state have been certified into the treasury as belongs to the state.[18]

In 1902 the legislature provided for a separate system of uniform accounting and auditing of all public offices, and for the annual examination of their finances, under the direction of a bureau of inspection in the office of the state auditor.[19] Since 1904 the county auditor has been required to report to the commissioners on the state of the county finances; on the first business day of each month he prepares in duplicate a statement of the county finances for the proceeding month, compares it with the treasurer's balance, and submits it to the commissioners to post one copy of it in the auditors office for thirty days for public inspection.[20]

During the development of the office additional duties in great diversity have been delegated to the county auditor. Since 1833 he has been authorized to discharge prisoners jailed for nonpayment of any fine or amercement due the county when in his opinion the amount cannot be collected.[21] In 1838 and act was passed making him county superintendent of schools. He was relieved of this duty in 1848 when a county superintendent of schools was authorized in each county.[22] Since 1846 he has served as a sealer of weights and measures, is responsible for the preservation of the copies of the original standards delivered to his office, and enforces in his county all state laws regulating weights and measures.[23]

---

17. *Laws of Ohio,* XCVII, 25; CVIII, pt.i, 272.
18. *Ibid.,* XXXIII, 44; LXVII, 103.
19. *Ibid.,* XCV, 511-515.
20. *Ibid.,* XCVII, 457.
21. G. C. sec, 2576; *Laws of Ohio,* XXXI, 18; LXVII, 103.
22. See p. 208.
23. G. C. Sec. 2615; *Laws of Ohio,* XLIV, 55; LVIII, 78; CI, 234.

In 1861 he was authorized to report to the state auditor statistics concerning the death, dumb, blind, insane, and idiots in his county, with the names and addresses of the parents or guardians.[24] Eight years later, in 1869, he was authorized to report to the same officer statistics concerning livestock in his county as returned to his office by assessors, and an abstract of the funded indebtedness of his county, and of each township, city, village, and school district.[25] Since 1827 he has been authorized to issue licenses to traveling public shows and exhibitions, although municipal authorities may impose an additional license.[26] In 1862 he was authorized to issue peddlers' licenses to persons who filed a statement of stock in trade in conformity with the law requiring the listing of such stock for taxation, and since 1917 has issued dog licenses.[27] The auditor has issued licenses to wholesale and retail dealers in cigarettes since 1893[28] in brewers' wort and malt since 1933[29] and cosmetic licenses from August 1, 1933, to June 30, 1936.[30]

From 1821 to 1908 the county auditor of Montgomery County served as clerk to the county commissioners; his duties included keeping an accurate record of their proceedings and preserving all documents, books, records, maps, and papers which were required to be filed in his office.[31] Since 1850 he has been official custodian of the reports submitted to the commissioners by the prosecuting attorney, the clerk of courts, the sheriff, and the treasurer; these reports are recorded by the auditor in books kept specifically for the purpose.[32] This record has apparently not been kept by the Montgomery County auditor but official reports are recorded the Commissioners' Journal from 1850 to date.[33]

---

24. *Laws of Ohio,* LVIII, 40.
25. G. C. sec. 2604.
26. Chase, *op. cit.,* III, 1582; *Laws of Ohio,* XXIX, 446; G. C. secs. 6374-6375.
27. *Laws of Ohio,* LIX, 67; LXXIX, 96; CVII, 534.
28. G. C. sec. 5894-5.
29. G. C. sec. 5545-5.
30. *Laws of Ohio,* CXV, 649; CXV, pt. ii, 83; CXVI, pt. ii, 323.
31. G. C. sec. 2566; *Laws of Ohio,* XIX, 147.
32. G. C. Sec. 2504; R. S., sec. 886; *Laws of Ohio,* XLVIII, 66.
33. See entry 1.

The county auditor is a member of the county board of revision established in 1825, secretary of the budget commission, and serves as a trustee and secretary of the board of trustees of the sinking fund established in 1919[34] and as bookkeeper of the county, he is a very important county official. The auditor of Montgomery County receives an annual salary of $5,790.[35]

---

34. See pp. 196, 197, 202.
35. Ohio Auditor of State, *Annual Report, 1939,* p. 366.

Property Transfers

313. TRANSFER BOOK
1847. 1 volume (1).
Record of transfers of real estate, showing date of transfer, name of grantor and grantee, location and description of property, and amount of consideration. Arranged chronologically by dates of transfers. No index. Handwritten. 350 pages. 18 x 12 x 3. Auditor's room E.

For subsequent records, see entry 334.

314. AUDITOR'S DEEDS
1820—. 5 volumes (1-5).
Record of deeds for land sold for delinquent taxes, showing name of taxing district, name of original owner, date of sale, name of purchaser, range, township, and section numbers, acreage, description of tracts, what portion sold, amount of sale, name of person to whom deed was made, date of deed, and signature of county auditor. Arranged chronologically by dates of deeds. No index. Handwritten on printed forms. Average 500 pages. 18 x 12 x 3. 4 volumes, 1820-1895, Auditor's room E.; 1 volume, 1896—, Auditor's office room 1.

Plats, Maps, and Surveys

315. COUNTY TAX MAP BY TOWNSHIPS
Approximately 1820—. 50 volumes. (151-200). Subtitled by names of townships.
Tax maps of townships and villages in Montgomery County, showing section number, fractional ranges, plat and lot numbers, description of property, and name of owner. Prepared by F. J. Cellarious. Arranged alphabetically by names of

townships and numerically thereunder by sections and lots of numbers. For index or key map, see entry 316. Lithographed by F. J. Cellarious and Sons. Scale vary. Average 20 pages. 24 x 26.5 x 1. Auditor's office room 1.

316. KEY TO TOWNSHIP MAPS
Approximately 1820—. 1 map.
Index or key map to County Tax Map by Townships, entry 315, showing name of township, range, section and lot numbers, and names of villages, streets, roads, and rivers. Prepared by F. J. Cellarious. Lithographed by F. J. Cellarious and Sons. Scale, 1 inch equals 1000 feet. 72 x 48. Auditors office room 1.

317. PLAT BOOK
1874-1896. 16 volumes.
Plats of additions, showing date of survey, name and address of property owner, lot and plat numbers, dates of transfers, dates map received and filed, name of witnesses, and name of auditor. Arranged chronologically by dates of surveys. No index. Handwritten and hand drawn. Scales vary. 450 pages. 18 x 13 x 3. Auditor's record room E.

318. COUNTY TAX ATLASES, CITY OF DAYTON
Approximately 1831—, revised to date. 146 volumes (1-146).
Sectional maps of the city of Dayton, showing ward number, lot number, name of owner, address, record of transfers, and widths of streets and alleys. Prepared by various engineers. Arranged numerically by ward and lot numbers. For index or key map, see entry 319. Handwritten and hand drawn on cloth. Scales vary. Average 8 pages. 26 x 18 x .5. Auditor's office room 1.

319. KEY MAP TO [County Tax Atlases, City of Dayton] PLATS
Approximately 1831—. 1 map.
Index or key map to County Tax Atlases, City of Daytona entry 318, showing name of street, lot number, and volume and page numbers of record. Prepared by F. J. Cellarious. Lithographed by F. J. Cellarious and Sons. 1 inch equals 1000 feet. 82 x 48. Auditor's office room on one.

320. REVISED PLATS
1809. 1 volume.
Plats of city lots and lands in immediate vicinity of the city of Dayton, showing

range, township, section and lot numbers, and names of streets. No obvious arrangement. No index. Hand drawn. Scales vary. 250 pages. 18 x 12 x 2. Auditor's record room E.

321. PLATS AND DESCRIPTION OF LAND IN MONTGOMERY COUNTY
[1820—]. 16 volumes. Subtitled by names of townships.
Tax plats, showing foot frontage or acreage, name of owner, address, description of property, and valuation; also shows old and new street lines, date replatted, kind of buildings or if vacant, and index number. Arranged alphabetically by names of townships and numerically thereunder by index numbers. No index. Hand drawn. Scales vary. Average 150 pages. 18 x 14 x 1.5. Auditor's office room 1.

322. ATLAS OF CITY OF OAKLAND, REVISED
n. d. 9 volumes.
Sectional maps of city of Oakland, showing location of lots by streets and lot numbers, name of owner and record of transfers (if any), and widths of streets and alleys. Prepared by various county engineers. Arranged numerically by lot numbers. No index. Handwritten and hand drawn on cloth. Scales very. Average 100 pages. 38 x 22 x 1. Auditor's record room 1.

323. NUMBER BOOK– MONTGOMERY COUNTY
1855-1875. 6 volumes. (labeled by contained lot numbers).
Lists of lots in county, showing name of property owner and lot number. Arranged numerically by lot numbers. No index. Handwritten. Average 250 pages. 18 x 12 x 2. Auditor's record room E.

324. NUMERICAL LIST FOR CITY OF DAYTON, LOT NUMBERS
1881—. 132 volumes. (labeled by contained lot numbers).
Record of lots in city of Dayton only, showing diagram of lot, lot number, name of original owner, date sold or transferred, and names of grantor and grantee. Arranged numerically by lot numbers. No index. Handwritten on printed forms. Average 500 pages. 18 x 12 x 3.5. Auditor's office room 1.

Taxes

Real Property

325. TAX LEVIES
1913—. 2 volumes (1, 2). Prior records destroyed.
Record of tax levies of townships, showing year, name of township, amount requested, amount reduced and amount allowed, and amount in sinking fund. Arranged chronologically by years and alphabetically thereunder by names of townships. No index. Handwritten on printed forms. Average 400 pages. 11 x 14 x 2. Auditor's vault.

326. REAL ESTATE CARDS
1931-1937. 104 file boxes. (labeled by contained lot numbers).
Card record of appraised value of real property in Montgomery County, showing a lot number, name and address of owner, foot frontage, depth of plot or lot, value per front foot, appraised value of land and buildings, total, amount of adjustments, and total appraisement. Arranged numerically by lot numbers. No index. Handwritten on printed forms. 12 x 12 x 36. Auditor's taxation department.

327. APPRAISER'S ASSESSMENTS OF REAL PROPERTY
1849-1901. 11 volumes.
Record of real property appraisements made by county appraisers, showing name of property owner, location and description of property, and date and amount of appraisal. Arranged chronologically by dates of appraisals. No index. Average 250 pages. 24 x 12 x 1.5. Auditor's record room E.

328. SPECIAL ASSESSMENTS FOR TOWNSHIPS
1881-1916. 33 volumes.
Record of special assessments for public improvements including sewers, showing date of assessment, purpose, amount, name of property owner, and location of property by street and lot number. Arranged chronologically by dates of assessments. Indexed alphabetically by names of property owners. Handwritten and typed. Average 250 pages. 18 x 12 x 2. Auditor's record room E.

329. SPECIAL ASSESSMENTS

1935—. 26 volumes. Subtitled by names of cities and townships.

Record of special assessments for the construction or improvement of streets and roads, showing purpose of assessment, amount, name of property owner, location of property, name of street or road, lot number, and acreage. Arranged numerically by lot numbers. No index. Handwritten. Average 1000 pages. (Loose-leaf) 18 x 12 x 4. Auditor's record room 2.

330. ASSESSMENTS FOR ROAD IMPROVEMENTS

1919—. 3 volumes (1-3).

Record of assessments for road improvements, showing name of property owner, range, township, section, number of acres owned, number of acres benefited, number of lots, front frontage, cost of assessment, and amount of assessment. Arranged alphabetically by names of property owners. Indexed alphabetically by names of improvements. Handwritten on printed forms. Average 250 pages. 18 x 12 x 2. 1 volume, 1919-1928, Auditor's record room E; 2 volumes, 1929—, Auditor's office 2.

331. SPECIAL ASSESSMENTS, CITY OF DAYTON

1923—. 41 volumes. (A1-S41).

Record of assessments for installation and maintenance of water lines, electricity, street paving, sanitary and storm sewer and sewer outlets, showing location of street and lot number, frontage, rate, plat number, name of owner and remarks. Arranged alphabetically by names of owners. No index. Handwritten. Average 400 pages. 16 x 9.5 x 3. Auditor's record room 2.

332. ASSESSMENTS, ELECTRIC LIGHTING VILLAGE OF OAKWOOD

1921-1924. 1 volume.

Record of assessments for electric lights for village of Oakwood, showing plat number, lot number, name of owner, amount of assessment, and remarks. Arranged numerically by lot numbers. Indexed alphabetically by names of owners. Handwritten. 300 pages. 18 x 12 x 2. Auditor's record room E.

333. THE MIAMI CONSERVANCY DISTRICT ANNUAL
ASSESSMENTS

1917—. 189 volumes. (dated, nine each year). Last assessment 1938.

Record of assessments to property owners in county benefiting from the
conservancy district protection, showing name of property owner, location and
description of property, value, and amount of assessment. Arranged alphabetically
by names of corporations and townships and alphabetically thereunder by names of
property owners. No index. Handwritten and typed on printed forms. Average 45
pages. 24 x 20 x 1.5. 153 volumes, 1917-1934, Auditor's record room E; 36
volumes, 1935—, Auditor's office room 2.

334. TAX DUPLICATE REAL PROPERTY

1810—. 495 volumes. (dated).

Tax duplicates of real property, showing name of taxing district, name of property
owner, address, location and description of property, lot number, value, and amount
of delinquent tax, penalties, and revisions; also includes, 1848—, a record of
property transfers, showing date of transfer, names the grantor and grantee, and
description and location of property. Arranged alphabetically by names of taxing
districts and alphabetically thereunder by names of property owners. No index.
1810-1910, handwritten on printed forms; 1910—, typed on printed forms. Average
250 pages. 18 x 12 x 2. 393 volumes, 1810-1929, Auditor's record room E; 102
volumes, 1930—, Auditor's office room 1.

For record of transfers, 1847, see entry 313.

335. TAX DUPLICATE REAL PROPERTY

1926—. 32 volumes (A-Z, 1-6). Twenty-six subtitled Dayton; six by names
of townships.

Combined auditor's and treasurer's tax duplicate, showing name of property owner,
address, location, lot number, description, value, amount paid or delinquent,
penalty, and date paid. Arranged alphabetically by names of property owners. No
index. Handwritten on printed forms. Average 250 pages. 18 x 12 x 2. Auditor's
office room 2.

336. AUDITOR'S TURNPIKE DUPLICATE

1870-1880. 1 volume.

Record of assessments for construction or improvement of turnpikes, showing name
of property owner, location of property, date of assessment, amount of assessment,

and penalty. Arranged chronologically by dates of assessments. No index. Handwritten. 300 pages. 24 x 12 x 2. Auditor's record room E.

Personal Property

337. PERSONAL TAX RETURNS
1930—. 26 volumes, 62 file boxes. (labeled by contained letters of alphabet).
Original returns filed by individuals on taxable personal property, showing name and address of property owner, date of return, items taxable value, total listed value, tax rate, and amount of tax due. Arranged alphabetically by names of property owners. No index. Handwritten on printed forms. Volumes average 75 pages. 18 x 12 x 1; file box, 12 x 15 x 36. 26 volumes, 1930-1932, Auditor's record room E; 62 file boxes, 1932—, Personal tax department.

338. PERSONAL TAX DUPLICATE
1820—. 79 volumes. (dated).
Record of assessments on personal property, showing name of owner, address, location and description of property, value, amount, and date of assessment; includes, 1932—, general and classified tax assessments. Arranged alphabetically by names of owners. No index. Handwritten and typed on printed forms. Average 500 pages. 18 x 12 x 3. 70 volumes, 1820-1931, Auditor's record room E; 9 volumes, 1932—, Personal tax department.

339. GENERAL [Personal] TAX
1838—. 2 volumes.
General tax list of tangible personal property, showing name and address of person or corporation taxed, name of taxing district, class of property as domestic animals, grain inventory, engines, machinery, tools, implements, manufacturing and merchandise inventory, other personal property, rate of tax, listed value, penalty assessment, total assessment, total tax, amount of advance payment, when due, date paid, and signature of county auditor. Arranged alphabetically by names of the corporations or individuals taxed. No index. Typed on printed forms. Average 1500 pages. 12 x 6 x 8.5. Personal tax department.

340. CLASSIFIED [Personal] TAX

1939——. 2 volumes.

Classified list of intangible property, showing name and address of corporation or individual, name of taxing district, class of investment, income yield, nonproductive investments, deposits, credits, money and other intangibles, rate of interest, listed value, penalty assessments, total tax, advance payment, amount due, date paid, and signature of auditor. Arranged alphabetically by names of corporations or individuals taxed. No index. Typed on printed forms. 1500 pages. 12 x 6 x 8.5. Personal tax department.

Adjustments

341. ADDITIONS AND DEDUCTIONS

1891-1896, 1914——. 8 volumes.

Record of additions to and deductions from the general tax duplicates, showing name of property owner, description of property, number of acres, value, amount of general and special tax, street improvements, delinquencies, penalties, and amount of addition or deductions. Arranged alphabetically by names of property owners. No index. Handwritten on printed forms. Average 1225 pages. 16 x 14 x 10. Auditors room 1.

Delinquent

342. DELINQUENT LIST FOR REAL AND PERSONAL PROPERTY, TOWNSHIPS

1890——. 49 volumes.

Record of delinquent real and personal property taxes in county, showing name of property owner, description and location of property, plat or lot numbers, name of township, value, amount of assessment, amount of delinquency, penalty, total, and date certified delinquent by county treasurer. Also contains Auditor's Delinquent Record for Real and Personal Tax for the city of Dayton, 1890-1911, entry 343. Arranged alphabetically by names of property owners. No index. Handwritten. Average 320 pages. 18 x 12 x 3. Auditor's office room 1.

343. AUDITOR'S DELINQUENT RECORD FOR REAL AND PERSONAL TAX FOR THE CITY OF DAYTON

1912—. 32 volumes. (A2-Z2, U-Z). 1890-1911 in delinquent list for real and personal property, townships, entry 342.

Record of delinquent real and personal property for the city of Dayton, showing information as in Delinquent List for Real and Personal Property, Townships, entry 342. Arranged chronologically by dates certified delinquent. Indexed alphabetically by names of property owners. Handwritten. Average 320 pages. 18 x 12 x 3. Auditor's office room 1.

344. COUNTY TREASURER'S DELINQUENT TAX LIST, CITY OF DAYTON

20 volumes. (labeled by contained letters of alphabet).

List of delinquent real property owners in the city of Dayton as certified by the county treasurer to the county auditor, showing name the taxing district, name of property owner, address, location and description of property, call value, amount of tax, amounts of delinquency and penalty, and date certified to the auditor. Arranged alphabetically by names of property owners. No index. Typed. Average 500 pages. 16 x 14 x 3.5. Auditor's office room 1.

345. CITY DELINQUENT LIST, DAYTON ANNEXATION, PERSONAL

August, 1931. 1 volume.

This volume is in two sections: first section, list of delinquent personal tax as certified delinquent in the August settlement, showing information as in County Treasurer's Delinquent Tax List, city of Dayton entry 344; the second section, county treasurer's returns on delinquent real property, showing information as in Delinquent List for Real and Personal Property, Township, entry 342. Arranged chronologically by dates certified delinquent. Indexed alphabetically by names of property owners. Handwritten. 1070 pages. 16.5 x 14.5 x 4.5. Personal tax department.

346. THE MIAMI CONSERVANCY DISTRICT ANNUAL ASSESSMENT DELINQUENCY

1935—. 8 volumes. (Two each 34-37 and labeled by contained assessment numbers 17-20).

Record of delinquent assessments for conservancy taxes on property located in Miami Conservancy District, showing name of property owner, location and description of property, amounts of assessments, delinquency, and penalty, date certified delinquent, and assessment number. Arranged alphabetically by names of property owners and numerically thereunder by assessment numbers. No index. Handwritten and typed on printed forms. Average 300 pages. 24 x 20 x 2. Auditor's office room 2.

347. CITY DELINQUENT LIST
1926—. 18 volumes.
List of delinquent property owners for the city of Dayton at certified to the prosecuting attorney for action, showing name and address of property owner, location and description of property, value of property, amount of assessment, penalty, total delinquent, and date certified delinquent. Arranged alphabetically by names of property owners. No index. Handwritten. Average 1700 pages. 16 x 14 x 10. Auditor's office room 1.

348. TREASURER'S TRIENNIAL LAND TAX CERTIFICATE OF DELINQUENT TRACTS OF LAND OR TOWN LOTS, MONTGOMERY COUNTY
1932—. 19 volumes. (dates).
Copies of triennial land tax certificates of delinquent property owners as certified by the county auditor to the prosecuting attorney and state auditor, showing date certified, certificate number, name and address of property owner, description and location of property, appraised value, amounts of assessment, delinquencies, penalty, and interest, and total amount due. Arranged alphabetically by names of townships and alphabetically thereunder by names of property owners. No index. Typed on printed forms. Average 700 pages. 17 x 14 x 5. 14 volumes, 1932-1935, Auditor's record room E; 5 volumes, 1936—, Auditor's office room 1.

For prosecuting attorney's records, see entry 288.

349. DELINQUENT TAX SALES
1847—. 14 volumes.
Record of property sold for delinquent taxes, showing name and address of property owner, location and description of property, appraised value, amount of unpaid taxes, penalty, date of sale, name of purchaser, and amount of sale. Arranged chronologically by dates of sales. Indexed alphabetically by names of purchasers. Handwritten and typed. Average 500 pages. 18 x 12 x 3. 13 volumes, 1847-1930, Auditor's record room E; 1 volume, 1931—, Auditor's office room 1.

Inheritance

350. CERTIFICATES OF INHERITANCE TAX
1919— . 19 volumes. (labeled by contained certificate numbers).
Copies of certificates of county auditor certifying inheritance tax charges, showing name of decedent, name of taxing district, certificate number, amount of tax, amount of discount or exemption, interest, and date of certificate. Arranged numerically by certificate numbers and chronologically by dates of certificate. No index. Handwritten on printed forms. Average 250 pages. 18 x 12 x 1. 16 volumes, 1919-1935, Auditor's record room E; 3 volumes, 1936—, Auditor's office room 1.

Utility

351. RAILROAD APPRAISEMENTS
1891-1910. 3 volumes (1-3). Discontinued; law repealed.
Minutes of board of appraisers and assessors, members of the board being auditors of the counties affected, showing date of appraisal and meeting, name of railroad, county, township, length of main track, value of main track per mile, length of second track, value of second track per mile, length of sidings, value of sidings per mile, value of rolling stock, description and location of buildings, value of buildings, amount and value of tools and machinery, amount of money and credits, value of all other property per mile, grand total of all taxable property, additions and deductions by the state board of equalization, and net value for taxation. Arranged chronologically by dates of appraisals. No index. Handwritten on printed forms. Average 275 pages. 18 x 12 x 2. Auditor's record room E.

Excise

352. LIQUOR AND CIGARETTE TRAFFIC
1884-1918. 56 volumes.
Record of assessments on merchants dealing in cigarette and liquor, showing license number, name of merchant or vendor, location of business, owner of premises, kind of license, amount of fee paid, and date of payment. Arranged numerically by license numbers. No index. Handwritten on printed forms. Average 40 pages. 24 x 16 x .5. Auditor's record room E.

353. CIGARETTE TRAFFIC, MONTGOMERY COUNTY

1913-1932. 10 volumes. (dated).

Record of assessments of state tax to vendors of cigarettes, showing name of vendor, location of business, amounts of quarterly installments, total assessments, and penalty; also includes a record of collections of assessments, showing date due, amount, and date of payment. Arranged alphabetically by names of vendors. No index. Handwritten on printed forms. Average 300 pages. 18 x 12 x 3. Auditor's record room E.

Financial Records

Budgets and Appropriations

354. BUDGET

1916—. 17 file drawers. (dated).

Copies of budgets of taxing or school districts, showing date, name of taxing or school district, and amount approved; also copies of county commissioners' resolutions pertaining to budgets. Arranged alphabetically by names of taxing or school districts. No index. 10.5 x 15 x 18. Auditor's office room 3.

355. SCHOOL FUNDS

1859-1890. 1 volume.

Record of funds needed for schools for fiscal year as requested in budget presented to the budget commission, showing date presented, amount needed for the various departments, and amount of anticipated expenses. Arranged chronologically by dates presented. No index. Handwritten. 250 pages. 18 x 12 x 1.5. Auditor's record room E.

356. APPROPRIATION LEDGER

1926—. 14 volumes (1-14).

Auditor's record of appropriations to each fund or department by the county commissioners and expenditures from each fund, showing name of fund or department, amount credited to fund or department, amount debited to each fund or department, date of entry, name of payee or vendor, warrant number, purpose, amount of warrants, and amounts of debits, credits, and unencumbered balance. Arranged alphabetically by the names of funds or departments and chronologically thereunder by dates of entries. No index. Handwritten on printed forms. Average

500 pages. 11.5 x 14.5 x 4. 12 volumes, 1926-1938, Auditor's record room E; 2 volumes, 1838—, Auditor's office room 3.

Settlements

357. SCHOOL SETTLEMENT RECORDS
1915—. 6 volumes (2-7).

Record of funds apportioned to county schools, showing name of school district, amount apportioned, dates and amounts expended with certification of expenditures and balances by officials of banks where funds are deposited, clerk's record of examination and certification, and date of settlement. Arranged chronologically by dates of settlements. No index. Handwritten on printed forms. Average 600 pages. 18.5 x 14 x 3. 5 volumes, 1915-1936, Auditor's record room E; 1 volume, 1937—, Auditor's office room 3.

358. SETTLEMENTS
1904—. 10 volumes (1-10).

Record of settlements with county treasurer, state auditor, townships, and taxing districts, showing amount of taxes paid, amount of village and township levies for school purposes, general and classified tax, auditor's fees, and total to be distributed; also date of settlement, dates bills received and approved, and date and amount paid. Arranged chronologically by dates of settlements. No index. Handwritten. Average 300 pages. 14 x 8 x 1.5. 4 volumes, 1904-1935, Auditor's record room E; 6 volumes, 1936—, Auditor's office room 2.

359. AUDITOR'S DAILY DISTRIBUTION OF MOTOR VEHICLE LICENSES FEES RECEIVED
1928-1932. 6 volumes. Discontinued; law revised.

Record of daily distribution and settlement of motor vehicle license fees received, showing date received, whether to municipal government or to county general funds, amount, to whom distributed, and certification of auditor's deputy. Arranged chronologically by dates of entries. No index. Handwritten on printed forms. Average 350 pages. 14 x 12 x 2. Auditors record room E.

General Accounts

360. AUDITOR'S RECORD OF ACCOUNTS
1875—. 5 volumes.

Record of accounts of funds, including townships, bridges, ditches, roads, children's home, auctioneers' licenses, schools, and liquor, showing date of entry, to whom paid, for what, total receipts and disbursements, balances, and overdrafts. Arranged chronologically by dates of entries. Indexed alphabetically by names of funds. Handwritten. Average 425 pages. 20 x 15 x 3. 2 volumes, 1875-1912, Auditor's record room E; 3 volumes, 1913—, Auditor's office room 1.

361. AUDITOR'S FINANCIAL REPORT BLOTTER
1918. 1 volume. Discontinued.

Record of money received by the auditor, showing date and amount of receipt; also expenditures for salaries and sundries, showing date, amount, purpose, and balance. Arranged chronologically by dates of receipts and expenditures. No index. Handwritten and typed. 75 pages. 18 x 12 x .5. Auditor's record room E.

362. DAILY CASH BALANCE, MONTGOMERY COUNTY
1913—. 20 volumes (10-39). Prior records destroyed.

Record of daily cash receipts and disbursements, showing amount on hand, date of receipt or disbursement, amount received, amount paid out or refunded, explanation of transaction, and balance. Arranged chronologically by dates of entries. No index. Handwritten on printed forms. Average 430 pages. 14 x 12 x 3. 16 volumes, 1913-133, Auditor's record room E; 4 volumes, 1934—, Auditor's office room 3.

363. JOURNAL OF PAYMENTS INTO TREASURY
1904—. 5 volumes (1-5).

Record of payments into treasury by auditor, showing date payment made, pay-in order number, name of payer, amount, and for what purpose. Arranged chronologically by dates of pay-ins. No index. Handwritten on printed forms. Average 250 pages. 20 x 16 x 1.5. 4 volumes, 1904-1939, Auditor's record room E; 1 volume , 1940—, Auditor's office room 3.

364. AUDITOR'S RECORD OF FEES
1907—. 1 volume (1).

Records of fees collected by the auditor, showing date, amount, by whom paid, and purpose, as general settlement, other settlements, transfers, additions, ditches, pikes, and sundries. Arranged chronologically by dates of entries. No index. Handwritten on printed forms. 240 pages. 16 x 11 x 1.5. Auditor's office room 3.

365. BONDED INDEBTEDNESS
1917—. 4 file boxes. (dated).
Copies of reports from the county auditor to the state auditor of the bonded indebtedness of cities and townships, showing purpose for which the debt was created, public utility debt, general and special assessment debt and summary, prior issue, new issue, total outstanding indebtedness, rate of interest, date of maturity, balance in sinking fund, name of city or township, and signature of county auditor. Arranged chronologically by years. No index. Typed on printed forms. 4.5 x 10.5 x 13.5. Auditor's vault.

366. REPORTS, JUSTICE OF PEACE
1929—. 4 file boxes.
Original reports of justices of the peace to the county auditor, showing date of report, itemized account of fines and cost from criminal cases, name of justice, and date report filed. Arranged chronologically by dates of reports. No index. Handwritten on printed forms. 10.5 x 5 x 18. Auditor's office room 1.

367. DEPOSITORY REPORTS
1926—. 2 file boxes. Prior records missing.
Reports to county auditor of township funds made by township clerks, showing date of report, name and address of depository, and amount of bond. Arranged chronologically by dates or reports. No index. Handwritten and typed on printed forms. 10.5 x 5 x 18. Auditor's office room 1.

368. FINANCIAL STATEMENTS
1939—. 4 file boxes. Prior records destroyed.
Copies of auditor's monthly and annual financial statements to the county commissioners, showing date of statement, itemized account of cash receipts from all sources credited to county funds, itemized account of expenditures, and amounts of debits, credits, and balance of each fund. Arranged chronologically by dates of statements. No index. Handwritten on printed forms. 10.5 x 5 x 18. Auditor's office room 3.

369. FINES AND FEES

1907—. 2 volumes.

Auditor's copies of county officials' reports on fines and fees, showing date of report, name of person paying fine, amount assessed, amount of recognizance forfeited, and total amount collected. Arranged alphabetically under tabs by names of offices and chronologically thereunder by dates of reports. Handwritten on printed forms. Average 450 pages. 18 x 12 x 2. 1 volume, 1907-1922, Auditor's record room E; 1 volume, 1927—, Auditor's office room 3.

Special Accounts

370. CLERK"S SCHOOL FUND–CHAUTAUQUA DISTRICT

1914-1926. 1 volume.

Record of funds received from tax collections, showing date of receipt, date of expenditure, name of payee, for what purpose, warrant number, year and month warrant was returned by depository, amount of teachers' salaries, aggregate days of attendance of pupils, amount of depository interest, amount from foreign tuition, from sales of bonds, and miscellaneous receipts. Arranged chronologically by dates of entries. No index. Handwritten. 75 pages. 24 x 12 x 2.5. Auditor's record room E.

371. AUDITOR'S RECORD OF COST CONSTRUCTION

1913-1921. 1 volume.

Auditor's record of estimated cost of projects under construction, showing project name or number, name of contractor, amounts for labor and material, date of contract, probable date of completion, and remarks. Arranged chronologically by dates of contracts. No index. Handwritten. 300 pages. 18 x 12 x 3. Auditor's record room E.

372. LEDGER [Infirmary]

1902—. 12 volumes.

Record of disbursements from fund allocated to the county home, showing date of expenditure, name of payee, amount, and purpose of expenditure. Arranged chronologically by dates of expenditures. Indexed alphabetically by names of payees. Handwritten. Average 500 pages. 18 x 12 x 3. 11 volumes, 1902-1936, Auditor's record room E; 1 volume, 1937—, Auditor's office room 3.

373. FEES FOR BURIAL COMMITTEE OF INDIGENT SOLDIERS
1908-1914. 1 volume.

Record of fees allowed members of the soldiers' burial committees, showing name and address of decedent, date of death, cost of burial, warrant number, and amount. Arranged numerically by warrant numbers. Indexed alphabetically by names of decedents. Handwritten on printed forms. 120 pages. 14 x 10 x 1.5. Auditor's record room E.

374. AUDITOR'S RECORD OF SOLDIERS' RELIEF
1887-1910. 3 volumes.

Record of monthly payments to indigent soldiers, sailors, marines, or their dependents, showing name of recipient, address, amount, date of payment, and warrant number. Arranged chronologically by dates of payments. Indexed alphabetically by names of recipients. Handwritten on printed forms. Average 200 pages. 24 x 13 x 3. Auditor's record room E.

375. BLIND RELIEF
1908- June 1936. 7 bundles. (dated). Discontinued.

Record of payments to blind beneficiaries, showing name and address of recipient, amount allowed, date payment authorized, warrant number, and date paid. Arranged chronologically by dates of payments. No index. Typed on printed forms. 18 x 12 x .5. Auditor's record room E.

376. MOTHERS' PENSIONS
1913- June-1936. 2 bundles. (dated). Discontinued.

Auditor's record of payments for mothers' pension fund, showing name and address of payee, amount authorized, amount paid, date of payment, and warrant number. Arranged chronologically by dates of payments. No index. Typed. 18 x 12 x .5. ADC office.

377. AID TO DEPENDENT CHILDREN
1936—. 1 volume.

Record of vouchers issued for aid to dependent children, showing date of voucher, voucher number, name and address of payee, and date of grant; also record of notifications or terminations of grant; total amount of receipts, total expenditures from fund, and balance. Arranged alphabetically by named of recipients. No index. Typed on printed forms. 500 pages. 12 x 9 x 3. Auditor's office room 1.

Bills and Claims

379. AUDITOR'S DOCKET OF BILLS FILED
1912—. 15 volumes. Prior records destroyed.
Docket of commissioners' bills filed, showing bill number, name of creditor, specific purpose, fund from which payable, amount, date of filing, dates of approval and entry, amount approved, date of payment, warrant number, and remarks. Arranged numerically by bill numbers. No index. Handwritten on printed forms. Average 500 pages. 18 x 12 x 3. 13 volumes, 1912-1928, Auditor's record room E; 2 volumes, 1929—, Auditor's office room 1.

380. DOCKET OF BILLS [Infirmary]
1904—. 4 volumes (1-4).
Auditor's record of bills filed with county commissioners against infirmary account, showing date of bill, name of creditor, for what purpose, amount of bill, date filed, date approved, amount approved, date paid, and warrant number. Arranged chronologically by dates of filing. No index. Handwritten on printed forms. Average 300 pages. 19 x 14 x 3.5. Auditor's office room 3.

381. ANIMAL CLAIMS
1892—. 2 volumes.
Record of claims filed for compensation for animals killed or injured by dogs, showing date claim filed, name of claimant, township, number of animals killed or injured, amount allowed by trustees, amount allowed by commissioners, names of witnesses, date paid, and order number. Chronological by dates of filing. No index. Handwritten on printed forms. Average 175 pages. 18 x 12 x 1.5. 1 volume, 1892-1930, Auditor's record room E; 1 volume, 1931—, Auditor's office room 1.

Vouchers and Warrants

382. EMERGENCY POOR RELIEF VOUCHERS
1934—. 299 file boxes. (labeled by contained voucher numbers).
Cancelled vouchers issued to indigents in the county, showing to whom issued, address, kind of assistance, voucher number, and amount of order. Numerical by voucher numbers. No index. Handwritten and typed on printed forms. 12 x 18 x 26. 298 file boxes, 1934-1939, Auditor's record room E; 1 file box, 1940—, Auditor's office room 1.

383. BLIND RELIEF VOUCHERS

1913—. 1 file box.

Cancelled vouchers for payment of blind relief, showing name and address of client, amount of payment, voucher number, date, remarks, and signature of commissioner in charge permitting payment. Arranged chronologically by dates of vouchers. No index. Handwritten and typed on printed forms. 12 x 15.5 x 25.5. Auditor's office room 1.

384. JOURNAL OF WARRANTS ISSUED

1904—. 18 volumes (1-18).

Journal of warrants issued on county treasurer, showing purpose of warrant, name of payee, warrant number, amount of warrant, and date of issue. Arranged chronologically by dates of issues. Indexed alphabetically by names of payees. Handwritten on printed forms. Average 500 pages. 18 x 12 x 3. 12 volumes, 1904-1936, Auditor's record room E; 6 volumes, 1937—, Auditor's office room 1.

385. RECORD OF [Court] WARRANTS ISSUED

1904—. 11 volumes (1-11).

Auditor's record of warrants issued for jury and witness fees, showing date issued, name of payee, warrant number for common pleas, petit jury, grand jury, witnesses, and witnesses in criminal cases; probate court jury, criminal witnesses, and witnesses in lunacy and epilepsy cases; also for witnesses in minor courts, and coroner's witnesses and jurors. Arranged chronologically by dates of issue. No index. Handwritten on printed forms. Average 500 pages. 20 x 16 x 3. 9 volumes, 1904-1935, Auditor's record room E; 2 volumes, 1936—, Auditor's office room 3.

386. AUDITOR'S RECORD OF POOR RELIEF WARRANTS ISSUED

1935—. 1 volume (1).

Auditor's record of poor relief warrants issued by county commissioners, showing date of warrant, name of person or firm to whom warrant issued, for what purpose, number of warrant, and from what fund payable (emergency poor relief fund or selective sales tax fund). Arranged chronologically by dates warrants issued. No index. Handwritten on printed forms. 500 pages. 18 x 12 x 2.5. Auditor's office room 3.

387. WARRANTS REDEEMED [General]
1904——. 3 cartons, 1file box.
Auditor's cancelled warrants on county treasurer, showing warrant number, date of warrant, name of payee, for what, from want fund, amount, and date cancelled. Arranged chronologically by dates cancelled. No index. Handwritten on printed forms. Cartons, 12 x 18 x 25; file box, 11 x 13 x 26. 3 cartons 1904-1938, Auditor's record room E; 1 file box, 1939——, Auditor's office room 1.

388. COURT WARRANTS REDEEMED
1904——. 4 cartons, 1 file box.
Cancelled warrants issued in payment of witnesses and juror fees in common pleas, probate, minor courts, and coroner's inquests, showing date issued, date redeemed, name of payee, kind of case, amount, and warrant number. Arranged chronologically by dates redeemed. No index. Handwritten on printed forms. Cartons, 12 x 13 x 16; file box, 11 x 13 x 26. 4 cartons, 1904-1938, Auditor's record room E; 1 file box, 1939——, Auditor's office room 1.

Licenses

389. DOG AND KENNEL REGISTER
1918——. 3 volumes, 10 file boxes. (dated).
Record of dog tags and kennel register, showing name of owner or harborer, address, number of dogs, description of dog, tag numbers, date issued, amount of fee, and dates and numbers of duplicate tags issued. Volumes and 7 file boxes, 1918——, arranged alphabetically by names of owners and chronologically thereunder by dates of licenses; 3 file boxes, 1937——, arranged numerically by license numbers. No index. Handwritten on printed forms. Volumes average 400 pages. 14 x 12 x 2.5; file box, 12 x 5 x 24. 3 volumes, 4 file boxes, 1918-1937, Auditor's record room E; 6 file boxes, 1937——, Auditor's dog license bureau.

390. COSMETIC LICENSES
1933——. 1 volume. Discontinued; law repealed.
Copies of cosmetic licenses issued to cosmetic vendors, showing name of vendor, place of business, license number, date issued, date effective, and amount of fee. Arranged chronologically by dates of issue. No index. Handwritten on printed forms. 500 pages. 15 x 9 x 2.5. Auditor's record room E.

391. CIGARETTE LICENSES
1933—. 5 volumes. (dated).

Copies of licenses issued to cigarette vendors, showing name and address of licensee, place of business, license number, amount of fee, and date of issue. Arranged chronologically by dates of issue. No index. Typed on printed forms. Average 1500 pages. 15 x 9 x 7. Auditor's vault.

392. PEDDLER'S LICENSES [Stubs]
1929—. 23 volumes.

Stubs of licenses issued to peddlers, showing name and address of vendor, date issued, and license number. Arranged chronologically by dates of issue. No index. Handwritten on printed forms. Average 100 pages. 15 x 6 x 1. 15 volumes, 1929-1934, Auditor's record room E; 8 volumes, 1935—, Vendor's license room.

393. VENDORS' LICENSES
1935—. 87 volumes. (labeled by contained license number).

Applications for vendors' licenses, showing date of application, name of vendor, license number, business and residence address, number of stores operating, kind of business, and date issued. Arranged numerically by license numbers. No index. Handwritten on printed forms. Average 500 pages. 11 x 8.5 x 3.5. Vendor's license room.

Enumerations and Statistics

394. ENUMERATION RETURNS
1923—. 2 file boxes.

Reports of school enumerators as returned to county auditor of all youths between the ages of 6 and 21 years, showing date of enumeration, name of township, city or village, name and address of youth, sex, age, date and place of birth, names of parents or guardians, address, name and address of school attending, grade in school, and if handicapped, shows the nature of the affliction, and how instructed or date of admission to an institution. Arranged alphabetically by names of townships, cities, or villages and chronologically thereunder by years of enumeration. No index. Typed on printed forms. 10 x 5 x 13.5. Auditor's office room 1.

395. REPORTS OF BOARD OF EDUCATION
1914—. 8 file boxes.

Annual reports of township, village, and district boards of education to county auditor, showing date of report, name of school district, number of subdistricts, school buildings, and school rooms; value of school property, number of teachers, average monthly wage of teachers, number of weeks in school year, number of pupils in district, number of boys, number of girls, average monthly enrollment, and average daily attendance. Arranged chronologically by dates of reports. No index. Handwritten on printed forms. 4 x 5.5 x 11. 6 file boxes, 1914-1938, Auditor's record room E; 2 file boxes, 1939—, Auditor's office room 3.

Bonds

396. FUNDING INDEBTEDNESS
1929—. 1 volume.

Copies of resolutions of the county commissioners to provide for funding the indebtedness, showing date of resolution, title or subject of the resolution, total amount of funded and unfunded debt, and total amount of indebtedness. Handwritten on printed forms. 250 pages. 15 x 15 x 2. Auditor's office room 3.

397. BOND RECORD
1908—. 7 volumes. (1-7).

Record of bonds authorized and issued by county commissioners for highways, county buildings, poor relief, road improvements, and refunding purposes, showing for what purpose issued, names of county commissioners and auditor authorizing same, amount of bond, date issued, bond numbers, date and number of bonds sold, name of purchaser, denomination, rate of interest, date of maturity, record of redemption, and amount of interest payments. Arranged chronologically by dates of issue of bonds. No index. Handwritten on printed forms. Average 250 pages. 14 x 9.5 x 2.5. Auditor's office room 2.

398. BONDS AND COUPONS
1936—. 22 file boxes.

Original bonds for retirement fund, road improvement, and poor relief, showing date of issue, rate of interest, date of maturity, bond number, full amount of bond, date of authorization, and signature of county commissioners and auditor.

Arranged chronologically by dates of issues and numerically by bond numbers. No index. Handwritten on printed forms. 10.5 x 5 x 18. Auditor's office room 2.

Weights and Measures

399. WEIGHTS AND MEASURES
1929—. 1 file box.

Copies of annual reports of deputy sealer of weights and measures to the county auditor, showing date of report, name and address of sealer, amount of his salary, summary of tests made, record of articles reweighed and measured, and in case of prosecution, shows name of defendant, amount of fine, and date paid. Arranged chronologically by years. No index. Handwritten on printed forms. 12 x 12 x 24. Auditor's office room 1.

Miscellaneous

400. APPOINTMENTS [Deputies]
1913—. 4 file drawers.

Copies of certificates of appointments as deputies to the various offices, showing name of appointee, date of appointment, office to which appointed, date appointment is effective, oath of appointee, and signature of appointee and clerk of courts. Arranged chronologically by dates of appointments. No index. Typed on printed forms. 3 x 9 x 18. Auditor's office room 1.

The office of county treasurer was established by an act of the Northwest Territory in 1792 and continued by the state of Ohio.[1] Although the constitution of 1802 made no provision for the office of county treasurer, it was created by the legislative act of 1803.[2] The treasurer, appointed by the associate judges in 1803 and by the county commissioners in 1804, was required to take an oath and give bond for the faithful performance of the duties of his office, and was subject to removal by the appointing power.[3] The treasurer remained and appointive official until 1827 when the office became an elective one by popular vote in the county.[4] Although it did not specifically create the office, the constitution of 1851 stated that no person should hold the office of treasurer for more than four years in any six. This provision was repealed in 1933 by an amendment authorizing any county to adopt a charter form of government.[5] Interpreting the constitutional provision, the legislature fixed the term of office at two years in 1859.[6] The term of office continued at two years until 1936 when it was extended to four years.[7] Until 1906 the county treasurer received his remuneration from fees; since that date his salary has been determined by law according to the population of the county.[8] In 1939 the Montgomery County treasurer's salary was $5,790.[9]

The duties of the treasurer were defined by statute in the earlier period and specified in detail by the acts of 1827 and 1831 repealing previous acts. The provisions of the latter act, although subject to amendment and repeal, furnished the basis for subsequent legislation and laid the foundation for the present duties of the treasurer, which do not differ greatly from those prescribed by the earlier statutes.

In 1803 the treasurer was given his present duty at giving public notice of the tax duplicate. On receiving from the county auditor a duplicate of the taxes assessed upon the property of the county, the treasurer prepares and post notices in three places in each township including the place in which elections are held; and

---

1. Pease, *op. cit.,* 68-69.
2. *Laws of Ohio,* I, 97.
3. *Ibid.,* I, 97-98; II, 145.
4. *Ibid.,* XXV, 25-32.
5. *Ohio Const. 1851,* Art, X, sec. 3 (Amendment, 1933).
6. *Laws of Ohio,* LVI, 105.
7. *Ibid.,* CXVI, pt. ii, 184.
8. *Ibid.,* XCVIII, 89.
9. Ohio Auditor of State, *Annual Report, 1939,* 368.

inserts the notice for six consecutive weeks in the newspaper having the largest circulation in the county.[10] He receives money and payment of taxes levied for the county, for the state, and for other purposes, and gives the payer a receipt.[11] In the earlier years of the office the treasurer was required to give announcement of the time he would be in the respective townships of the county and in his office at the seat of justice to receive tax collections. Since 1858 the treasurer has been authorized to receive the semiannual payment of taxes or assessments levied upon real estate or upon delinquent real estate taxes or assessments.[12] Moreover, since 1908, the commissioners have been authorized to extend the time for paying taxes for not more than 30 days after the time fixed by law.[13]

After each semiannual collection of taxes, the treasurer is required to report to the auditor showing the amount of taxes received in each taxing district in the county since the last settlement. Since 1904 the semiannual settlements have been made under the heads of liquor, cigarette, inheritance, delinquent personal, road, and general taxes. The treasurer keeps his account in books which enable him to compile such reports.[14]

After the taxes are collected and immediately after each settlement with the county auditor, the county treasurer, upon the presentation of the proper warrant from the auditor, pays to the township treasurer, city or village treasurer, the treasurer of the school district, or treasurer of any "legally constituted board authorized by law to receive the funds or proceeds of any special tax levy," or other officer delegated with authority to receive such funds, all money in the treasury belonging to such boards and subdivisions.[15] In addition, after the treasurer has made each settlement with the county auditor, he is required to pay to the state treasurer, on warrant from the state auditor, "the full amount of all sums" found by the latter to belong to the state.[16]

10. *Laws of Ohio*, I, 98; XXIX, 291; LII, 124.
11. G. C. sec. 2650; *Laws of Ohio*, XXIX, 292; LXXVI, 70; LXXXV, 237.
12. *Laws of Ohio*, LV, 62; LVI, 101.
13. *Ibid.*, XCIX, 435; CXIV, 730; CXV, pt. ii, 226.
14. G. C. sec. 2643; *Laws of Ohio*, XXIX, 296; XCVII, 458.
15. G. C. sec. 2689; *Laws of Ohio*, LVI, 101.
16. *Laws of Ohio*, LVI, 101; CXIV, 732.

Another function of the county treasurer, which had its inception in the earlier years of the office, is the collection of delinquent taxes. It was and is his duty to assess a penalty on the tax duplicate for nonpayment of taxes–which penalty when collected, is paid to the treasurer's fund. If the treasurer is unable to collect the delinquent taxes, he is authorized to apply to the clerk of court of common pleas who serves notice to show cause why such taxes were not paid. The court may enter a rule against the delinquent taxpayer for the payment and cost and enforce it by attachment.[17]

During the last decade provision has been made for the installment payment of delinquent taxes without interest or penalty. In 1931 it was provided that delinquent taxes, assessments, and penalties charged on the tax duplicate against any entry of real estate might be paid in installments during five consecutive semiannual taxpaying periods, "whether such real estate had been certified as delinquent or not."[18] The Wittemore act, passed as an emergency measure in 1933, provided for the collection in installments, without interest or penalty, of delinquent real estate assessments. Anyone electing to pay such delinquent real property taxes and assessments in installments pursuant to this act may, at any installment period, pay the entire unpaid balance, in which event no interest shall be charged or collected on the amount so paid. In 1934 the benefits of the act were extended to include delinquent personal and classified taxes.[19] With slight alterations the law was re-enacted in 1935 and again in 1936.[20] An act was passed in 1937 providing for the settlement of taxes delinquent prior to 1936 without interest or penalty, in one payment or in ten annual installments. Similar laws were enacted in 1938 and 1939; the latter act is still in effect.[21]

The county treasurer has charge of the funds collected by taxes, and also of other funds belonging to the county. Although earlier acts made provision for storage vaults in the county treasury for county deposits, the commissioners have been authorized, since 1894, to receive sealed bids for the deposit of county funds; and the banks or trust companies offering the highest rate of interest are selected as the county depositories.[22]

---

17. G. C. sec. 2660; *Laws of Ohio,* LVI, 175; XCIX, 435.
18. G. C. sec. 2672; *Laws of Ohio,* CXIV, 827.
19. *Laws of Ohio,* CXV, 161-164; CXV, pt. ii, 230, 332.
20. *Ibid.,* 199, 468; CXVI, pt. ii, 14-21.
21. *Ibid.,* CXVII, 32, 832.
22. *Ibid.,* XCI, 403; CII, 59; CXV, pt. ii, 215.

The treasurer is required to keep an account concurrent with the county auditor–a practice which originated in 1831. Each day the treasurer makes a statement to the county auditor for the previous day's business showing the amount of taxes received on auditor's drafts, the amount received from other sources, together with the amount of money deposited in the depository, the total amount paid out by check and by cash, and the balance in the treasury.[23]

The treasurer, as well as the sheriff, prosecuting attorney, and clerk of courts, have been required since 1850 to report annually to the county commissioners.[24] Since 1874 the county auditor and county commissioners have been required to make a thorough examination of all books, vouchers, accounts, moneys, bonds, securities, and other property in the treasury at least every six months.[25] Besides being under the supervision of the county commissioners and county auditor, the treasurer is subject to the supervision of state auditor. In 1902 an act was passed providing for a uniform system of accounting and auditing for all public offices in the state, under the direction of a bureau of inspection in the office of the state auditor and for the annual examination of the finances of all public offices.[26]

The treasurer is a member of the budget commission, the county board of revision, and serves as trustee of the sinking fund.[27] Since the early days of the office the treasurer has been the official custodian of the bonds furnished to the state by the county auditor, county commissioners, and other officials. Since 1869 he has been required to record and preserve a record of the deputies appointed and removed by the county auditor[28] but such record was not found in Montgomery County treasurer's office.

Like other county officials, the treasurer is required at the expiration of his term to turn over to his successor all books, papers, moneys, and records appertaining to his office.[29]

----

23. G. C. sec. 2642; *Laws of Ohio,* XCVII, 457.
24. G. C. sec. 2504.
25. G. C. sec. 2699; R. S. 1129; *Laws of Ohio,* LXII, 137.
26. G. C. sec. 2641; *Laws of Ohio,* CXIV, 728; XCV, 511-515.
27 G. C. secs. 5625-19, 2976-18, 5580. See also pp. 196, 197, 202.
28. G. C. sec. 2563; *Laws of Ohio,* LXVI, 35.
29. G. C. sec. 2639.

Real Property

401. COUNTY TAX LIST, TREASURER'S REAL AND PERSONAL PROPERTY
1920—. 868 volumes. (dated). Subtitled by names of taxing districts.

Treasurer's tax list, showing name and address of property owner, lot number, description and location of property, amount of tax due, penalty, and date and amount paid; also includes record of personal property assessments. Arranged alphabetically by names of taxing districts and alphabetically thereunder by names of property owners. No index. Handwritten on printed forms. Average 50 pages. 24 x 18 x 1. 827 volumes, 1920-1931, Auditor's record room E; 41 volumes, 1932—, Treasurer's office.

402. TURNPIKE DUPLICATE
1871-1874. 2 volumes.

Record of road contracts, estimates, and levies on property affected to meet cost of improvement, showing name of township, amount due on contract, date due, name of property owner, description and location of property, and estimated amount of assessment. Arranged alphabetically by names of townships and alphabetically thereunder by names of property owners. No index. Handwritten. 300 pages. 24 x 12 x 3. Auditor's record room E.

403. SPECIAL ASSESSMENTS DUPLICATE
1921-1928. 14 volumes. (labeling varies). One subtitled Shakertown.

Record of special assessments for public improvements showing name of property owner, location and description of property, kind of improvement, name of improvement, value, amount of assessment, and date paid. Arranged alphabetically by names of property owners. No index. Handwritten. Average 250 pages. 20 x 12 x 2. Auditor's record room E.

404. CONSERVANCY TAX DUPLICATE
1935—. 32 volumes.

Record of property in Miami Conservancy District, showing location in block, rural or urban, value, name of property owner, amount of current and delinquent taxes due, and date of payment. Arranged alphabetically by names of property owners.

No index. Typed. Average 150 pages. 18 x 12 x .75. Treasurer's office.

Personal Property

405. TREASURER'S LIST OF TANGIBLE PERSONAL PROPERTY
1932—. 6 volumes. (dated).

Record of tangible personal property taxes, showing assessment certificate number, name of taxing district, name of property owner, address, final assessment, total tax for the year, amount of advanced pavement, and amount of tax due. Arranged alphabetically by names of taxing districts and alphabetically thereunder by names of property owners. No index. Handwritten on printed forms. Average 500 pages. 22 x 14 x 3. Treasurer's office.

406. TREASURER'S LIST OF INTANGIBLE PERSONAL PROPERTY
1932—. 6 volumes. (dated).

Record of intangible personal property taxes, showing assessment certificate number, name of taxing district, name and address of property owner, amounts of productive and non-productive investments, deposits, credits, money, and other taxable and intangibles, amount of advance payment, and amount due. Arranged alphabetically by names of taxing districts and alphabetically thereunder by names of property owners. No index. Handwritten on printed forms. Average 500 pages. 22 x 14 x 3. Treasurer's office.

407. GENERAL TAX DUPLICATE
1932—. 5 volumes.

Record of tangible personal tax assessments, showing name of taxing district, name and address of property owner, list of taxable property, total tax, amount of advance payment, and balance due. Arranged alphabetically by names of taxing districts and alphabetically thereunder by names of property owners. No index. Typed on printed forms. Average 250 pages. 18 x 12 x 2. Treasurer's office.

408. CLASSIFIED TAX DUPLICATE
1932—. 5 volumes.

Record of intangible, classified, personal tax assessments, showing name of taxing district, name and address of property owner, list of taxable property, amount of tax, amount of advanced payment, and balance due. Arranged alphabetically by names of taxing districts and alphabetically thereunder by names of property owners.

No index. Typed on printed forms. Average 250 pages. 18 x 12 x 2. Treasurer's office.

Adjustments

409. ADDITIONS BY TAX INQUISITOR
1892-1900. 2 volumes.

Record of additional assessments of property listed on tax duplicates, showing name of property owner, name of taxing district, value, amount of added assessment, and date addition filed. Arranged chronologically by dates of filing. Indexed alphabetically by names of property owners. Handwritten. Average 75 pages. 24 x 16 x .25. Treasurer's office.

410. DIRECT HOUSING RELIEF ABSTRACT
1934—. 3 volumes. (1-3).

Record of remittance on current real property taxes of property owners housing relief tenants, showing name and address of property owner, date and amount of warrant for tax remit, description and location of property, name of indigent tenant, and date remit filed. Arranged chronologically by dates of filing. Indexed alphabetically by names of property owners. Handwritten. Average 200 pages. 26 x 12 x 2. Treasurer's office.

Delinquent

411. TREASURER'S DELINQUENT REAL ESTATE TAX DUPLICATE
1918—. 702 volumes. (dated).

Record of delinquent real estate taxes, showing name of property owner, description and location of property, appraised value, amount of regular tax delinquent, special assessments, penalties, and total amount due. Arranged alphabetically by names of property owners. No index. Handwritten and typed. Average 150 pages. 16 x 14 x 1. 624 volumes, 1918-1934, Auditor's record room E; 78 volumes, 1935—, Treasurer's office.

412. AUGUST SETTLEMENT
1930—. 26 volumes. (dated).

Record of treasurer's returns to the auditor of delinquent property taxes, showing receipt number, amounts of current, miscellaneous current, and special taxes, date of return, amount delinquent, penalty, and total delinquent. Arranged numerically by receipt numbers. Handwritten on printed forms. Average 2000 pages. 15 x 18 x 2. 22 volumes, 1930-1935, Auditor's room E; 4 volumes, 1936—, Treasurer's office.

413. TRIENNIAL LAND TAX
1934—. 6 volumes. Subtitled by names of townships.
Record of taxpayers delinquent three years or more, showing name and address of property owner, description and location of property, name of township, dates and amounts delinquent, and penalties. Arranged alphabetically by names of townships and alphabetically thereunder by names of property owners. No index. Handwritten and typed. Average 700 pages. 18 x 15 x 5. Treasurer's office.

414. PERSONAL PROPERTY LIST
1875-1882. 5 volumes.
Record of delinquent personal property taxes, showing year, name and address of property owner, description and location of property, valuation, and amount due. Arranged chronologically by years and alphabetically thereunder by names of property owners. No index. Handwritten on printed forms. Average 200 pages. 18 x 14 x 1. Treasurer's office.

415. DUPLICATE OF DELINQUENT PERSONAL PROPERTY
1904—. 8 volumes.
Duplicate of personal property taxes unpaid in August settlement, showing name of property owner, year, valuation, penalty, total, dates and amounts of payments, and 1932—, amount of general and classified personal taxes. Arranged chronologically by years and alphabetically thereunder by names of property owners. No index. Handwritten on printed forms. Average 200 pages. 18 x 12 x 1.5. Treasurer's office.

Inheritance (See also entry 422)

416. INHERITANCE TAX CHARGE
1919—. 9 volumes.
Record of inheritance tax charges, showing name of taxing district, name of decedent, amount of tax as fixed by the probate court and auditor, name of executor, administrator, or trustee, date of accrual, discount, interest, total amount paid, date,

name of payer, and remarks. Arranged alphabetically by names of decedents. No index. Handwritten on printed forms. Average 375 pages. 12 x 15 x 3. Treasurer's office.

Excise

417. LIQUOR TRAFFIC TAX
1887-1917. 3 volumes. (dated).
Treasurer's liquor tax duplicate, showing name of dealer, location by city, village, township, street and number, name of owner of real estate, description of real estate, date commencing business, amount of assessment, amount due June 20, amount to be accounted for after June settlement, date payment made, and names of successors in same location. Arranged alphabetically by names of dealers. No index. Handwritten on printed forms. Average 60 pages. 16 x 14 x 1. Treasurer's office.

418. CIGARETTE TRAFFIC
1913—. 25 volumes. (dated).
Treasurer's duplicate of assessments in cigarette traffic, showing treasurer's receipt number, name of person engaged in traffic, description of premise whereon the assessment is a lien, name of owner of the premise, effective date of assessment, date of assessment, amount of assessment, amount added by certificate, certificate number, total amount, and date paid. Arranged chronologically by dates of assessments. No index. Handwritten on printed forms. Average 50 pages. 18 x 11 x 1. Treasurer's office.

419. SALES TAX AND INVENTORY
1935—. 10 bundles, 1 volume (1).
Daily inventory of sale tax stamps, showing dates, number on hand, number and denomination of stamps received, and total; also record of sales tax stamps, showing date, name of vendor, license number, number of denomination of stamps sold, total amount of sale, amount of vendors discount, and total collected. Arranged chronologically by dates of entries. No index. Handwritten on printed forms. Bundles, 12 x 16 x 24; volumes, 530 pages 14 x 12 x 3. 10 bundles, 1935-1937, Auditor's record room E; 1 volume, 1937—, Treasurer's office.

Collections

420. TREASURER'S TAX BLOTTER
1914-1922. 16 volumes. (dated, 1-16).
Record of daily tax collections, showing date collected, tax receipt number, amount, and total amount of daily collection. Arranged chronologically by dates of collections. No index. Handwritten on printed forms. Average 400 pages. 16 x 9.5 x 1.5. Auditor's record room E.

421. RECEIPT STUBS
1923—. 702 file boxes. (dated).
Treasurer's receipt stubs for taxes paid, showing date paid, receipt number, amount of payment, and kind of tax. Arranged numerically by receipt numbers. No index. Typed on printed forms. 3 x 8 x 12. 624 file boxes, 1923-1934, Auditor's record room E; 78 file boxers, 1935—. Treasurer's office.

422. TAX RECEIPTS FILE
1933—. 8 file boxes.
Receipt stubs for inheritance taxes paid, showing receipt number, date of payment, amount of tax, name of the estate, and name of payer. Arranged numerically by receipt numbers. No index. Handwritten on printed forms. 4 x 8 x 18. Treasurer's office.

423. CONSERVANCY COLLECTION BLOTTER REGISTER
1934—. 2 volumes.
Record of conservancy taxes collected daily, showing name of taxpayer, date of payment, amount collected, amount banked, and balance on hand at end of each business day. Arranged chronologically by dates of receipts. No index. Handwritten on printed forms. 250 pages. 18 x 12 x 2. Treasurer's office.

424. DAILY CONSERVANCY CASH BOOK
1917—. 1 volume.
Record of daily cash collections, showing name of taxpayer, amount collected, date, and record of refunds. Arranged chronologically by dates of receipts. No index. Handwritten. 200 pages. 18 x 10 x 2. Treasurer's office.

425. RETAINER
1903-1911. 1 volume (1). Discontinued.

Record of taxes collected through court action for road construction, showing names of litigants, location of property, case number, and date and amount paid. Arranged numerically by case numbers. No index. Handwritten. 300 pages. 11 x 10 x 2. Auditor's record room E.

426. PARTIAL PAYMENT RECORD
1934—. 7 file boxes. (1-7).

Record of accounts of property owners paying taxes on the installment plan, showing name of property owner, description and location of property, name of taxing district, lot number, total amount of taxes, date and amount of each payment, receipt number, and balance due. Arranged numerically by receipt numbers. No index. Handwritten on printed forms. 5.5 x 4 x 12. Treasurer's office.

Financial Records
(See also entries 420-426)

427. DAILY CASH BOOK
1860—. 21 volumes (1-21).

Daily cash record of receipts and disbursements, showing balance forward, date of receipt, pay-in orders, amounts of current tangible and intangible personal tax, general tax, delinquencies, licenses, and special taxes; also amounts checked from depository, total receipts, and balance. Disbursements include general and court warrants, showing date of warrant, warrant number, amount, total to depository, total disbursements, record of refunds, total debts, total credits, and balance forward. Arranged chronologically by dates of entries. No index. Handwritten on printed forms. Average 450 pages. 13.5 x 11.5 x 2. Volumes, 1860-1937, Auditor's record room E; 10 volumes, 1938—, Treasurer's office.

428. JOURNAL OF RECEIPTS INTO COUNTY TREASURY
1904—. 10 volumes. (1-10).

Record of daily receipts into the treasury, showing date, source, pay-in order number, amount, and fund classification. Arranged chronologically by dates of entries. No index. Handwritten. Average 250 pages. 24 x 18 x 2. 7 volumes, 1904-1936. Auditor's record room E; 3 volumes, 1937—, Treasurer's office.

429. DAILY CASH BALANCE RECORD
1935—. 3 volumes. (26-28). Prior records missing.
Cashier's daily cash balance record, showing date of receipt, source, and amount; expenditures, showing date and amount; also total debits, credits, and balance. Arranged chronologically by dates of entries. No index. Handwritten on printed forms. Average 200 pages. 12 x 8 x 2. Treasurer's office.

430. COLLECTION REGISTER–FORM 7
1902, 1913-1923—. 7 volumes. (5 numbered; 1, 2).
Ledger account of daily receipts of cash, showing date, source, amount, and receipt number. Arranged chronologically by dates of receipts. No index. Handwritten. Average 250 pages. 18 x 12 x 3. 4 volumes, 1902-1923, Auditor's record room E; 3 volumes, 1933—, Treasurer's office.

431. INHERITANCE TAX PAY IN ORDERS
1921—. 10 volumes (labeled by contained pay-in order numbers).
Stubs of orders issued by the auditor to the treasurer for acceptance of inheritance tax payments, showing pay-in order number, date of order, amount, auditor's charge number, case number, name of taxing district, name of payer, name of estate, and net amount paid. Arranged numerically by pay-in order numbers. No index. Handwritten on printed forms. Average 500 pages. 8.5 x 3.5 x 1.5. Treasurer's office.

432. WARRANTS REDEEMED
1913—. 13 volumes (5-17). Prior records missing.
Record of warrants redeemed, showing date of warrant, name of payee, name of fund, purpose for which issued, amount, warrant number, and date redeemed. Arranged chronologically by dates redeemed. No index. Handwritten. Average 500 pages. 18 x 12 x 3. Treasurer's office.

433. COURT WARRANTS REDEEMED
1904—. 14 volumes. (1-14).
Record of court warrants redeemed, showing date of warrant, name of payee, name of court, purpose for which issued, amount, warrant number, and date redeemed. Arranged chronologically by dates redeemed. No index. Average 500 pages. 18 x 12 x 3. 12 volumes, 1904-1928, Auditor's record room E; 2 volumes, 1929—, Treasurer's office.

434. EMERGENCY POOR RELIEF RECORD JOURNAL

1936—. 2 volumes. (1, 2).

Journal of poor relief warrants redeemed, showing date issued, name of payee, purpose for which issues, amount, warrant number, and date redeemed. Arranged chronologically by dates redeemed. No index. Handwritten. Average 200 pages. 16 x 12 x 1.5. Treasurer's office.

435. GENERAL FUND

1926—. 181 file boxes. (labeled by contained voucher numbers and dated).

Canceled vouchers with purchase orders attached: vouchers show date, voucher number, name of payee, and amount; purchase orders show date, by whom purchased, source of supply, itemized list of purchases, names of county commissioners authorizing payment, and date voucher issued. Arranged numerically by voucher numbers. No index. Handwritten on printed forms. 15 x 15 x 25.5. 60 file boxes, 1926-1934, Auditor's record room E; 121 file boxes, 1935—, Treasurer's office.

436. UNCLAIMED COST RECORD

1908-1917. 11 volumes.

Treasurer's record of unclaimed witness fees and court cases, showing case number, amount of fee, to whom due, name of court, and if subsequently paid. Arranged numerically by case numbers. No index. Handwritten. Average 75 pages. 14 x 8 x .5. Auditor's record room E.

Bonds

437. BOND RECORD

1897—. 2 volumes. (1, 2).

Record of official bonds of county and township officers, showing name of official or deputy, office to which elected, date bond filed, amount of bond, and names of sureties to bond. Arranged chronologically by dates of filing. Indexed alphabetically by names of officials or deputies. Handwritten. Average 350 pages. 18 x 10 x 4. 1 volume, 1897-1913, Auditor's record room E; 1 volume, 1914—, Treasurer's office.

438. BONDS

1895—. 150 bonds in 3 bundles.

Original bonds of all county officials except treasurer, showing date of bond, name of official, name of office, names of sureties to bond, amount of bond, and date filed. Arranged chronologically by dates of filing. No index. Handwritten and typed on printed forms. 8 x 6 x 4. Treasurer's office.

Miscellaneous

439. DEPOSITORY BIDS

1900—. 3 file boxes.

Original bids submitted by banking institutions for deposits of county funds, showing name of bank, date submitted, term of agreement, and date bid filed. Arranged chronologically by dates of filing. No index. Typed on printed forms. 3 x 8 x 12. Treasurer's office.

A budget commission was established in Montgomery County in 1911 under the provisions of the act of that year which authorized the establishment in each county of a budget commission to be composed of the county auditor, the mayor of the largest municipality, and the prosecuting attorney.[1] In 1915 the county treasurer replaced the mayor as a member of the commission.[2] It was not until after the World War, when county expenditures steadily increased, that the importance of improved methods of finance were forcibly brought to the attention of the legislature. This need was met in 1923 by enlarging the powers minutely prescribing the duties of the budget commission. As in 1915 the county auditor, county treasurer, and county prosecuting attorney were made ex-officio members of the commission.[3] Under the present law, passed in 1927, the commission, consisting as before of the county auditor, the county treasurer, and the county prosecuting attorney, receives and examines the annual budgets of the county, municipal, township, and school authorities, with an estimate of the amount to be raised for state purposes in each subdivision.[4] If the total amount exceeds the sum authorized to be raised, the commission adjusts the amount to be raised and may change and revise the estimates. The commission may reduce all items in the budget, but is prohibited from increasing the total of any budget or any item.

The adjusted budget is certified to the taxing authority in each subdivision. If the work of the commission is satisfactory, each taxing authority by ordinance or resolution authorizes the necessary tax levies and certifies them to the county auditor. On the other hand, the taxing authority in any subdivision may appeal, through its fiscal officer, from the decision of the budget commission to the state tax commission of Ohio, which is empowered to adjust the estimate of revenues and balances in fixing the tax rates.[5]

The county auditor, as secretary to the commission, is required to keep a full and accurate record of the proceedings of the commission.[6]

---

1. *Laws of Ohio*, CII, 271.

2. *Ibid.*, CVI, 180.

3. *Ibid.*, CX, 459. Under the provisions of this act elective commissioners might be substituted for the ex-officio members, at the option of the electors of the county.

4. *Laws of Ohio*, CXII, 399.

5. G. C. secs. 5625-25, 5625-28.

6. G. C. sec. 5625-19.

440. BUDGET COMMISSION

August 1927—. 2 volumes. (1 unlabeled; 1 dated).

Minutes of the budget commissioners, showing date of meeting, names of members present, action on resolutions and motions, and record of all business transacted. Arranged chronologically by dates of meetings. No index. 1927-1935, handwritten; 1935—, typed. Average 150 pages. 15 x 12 x 1.5. Auditor's office room 3.

The county board of revision, the object of which was to correct some of the defects and inequalities of tax assessments, was established by the legislature in 1825. The first board of revision, or equalization as it was sometimes called, was composed of the county commissioners, the county auditor, and the assessor. The board was authorized to meet at the seat of justice on the first Monday in June annually "to hear and determine the complaint of any owner of property listed and valued by the assessor . . . and shall correct any list or evaluation made by the assessor, either by adding two or deducting from the evaluation."[1] The act of 1831, repealing the act of 1825, left the duties and personnel of the board unchanged.[2]

In 1859 the legislature made provision for two county boards of equalization. One board, composed of the county auditor and the county commissioners, was directed to meet annually for the purpose of equalizing real and personal property, and moneys and credits in the county. The other board, composed of the county auditor, the county surveyor, and the county commissioners, was authorized to meet sexennially for the same purpose.[3]

The act of 1863, amending the act of 1859, left the personnel and duties of the annual county board unchanged. The second county board, although continuing without alterations in composition of or duty, was directed to meet decennially, rather than sexennially.[4] The legislative act of 1868, amending the act of 1863, left the membership of the annual and special boards, as well as their duties, practically unchanged.[5]

The annual and special boards of equalization were abolished, when, in 1913, the tax commission of Ohio was given the task of supervising the assessment of real and personal property in the state.[6] Under this arrangement each county constituted a district. In each district containing less than 60, 000 inhabitants there was to be appointed by the governor one state tax commissioner. In all other districts, which included Montgomery County, they were appointed in the same matter, two state deputy tax commissioners. In each district there was appointed a district board of complaints.

---

1. *Laws of Ohio*, XXIII, 64.
2. *Ibid.,* XXIX, 278.
3. *Ibid.,* LVI, 193-194.
4. *Ibid.,* LX, 57, 59.
5. *Ibid.,* LXV, 168-170.
6. See also pp. 31-32.

This board, appointed by the state tax commission with the consent of the governor, took over the duties and powers formerly vested in the boards of equalization. The county auditor, made secretary to the board of complaints, was required to be present at each meeting in person or by deputy, and keep an accurate record of their proceedings in a book kept for that purpose.[7] Moreover, the board was directed to take full minutes of all evidence given before it and might have such evidence taken in shorthand and extended into typewritten form. The auditor was required to preserve in his office separate records of all minutes and documentary evidence offered in each complaint.[8]

This arrangement, after being in operation for two years, was abrogated by the legislature in 1915. In that year the county auditor, under the supervision of the tax commission of Ohio, became the chief assessing officer in the county. The county treasurer, the county prosecuting attorney, the probate judge, and the president of the county commissioners were to serve as a board for the purpose of appointing three members to constitute a board of revision. Again the county auditor was made secretary of the board and was directed to keep a record of their proceedings and to preserve in his office a separate record of all minutes and documentary evidence offered in each complaint.[9]

Under the present system, inaugurated in 1917, the county treasurer, the county auditor, and the president of the county commissioners constitute a board of revision. This board organizes annually on the second Monday in June by electing a chairman for the ensuing year. The county auditor serves as secretary to the board.[10] The county board of revision may, with the consent and approval of the tax commission of Ohio, employ experts, and other employees.[11]

The duties of the board, not differing in detail from those prescribed in 1825, include the hearing of all complaints relating to valuation or assessments of both real and personal property as it appears upon the tax duplicate of the "then current year." The board is authorized to investigate all complaints and may increase or decrease any valuation or correct any assessment complained of, or may order a reassessment by the original assessing official.[12]

---

7. *Laws of Ohio,* XXIII, 64.
8. *Laws of Ohio,* CIII, 794.
9. *Ibid.,* CVI, 254-258.
10. G. C. sec. 5580.
11. G. C. sec. 5587.
12. G. C. sec. 5597.

However, no valuation is increased without giving notice to the person in whose name the property affected is listed.[13] The board of revision, in all respects, is governed by the laws relating to the valuation of real property and makes no change of any valuation "except in accordance with such laws."[14]

On the second Monday in June, annually, the county auditor lays before the board of revision the statements and returns of assessments of any personal property for the current year, and the board proceeds to review the returns. On the first Monday in July, annually, the auditor lays before the board the returns of assessments of any real property for the current year. The board of revision reviews the assessments and certifies its action to the county auditor, who corrects the tax list and duplicate according to the additions and deductions ordered by the board. The auditor is prohibited by statute from making up his tax list and duplicate, until the board has completed its work and has submitted to him all returns laid before it with revisions.[15] But in the event the tax duplicate has been delivered to the county treasurer, the auditor is required to certify such corrections to him and enter such corrections in his tax duplicate.[16]

In its investigations the board may examine, under oath, persons as to their or others' real property. In the event witnesses fail to appear or refuse to testify, the board through its chairman is authorized to make a complaint in writing to the probate judge, who, by statue, is directed to institute proceedings against them.[17] The decisions of the board are subject to appeal to the state tax commission of Ohio, within thirty days after a decision is served.[18]

The secretary of the board is required to keep "an accurate record of the proceedings of the board in a book to be kept for that purpose."[19] The county auditor, as in 1913, is required to preserve in his office separate records of all minutes and documentary evidence offered in each complaint.[20] The record of the board are open to the inspection of the public.[21]

---

13. G. C. sec. 5599.
14. G. C. sec. 5596.
15. G. C. sec. 5605.
16. G. C. sec. 5602.
17. G. C. sec. 5596.
18. G. C. sec. 5610.
19. G. C. sec. 5592.
20. G. C. sec. 5603.
21. G. C. sec. 5591.

441. MINUTES [Board of Revision]

1892—. 15 volumes. 5 subtitled city of Dayton. Title varies: Settlements, County Board of Equalization, 1892-1904, 4 volumes; Journal, County Board of Revision, 1903-1908, 5 volumes; Expenses and Business, 1909-1935, 5 volumes.

Minutes of the county board of equalization, 1892-1912, district board of complaints, 1913-1914, and the board of revision, 1915—, showing date of meeting, names of members present, record of all business transacted, and for adjustments made, shows the name and address of the property owner, location and description of property, and amount added or deducted; also includes 1909-1935, a record of expenses, showing date of entry, amount of the expense, and purpose. Arranged chronologically by dates of meetings or entries. No index. Handwritten. Average 300 pages. 18 x 12 x 2. 14 volumes, 1892-1934, Auditor's record room E; 1 volume, 1935—, Auditor's office room 3.

442. PERSONAL MERCHANDISE, BOARD OF REVIEW

1909-1911. 1 volume. Discontinued.

Record of complaints on personal property assessments coming before the board of review, showing kind and location of property, name of owner, value, amount of assessment, date of complaint, and findings of the board. Arranged chronologically by dates of complaints. No index. Handwritten. 375 pages. 18 x 12 x 2. Auditor's record room E.

443. REAL ESTATE COMPLAINT

1903-1909. 1 volume. Discontinued.

Record of complaints on ownership, exorbitant appraisements, and faulty surveys, showing name of owner, location and description of property, date of complaint, value and remarks. Arranged chronologically by dates of complaints. No index. Handwritten. 250 pages. 18 x 16 x 2. Auditor's record room E.

The board of trustees of the sinking fund, composed of the prosecuting attorney, auditor, and treasurer, was organized in 1919 in Montgomery County and in each county owing a bonded debt. The county prosecuting attorney serves as president of the board and the auditor as secretary. It is the duty of the trustees to provide for the payment of all bonds issued by the county and the interest maturing their on.[1]

From 1919 all bonds issued by the county were required to be recorded in the office of the trustees of the sinking fund, and to bear a stamp containing the words "Recorded in the office of the sinking fund trustees" and be signed by the secretary before they became valid in the hands of the purchaser. In 1921 the act was amended to allow such recording and authenticating to be performed by the county treasurer and in 1935 such provisions were abrogated by the legislature.[2]

On or before the first Monday in May of each year, the trustees certify to the county commissioners the rate of tax necessary to provide a sinking fund both for the payment and maturity of bonds heretofore issued by the county and for the payment of interest on the bonded indebtedness. The amount certified by the trustees is set forth without diminution in the annual budget of the commissioners.[3] Then, after each semiannual statement of taxes and assessments, the county auditor reports to the trustees the amount of money in the treasury of the county charged to the credit of the sinking fund. Money is drawn from the county treasury for investment or disbursements by the issuance of a voucher signed by all the members of the board and directed to the county auditor. The trustees are directed, by statute, to invest all moneys subject to their control in United States bonds, Ohio bonds, or bonds of a municipal corporation, school district, township, or county in the state.

The board members are required to keep "a full and complete record of their transactions, a complete record of the funded debt of the county specifying the dates, purposes, amounts, numbers, maturities, and rates of maturities of interest and installments thereof, and were payable, and an account exhibiting the amount held in the sinking fund for the payment thereof."[4]

---

1. G. C. secs. 2976-18, 2976-19; Commissioners' Journal, volume 26 [1919], p. 1, see entry 1.
2. *Laws of Ohio,* CIX, 16; CXVI, 442.
3. G. C. sec. 2976-26.
4. G. C. sec. 2976-24.

The meetings of the trustees are open to the public. All questions relating to the purchase or sale of securities or the payment of bonds or interest are decided by a yea and nay vote, which is recorded in their journal.[5]

---

5. G. C. sec. 2976-22.

444. SINKING FUND JOURNAL
1919—. 1 volume.

Minutes of sinking fund trustees showing date of meeting, record of all business transacted, bonds issued or sold, bond numbers of each issue, maturity date of each issue, and interest coupon due dates. Arranged chronologically by dates of meetings. No index. Typed. 300 pages. 15 x 10 x 2. Auditor's office room 3.

(State Deputy Supervisors of Elections)

The responsibility for supervising and conducting elections in the county is delegated to state deputy supervisors of elections - the county board of elections. This board, created by the legislature in 1891 and consisting of four qualified voters in the county, is appointed for a four-year term by the secretary of state, who, by virtue of his office, is the chief election official of the state.[1] On the first day of March in the even numbered years, the secretary of the state appoints two board members, one of whom is from the political party which polled the highest number of votes in the state for the office of governor at the last preceding state election, and the other from the political party which polled the next highest vote at such election.[2] The board members may be removed by the secretary of state for the neglect of duty, malfeasance, misfeasance in office, or willful violation of the election laws, or for other good and sufficient causes.[3] The compensation of the members is determined on the basis of population of the county and is paid by the county.[4] Similarly the expenses of the county board are paid from the county treasury, "in pursuance of appreciation by the county commissioners," in the same matter as other expenses are paid.[5]

The persons so appointed by the secretary, meeting five days after their appointment, select one of their members as chairman and a resident elector of the county who is not a member of the board as clerk.[6] The board is vested with authority to establish, define, and provide election precincts; fix places of registration; provide for the purchase, preservation, and maintenance of voting booths, ballot boxes, books, maps, flags, blanks, cards of instruction, and other equipment used in registration; and to issue rules, regulations, and instructions not inconsistent with the law or contrary to the rules and regulations as established by the chief election official.[7]

---

1. *Laws of Ohio*, LXXXVIII, 449.
2. G. C. sec. 4785-8. For the method of appointment when the term of each of the four members of the board expires on the same date see G. C. sec. 4785-8a.
3. G. C. sec. 4785-11.
4. G. C. sec. 4785-18.
5. G. C. sec. 4785-20.
6. G. C. sec. 4785-10.
7. G. C. sec. 4785-13.

Besides providing places of voting and equipment, the board is authorized to appoint clerks and other officers of elections. On or before the first day of September before each November election the board by a majority vote is authorized, after careful examination and investigation as to their qualifications, to appoint for each precinct six "competent persons, four as judges and two as clerks, who shall constitute the election officers of such precinct." Not more than two of the judges and one of the clerks, states the law, "shall be members of the same political party." Precinct election officers, appointed for a one-year term, may be removed by the board for neglect of duty, malfeasance, or misconduct in office.[8]

The county board of elections is authorized to receive and examine nominating petitions and to certify their sufficiency and validity. They receive the election returns, canvas the returns, then make abstracts therefrom and transmit them to the proper authorities. They issue certificates of elections on forms prescribed by the secretary of state and report annually to the same official on forms prescribed by him, the number of voters registered, elections held, votes cast, appropriations received, expenditures made, and such other information as the secretary of state may require. Moreover, the board prepares and submits to the proper authorities a budget estimating the cost of elections for the ensuing year.[9]

Finally the board is empowered to investigate irregularities, nonperformance of duty, or violation of election laws by election officials. For the purpose of conducting investigations they may administer oaths, issue subpoenas, summon witnesses, and compel the presentation of books, papers, and records in connection with any investigation and report the facts to the prosecuting attorney.[10]

The secretary of state, in 1930, ruled that the members of the various boards of elections were to be considered as state officers. This ruling had reference to appointments made under section 4785-8a of the General Code.[11]

The clerk of the board is required to keep a record of the proceedings of the board and all moneys received and expended, and to file and preserve in his office all records of the board. Poll lists and tally sheets are to be preserved for two years; ballots for thirty days.

---

8. G. C. sec. 4785-25.
9. G. C. sec. 4785-13.
10. G. C. sec. 4785-13.
11. See George C. Trautwein, ed., *Supplement to Page's Annotated General Code 1926-1935* (Cincinnati, 1935), note on p. 688.

These records are open to the inspection of the public under regulations established by the board.[12]

---

12. G. C. secs. 4785-14, 4785-147.

Minutes

445. MINUTES
1911—. 2 volumes.

Minutes of county board of elections (deputy state supervisors of elections), showing date of meeting, names of members present, and full account of all business transacted. Arranged chronologically by dates of meetings. No index. Typed. Average 500 pages. 16.5 x 12.5 x 3.5. Board of elections office.

Registrations and Votes

446. POLL BOOKS AND TALLY SHEETS, CITY OF DAYTON
1936—. 232 volumes. (dated). Subtitled by voting districts.

Poll books of general elections, showing date of election, name and address of voter, voting district; also poll books of primary elections, showing date of election, name and address of voter, voting district, and name of political party affiliation. Tally sheets, show date of election, total number of votes for each candidate and issue in each voting district and a summary of votes cast. Poll books arranged by voting districts and alphabetically thereunder by names of voters; tally sheets arranged by offices and issues in order of importance. No index. Handwritten on printed forms. Average 36 pages. 17 x 10 x .25. Board of elections office.

447. REGISTER OF ABSENT VOTERS
1936—. 8 volumes. Prior records legally destroyed.

Record of voters absent from city and county desiring to cast vote by mail, showing name of voter, permanent and temporary address, sex, age, ward, precinct, date application mailed, date returned, and date of election. Arranged chronologically by dates returned. No index. Handwritten. Average 100 pages. 14.5 x 9 x .75. Board of elections office.

448. ABSTRACT OF ELECTIONS
1909—. 3 volumes.

Copies of condensed reports of elections as forwarded to the secretary of state by the judges of the elections, showing names of candidates, name of votes for and against each candidate, question, and issue, and date of election report. Arranged chronologically by dates of reports. No index. Handwritten on printed forms. Average 800 pages. 23 x 18 x 4. Board of elections office.

Financial Records

449. APPROPRIATION LEDGER
1904—. 3 volumes.

Record of appropriations for election expenses, showing date of appropriation, and amount of appropriation; also includes a record of expenditures, showing date of expenditure, name of payee, amount, and purpose of expenditure, as salaries, printing, traveling expenses, and sundries. Arranged chronologically by dates of entries. No index. Handwritten on printed forms. Average 150 pages. 15 x 12 x 1. Board of elections office.

450. CASH BOOK
1930—. 1 volume.

Record of fees paid by candidates for election, showing name of candidate, date of fee, office desired, annual salary upon which the filing fee is computed, amount of fee, and date paid. Arranged chronologically by dates of payments. No index. Handwritten on printed forms. 200 pages. 16.5 x 12 x 1.5. Board of elections office.

451. EXPENSE REPORTS AND RECORDS OF FILING FOR CANDIDACY
1934—. 33 file boxes.

Expense reports of candidates for office, showing date of election, name of candidate, name of office, and itemized list of expenditures; also includes record of fees for candidacy, showing name of candidate, office desired, salary of office sought, amount of fee, and date filed. Arranged chronologically by dates of filing. No index. Handwritten on printed forms. 10.5 x 5 x 12. Board of elections office.

The county board of education, a modern administrative and supervisory agency developed during the last two decades, supplanted the smaller educational units, which, established during the early period of Ohio history, became inefficient and unable to meet the modern requirements as demanded by real communities.

During the earlier period of Ohio history, educational administration, because of the newness of the state, the sparseness of the population, and the undeveloped means of transportation was, by necessity, local in character. For fourteen years after the accession of Ohio to statehood, though the constitution stated that means of education should be encouraged by the general assembly no legislation was enacted for public schools.[1] It was not until 1817 that the legislature authorized six or more people to form associations to build schoolhouses and to be incorporated for educational purposes.[2]

The first permanent law for the organization of schools in Ohio was passed in 1821. Under the provisions of this act, the electors of the township were authorized to vote on the proposition of dividing the townships into school districts. If the proposal carried, there were to be elected three school commissioners, who, in turn, were authorized to select a clerk and a collector who should act as a treasurer. They were instructed also, to levy taxes for the support of schools and to hire teachers.[3]

As education began to advance in the early years of the nineteenth century, some kind of state control was needed. Accordingly, in 1837, the office of state superintendent of schools was established.[4] A year later an act was passed making the county auditor ex-officio county superintendent of the schools; and in each township the clerk became superintendent of the smaller unit. The county superintendent was made responsible to the state superintendent in all educational affairs. In the same year each incorporated city, town, or borough not regulated by a charter was made a separate school district. The voters in each division were authorized to elect three directors.[5]

---

1. *Ohio Const. 1802,* Art. VIII, secs. 3, 25, 27.
2. *Laws of Ohio,* XV, 107.
3. *Ibid.,* XIX, 52.
4. *Ibid.,* XXXV, 82.
5. *Ibid.,* XXXVI, 81.

The effectiveness of this organization, however, was destroyed in 1840, when the legislature abolished the office of state superintendent and the secretary of state took over his functions of tabulating and transmitting school statistics.[6]

Seven years later, twenty-five counties exclusive of Montgomery were allowed to have county superintendents,[7] and in 1848 the provisions of the previous act were extended to Montgomery and all other counties in the state.[8]

Although marked changes were made in the curricula of the schools, the history of education in Ohio from 1850 to the early part of the twentieth century was largely one of the gradual transference of power from districts to townships, and from townships to county in the interest of a better system of education. It was not, however, until within the last three decades that the county became the unit for educational administration.[9]

The county board of education was authorized to change school district lines; afford transportation for children living more than two miles from a schoolhouse; appoint a county superintendent; and certify annually to the county auditor the number of teachers and superintendents employed, their salaries, and the amount apportioned to each school district for the payment of the salaries of the county and district superintendents. The county superintendent, acting as secretary of the board, was required to keep in a book provided for that purpose a full record of the proceedings of the board properly indexed. Each motion, together with the name of the person making it and the vote thereon, was to be entered on the record.[11]

The county was divided into administrative divisions containing one or more village or rural school districts. Each district was to be under the supervision of a district superintendent, who was required to visit the school in his charge, direct and assist teachers in the performance of their duties, and classify and control promotions of pupils. Moreover, he was required to report annually to the county superintendent on matters under his charge, and assemble teachers for the purpose of referring on curricular matters, discipline, and school management.[12]

---

6. *Ibid.,* XXXVIII, 130.
7. *Laws of Ohio,* XLV, 32.
8. *Ibid.,* XLVI, 86.
9. *Ibid.,* LXX, 195, 242; XCVII, 354.
10. *Ibid.,* CIV, 133.
11 *Ibid.,* CIV, 133; CVIII, pt. i. 704.
12. *Ibid.,* CIV, 133-145.

Significant changes were made by the act of 1921, under which the board members became elective by popular vote. They were authorized to appoint one or more assistant county superintendents for a term of three years. There is an assistant superintendent in Montgomery County. The board was authorized to publish, with the advice and consent of the county superintendent, a minimum course of study to serve as a guide to local board members. The same act abolished the office of district superintendent.[13]

The county organization has placed the rural schools on a plane of equality with the city schools. The consolidation of the smaller units has eliminated small, ill-equipped schools, and provides under one roof facilities and instructions suited to the needs of the rural children under the supervision of educational specialists.

---

13. G. C. secs. 4728-1, 4729; *Laws of Ohio,* CIX, 242.

452. MINUTES, BOARD OF EDUCATION
1914—. 10 volumes. (dated).

Minutes of county board of education, showing date of meeting, names of members present, full account of proceedings, and record of aye and nay votes of each member. Arranged chronologically by dates of meetings. No index. Handwritten and typed. Average 100 pages. 11 x 8.5 x 1. Board of education office.

453. CERTIFICATIONS
1914—. 2 file boxes.

Record of teachers' certificates, showing name of teacher, name of district, date certificate issued, certificate number, names of subjects teaching, number of years attended school, degrees held, and number of years of teaching experience. Arranged alphabetically by names of teachers. No index. Handwritten on printed forms. 4 x 5.5 x 11. Board of education office.

454. ATTENDANCE RECORD
1914—. 4 file boxes.

Teachers' monthly reports to county superintendent on attendance, showing name of pupil, and number of days absent, and present; also record of children leaving school, showing name of child, grade, and reason for withdrawal; also record of pupils absent from school, showing name of pupil, school district, and reason for absence. Arranged alphabetically by names of pupils. No index. Handwritten on printed forms. 4 x 5 x 11. Board of education office.

455. SCHOOL ENUMERATION
1914——. 2 file boxes.

Enumeration of youths in county, showing year, name and address of youth, sex, and names of parents or guardians. Arranged chronologically by years and alphabetically thereunder by names youths. No index. Handwritten on printed forms. 4 x 5 x 11. Board of education office.

456. WORK PERMITS
1914——. 4 file boxes.

Record of work permits issued to undergraduates, showing date of permit, name of student, address, age, scholastic rating, physical condition, and reason for discontinuing education. Arranged alphabetically by names of students. No index. Handwritten on printed forms. 4 x 6 x 18. Board of education office.

The general health district, or county health department, is one of the recent developments in county health administration. An act of the legislature in 1919 provided that townships and municipalities in each county, exclusive of any city with 25,000 or more population, to constitute a general health district; cities with 25,000 or more population a municipal health district; municipalities of not less than 10,000 nor more than 25,000 population, and maintaining a board of health meeting the qualifications of the legislative act, were authorized after examination by the state health department to continue operation as separate health districts.[1]

An amendment in December 1919 made each city a health district; the township and villages in each county were combined into a general health district; and a city and general health district might combine for administrative purposes.[2] The mayor of each municipality not constituting a city health district, and the chairman of the trustees of each township, are authorized to meet at the seat of justice and by selecting a chairman and a secretary organize a district advisory council which selects and appoints a district board of health compose the five members, one of whom must be a physician, who serves without compensation.[3]

Within thirty days after their appointment the members of the district board of health–the county board of health–organized by appointing one of their members president and another president *pro tempor*. The board is authorized to appoint a district health commissioner a licensed physician who serves as secretary to the board. This official is designated deputy state registrar of vital statistics and is required to report monthly to the state registrar of vital statistics.[4]

On recommendations of the district health commissioner the board appointments a full-time public health nurse, a clerk, and such additional public health nurses, physicians, and others as may be necessary for the proper conduct of its work. The board studies the prevalence of diseases, especially communicable diseases, provides treatment for venereal diseases, and is authorized to make any and all regulations it deems necessary for the prevention or restriction of disease, and the prevention, abolition, or suppression of nuances. It provides for inspection of public charitable, benevolent, correctional, and penal institutions; and may provide inspection of dairies, stores, restaurants, hotels, and other places where food is manufactured, handled, stored, sold, or offered for sale.

---

1. *Laws of Ohio,* CVIII, pt. i, 238.
2. *Ibid.,* CVIII, pt. ii, 1085.
3. *Ibid.,* CVIII, pt. ii, 1085.
4. G. C. sec. 1261-32; *Laws of Ohio,* CVIII, pt. i, 238-242.

The board is authorized to carry on necessary laboratory test by establishing a laboratory or contracting with existing laboratories, and all state institutions supported in whole or in part by public funds must furnish such laboratory service to a county board of health under the terms agreed upon.[5]

The health department is financed by public taxation. The district board of health annually estimates in itemized form the amount needed for the fiscal year, and these estimates are certified to the county auditor and submitted by him to the county budget commissioner who may reduce any item but cannot increase any item or the aggregate of all items. The total amount fixed by the budget commissioners is apportioned by the county health department on the basis of taxable valuations in the townships and municipalities composing the district.[6]

---

5. *Laws of Ohio,* CVIII, pt. ii, 1088, 1089.
6. *Ibid.,* CVIII, pt. ii, 1091.

Minutes

457. MINUTES, DISTRICT BOARD OF HEALTH
1920—. 3 volumes.

Minutes of board of health, showing date of meeting, names of members present, and record of business transactions. Arranged chronologically by dates of meetings. No index. Handwritten and typed. Average 150 pages. 11 x 9 x 1. Board of health office, Cooper Building, Dayton.

Case Records

458. DAILY REPORT OF NURSES AND SANITARY OFFICER
1920—. 4 file boxes.

Daily reports of visiting county nurses, showing name of nurse, name of township, name and address of patient, and detailed report; also reports of inspectors. Arranged alphabetically by names of townships and alphabetically thereunder by names of patients. No index. Handwritten on printed forms. 14.5 x 9 x 15. Board of health office, Cooper Building, Dayton.

459. CRIPPLED CHILDREN

1922—. 1 file drawer.

Records of children in county with physical defects, showing name of child, age, sex, name of parents, family history, nature of affliction, cause and nature of treatment. Arranged alphabetically by names of children. No index. Typed on printed forms. 14.5 x 9 x 15. Board of health office, Cooper Building, Dayton.

460. SCHOOL REPORTS

1926—. 1 file drawer. (labeled by contained letters of alphabet)

Card record of physical condition of all school children in the county with the exception of the city of Dayton, showing name of school district, physical rating as determined by regular examinations of each child by school nurse from preschool age to graduation, name of child, age, date of examination, and nurses findings and recommendations. Arranged alphabetically by names of school districts and alphabetically thereunder by names of children. No index. Typed on printed forms. 14.5 x 9 x 15. Board of health office, Cooper Building, Dayton.

Immunizations

461. SCHICK [Tests]

1936—. 1 file drawer.

Report on Schick test made for susceptibility to diphtheria, name of township, name of patient, date of test, and result; also includes consents of parents or guardians to immunizations to diphtheria. Arranged alphabetically by names of townships and alphabetically thereunder by names of patients. No index. Typed on printed forms. 14.5 x 9 x 15. Board of health office, Cooper Building, Dayton.

Contagious Diseases

462. [Contagious] DISEASES

1936—. 1 file drawer.

Record of contagious and reportable diseases treated in the county, showing name of disease, date reported, name of patient, name of doctor, length of quarantine, and remarks. Arranged alphabetically by names of patients. No index. Typed on printed forms. 14.5 x 9 x 15. Board of health office, Cooper Building, Dayton.

463. CLUBS, INSTITUTIONS, AND MUNICIPAL SEWAGE [Reports]
1937—. 1 file drawer.

Reports on sanitary conditions of clubs and institutions in county and sewage systems in Dayton and villages, showing name of club, institution, or sewer inspected, location, investigations and test, date of report, findings, and recommendations for improvements. Arranged alphabetically by names of clubs, institutions, and cities or villages. No index. Typed. 14.5 x 9 x 15. Board of health office, Cooper Building, Dayton.

464. SCHOOLS [Inspections]
1937—. 1 file drawer.

Reports of health conditions as found in all county schools, showing name of school, condition of sewage disposal, water, lighting, and cleanliness, name of principal in charge, and recommendations for changes. Arranged alphabetically by names of schools. No index. Typed. 14.5 x 9 x 15. Board of health office, Cooper Building, Dayton.

465. SANITARY REPORTS
1932—. 1 file drawer.

Record of investigations made pertaining to sanitary conditions of county, showing kind of complaint, name of complainant, date filed, date investigated, findings, and recommendations or improvements made; also includes a report of persons bitten by dogs in county, with statement of facts concerning extent of injury and findings of investigating officer as to cause and condition of dog involved and test made to ascertain whether animal was infected. Arranged chronologically by dates of filing. No index. Handwritten and typed. 14.5 x 9 x 15. Board of health office, Cooper Building, Dayton.

466. WATER REPORTS
1936—. 1 file drawer.

Reports of analysis of water taken from various sources in county, showing source, name of person requesting analysis, result of test, date of report, and remarks. Arranged alphabetically by names of persons requesting analysis. No index. Typed on printed forms. 14.5 x 9 x 15. Board of health office, Cooper Building, Dayton.

467. MISCELLANEOUS
1920—. 1 file drawer.

Miscellaneous papers including inspection reports of dairies, analysis of water from private wells, and sanitary inspections, showing date of inspection, subject covered, and date filed; also includes copies of contract with the city of Miamisburg to look after health conditions, showing date of contract, names of principles, terms, and date filed. Arranged chronologically by dates of filing. No index. Typed on printed forms. 4 x 10 x 24. Board of health office, Cooper Building, Dayton.

468. REPORTS AND PERMITS
1922—. 1 file drawer.

Record of inspections of dairies for permits to sell milk at wholesale and retail in county, showing date of permit, name of dealer, terms of permit, and date filed. Arranged alphabetically by names of dealers and chronologically thereunder by dates of filing. No index. Typed on printed forms. 14.5 x 9 x 15. Board of health office, Cooper Building, Dayton.

Vital Statistics

469. BIRTH RECORD
1920—. 1 file drawer,

Copies of birth certificates, showing the name of township, name of infant, date of birth, sex, color or race, birthplace, mother's maiden name, name of father, and name of attending physician or midwife. Arranged alphabetically by names of townships and alphabetically thereunder by names of infants. No index. Handwritten and typed on printed forms. 14.5 x 9 x 15. Board of health office, Cooper Building, Dayton.

470. DEATH CERTIFICATE
1920—. 1 file drawer.

Copies of death certificates, showing name of township, name of descendant, sex, color, residence, date and place of birth, occupation, date and cause of death, and name of physician or mortician reporting same. Arranged alphabetically by names of townships and alphabetically thereunder by names of decedents. No index. Handwritten on printed forms. 14.5 x 9 x 15. Board of health office, Cooper Building, Dayton.

471. MISCELLANEOUS FILE
1920——. 4 file boxes.
Copies of monthly and annual reports of activities of the county board of health to the state board of health, showing date of report, statistics on births and deaths, health statistics, and itemized financial accounts. Arranged chronologically by dates of reports. No index. Handwritten and typed. 11.5 x 3 x 12. Board of health office, Cooper Building, Dayton.

472. MISCELLANEOUS FILE [Correspondence]
1920——. 28 letter files.
Copies of correspondence relative to activities of the county board of health, showing date, name of correspondents, and text of letter. Arranged alphabetically by subjects. No index. Handwritten and typed. 11.5 x 3 x 12. Board of health office, Cooper Building, Dayton.

The Stillwater Sanatorium, also known as District Tuberculosis Hospital, was found July 14, 1909 under terms of an act of March 12, 1909.[1] The county commissioners of Montgomery and Preble Counties met in Dayton and formed a joint-county board for the purpose of establishing and maintaining a district hospital for the care and treatment of persons suffering from tuberculosis.[2] On the date of organization the joint board purchased the Brookside Sanatorium which was soon inadequate to meet the needs and on June 10, 1912 a site was ordered purchased for a new hospital[3] but it was not used for this purpose and was sold by the commissioners November 20, 1915.[4] New grounds were purchased April 5, 1916,[5] and operation were begun for the erection of a permanent hospital. The new buildings were occupied April 15, 1918 and a dedication held June 22, 1918, at which time the hospital was filled to capacity and the need for additional beds were apparent. In the spring of 1920, a contract was let for a third hospital which was completed in the fall of 1922. Additional facilities again became essential and in January 1938, a one-hundred-bed edition was built. This edition is entirely modern and of fireproof construction.[6]

The hospital is governed by the board of trustees, one member for each county represented. They are elected annually by the joint board which is composed of the county commissioners of both counties. Additional officers are the medical superintendent who is in charge of all medical matters and the maintenance superintendent who is in charge of administrative affairs and nursing service. A dentist is included on the staff, and visiting consultants are available. By an agreement with the Miami Valley Hospital, its interns in residence are given a term of service at the sanitarian.

The patients of the two counties are admitted without respect to color, race, or creed. One building is dedicated entirely to the use of children, and there is a school maintained for them which is financed from school funds as provided by section 7644 of the General Code. This law was drafted and passed through the efforts of the officers of the Stillwater Sanatorium.

---

1. *Laws of Ohio,* C, 87.
2. Commissioners' Journal, volume 19 (1909), p. 227.
3. *Ibid.,* volume 21 [1912], p. 21.
4. *Ibid.,* volume 22 [1915], p. 337.
5. *Ibid.,* volume 23 [1916], p. 30.
6. *Ibid.,* volume 44 [1938], p. 60.

Close co-operation is maintained with other agencies. Funds for support of the hospital are secured from taxation of the two counties and from private sources. The hospital was organized principally for indigent patients and usually no charge is made for services. A financial investigation is made before admittance and small fees are collected from those able to pay.[7]

---

7. Council of social agencies, *Social Service Directory for Dayton and Montgomery County* (Dayton, March 1938), III, 68.

Admissions and Registers

473. PRELIMINARY REPORTS OF ADMISSION
1919—. 415 volumes.
Record of patients admitted to the institution. Stubs, showing name of patient and date of admission; detachable cards which are sent to State Medical Board show case number, name of patient, sex, color, date of birth, marital status, date of admission, legal residence, and name and address of attending physician. Arranged chronologically by dates of admission. No index. Handwritten on printed forms. Average 100 pages. 8.5 x 3.5 x .5. 430 volumes, 1919-1938, Hospital basement vault, 20 volumes, 1939—, Hospital office, Covington Pike, Dayton.

474. ALPHABETICAL BOOK
1908—. 1 volume.
Index record of patients treated in hospital, showing name and address of patient, case number, condensed case history, and length of time and hospital. Serves as an index to Admission Cards, entry 475, Record of Patients, entry 477, Census Cards [Nurses Reports], entry 478, X-rays, entry 479, Case Data [Examinations], entry 480, Discharge record, entry 483, and Financial Record, entry 487, by showing case number. Arranged alphabetically by names of patients. Handwritten. 200 pages. 14 x 10 x 1. Hospital office, Covington Pike, Dayton.

475. ADMISSION CARDS
1919—. 1 file box.
Card record of condensed information regarding admission of patient, showing case number, X-ray number, name and address of patient, date of admission, name and address of physician, result of treatment, and if discharged, show date of discharge

and condition of discharge. Arranged numerically by case numbers. For index, see entry 474. Handwritten and typed on printed forms. 4.25 x 6 x 11.5. Hospital office, Covington Pike, Dayton.

476. EMERGENCY ADDRESS
1919—. 2 file boxes

Card record of emergency addresses, showing name of patient receiving treatment, case number, and names and addresses of persons to be notified in case of emergency. Arranged alphabetically by names of patients. No index. Handwritten and typed. 4.5 x 6 x 11.5. Hospital office, Covington Pike, Dayton.

Case Records
(See also entry 487)

477. RECORD OF PATIENTS
1909—. 3 volumes.

Record of patients admitted to hospital, showing case number, date of admission, name of county, name and address of patient, age, religion, social conditions, birthplace, occupation, diagnosis at admission, and complications. When discharged, also shows date of discharge, reason, and diagnosis on discharge. Arranged numerically by case numbers. For index, see entry 474. Handwritten and typed on printed forms. Average 150 pages. 12 x 9 x 1.5. 2 volumes, 1909-1936. Hospital basement vault, 1 volume, 1937—, Hospital office, Covington Pike, Dayton.

478. CENSUS CARDS [Nurses' Reports]
1932—. 1 file box.

Nurses' card record of patients treated in hospital, showing name and address of patient, case number, and nature of treatment. This record used in compiling annual report. Arranged numerically by case numbers. For index, see entry 474. Handwritten and typed. 4.5 x 6 x 11.5. Hospital office, Covington Pike, Dayton.

479. X-RAYS
1920—. 6 file drawers.

Shadow prints of congested areas of patients suffering from tuberculosis, showing name of patient, case number, date admitted to hospital, date of X-ray, and X-ray number. X-rays taken by examining physician or nurse in charge. Arranged numerically by case numbers. For index, see entry 474. X-rays, 17 x 14 and unmounted; file drawer, 15 x 18 x 28. Hospital office, Covington Pike, Dayton.

480. CASE DATA [Examinations]
1908—. 3086 envelopes in 10 file drawers. (labeled by contained case numbers).
Case records of patients treated in hospital, including sputum examination, urine analysis, weight charts, nurses' clinical charts, case history, and X-ray findings. All papers of each case are filed together in a separate envelope, showing name of patient and case number. Arranged numerically by case numbers. For index, see entry 474. Handwritten and typed on printed forms. Envelopes, 12 x 9; File drawers 1939—, Hospital office, Covington Pike, Dayton.

481. NARCOTIC RECORD BOOK
1939—. 1 volume. Records destroyed every two years.
Record of narcotics dispensed in institutions for the treatment of tuberculosis and its kindred ailments, showing name of patient, kind of narcotic, amount given and date. Arranged chronologically by dates of treatments. No index. Handwritten. 200 pages. 15 x 6 x 1. Hospital office, Covington Pike, Dayton.

482. NIGHT ORDERS
1939—. 1 volume. Record destroyed every two years.
Record of treatment and special attention recommended by physician, head nurse, or nurse in charge of night force, showing name of patient, date of order, and text of same. Arranged chronologically by dates of orders. No index. Handwritten. 200 pages. 12 x 7 x 1. Hospital office, Covington Pike, Dayton.

483. DISCHARGE RECORD
1917—. 10 bundles.
Record of patients discharged from hospital, showing name of patient, case number, case history, progress of case, and destination on discharge. Arranged numerically by case numbers. For index, see entry 474. Handwritten and typed on printed forms. 4 x 8 x 11. Hospital office, Covington Pike, Dayton.

Statistics

484. STATE REPORTS
1915—. 500 volumes.

Stub record of reports sent to state commissioner of health regarding treatment for tuberculosis. Stub shows date of report, name and address of patient, and remarks. Detachable card shows date of report, name of disease, probable date of onset, age, name and address of patient, directions for finding address, name and address of parents, and signature of person making report. Arranged chronologically by dates of reports. No index. Handwritten on printed forms. Average 50 pages. 8.25 x 5.25 x .5. 450 volumes, 1915-1938, Hospital basement vault; 50 volumes, 1939—, Hospital office, Covington Pike, Dayton.

485. ANNUAL REPORTS
1919—. 1 volume.

Triplicate copies of annual reports covering movements of patients in the institution for the year, showing number of admissions and dismissals, date of report, stages of disease by percentage of all patients treated, different types of disease with figures of previous years inserted for comparison, number of cures, number of deaths, and period covered by reports. Arranged chronologically by dates of reports. No index. Typed on printed forms. 200 pages. 14 x 10 x 1. Hospital office, Covington Pike, Dayton.

486. SEWAGE REPORTS
1923—. 1 file box.

Copies of monthly reports sent to the state department of health, showing day by day report on condition of sewage disposal plant at hospital, record of sewage flow, weather, condition of tanks, sludge beds, filters, settleable solids, dissolved oxygen, disinfection, and remarks. Arranged chronologically by dates of reports. No index. Handwritten and typed on printed forms. 14 x 15 x 25. Hospital office, Covington Pike, Dayton.

Financial Records

487. FINANCIAL RECORD
1919—. 1 file box.
Patient financial records and account card, showing card number, name and address of person responsible for payment, case number, name and address of patient, occupation, age, name of county, whether free or pay patient, date of admission, time in hospital, date of discharge or death, and amounts of debits and credits. Arranged numerically by case numbers. For index, see entry 474. Handwritten and typed on printed forms. 6 x 9 x 15. Hospital office, Covington Pike, Dayton.

488. FOOD AND DRUG
1929—. 2 file boxes. One subtitled General.
Record of cost for food and drugs used in hospital, showing date of purchase, name of food or drug, amount purchased, and cost; also a record of general purchases made for the hospital, showing whether food, clothing, drugs, linen, equipment, or miscellaneous, from whom purchased, and cost. Arranged alphabetically by names of items. No index. Handwritten. 4.5 x 6 x 11.5. Hospital office, Covington Pike, Dayton.

489. INVOICES
1919—. 5 file boxes.
Invoices for supplies used in hospital, showing name of vendor, date of purchase, and amount; also voucher authorizing payment and cancelled check for same. Arranged alphabetically by names of vendors. No index. Handwritten and typed. 14 x 15 x 25. 4 file boxes, 1919-1938, Hospital basement vault; 1 file box, 1919—, Hospital office, Covington Pike, Dayton.

Personnel

490. PERSONNEL CARDS
1919—. 1 file box.
Record of employees of the hospital, showing name and address of employee, duties performed, length of service, and remarks. Arranged alphabetically by names of employees. No index. Handwritten. 4.5 x 6 x 11.5. Hospital office, Covington Pike, Dayton.

In December 1825 the county commissioners appointed a committee of representative citizens to purchase a site for the Montgomery County Home[1] as provided for by the legislature in 1816.[2] In April 1826 the committee recommended the purchase of 160 acres in the northeast corner of Jefferson Township at a cost of $9 per acre, including lands and buildings.[3] The institution opened with seven inmates. Since that time, additional land has been purchased until the present site, located at 601 Infirmary Road, now contains 244 acres. New buildings have been erected, including the administration building in 1908, and additions and wings have been added as needed.[4]

By the provision of the legislative act of 1816, the county commissioners were authorized to build a "poor house," and to appoint annually seven persons to constitute a board of directors. This board, a corporate body, was authorized to make such rules and regulations as were necessary for the management of the institution, and to appoint a superintendent. This officer was directed to receive only persons who had the required order from the township trustees. He was directed to keep a book listing the name and age of every person received, together with the date of admission.[5] The board of directors, or a committee of that board, was required to visit the "poor house" monthly to examine the condition of the paupers and to make a report on such matters as the food, clothing, and treatment of the inmates. Moreover, they were required to inspect the books and accounts of the superintendent. Annually the board was required to report to the county commissioners the "state of the institution" with a full and correct account of all their proceedings, contracts, and disbursements; and the expenses of establishing and supporting the institution were to be paid on the order of the county commissioners out of the money and a treasury not otherwise appropriated.[6]

By the legislative act of 1831, the membership of the board was reduced to three. This board, like its predecessor, was authorized to appoint a superintendent.

---

1. Road and Commissioners' Record, volume B [1823-1840], p. 28.
2. *Laws of Ohio,* XIV, 447.
3. Road and Commissioners' Record, volume B [1823-1840]. p. 32.
4. Commissioners' Journal, volume 18 [1908], p. 387; volume 8 [1885], p. 168; volume 10 [1893], p. 283; volume 22 [1915], p. 149.
5. *Laws of Ohio*, XIV, 447.
6. *Ibid.,* XIV, 499.

It was his duty, upon the order of the board, to discharge from the poorhouse any person who had been admitted because of illness when he had sufficiently recovered.[7] Moreover, the directors were authorized to remove paupers to the legal place of residence.[8] Besides this, any pauper rejected by the board of directors could be turned over to the township overseers to be cared for by contracting with the lowest bidder.[9] In 1842 the board was made elected for a three-year term.[10]

In 1850 the name poorhouse was changed to that of county infirmary.[11] Fifteen years later, in 1865, the board of infirmary directors, consisting of three resident electors, was to be elected by the voters of the county for a three-year term. The board was still authorized to appoint a superintendent, and was still required to make inspection visits, and report their findings to the county commissioners.[12]

Although reports have been required in previous years, it was not until the decade of the seventies that the legislature enacted measures looking forward to some business-like management of this ancient institution. Accordingly, in 1872, an act was passed which required each infirmary director, as well as the superintendent, to give bond conditioned for the faithful performance of the duties of his office. Under this act the directors were required to report semiannually to the county commissioners the condition of the infirmary, the number of inmates, and such other information as the county commissioners believed proper. Furthermore, the board of directors was required to file a full account "of all money's received and paid out, together with the vouchers . . . from whence received, to whom and for what paid out" with the county commissioners, who, after examining it, entered the report in the minutes of their proceedings. This report, as well as the vouchers, was filed in the auditor's office, and was to be "safely preserved" by that officer.[13]

The county infirmary served also as a place for the confinement of children, the mentally ill, and persons afflicted with epilepsy.

---

7. *Ibid.,* XXIX, 316.
8. *Ibid.,* XXIX, 316.
9. *Laws of Ohio,* XXIX, 321-322.
10. *Ibid.,* XL, 35.
11. *Ibid.,* XLVIII, 62.
12. *Ibid.,* LXII, 24-25.
13. *Ibid.,* LXIX, 120-122. See entry 5.

Although the state assumed responsibility for the mentally ill in the early years of the nineteenth century it was not until 1898 that it was made unlawful to confine adult insane and the epileptics in the county home.[14] Previously in 1884, the legislature prohibited the housing of children in the county infirmary who were eligible to the county children's home or to some other charitable institution unless separated from adults.[15] However, exceptions were made in the case of insane, idiotic, and epileptic children.[16] The latter provision is still effective in Ohio.[17]

By an act of May 31, 1911, effective January 1, 1913, the board of infirmary directors was abolished and the power formerly exercised by this body were transferred to the county commissioners and the infirmary superintendent.[18] The superintendent is still required to keep a record of the inmates, as prescribed by statute and to report annually to the county commissioners. This report, the acceptance of which is evidenced by an entry in the commissioners' journal, is filed with the county auditor and by him preserved.[19] In 1919 the name county infirmary was changed to that of county home.[20]

The county commissioners still make provisions for the establishment and maintenance of the county home, appoint a superintendent, and make regular inspections visits. The superintendent is appointed from the list of names of persons eligible under civil service regulations.[21] The superintendent is authorized to appoint a matron and other employees.[22] In Montgomery County, in addition to the superintendent and matron, an office assistant, a physician, and 26 others are on the maintenance staff.[23] Since 1882 the county commissioners have been authorized to appoint an infirmary physician, who, like the superintendent, is required by statute to report to them.

---

14. *Laws of Ohio*, XCIII, 274. Children were housed in Montgomery County Home, 1854-67, Minutes volume A, *passim.*

15. *Laws of Ohio*, LXXXI, 92.

16. *Ibid.,* CIII, 890.

17. G. C. sec. 3091.

18. *Laws of Ohio*, CII, 433.

19. G. C. sec. 2535. See entry 5.

20. *Laws of Ohio*, CVIII, pt. i, 68.

21. Ohio Attorney General, *Opinions,* III, 2021.

22. G. C. sec. 2522.

23. Interview with J. W. Morris, Superintendent of Montgomery County Home.

This report, made quarterly, includes such information as the nature and extent of medical services rendered, to whom, and the character of the disease treated.[24]

Although there is some relation between the old age pension system and the county home the newer form of aid is merely supplementary to the institution. As always the county home cares for those whose condition is such that they cannot be satisfactory cared for except in an institution.[25] Since the inauguration of aid for the aged there has been a slight reduction in the population of many county homes; however, the social aid programs have resulted in no reduction in the cost of operating county homes.[26] The Montgomery County home has an average population of 358 inmates with operating and maintaining cost of $71,100.84 and a per capita cost of $198.61.[27] Relatives whose income is sufficient to defray the cost of care are required to pay for the maintenance of the inmates in the home. These accounts range from $4 to $15 per month and the total income to the county treasurer does not exceed $62.50 per month from this source.[28]

---

24. G. C. Sec. 2546; *Laws of Ohio,* LXXIII, 233; LXXIX, 90; CII, 436; CVIII, pt. i, 269.

25. *The Reorganization of County Government in Ohio* . . . 132, 135.

26. Ohio Auditor of State, *Comparative Statistics, Counties of Ohio* (Columbus, 1934-1937), *passim.*

27. *Ibid.,* 1939, p. 41.

28. Council of Social Agencies, *Social Service Directory for Dayton and Montgomery County* (Dayton, March 1938), III, 53.

Minutes

491. MINUTES
1854-1912. 6 volumes. (A-F).

Minutes of the board of directors of the county infirmary, showing date of meeting, names of members attending, record of appointments made, bills allowed, and other business transacted. 1854-1867 also includes a record of children housed at the infirmary, showing name of child, date of birth, name of person to whom indentured, and when child left home upon becoming of age, shows date of departure and amount of money in clothing given. Arranged chronologically by dates of meetings. No index. Handwritten. Average 350 pages. 18 x 12 x 2. County courthouse. commissioners record room F.

For subsequent records, see entry 5.

492. REGISTER OF INMATES
1888—. 5 volumes.
Register of inmates, showing name and address of inmate, case history, name of person to notify in case of death, and remarks. Arranged alphabetically by names of inmates. No index. Handwritten. Average 500 pages. 17 x 14 x 2. County home office, 601 Infirmary Road, Dayton.

793. RECORDS OF INMATES
1892—. 2 file boxes. (labeled by contained letters of alphabet). 1 subtitled Active; 1 Dead or Checked Out.
Card record of inmates of county home, showing name and former residence, date of arrival, amount of aid extended, and date checked out or date of death. Arranged alphabetically by names of inmates. No index. Handwritten and typed on printed forms. 7 x 5.5 x 9. County home office, 601 Infirmary Road, Dayton.

494. RESIDING IN
1892—. 26 file boxes. (labeled by contained letters of alphabet).
Case papers of inmates in county home, including case history and application; all showing date of admission, name and former address of inmate, case number, and remarks. Arranged alphabetically by names of inmates. No index. Handwritten and typed on printed forms. 5 x 4.5 x 9.5. County home office, 601 Infirmary Road, Dayton.

495. DEATHS
1892—. 26 file boxes. (labeled by contained letters of alphabet).
Case papers of deceased county home inmates, showing information as in Residing In, entry 494, amount of aid received, date and cause of death, and place of burial. Arranged alphabetically by names of deceased inmates. No index. Handwritten and typed on printed forms. 5 x 4.5 x 9.5. County home office, 601 Infirmary Road, Dayton.

496. CHECK OUTS
1892—. 26 file boxes. (labeled by contain letters of alphabet).
Case papers of former inmates who have left the county home, showing information as in Residing In, entry 494, also amount of aid received, date checked out, and place of residence after leaving the home. Arranged alphabetically by names of former inmates. No index. Handwritten and typed on printed forms. 5 x 4.5 x 9.5. County home office, 601 Infirmary Road, Dayton.

497. BIRTH AND DEATH RECORD
1886—. 2 volumes.
Record of birth and deaths at the county home; record of births, showing date of birth, maiden name of mother, name of father, and date of admission of mother to home; also a record of deaths, showing name of decedent, date of admission to county home, date and cause of death, place of burial, and remarks. Arranged chronologically by dates of births or deaths. No index. Handwritten. Average 200 pages. 14 x 9 x 1. County home office, 601 Infirmary Road, Dayton.

498. INSANE RECORD
1866—. 3 volumes.
Record of inmates who had been housed in the county home and were committed to the state hospital, showing name of inmate, date committed to state hospital and nature of case. Arranged chronologically by dates of commitments. No index. Handwritten. Average 500 pages. 16 x 11 x 3. County home office, 601 Infirmary Road, Dayton.

499. COMMISSARY DEPARTMENT
1910—. 4 volumes.
Record of clothing issued to county home inmates by the stewart, showing date of issue, kind of clothing issued, and name of inmate. Arranged chronologically by dates of issue. No index. Handwritten. Average 500 pages. 16 x 11 x 3. County home office, 601 Infirmary Road, Dayton.

Financial Records

500. RECORD OF EXPENDITURES AND RECEIPTS
1920—. 2 volumes. (dated).
Record of expenditures from county home fund for salaries, food, clothing, medical,

equipment, maintenance, and burial expenses, showing date of expenditure, amount, and classification of same; also includes a record of receipts, showing date of received, from whom received, source of receipt, and amount. Arranged chronologically by dates of receipts or expenditures. No index. Average 200 pages. 17 x 14 x 2. County home office, 601 Infirmary Road, Dayton.

Personnel

501. EMPLOYMENT RECORD
1887—. 3 volumes.

Record of employees of the county home, showing name of employee, position held, amount of wage, date employed, and date discharged; also includes a record of payment of salaries, showing date and signature of employee certifying receipt of payment of salary. Arranged chronologically by dates of payments. Indexed alphabetically by names of employees. Handwritten. Average 400 pages. 14 x 9 x 2. County home office, 601 Infirmary Road, Dayton.

Miscellaneous

502. VISITORS REGISTER
1909. 1 volume.

Register of visitors to the county home, showing name and address of visitor, date of visit, name of inmate visited, and remarks. Arranged chronologically by dates of visits. No index. Handwritten. 400 pages. 16 x 11 x 2. County home office, 601 Infirmary Road, Dayton.

503. MOVEMENT OF INMATES
1933—. 5 volumes. (dated).

Copies of reports of census of inmates to state division of charities, showing date of report, number of males and females at beginning of period, number admitted, number of deaths, number checked out, number of males and females at end of period, dates covered by report, and remarks. Arranged chronologically by dates of reports. No index. Handwritten on printed forms. Average 100 pages. 12.5 x 9 x .5. County home office, 601 Infirmary Road, Dayton.

Although the legislature made provision for the institutional care of the county's indigent as early as 1816, it was not until after the middle of the nineteenth century, when hundreds of Ohio school children were left homeless by the scourge of civil war, that the legislature enacted measures for the care of dependent children. Previous to this time the Ohio statutes related to the care of children have been taken from the territorial code which authorized the overseers of the poor, and later the trustees of the "poor house," to apprentice the children of the indigent, boys until twenty-one and girls until eighteen years of age.[1] The fact that the system was not only inhumane, but entirely unsatisfactory, is evidenced by the innumerable advertisements for run-away apprentices appearing in the press.

In 1865 the legislature authorized the county commissioners to receive request for orphans' asylums, and, when funds accumulated in sufficient quantities, to construct such a home, and appoint a board of directors consisting of six persons who were given the task of managing the institution, subject to the rules and regulations of the county commissioners. This board, electing a president and a treasurer from its own number, was required annually to make a report of the receipts and disbursements of the asylum, together with the number of orphans received into and discharged from the institution. This report was to be published by the commissioners in the newspaper having a general circulation.[2]

A year later, in 1866, the commissioners were authorized, when in their judgment the best interest of the wards of the county would be served, to establish children's homes, and to provide by means of taxation, funds to be used for the purchase of a site, to construct buildings, and to maintain such charitable institutions.[3] Then, in 1876, and act was passed which repealed all previous legislation and established the present duties of the county commissioners, trustees, superintendent, and matron in respect to children's home. The act authorized the county commissioners to appoint a board of trustees and a superintendent of each children's home.[4]

In the early 1860s, with funds received from citizens of the county, a lot was purchased on Magnolia Street, Dayton, upon which a small brick building was erected, the first "Orphans Home" in the county.

---

1. Pease, *op. cit.,* 219; *Laws of Ohio,* III, 276; VIII, 223-224; XXIX, 318.
2. *Laws of Ohio,* LXII, 97.
3. *Ibid.,* LXIII, 45.
4. *Ibid.,* LXXXIII, 67.

By legislative act of March 20, 1866, covering establishment of children's home in the counties, Montgomery County took over the care of its orphaned and dependent children in the "Dayton Association" under the supervision of Robert W. Steele, C. Herchelrode, and Dr. C. McDermot. In March 1867 land was purchased on Summit Street by the county commissioners and a contract was let two months later for a $32,800 building to be devoted to the care of indigent children. This was the first nonsectarian children's home in the state of Ohio.[5] Several additions were made to this home which served until 1927 when the present home known as "Shawne Acres–Children's Village" was built on the site presented to the county commissioners by Dr. Shawne.[6] The home occupies a 20-acre tract at 3304 North Main Street, Dayton. There are 10 cottages, administrative buildings, playgrounds, swimming pool, auditorium, and laundry. The grounds are beautifully landscaped and have winding walks and well kept lawns.

The board of trustees consists of five members appointed for a five-year term. The trustees, besides appointing a superintendent, hold monthly meetings at which time they examine all accounts presented for payment, examine into the condition of the property and the manner of care offered to the wards. Annually or oftener, they are required to file with the state board of charities a detailed account giving to the whereabouts of each child and the physical condition of each ward under their care.[7]

The superintendent, operating under the rules and regulations of the trustees, has entire charge and control of the home and its wards. He may appoint a matron, assistant matron, and other necessary employees, subject to the approval of the board of trustees. It is the duty of such employees to care for the inmates in the home, direct their employment, and give suitable physical, mental, and moral training. Under the direction of the superintendent, the matron has general management and supervision of the household duties of the home. The matron, like other employees, receives such salaries as the trustees made direct and may be removed by the superintendent or at the pleasure of a majority of the trustees.[8]

---

5. Charlotte Reeves Conover, ed., *History of Dayton and Montgomery County- Resources and People* (New York, 1932), I, 632-633.
6. Commissioners' Journal, volume 32 [1926], p. 232.
7. G. C. sec. 3082-1.
8. G. C. sec. 3085.

The county children's home serves as a refuge for children under eighteen years of age who have resided in the county one year and who are, in the opinion of the trustees, eligible to admission by reason of orphanage, abandonment, or neglect by parents, or the inability of parents to provide for them.[9] Children are admitted to the home on orders of a juvenile court or upon the order of a majority of the board of trustees. Since 1876 each child committed to children's home must be accompanied by a statement of the facts setting forth his name, age, birthplace, and physical condition. These facts, recorded by the superintendent in a book kept for that purpose are confidential and open to inspection only at the discretion of the board of trustees.[10] All wards of the children's home who have been committed to the institution by the juvenile court because of abandonment, neglect, or dependency, or who have been voluntarily surrendered by their parents are under the exclusive jurisdiction, guardianship, and control of the trustees until they have become of lawful age.[11]

The county commissioners may, subject to the approval of the board of state charities, after an opportunity has been given to the electorate to demand a referendum on the proposition, abandoned the children's home. If the home is discontinued, they may sell the site and buildings and use the funds for care of neglected and dependent children, providing that the wards in the children's home who are placed in foster homes and those who are under the guardianship of the trustees are legally committed to the guardianship of the board of state charities.[12]

The board of trustees of the Montgomery County Children's Home, comprised of five members appointed by the county commissioners, govern the policies of the home and serve without compensation. The staff consists of the superintendent, matron and cottage mothers, case supervisor and six case workers, registered nurse, doctor, dentist, recreational director, dietitian, secretary, bookkeeper, stenographer, and eight specialists on the consultant staff.

The home is a member of the council of social agencies and receives all its funds from the Montgomery County general fund. The Four Seasons Garden Club has supported and is in charge of the beautification of the grounds. Other organizations and individuals contribute funds for the children's picnics, recreational projects, and for Christmas festivities.

---

9. G. C. sec. 3089.
10. G. C. Sec. 3089; *Laws of Ohio*, LXXIII, 64; LXXXIII, 196; XCIX, 187; CIII, 889.
11. G. C. sec. 3093.
12. *Laws of Ohio*, CIX, 533.

Besides the children in the home there are 345 children who have been placed in foster homes. These children are wards of the county and the homes are under supervision of the children's home.[13] In 1939 there was an average of 534 children in the home, and the operation and maintenance costs were $110,015.97, making a per capita cost of $206.08.[14] Fees for services are not charged by the children's home but parents are required to pay all or part of the cost of the child's care when they are able. The home offers institutional observation and training, educational advantages, and supervision of foster and boarding homes.

---

13. Cancel of Social Agencies, *Social Service Directory for Dayton and Montgomery County, Ohio* (Dayton, March 1938). III, 52-53.
14. Ohio Auditor of State, *Comparative Statistics, Counties of Ohio* (Columbus, 1939), 43.

Minutes

504. MINUTES
1867—. 6 volumes. (dated).
Minutes of the board of trustees of the children's home, showing date of meeting, names of members present, and record of business transacted. Arranged chronologically by dates of meetings. No index. Handwritten and typed. 5 volumes average 200 pages. 14 x 8 x 1.5; 1 volume (loose-leaf) 400 pages. 14 x 8 x 12. Children's home office, 3304 North Main Street, Dayton.

Case Records

505. REGISTER OF ADMISSION AND INDENTURES
1867-1928. 3 volumes. (dated).
Register of children admitted to the home, showing name, sex, age, race, birthplace, case history of child and parents, and date of admission; also includes a record of indentures, showing date indentured, name of child, terms, and name of person to whom indentured. Arranged alphabetically by names of children. No index. Handwritten. Average 250 pages. 18.5 x 12 x 3.5. Children's home office, 3304 North Main Street, Dayton.

506. ADMISSIONS
1912—. 13 file drawers. (labeled by contained letters of alphabet).
Case records of children admitted to the home including complete case history of

the child and parents and health record of child, all showing name of child, names of parents, and date of admission. Arranged alphabetically by names of children. No index. Handwritten and typed, some on printed forms. 15 x 15 x 25. Children's home office, 3304 North Main Street, Dayton.

507. SOCIAL SERVICE DEPARTMENT
1928—. 26 file drawers. (labeled by contained letters of alphabet).
Social service history of each child admitted to the home, showing name of child, health facts, results of mentality test, and special characteristics of child. Arranged alphabetically by names of children. No index. Typed. Handwritten. 15 x 12.5 x 24.5. Children's home office, 3304 North Main Street, Dayton.

Financial Records

508. BOARDING HOME ACCOUNT
1928—. 1 volume.
Record of children boarded in private homes but still under the jurisdiction of the children's home, showing name of child, location of boarding home, names of person or persons responsible for care of the child, and rate of charge per week. Arranged alphabetically by names of children. No index. Handwritten on printed forms. 200 pages. 10.5 x 8.5 x 1. Children's home office, 3304 North Main Street, Dayton.

509.CLASSIFICATION OF EXPENDITURES
1907—. 6 volumes. (dated). Title varies: Expenditures, 1907-1917, 3 volumes.
Records of expenditures from the children's home appropriation, showing date of expenditure, name of payee, purpose for which expended, and amount. Expenditures are classified as salary of superintendent and matron, salaries of all other employees, food, fuel, light, water, clothing, drugs, education, recreation, and vehicles. 1907-1917, arranged chronologically by dates of expenditures; 1917—, alphabetically by expense classification and chronologically thereunder by dates of expenditures. No index. Handwritten. 3 volumes average 300 pages 15 x 12 x 1.5; 3 volumes 140 pages 17.5 x 12 x 1. Children's home office, 3304 North Main Street, Dayton.

510. CANCELLED VOUCHERS

1904—. 6 file drawers.

Cancelled vouchers for payment of invoices and services rendered, showing date issued, name of payee, purpose, amount, date cancelled, and date filed. Arranged chronologically by dates of filing. No index. Handwritten and typed on printed forms. 15 x 12.5 x 24.5 Children's home office, 3304 North Main Street, Dayton.

511. STORE-ROOM RECORDS COMMISSARY

1935—. 2 file boxes.

Record of all food, supplies, clothing, and shoes rationed to various departments in the institution or to cottages, showing to whom issued, name of child receiving same, cost and description of article, date issued, and remarks; also includes copies of invoices covering food and supplies. Arranged alphabetically by names of departments or cottages and chronologically thereunder by dates of issue. No index. Handwritten and typed on printed forms. 11.5 x 10 x 15. Children's home office, 3304 North Main Street, Dayton.

Miscellaneous

512. MISCELLANEOUS

1920—. 1 file box.

Miscellaneous papers, including applications offering shelter to charges of the county, showing name of applicant, address, number of persons in applicant's family, extent of worthiness of applicant, and date filed; case reports from the home mothers to the superintendent in charge, showing number of children in her care, their names, dates of admission and release, either from the home or transferred to another division, approximate cost of children's upkeep, both as individual (itemized) and as a group, remarks and date filed; also copies of reports as compiled by the superintendent of the home and presented to commissioners and the state division of charities, showing name of institution, date report filed, period covered, location of home, number of children, number of each sex, average cost of child per day, per week, and per period, health report, number of children boarded out, but still under the jurisdiction of home, and remarks. Arranged chronologically by dates of filing. No index. Typed on printed forms. 12.5 x 15 x 24.5. Children's home office, 3304 North Main Street, Dayton.

The board of county visitors, an agency for the examination and inspection of county institutions supported wholly or in part by county or municipal taxation, was created by an act of the general assembly in 1882. Under this act, the judge of the court of common pleas was authorized to appoint five persons, three of whom were to be women, who were to visit periodically such county institutions as the county infirmary, county jail, municipal prisons, and children's home, and file annually a report of their proceedings and recommendations for changes with the clerk of courts, and to forward a copy to the state board of charities. The members, appointed for an indefinite period, were to serve without compensation.[1]

By the act of 1892 the personnel of the board was increased to six persons, three of whom were to be women, and not more than three to have the same political affiliations. Furthermore the act made it the duty of the probate judge, whenever proceedings were instituted in his court to commit a child under sixteen years of age to the boys' industrial home or to the girls' industrial home, to have notice given to the board of such proceedings; and it was made the duty of the board of visitors to attend the meeting of the court, as a body or as a committee, to protect the interest of the child.[2]

While the provisions of the act of 1892 were amended by the acts of 1898 and 1900, these acts did not, in the main, affect the duties of the board.[3] The latter act, however, made the board a continuous body with two members serving for one year, two members serving for two years, and two members serving for three years. The members were allowed expenses not to exceed $50 annually.[4]

Six years later in 1906, the power of appointment of the board members was given to the judge of the probate court. The board was authorized to recommend to the county commissioners measures for the more economical administration of county institutions. Their report, together with their recommendations, were to be filed each year with the judge of the probate court, the county prosecuting attorney, and the state board of charities at Columbus.[5]

---

1. *Laws of Ohio*, LXXIX, 107.
2. *Ibid.*, LXXXIX, 161.
3. *Ibid.*, XLIII, 57; XCIV, 70.
4. *Ibid.*, XCIV, 70; XCIII, 57.
5. *Ibid.*, XCVIII, 28, 29.

Under the act of 1913, the manner of appointment, qualifications, and number of board members remained unchanged but the term of office was changed to three years for all members, two to be appointed each year and vacancies were to be filled by the probate judge for the unexpired term. By provisions of this act the juvenile judge, like the probate judge under the act of 1892, was authorized to notify the board of visitors when any proceedings were instituted in his court for the commitment of any child to a state institution for correction.[6]

The members of the board served without compensation but necessary expenses incurred in the discharge of their duties are allowed by the county commissioners from the general funds, however, the maximum allowance is $100 per annum payable only upon certification of the probate judge that the board member has satisfactorily performed his duties.[7]

Although the annual reports are still required to be filed with the probate judge and the county prosecuting attorney, they were not found in the inventory of Montgomery County archives.

---

6. *Laws of Ohio,* CIII, 174, 888.
7. *Ibid.,* XCVIII, 28.

The soldiers' relief commission was established by the legislative act of May 19, 1886 to provide for the relief of indigent Union soldiers, sailors, and marines, and the indigent wives, widows, and minor children of indigent or deceased Union soldiers, sailors, and marines. The judge of the court of common pleas was authorized to appoint a commission of three county residents, at least two of whom were honorably discharged Union soldiers, to serve for a term of three years, and the county commissioners were authorized to levy a special tax for the purpose of creating a fund for this relief.[1]

An amendment passed March 4, 1887, provided that the councilman of the city wards as well as the board of trustees of each township certify to the soldiers' relief commission the names of those requiring and entitled to aid.[2] By an act of April 28, 1890, the commission was authorized to appoint annually a committee of three in each township and ward, in any city in the county to receive applications for aid and certify them to the commission.[3]

Membership of the commission was changed by the amendment of March 6, 1917, to include one member who was the wife, widow, son, or daughter of an honorably discharged soldier, sailor, or marine of the Civil War or Spanish American War, the other two members to be honorably discharged soldiers, sailors, or marines of the United States, and one member of the township and ward committee to be a wife, or widow of a soldier, sailor, or marine of the United States.[4] On April 6, 1929, the membership of the commission was again changed to include one member who is the wife, widow, son, or daughter of an honorably discharged soldier, sailor, or marine of the Civil War, of the Spanish-American War, or of the World War; the other two to be honorably discharged soldiers, sailors, or marines of the United States, one of whom should, if possible, be a member of the Spanish-American War Veterans any other of the American Legion.[5]

In 1919 the provisions of the act were extended to include indigent veterans of the World War and indigent parents, wives, widows, or minor children of such veterans.[6]

---

1. *Laws of Ohio,* LXXXIII, 232.
2. *Ibid.,* LXXXIV, 100.
3. *Ibid.,* LXXXVII, 352.
4. *Ibid.,* CVII, 27.
5. *Ibid.,* CXIII, 466.
6. *Ibid.,* CVIII, pt. i, 633.

513. MINUTES OF SOLDIERS' RELIEF COMMISSION
1886—. 3 volumes.

Minutes of the soldiers' relief commission, showing date and place of meeting, applications considered and action taken on same, giving name and address of applicant, and amount of award for cases approved and cause for those denied; also copies of reports to county commissioners and auditor with list of applicants recommended and amount of grant as approved by the commission. Arranged chronologically by dates of meetings. No index. Handwritten and typed. Average 300 pages. 18 x 12 x 3. Soldiers' relief commission office.

514. APPLICATIONS
1933—. 1 file box.

Original applications for soldiers' relief filed with the commission, showing date of application, name and address of applicant, military record, personal history of applicant, number of dependents, and financial statements. Arranged alphabetically by names of applicants. No index. Handwritten and typed on printed forms. 12 x 3 x 11.5. Soldiers' relief commission office.

515. RELIEF CARDS
1930—. 3 file boxes.

Card record of recipients of soldiers' relief, showing name and address of recipient, date of discharge from military service, amount of relief, names of dependents, date allowed, and remarks. Arranged alphabetically by names of recipients. No index. Handwritten and typed on printed forms. 12 x 12 x 35. Soldiers' relief commission office.

516. CORRESPONDENCE
1933—. 1 file box.

Correspondence of the relief commission, showing date of letter, name of correspondent and addressee, and text of letter. Arranged alphabetically by names of correspondence. No index. Handwritten and typed. 12 x 3 x 11.5. Soldiers' relief commission office.

In 1884 the legislature made provision for a soldiers' burial commission in each county, to consist of three persons in each township appointed by the county commissioners, which was directed to defray the expense incurred in the internment of any honorable discharge Union soldier, sailor, or marine who died in poverty. The commission, serving at the pleasure of the appointing power, was required to report to the county commissioners the name, rank, and command of the decedent, which report was transcribed by the county commissioners in a book kept for that purpose.[1] The original act, amended in 1891, extended the provisions of the act to include the internment of the wives or widows of Union soldiers.[2] In 1893 the act was again amended to provide for the internment of mothers of Union soldiers, sailors, and marines, and army nurses.[3] In 1908 the personnel of the commission was reduced to two.[4]

Under the present law which became effective in 1921 the county commissioners are authorized to appoint two suitable persons in each township and ward in the county, who are directed to contract with the undertaker selected by the family or friends of the deceased, and to direct the burial in a respectable manner of the body of any honorably discharged soldier, sailor, or marine having at any time served in the army or navy of the United States, or the mother, wife, or widow of any soldier, sailor, or marine, or that of any war nurse who served at any time in the army of the United States who died in poverty.[5]

The soldiers' burial commission is also given the duty of caring for the graves are those persons certified by them and the expense is borne by the city, village, or township in which the person is buried but in no case is to exceed an annual cost of fifty cents for each grave to be paid to the cemetery association.[6] Furthermore, the graves of the ex-servicemen are marked and recorded.[7]

---

1. *Laws of Ohio,* LXXXI, 146-147.
2. *Ibid.,* LXXXVIII, 330-331.
3. *Ibid.,* XC, 177.
4. *Ibid.,* XCIX, 99.
5. G. C. sec. 2950; *Laws of Ohio,* CVIII, pt. i. 34; CIX 211.
6. *Laws of Ohio,* CII, 75.
7. *Ibid.,* XC, 178.

The burial commission is instructed to enforce all laws relative to the burial of indigent veterans, investigate the financial status of the decedent's family, and report its findings to the county commissioners, together with the name, rank, and command to which the deceased belonged, date of death, place of burial, occupation while living, and an itemized statement of the cost of burial.[8]

Upon receiving this report of the burial commission, the county commissioners transcribe the information in a book kept for that purpose and certify the expense to the county auditor who draws his warrant for payment to the person or persons specified by the county commissioners.[9]

The amount contributed by the county for the burial of an indigent veteran set by the legislature at $35 in 1884 was increased to $75 in 1908, and to $100 in 1921.[10] Since 1908 each member of the burial commission has been allowed one dollar for each service performed.[11]

The soldiers' burial commission keeps no separate records; for records in other offices, see entries 8, 373.

---

8. *Ibid.,* XCIX, 100.
9. *Laws of Ohio,* XCIX, 101.
10. *Ibid.,* LXXXI, 146-147; XCIX, 99; CIX, 212; G. C. sec. 2951.
11. *Laws of Ohio,* XCIX, 99; G. C. sec. 2951.

Provision for the relief of the indigent was made in 1805, but it was not until 1898 that the legislature provided separate relief for the indigent blind. The act authorized the township trustees to certify to the county commissioners an amount not to exceed $100 per person per annum for such relief, the certification to be made a record listing the name of the beneficiary and the amount required; and directed the county commissioners to levy on the township to the amount certified, this amount to be paid into the county treasury and thence to the township treasurer to be used for blind relief.[1]

Six years later, in 1904, certification authority was transferred from the township trustees to the probate judge, who was required to register the name and address of beneficiaries and to issue to each a certificate giving his name, address, and the amount to be drawn. Persons eligible for relief were blind males over twenty-one and blind females over eighteen years of age, without property or means of support. Not less than two county citizens, one a physician selected by the court, were required to testify that the applicant had been a resident of the state for five years and a resident of the county for one year immediately proceeding the filing of an application for relief as a condition for granting aid.[2]

The act of 1904 was declared unconstitutional for the reason that it required spending for a private purpose public funds raised by taxation.[3] Hence, in 1908, an act was passed authorizing the county commissioners to levy a stipulated tax to create a fund for relief of the needy blind, the maximum benefits not to exceed $150 per person per annum to be paid quarterly; and authorizing the probate judge to appoint a blind relief commission consisting of three members to serve for a three-year term, directed to me annually in the office of the county commissioners to examine applications recorded in order of their receipt in a book furnished by the county commissioners. This record was required to be kept open for public inspection.[4]

The blind relief commission was abolished by the legislature in 1913 and its powers and duties were transferred to the county commissioners. No records of the defunct commission were found in Montgomery County.[5]

---

1. *Laws of Ohio*, XCIII, 270.
2. *Ibid.*, XCVII, 392-394.
3. *Auditor of Lucas County* v. *The State, Ohio State Reports*, LXXV, 114-137.
4. *Laws of Ohio*, XCIX, 56-58.
5. *Ibid.*, CIII, 60. See also pp. 3, 4.

Old age pensions, although well known in Europe at the end of the nineteenth and beginning of the twentieth century and in a few American states during the same period, were not provided for in Ohio until recently.[1] In 1933 an "Old Age Pension" law, proposed by initiative petition, was voted upon at the general assembly of that year, providing for the granting of aid to the aged in Ohio under certain conditions. The law was adopted by a majority of the electors voting thereon.[2] The act, as mentioned in 1936, provides, among other things, that any person sixty-five years of age or upward (unless confined in a penal or correctional institution or the state hospital) who is a citizen of the United States, who has resided in Ohio not less than five years during the nine prior to making application for aid, and who has resided for one year in the county wherein application for aid is made, is eligible to receive a pension, providing his income from all and every source does not exceed $360 per year.[3] Moreover, the applicant must be unable to support himself, and have no husband, wife, child, or other person who is legally responsible for his support, and found by the division of aid for the aged able to support him. In addition to this, the net value of all real and personal property of the unmarried applicant, less all encumbrances and liens, must not exceed $3,000; if the applicant is married the net value of the property of husband and wife shall not exceed $4,000. It may be required that such property, as a condition precedent to payment of aid, be transferred in trust to the division of aid for the aged. This provision does not, however, prohibit the applicant or his wife from occupying such property during their lifetime.[4] An amendment to the act in 1937 eliminated the transfer of property as a possible condition precedent to granting aid, leaving the transfer optional. The amendment act further states that any property, either real or personal, which has heretofore been conveyed to the division in trust could be reconveyed to the grantor or the division.[5]

For the purpose of administering the old age pension law there was created in 1933 in the state department of public welfare a division for aid for the aged.

---

1. Arthur Lyon Cross, *A Shorter History of England and Greater Britain* (New York, 1925). 746-747; J. Salwyn Schapiro, *Modern and Contemporary European History, 1815-1928* (New York, 1931), - 275, 347, 396, 790.

2. *Laws of Ohio,* CXV, pt. ii, 431-439.

3. *Ibid.,* CXVI, pt. ii, 86-88, 216-221.

4. *Ibid.,* CXV, pt. ii, 431-439.

5. G. C. sec. 1359-6.

The chief of the division of aid for the aged, appointed by the director of public welfare with the approval of the governor, is authorized to appoint all necessary assistance, clerks, stenographers, and other employees and fix their salaries, subject to approval of the director of public welfare.[6]

In each county the commissioners constitute a board for administering the act. However, if the commissioners by a majority vote declined to serve in such capacity, the chief of the division of aid for the aged is authorized, with the consent of the director of public welfare, to appoint a board consisting of three or five members, who, like the county commissioners, serve without compensation. The local boards are required to keep such records and make such reports as the division may prescribe, and are also authorized to employ, subject to the approval of the division, such investigators, clerks, and other employees as are necessary for performance of their duties.[7]

In 1937 the chief of the division was directed to appoint an advisory board in each county consisting of five citizens of such county. The members of the board, appointed for two years, are required to take an oath of office before entering upon their duties. This board succeeded to the duties formerly performed by the county commissioners.[8]

Applications for relief were made annually to the local board but an act of the legislature in 1937, reorganizing the division of aid for the aged, omitted the provision for annual reapplication.[9] Each applicant is thoroughly investigated. In its investigation the local board is not bound by common law or statutory rules of evidence, but is authorized to make inquiries in such a matter as seems "best calculated to conform to substantial justice." For the purpose of its investigations, each county board has the power to compel the attendance and testimony of witnesses. Decisions of the local boards may be appealed to the division.[10]

After the applicants have been investigated by the local board, "certificates of aid" are granted to persons entitled to relieve in conformity with the provision of the law.

---

6. *Laws of Ohio,* CXV, pt. ii, 431-439.
7. *Laws of Ohio,* CXV, pt. ii, 431-439.
8. G. C. sec. 1359-12.
9. G. C. sec. 1359-14.
10. *Laws of Ohio,* CXV, pt. ii, 431-439

Each certificate, bearing the applicant's name and the pension allowed, as well as the records pertaining to the investigation, is forwarded to the division, which may approve, modify, or reject the certificate and findings of the board.[11]

In February 1934 the general assembly made its first appropriation for old age pensions covering the last half of the calendar year 1934.[12] The total cost to the state and federal governments for old age pensions and the administration of the old age pension system in Ohio since its inauguration has been $99,509,315.43. The cost to the state of Ohio for the year 1937 exclusive federal grants was $14,993,155.53.[13]

---

11. *Ibid.,* CXV, pt. ii, 435.
12. *Ibid.,* CXV, pt. ii, 186.
13. Ohio Auditor of State, *Annual Report, 1934,*244; *ibid., 1935,* 269; *ibid., 1936,* 202; *ibid., 1937,* 130, 131; *ibid., 1938,* 7, 36, 58, 144.

Applications and Investigations

517. APPLICATIONS RECEIVED
1934—. 3 volumes. (labeled by contained application numbers).
Register of applications received for aid for aged, showing application number, date of application, name and address of applicant, sex, type of case (new, old denied, reopened, or transferred from another county), and final action taken. Arranged numerically by application numbers, and chronologically by dates of applications. No index. Handwritten on printed forms. Average 225 pages (loose-leaf) 12 x 18 x 1.5. Aid for the aged office, 104 East Third Street, Dayton.

518. APPLICATIONS PENDING
1934—. 1 file drawer.
Case papers of applications pending investigation and approval, showing name and address of applicant, application number, date of application, and case history. Arranged numerically by application numbers. No index. Handwritten and typed on printed forms. 12.5 x 15 x 25.5. Aid for the aged office, 104 East Third Street, Dayton.

519. ABEYANCE

1934—. 2 file drawers.

Case papers of applications investigated but held in abeyance pending more complete information, showing information as in Applications Pending, entry 518. Arranged numerically by application numbers. For index, see entry 524. Handwritten and typed on printed forms. 12.5 x 15 x 25.5. Aid for the aged office, 104 East Third Street, Dayton.

520. APPLICATIONS DENIED AND WITHDRAWN

1934—. 1 volume.

Register of applications denied and withdrawn, showing date of application, reason for denial, date denied or withdrawn, name and address of applicant, sex, and remarks. Arranged chronologically by dates denied or withdrawn. No index. Handwritten on printed forms. 150 pages. 16 x 10 x 2. Aid for the aged office, 104 East Third Street, Dayton.

521. CANCELLATIONS AND WITHDRAWALS

1934—. 10 file drawers.

Case papers of applications denied and withdrawn, showing information as in Applications Pending, entry 518, and date and reason for denial or date withdrawn by applicant. Arranged numerically by application numbers. No index. Handwritten and typed on printed forms. 12.5 x 15 x 25.5. Aid for the aged office, 104 East Third Street, Dayton.

522. INVESTIGATIONS

1934—. 2 file drawers. 1 subtitled to be Investigated; 1, Investigations Completed.

Case workers' file of applications to be investigated and investigations completed including case papers, showing information as in Applications Pending, entry 518; investigations completed, showing date, and case workers' report. Arranged alphabetically by names of case workers. No index. Handwritten and typed on printed forms. 12.5 x 15 x 25.5. Aid for the aged office, 104 East Third Street, Dayton.

523. RECIPIENTS

1934—. 27 file drawers. (labeled by contain case numbers).
Case papers of active aid for aged cases, showing name and address of recipient, application number, certificate or case number, case history, date certificate of award issued, and amount of award. Arranged numerically by case numbers. For index, see entry 524. Handwritten and typed on printed forms. 12.5 x 15 x 25.5. Aid for the aged office, 104 East Third Street, Dayton.

524. MASTER FILE, ACTIVE CASES

1934—. 2 file drawers, 6 file boxes. (labeled by contained letters of alphabet).
Case record of active cases, showing name and address of applicant, application number, sex, age, certificate of award or case number, and amount of award. Serves as an index to Abeyance, entry 519, Recipients, entry 523, and Unawarded Cases, entry 525, by showing application and case numbers. Arranged alphabetically by names of applicants and recipients. No index. Handwritten and typed on printed forms. 2 file drawers, 6.5 x 12.5 x 25.5; 6 file boxes, 4.5 x 6 x 11.5. Aid for the aged office, 104 East Third Street, Dayton.

525. UNAWARDED CASES

1934—. 2 file drawers.
Case papers of cases approved but not yet placed on active list, showing information as in Recipients, entry 523. Arranged numerically by case numbers. For index, see entry 524. Handwritten and typed on printed forms. 12.5 x 15 x 25.5. Aid for the aged office, 104 East Third Street, Dayton.

526. INACTIVE CASES

1934—. 4 file drawers. (labeled by contained letters of alphabet).
Case papers of inactive cases, showing information as in Recipients, entry 523, and date and reason inactive. Arranged alphabetically by names of former recipients. No index. Handwritten and typed on printed forms. 12.5 x 15 x 25.5. Aid for the aged office, 104 East Third Street, Dayton.

527. CANCELLATIONS AND DEATHS

1934—. 4 file drawers.

Case papers of former recipients who are deceased and of cases closed, showing information as in Recipients, entry 523, and date and the reason for closing or date of death. Arranged numerically by case numbers. No index. Handwritten and typed on printed forms. 12.5 x 15 x 25.5. Aid for the aged office, 104 East Third Street, Dayton.

Miscellaneous

528. DECEASED

1934—. 1 file drawer.

Financial records of deceased clients, showing amount of money received as aid while a recipient of aid for aged relief, and record of money collected or in process of collection to reimburse the state. Arranged alphabetically by names of decedents. No index. Handwritten and typed. 12.5 x 15 x 25.5. Aid for the aged office, 104 East Third Street, Dayton.

529. CORRESPONDENCE

1934—. 3 file drawers. (labeled by contained letters of alphabet).

Interoffice communications, bulletins, and general correspondence, showing date, name of correspondent or subject, and text of communication or bulletins. Arranged alphabetically by names of correspondents or subjects. No index. Handwritten and typed. 12.5 x 15 x 25.5. Aid for the aged office, 104 East Third Street, Dayton.

The office of county surveyor, another English institution transplanted to America during the colonial period, became an important office in frontier Ohio where land titles and boundary lines were often in dispute. The office is purely a creature of statute, there being no constitutional provision for its establishment.

The first act of the general assembly pertaining to the surveyor was passed during the first legislative session of 1803. Under this act the court of common pleas was authorized to appoint a person well qualified to act as county surveyor. He received his commission from the governor, was required to give bond conditioned for the faithful performance of the duties of his office, and was directed to survey all lands which were sold or were to be sold for taxes, and was authorized to appoint chainmen or markers who function it was to establish corners. The surveys made by the surveyor or his deputies were the only ones to be accepted as legal evidence in a court of law or equity. For remuneration, the surveyor was permitted to retain all fees collected by him in the operation of his office.[1]

Although it made no fundamental change in the duties of the surveyor, the act of 1816 fixed his term of office at five years; authorized him to appoint deputies, and made him responsible for their official acts; and made him liable to removal by the court for negligence or incompetency, and liable to suit by persons believing themselves damaged by his negligence or that of his deputies.[2] A year later, in 1817, provision was made for the appointment of a successor in the event the office became vacant because of death, resignation, or removal.[3]

The act of 1831 consolidated the previous acts, redefined the duties of the surveyor, increased the amount of his bond, and authorize him, when directed by the county commissioners, to procure from the surveyor general's office a "certified plat, together with the field notes of corners, and bearing trees to each section, quarter section, lot, or original survey in his county, and cause the same to be preserved in a book by him provided for that purpose; which shall be deposited in the county auditor's office, for the use of the land holders in the county." It provided further, that the surveyor shall keep "a fair and accurate record of all official surveys made by himself or by his deputies," in a suitable book to be kept by him for that purpose, and that he should number his surveys progressively. More significant, however, was the fact that the office was made elected for a three-year term by the act of 1831.

---

1. *Laws of Ohio,* I, 90-93.
2. *Ibid.,* XIV, 424-431.
3. *Ibid.,* XV, 64.

The term remained at three years till 1906 when it was reduced to a two-year period; and by the act of 1927, effective with the term of the surveyor elected in 1928, the term was increased to four years.[4]

During the years of the development of the office other duties have been delegated to the surveyor. In 1842 he was given the duty of ascertaining and reporting trespassing on public lands.[5] Later, in 1854, he was given the same powers as the justices of the peace to take acknowledgments of and certify deeds, mortgages, powers of attorney, and other instruments affecting real estate, to administer oaths, and to take and certify affidavits.[6] In 1867 he was given authority, when directed by the county commissioners, to transcribe any and all dilapidated maps, records of plats, and field notes and surveys of other counties.[7] Similarly, in 1881, he was authorized to procure from any office in the state a certified plat together with the field notes of corners, quarter sections, lots, or original surveys and place them in a book provided for that purpose. Certified copies from his book were to be taken as *prima facie* evidence.[8]

With the increase in modern means of transportation, there developed a growing need for more efficient methods of road construction and maintenance. Accordingly, in 1906, the surveyor was directed to act, whenever the services of an engineer were required, in the capacity of an engineer with respect to roads, turnpikes, bridges, or ditches, except in cities of the first grade.[9] He was directed by statute to perform all duties in his county which would be done by a civil engineer or surveyor, to prepare all plans, specifications, and estimates of cost, and to submit forms for contracts for the construction and repair of all bridges, culverts, roads, draws, ditches, and other public improvements (except buildings) over which the county commissioners had authority. At the same time, he was made responsible for the inspection of all public improvements, and was directed to keep a complete list of all estimates and bids received for such work, as well as of contracts awarded for improvements.[10]

---

4. *Ibid.,* XXIX, 399; XCVIII, 245-247; CXII, 179.
5. *Laws of Ohio,* XL, 57.
6. *Ibid.,* LII, 70.
7. *Ibid.,* LXIV, 216-217; LXXVIII, 285.
8. *Ibid.,* XXIX, 399; LXXVIII, 285.
9. *Ibid.,* XCVIII, 245-247.
10. *Ibid.,* XCVIII, 245-247.

Similarly, another measure enacted in 1919 increased the duties of the surveyor regarding road construction and road maintenance. Under this act the surveyor was authorized to designate one of his deputies as maintenance engineer. This engineer, under the direction of the surveyor, was to have charge of all "road maintenance and repair work" in his county. Furthermore, when authorized by the county commissioners, the surveyor was to appoint a maintenance supervisor or supervisors to have charge of the maintenance of improved highways within a district or districts established by the commissioners or the surveyor, and containing not less than ten miles of improved county roads.[11] In 1923 the surveyor was delegated to assist the county planning commission wherever such commission was established.[12]

Thus the general responsibility of planning and directing county road construction is vested, by statute, in the county surveyor. Because of this increased responsibility placed on this office there has been an attempt to raise the general qualifications of those seeking elections to it. In 1935 an act was passed changing the the title of the office to that of "county engineer," and eligibility to the office was restricted to "*a registered professional engineer and registered surveyor licensed to practice in the state of Ohio.*"[13] This act was amended in 1936 to permit the incumbent to continue in office upon reelection, regardless of the lack of these qualifications.[14]

---

11. *Laws of Ohio,* CVIII, pt. i, 497.
12. *Ibid.,* CX, 312.
13. *Ibid.,* CXVI, 283.
14. *Ibid.,* CXVI, pt. ii, 152.

Surveys, Plats, and Maps

530. ORIGINAL SURVEYS
1823—. 2 volumes.
Record of surveys of land tracts, showing date of survey, survey number, description of tract surveyed, and names of person ordering the survey; also plat of surveyed tract, showing boundary lines, length of each line, area of tract, streams, and locations of landmarks. Prepared by county surveyors. Arranged numerically by survey numbers. No index. Record, handwritten; plats, hand drawn. Scales vary. Average 300 pages. 20 x 18 x 2. Engineer's office.

531. PLATS

1864——. 20 volumes. (1, 2, 3A, 1, 2, 3B, C-P).

Survey plats of townships, corporations, city wards, and other land tracts, showing size, location, name of plat, date of plat, name of landowner, and streets or roads bordering thereon. Prepared by county surveyors. Arranged chronologically by dates of plats. For index, see entry 532. Record, handwritten; plats, hand drawn. Scales vary. Average 100 pages. 20 x 28.5 x 2. Sanitary department.

532. PLAT INDEX

1864——. 3 volumes.

Index to Plats, entry 531, showing name of plat, location, date of plat, name of landowner, and in some cases boundaries of roads and streams, and volume and page numbers of record. Arranged alphabetically by names of plats or landowners. Handwritten. Average 200 pages. 17 x 14 x 2. Engineer's office.

533. ACCIDENT SPOT MAPS

1934——. 4 maps (dated).

Maps showing location of all accidents in the county by use of red thumb tacks placed on a site on a regulation county map. Basic map prepared by F. J. Cellarious and Company, Dayton, Ohio. Printed on linen. Scale, 1/4 inch equals 1 mile. 42 x 36. Engineer's office, on wall.

Improvements

Roads, Bridges, and Ditches

534. ROAD RECORDS

1803——. 7 volumes. (A-G).

Record of roads built in the county including record of original roads and subsequent extensions, showing name of township, name and number of road, date established, date and kind of improvement to original road, and location; also includes plat of each road. Prepared by county surveyors. Arranged chronologically by dates of entries. For index, see entry 535. Record, handwritten; plats hand drawn. Average 400 pages. 18 x 12 x 3. Engineer's office.

535. INDEX TO ROAD RECORDS

1803—. 1 volume.

Index to Road Records, entry 534, showing name or number of road, location by township, a few scattered dates of establishment, and volume letter and page number of record. Arranged alphabetically by names of roads. Handwritten. 100 pages. 20 x 20 x 2. Engineer's office.

536. ROAD IMPROVEMENTS

1803-1864. 1 volume.

Record of improvements to county roads by grading, draining, and bridge construction, showing name of road or bridge, name of township, and date and kind of improvement. Arranged chronologically by dates of entries. No index. Handwritten. 500 pages. 20 x 20 x 3. Engineer's office.

537. BRIDGE ATLAS

1900—. 1 volume.

Record of bridges in the county, showing date, exact location, type and description of bridge, and kind of materials used; also includes plats of roads on which bridges are located, showing name or number of road, dates of improvements, and whether built by the state, county, or township. Prepared by county surveyors. Arranged chronologically by dates of entries. No index. Record, handwritten; plats, hand drawn. Scale, 1 inch equals 2 miles. 50 pages. 30 x 30 x 1. Engineer's office.

538. GUARD RAIL ATLAS

1934—. 1 volume.

Record of guard rails along county roads, showing location of each by township, date of installation, complete description of guard rail and road, and recommendations for additional rails at hazardous points. Prepared to by county engineers. Arranged alphabetically by names of township. No index. Record, handwritten; plats, hand drawn. 50 pages. 26 x 18.5 x 1. Engineer's office.

539. DRAINAGE ATLAS

1900—. 1 volume.

Record of sewers and drains in the county, showing date of entry, section controlled by each drain, exact location, size, outlets, depth, kind of material, and recommendation and proposals for additional drains; also includes plats, showing location of ditch.

Prepared by county engineers. Arranged chronologically by dates of entries. No index. Record, handwritten; plats, hand drawn. 100 pages. 24 x 26.5 x 1.5. Engineer's office.

540. MONTGOMERY COUNTY IMPROVEMENT AND CONSTRUCTION DRAWINGS

1803—. 1400 drawings in 4 map cabinets. (14; drawers, A-M). 1 cabinet subtitled ditches.

Drawings and plans of improvements of roads, highways, bridges, ditches, streets, and rivers, showing name of improvement, location, name or number of road or highway, drawing number, and date filed. Prepared by county engineers. Arranged numerically by drawing numbers, and chronologically thereunder by dates of filing. For index, see entry 541. Hand drawn, some on linen; and blueprinted. Scales vary. Cabinet, 72 x 55 x 40; sizes of drawings vary. Engineer's office.

541. DRAWING INDEX

1803—. 2 file boxes. (labeled by contained letters of alphabet).

Card index to Montgomery County Improvement and Construction Drawings, entry 540, showing name of improvement, location by township, town, range, or road number, description of improvement, showing number, and cabinet number and drawer letter of map cabinet. Arranged alphabetically by names of improvements. Typed on printed forms. 5.5 x 4.5 x 12. Engineer's office.

Contracts

542. STATE [Road Contracts]

1912-1924. 3 file drawers. (labeled by contained letters of alphabet).

Copies of contracts for construction and repair of state aid roads, culverts, and bridges, showing name of project, date, name of contractor, and terms of contract. Arranged alphabetically by names of projects. No index. Handwritten, typed, and printed. 18 x 10 x 25. Engineer's office.

543. CONTRACTS

1925—. 8 file drawers. (labeled by contained letters of alphabet).

Copies of contracts, showing purpose for which contract was let, name of contractor, date, name and location of project, amount and kind of materials specified, probable date of completion, and remarks. Arranged alphabetically by names of projects. No index. Typed and printed. 18 x 10 x 25. Engineer's office.

Financial Records

544. PAID INVOICES
1933—. 13 file drawers. (dated).
Duplicates of paid or cancelled invoices for equipment and supplies, showing name of vendor, date of bill, kind of merchandise, amount, total, and date of filing. Arranged chronologically by dates of filing. No index. Handwritten and typed, some on printed forms. 18 x 10 x 25. Engineer's office.

Miscellaneous

545. MISCELLANEOUS
1923—. 11 file drawers. (labeled by contain letters of alphabet).
Miscellaneous papers including complaints from township trustees or taxpayers on condition of roads and asking for repair of same; road supervisors reports on complaints and investigations with the recommendations; record of oil and gas used by the engineers office, showing date, to whom issued, and purpose. Arranged alphabetically by subjects. No index. Handwritten, typed, and printed. 18 x 10 x 25. Engineer's office.

546. CORRESPONDENCE
1933—. 5 file drawers. (labeled by contained letters of alphabet).
Correspondence of engineer's office, showing date, name of correspondent, and text of letter. Arranged alphabetically by names of correspondents. No index. Handwritten and typed. 18 x 10 x 25. Engineer's office.

The legislature at its 1914 session, following the disastrous floods of the previous year, made provision for the establishment of conservancy districts in Ohio the objects of which were to prevent floods, to protect cities, villages, farms, and highways from inundation. This act, authorized by the constitutional amendment of 1912,[1] was upheld by the courts as a valid exercise of the police power of the state.[2] The conservancy districts, according to the act, may be established not only to prevent floods but to regulate streams, reclaim overflowed lands, provide irrigation, regulate the flow of streams, or divert watercourses.

The court of common pleas of any county in the state or any judge in vacation is authorized, after a petition signed either by 500 freeholders or by a majority of freeholders has been filed with the clerk of courts, to establish a conservancy district which might be within or without the county where the court is located. The court, after conducting hearings on the petition as to the purpose of the district, may declare the district organized and give it a corporate name. The clerk of court, within 30 days after the district has been declared a corporation by the court, transmits to the secretary of state, and to the county recorder in each county having lands in the district, copies of the finding and the decree of the court incorporating the district which, according to statute, is considered a political subdivision.

Within thirty days after the decree of incorporation the court is authorized to appoint three persons, at least two of whom are freeholders in the district, to serve as a board of directors of the districts to serve three, five, and seven years respectively. After the expiration of their terms the tenure of office is five years. The board of directors, after taking an oath that they "will not be interested directly or indirectly in any contact led by the district," organized by selecting one of their members as president and some person, not a member of the board, as secretary. The board is authorized to employ a chief engineer who may be an individual, copartnership, or corporation; an attorney; and such other engineers and attorneys as maybe necessary for carrying on the work. The board may provide for their compensation, which, with all other necessary expenditures, shall be taken as a part of the cost of improvement. While the chief engineer prepares plans and specifications of work, all contracts which exceed $1,000 are let by competitive bidding.

------

1. *Ohio Const. 1851,* Art. II sec. 36.
2. *County of Miami* v. *Dayton, Ohio State Reports,* XCII, 223-224, 236.

The board, or its agents, is authorized to enter upon lands within or without the conservancy district for the purpose of making surveys. They are authorized to exercise the right of eminent domain; condemn property, after appraisal, for the use of the district; make regulations to protect their work by prescribing the method of building roads, bridges, or fences; to remove bridges, cemeteries, or other structures impeding their work; and to co-operate with the federal government, with persons, railways, corporations, the state government of Ohio or other states, for assistance for drainage, conservancy, or other improvements.

To finance such improvements the board is authorized to levy upon the property of the district a tax not to exceed three-tenths of a mill on the assessed valuation. This tax is certified to the county auditor, and to the various treasurers of the counties within the district and is used to pay for the expenses of organization, surveys, and plans. The commission is authorized further to borrow money at a rate not to exceed six percent per annum and levy assessments for a bond fund.[3]

The board is required to "keep in a well-bound book a record of all its proceedings, minutes of all meetings, certificates, contracts, bonds given by employees and all corporate acts, which shall be open to the inspection of the owners of the property in the district, as well as to all other interested parties." The secretary, who may serve also as treasurer, is designated as the "custodian of the records of the district and its corporate seal."[4]

The Miami Conservancy District was established June 28, 1915, under the provision of the Conservancy Act for the purpose of building and maintaining flood control in the Miami Valley.[5] It includes portions of nine counties; Montgomery, Shelby, Miami, Clark, Greene, Warren, Preble, Butler, and Hamilton Counties.

The Miami River drains the southwestern portion of Ohio. Its source is in Logan County, just west of the center of the state, and it empties into the Ohio River at Cleves, a few miles below Hamilton. With its most important tributary, the Whitewater, its total length is 163 miles. The tributaries of the Miami above Hamilton, are Four Mile, Seven Mile, Twin, and Wolf Creeks; The Stillwater River and Loramie Creek from the west, and Mad River from the east.

---

3. *Laws of Ohio,* CIV, 18.
4. *Ibid.,* CIV, 18.
5. Common Pleas Record, volume 90, pp. 222-227, see entry 150.

The Miami Drainage area is about 120 miles long; above Hamilton its area is 3,672 square miles, and above Dayton, 2,525 square miles. The draining of swamp land, cultivation of farms, and possibly the destruction of forests has increased the flood runoff. The tremendous floods that swept down the valley are primarily due to the great storms which occur at intervals in this section.[6]

From March 23 to 27 in 1913, the Miami Valley was swept by a tremendous storm. The streams of the valley fed by this downpour rose rapidly and soon over topped the levees. More than 400 lives were lost and $100,000,000 worth of property was destroyed. Before the wreckage was cleared from the streets, several citizens relief committees were organized, funds were raised, and engineers were employed to study the problem of preventing a similar calamity. Within 60 days, Dayton alone raised $2,000,000. The Morgan Engineering Company of Memphis was employed to work out the problem of flood prevention but it was soon apparent that the cooperation of the entire valley was necessary.[7]

As soon as the governor has signed the Conservancy Act on February 18, 1914, a petition was filed and the court of common pleas of Montgomery County, asking for the establishment of the Miami Conservancy District. After a legal battle on the constitutionality of the law, the district was established on June 28, 1915, as previously stated, by a court decree and the directors were selected. On November 25, 1916, the official plan of improving channels and retarding basins was approved by the court. The appraisal roll was filed on May 9, 1917; on September 1, 1917, the directors of the district levied an assessment on property in the district, and on December 3, they sold the first installment of bonds, amounting to $15,000,000. The actual work consisted of the construction of five dams, levees and channels improvements at nine villages and towns, the relocation of four railroad lines and of many highways and wire lines, the elimination or removal of one village, the lowering of water and gas mains, and many minor pieces of work.[8]

Legally, the conservancy district, under the provisions of the Conservancy Act, is a public corporation, with powers to levy taxes, borrow money, condemn land, or to do whatever may be necessary to the accomplishment of flood prevention work.

---

6. *The Story of the Miami Conservancy District* (Dayton, Ohio, 1931), 5, 6.
7. *Ibid.,* 8.
8. *Ibid.,* 10.

About one-half of the total benefits was assessed to the cities and counties; the other half was assessed to the individual pieces of property subject to actual flooding. The value of property, degree of protection needed and provided, and depth of flooding in the 1913 flood, were all considered. About 60,000 pieces of property belonging to nearly 40,000 different owners were assessed. The benefits totaled $77,000,000. Construction costs are being paid from the proceeds of the sale of bonds worth $33,809,990.83. These bonds will be retired by 1949. The money to take up the bonds and to pay the interest on the bonds and maintenance of the works, is provided by a tax against the benefited property. About 30,000 acres of land was purchased outright by the district. This land, however, is available for agriculture, and is being resold with a flood easement attached.[9]

Construction work was of two main types: Public service relocation which included 2,500, 000 cubic yards of excavation; 30,000 cubic yards of concrete; and 55 miles of railroad track; and flood prevention works which included 8,200,000 cubic yards of embankment in dams; 2,500,000 cubic yards of embankment in levees; 5,330,000 cubic yards of excavation in river channels; 162,000 cubic yards of concrete in outlet works at dams; and 89,000 cubic yards of concrete in walls and levees revetment. Some of the principal items purchased for 450,000 barrels of cement, 70,000 tons of coal, 10,000,000 feet of lumber and 400,000 gallons of gasoline. The total spent on material and supplies, not including construction plant, was over $6,000,000. The maximum number of men employed at one time was 2,000 and the minimum 750.[10]

The five dams are located at Englewood, on the Stillwater; at Taylorsville on the Miami; and at Huffman on the Mad, all just above Dayton; and at Germantown, on Twin Creek, protecting Middletown and Hamilton; and at Lockington on Lorain Creek. The dams built of earth by the hydraulic method, are pierced by concrete conduits, which carry the normal stream flow through the embankment. The last dam was completed December 31, 1921 and the various channel jobs were completed within the next year.[11]

---

9. *Ibid.,* 12, 13.
10. *The Story of the Miami Conservancy District,* 14, 15.
11. *Ibid.,* 15-27.

The first test of the work of the district came on April 11-14, 1922, when a severe storm brought a rainfall of 3.5 inches of rain on saturated ground. Under the old conditions, the Dayton flood stage of 18 feet would have been exceeded and flood would have resulted. Actually, the river reached a stage of only 9.6 feet in Dayton. Only 32 percent of the channel capacity at Dayton was used, and 4 percent of the basin storage capacity was utilized. Near cloudburst and heavy rainfall no longer brings raging floods, and loss of life and property.[12]

---

12. *Ibid.*, 29-31.

Property and Tax Records

547. ABSTRACTS

1918—. 9 file drawers. Subtitled by names of basins.
Copies of abstract drawn in conjunction with obtaining and using land needed for storage or excess water within the boundaries of the district, showing name of property owner, description and location of land conveyed, date of filing, and name of storage basin. Arranged alphabetically by names of basins and chronologically thereunder by dates of filing of abstracts. No index. Typed on printed forms. 16 x 12 x 24. District office, 38 East Monument Avenue, Dayton.

548. COURT CASES

1918—. 7 file boxes. Subtitled by names of counties.
Records of court cases pertaining to acquisition of land for the purpose of water storage and dam construction and legality of acquisition, showing name of court, text of paper, and date filed. Arranged chronologically by dates of filing. No index. Handwritten. 6 x 12 x 24. District office, 38 East Monument Avenue, Dayton.

549. TAX DUPLICATES

1919—. 1664 volumes. (dated).
Record of taxable property in the conservancy district, showing identification number, name of property owner, description and location of property, total amount of appraised benefits, amount of levy, annual assessment, maintenance, semiannual division, total amount due, and remarks. Arranged alphabetically under tabs of names of property owners. No index. Typed on printed forms. Average 150 pages. 24 x 20 x 1. District office, 38 East Monument Avenue, Dayton.

550. TAX RECEIPTS
1919—. 1584 volumes. (dated).

Duplicates of tax receipts, showing identification number, name of property owner, lot number, amount, and date paid. Arranged alphabetically by names of property owners. No index. Typed on printed forms. Average 150 pages. 17 x 14 x 2. District office, 38 East Monument Avenue, Dayton.

551. AUDITOR'S REPORTS
1918—. 5 file boxes.

Copies of court reports confirming legality of tax collections and auditor's reports, showing amount collected and questioned, cost of maintenance, financial status and progress of the work in the district, and date report filed. Arranged chronologically by dates of filing. No index. Handwritten on printed forms. 6 x 12 x 24. District office, 38 East Monument Avenue, Dayton.

Financial Records

552. GENERAL LEDGER
1915—. 9 volumes. (dated).

General administrative ledger, showing date of audit, amount of investments, accounts receivable, other assets, accounts payable, reserves, and expenses classified by departments and revenues classified as to general types and sources. Arranged chronologically by dates of audits. No index. Handwritten on printed forms. Average 200 pages. 11 x 8.5 x 2. District office, 38 East Monument Avenue, Dayton.

553. DAILY BANK BALANCE
1918—. 19 volumes. (1-19).

Record of receipts and disbursements supported by a daily bank statement, showing date of entry, amounts of withdrawals and deposits, and certification of correctness by bank official. Arranged chronologically by dates of entries. No index. Typed on printed forms. Average 200 pages. 11 x 8.5 x 2. District office, 38 East Monument Avenue, Dayton.

554. DISTRIBUTIONS

1918—. 33 volumes. (dated).

Cost distribution sheets, showing date of entry, location and type of work to be done, amount of money appropriated, and a breakdown of expenses, giving date and amount for each part of the work completed. Arranged chronologically by dates of entries. No index. Handwritten and typed on printed forms. Average 200 pages. 11 x 8.5 x 1.5. District office, 38 East Monument Avenue, Dayton.

555. DISBURSEMENT VOUCHERS

1918—. 31 volumes. (1-31).

Copies of vouchers issued authorizing the disbursements of cash for maintenance and services rendered, showing date of voucher, voucher number, name of payee, and amount. Arranged numerically by voucher numbers. No index. Typed on printed forms. Average 150 pages. 11 x 8.5 x 2. District office, 38 East Monument Avenue, Dayton.

556. DISBURSEMENT VOUCHERS [Cancelled]

1918—. 142 file drawers. (labeled by contained voucher numbers).

Original vouchers which have been cancelled, showing information as in Disbursement Vouchers, entry 555. Arranged chronologically by dates of vouchers and numerically by voucher numbers. For index, see entry 557. Handwritten and typed on printed forms. 6 x 12 x 24. District office, 38 East Monument Avenue, Dayton.

557. INDEX TO DISBURSEMENT VOUCHERS

1918—.10 file drawers. (labeled by contained letters of alphabet).

Card index to Disbursement Vouchers [Cancelled], entry 556, showing name and address of payee, amount, date of voucher, date cancelled, and voucher number. Arranged alphabetically by names of payees. Typed, 6 x 4.5 x 12. District office, 38 East Monument Avenue, Dayton.

558. BILLS, VOUCHERS, RECORDS [Inactive]
1918—. 44 file drawers. (dated).
Cancelled freight bills, engineer's vouchers, and a record of construction work completed, all showing date of cancellation or completion, project or subject, and text record. Arranged chronologically by dates of cancellation or completion. No index. Handwritten and typed on printed forms. 6 x 12 x 24. District office, 38 East Monument Avenue, Dayton.

559. PERSONNEL
1917—. 9 file drawers. (labeled by contain letters of alphabet).
Record of personnel connected with the Miami Conservancy District, showing name of employee, position, salary, date entered service, change in rate, pay-off slips, and remarks. Arranged alphabetically by names of employees. No index. Typed on printed forms. 6 x 12 x 24. District office, 38 East Monument Avenue, Dayton.

560. STATE OF OHIO–MIAMI CONSERVANCY DISTRICT PAYROLL
1918—. 31 volumes. (1-31).
Record of payments made for services rendered, showing name of employee, beginning and ending dates of pay-roll period, hours of service rendered, rate per hour, total amount earned, amount deducted, net amount, and date of payment. Arranged chronologically by dates of payments. No index. Handwritten on printed forms. Average 300 pages. 24.5 x 16 x 3.5.

561. CANCELLED CHECKS
1917—. 24 file drawers. (labeled by contained check numbers). Subtitled by names of banks.
Cancelled checks drawn to meet payrolls or services rendered, showing name of employee, amount, check number, date, name of bank, and signatures of payer and payee. Arranged numerically by check numbers. No index. Types on printed forms. 6 x 12 x 24. District office, 38 East Monument Avenue, Dayton.

562. RECEIPTS
1918—. 75 volumes. (1-75).
Record of receipts for construction, maintenance, and assessments, showing file number, name of division, date entered, whether cash, money order, or check, total amount, name of remitter, signature of person familiar with the transaction, and

distribution of amounts to the accounts affected. Arranged chronologically by dates of entries. No index. Handwritten on printed forms. Average 150 pages. 11 x 8.5 x 1.5. District office, 38 East Monument Avenue, Dayton.

563. TREASURY CORRESPONDENCE AND FARM DISTRICT VOUCHERS
1918—. 17 file drawers.

Vouchers certifying disbursements of funds from the farm district treasury, showing nature of disbursement, if for lands purchased from the district, shows names of original owners, amount of land purchased, purchase price, and date filed; if for other disbursements relative to farm district, such as salaries or special services, shows for each item, the number of man hours, amount per hour, and total amount due to date; also includes a record of receipts as apportioned to the farm district, showing nature of receipt, from where and for what purpose, such as sale of dismantled buildings, special farming rights on lands subject to inundation or taxes received from property owners; correspondence between the treasury and residence or property owners in affected area, relative to the acquiring or sale of property, or taxation in the conservancy district, and date filed. Arranged chronologically by dates of filing. No index. Typed. 6 x 12 x 24. District office, 38 East Monument Avenue, Dayton.

Maps and Photographs

564. MAPS
1918—. 6000 maps in 5 map cabinets.

Topographical maps of Miami Conservancy District, showing file number of map, construction feature, and accession numbers; includes maps of rivers, dams, reservoirs, retaining walls, river channels, levees, relocations, bridges, railroads, highways, and detailed construction maps. Prepared by various engineers. Arranged by construction features and numerically thereunder by filed numbers. (Dewey Decimal System). For index, see entry 565. Hand drawn. Scales vary. Cabinets, 28 x 14 x 17.5; sizes of maps vary. District office, 38 East Monument Avenue, Dayton.

565. MAP INDEX

1918—. 25 file boxes. Subtitled by names of construction features.

Card index to maps, entry 564, showing name of construction feature, filed number of map, size of map, and accession numbers. Arranged alphabetically by names of construction features. Typed on cards. 6 x 4.5 x 12. District office, 38 East Monument Avenue, Dayton.

566. RELIEF MAP

1918—. 1 map.

Relief map of the topographical representation of the Miami Conservancy District, showing lowlands and parts affected most by rise and water. Prepared by conservancy engineers. Made of composition. Scale, horizontal, 1 inch equals 2 miles; vertical, 1 inch equals 528 feet. Sealed in glass case, 144 x 60 x 1. District office, 38 East Monument Avenue, Dayton.

567. PHOTOGRAPHS

1918—. 27 albums.

Photographic history of the entire conservancy district, showing date of photograph, dam sites before and after construction, topographical features, obstacles overcome, and unusual conditions. Arranged chronologically by dates of photographs. No index. Average 150 photographs. 11 x 7 x 3. District office, 38 East Monument Avenue, Dayton.

Orders and Contracts

568. ORDERS

1918—. 17 file boxes. (labeled by contained order numbers). 9 subtitled Shop; 8 Warehouse.

Original orders from construction engineers to shop foreman for repairs of equipment and maintenance, showing order number, kind of equipment, nature of work to be done, and date; also includes warehouse orders of construction engineers for supplies and equipment, showing kind of material or supply, date, and remarks pertaining to specifications. Arranged numerically by ordered numbers. No index. Handwritten on printed forms. 12 x 14 x 24. District office, 38 East Monument Avenue, Dayton.

569. CLOSED CONTRACTS
1918—. 4 file boxes. (labeled by contained contract numbers).
Closed and cancelled contracts for construction, showing name of contractor, contract number, terms of contract, and remarks. Arranged numerically by contract numbers. For index, see entry 570. Typed on printed forms. 6 x 12 x 24. District office, 38 East Monument Avenue, Dayton.

570. INDEX TO CLOSED CONTRACTS
1918—. 3 file boxes. (labeled by contained letters of alphabet).
Card index to Closed Contracts, entry 569, showing name of contractor, contract number, and date cancelled or closed. Arranged alphabetically by names of contractors. Typed. 6 x 4.5 x 12. District office, 38 East Monument Avenue, Dayton.

Miscellaneous

571. ENGINEER'S REPORT
1918—. 5 file boxes. (dated).
Engineers' reports to the board of conservancy directors, showing progress made on construction work as outlined in the official plans, percentages of work to be completed, duplicates of orders to shop foreman for the repair and maintenance of equipment, duplicates of orders on warehouses for supplies, record of men employed on job by name and total number employed, hours worked, rate of pay, and date of report. Arranged chronologically by dates of reports. No index. Handwritten on printed forms. 12 x 14 x 24. District office, 38 East Monument Avenue, Dayton.

572. CONSTRUCTION TRANSMITTAL JOURNAL
1918—. 17 volumes.
Copies of letters for state treasurer authorizing transfer of bonds and coupons, showing bond or coupon number, amount, date, and authorization for transfer. Arranged chronologically by dates of entries. No index. Handwritten and typed on printed forms. Average 150 pages. 11 x 10.5 x 1.5. District office, 38 East Monument Avenue, Dayton.

573. GENERAL ADMINISTRATIVE

1918—. 9 file drawers. (labeled by contained letters of alphabet).
Miscellaneous papers pertaining to the general administration of the conservancy district including correspondence, complaints, and investigations with record of answers and findings. All papers show date, names of principles, subject, and date filed. Arranged chronologically by dates of filing. No index. Handwritten and typed. 6 x 12 x 24. District office, 38 East Monument Avenue, Dayton.

574. CORRESPONDENCE

1918—. 21 File drawers. (labeled by contained letters of alphabet).
Inquiries from individuals and firms pertaining to dam and basin construction together with interoffice communications regarding the same, all showing date of communication, names of correspondents, text of the message, and date filed. Arranged chronologically by dates of filing. No index. Handwritten and typed. 6 x 12 x 24. District office, 38 East Monument Avenue, Dayton.

The first agricultural society was organized in Montgomery County in 1839 and on October 17and 18 of the same year, the first agricultural exhibit was held at Swanie's Hotel on East First Street, Dayton.[1] For several years these exhibits were held at this location but receipts were not sufficient to balance expenditures. When such was the case, public spirited citizens usually made up to difference. In 1846, under the provisions of the legislative act of that year, the society was re-organized and new officers placed in charge. For three or four years the fairs were held in North Dayton but were discontinued due to lack of public patronage.[2]

In August of 1852, a public meeting was held in the Dayton city hall for the purpose of reviving the association and new officers were elected. On October 21, 1852 a fair was held on the original fairgrounds (Swanie's) and for the first time the receipts exceeded the expenditures. In October 1853 a fair was held in the bottoms south of Washington Street on the site of the state fair. In 1855 ten acres of the present fairgrounds were purchased. The debt of the association grew to such proportions during these years that the association was forced to lease part of the land to Montgomery County in 1862 and in 1866 they sold the remainder of their holdings to the county and in 1873 the last annual fair was held by the Montgomery County Association.[3]

The Southern Ohio Fair Association was organized in May 1874 and held its first annual exhibit in the autumn of that year and fairs were held regularly until 1880 and the organization held together until 1889.[4] The present Montgomery County Agricultural Society was formed in 1890[5] and with the exception of three years, 1895 to 1897 inclusive, fairs have been held each year.[6]

County agricultural societies in Ohio were provided for by statute as early as 1846. On February 28 of that year the legislature passed an act authorizing the forming of such societies and making provisions for their aid by the counties.[7]

---

1. Ohio Department of Agriculture, *Annual Report, 1936,* 35.
2. A. W. Drury, *History of the City of Dayton and Montgomery County, Ohio* (Chicago and Dayton, 1909), I, 806-809.
3. Drury, *op. cit.,* I, 806.
4. Drury, *op. cit.,* I, 806.
5. Commissioners' Record, volume 9 [1890] p. 209.
6. Drury, *op. cit.,* I, 806-809.
7. *Laws of Ohio,* XLIV, 70.

On February 15, 1853 the legislature declared such societies to be bodies corporate and politic, capable of suing and being sued, and capable of holding in fee simple such real estate as they might purchase for sites whereon to hold fairs, such sites to be paid for by the county commissioners.[8]

By an act of the legislature passed in February 1861, county agricultural societies were required to report annually to the state board of agriculture, and to send a delegate to meet with the state board at Columbus once each year.[9] In 1853 the legislature provided for the organization of district or county agricultural societies. The act making this provision stipulated that with thirty or more persons, residents of any county or district embracing two counties, organized themselves into an agricultural society, under the rules and regulations of the state board of agriculture, the county might aid such society with a grant not to exceed $400 per year.[10] By act of April 21, 1896, provision was made for representation in a county society of thirty or more residents of any county or district embracing two or more counties.[11] In 1900 the legislature extended the amount of county aid to $800 per year.[12] Later, on May 6, 1902, the legislature passed an act authorizing thirty or more residents of a county or of a district embracing one or more counties, to organize themselves into an agricultural society.[13]

On April 17, 1919, the legislature provided for the organization of county and independent agricultural societies, the payment of class premiums; defined the duties of persons competing for premiums; prescribed the publication of treasurers' accounts and the list of awards by societies; designated conditions of membership in a county agricultural society; authorized the society to elect a board of directors consisting of eight members, and prescribed their term of office and the matter of their election. The act further stipulated how such societies might obtain state aid, and authorized the county commissioners to insure all buildings belonging to the agricultural societies.[14]

---

8. *Ibid.*, LI, 333.
9. *Laws of Ohio,* LVIII, 22.
10. *Ibid.*, LXXX, 142.
11. *Ibid.*, XCII, 205.
12. *Ibid.*, XCIV, 395.
13. *Ibid.*, XCV, 403.
14. *Ibid.*, CVIII, pt. i, 381-358.

The legislature of 1921 passed an act stipulating that the total amount of county aid to county agricultural societies should equal 100 percent of the amount paid by the society in regular class premiums but not to exceed $800.[15] By act of March 27, 1925, the county commissioners were authorized to purchase or lease, for a term of not less than twenty years, real estate whereon to hold fairs under the management of the county agricultural societies, and to erect thereon suitable buildings.[16] On March 10, 1927, the legislature authorized the county commissioners to appropriate annually on the request of the agricultural society a sum not less than $1,500 or more than $2,000 from the general fund for the purpose of "encouraging agricultural fairs."[17]

The most recent legislature affecting agricultural societies was that of March 19, 1935. This act provides that where no duly organized county agricultural society existed, and when no fair was held by a duly organized county agricultural society which had held an annual exposition for three years previous to January 1, 1933, the county commissioner should, on the request of an independent society, appropriate annually from the general fund a sum not more than $2,000 nor less than $500 for the encouragement of independent agricultural fairs.[18]

---

15. *Ibid.*, CIX, 240.
16. *Ibid.*, CXI, 238.
17. *Ibid.*, CXII, 84.
18. *Laws of Ohio*, CXVI, 47.

575. COUNTY AGRICULTURAL SOCIETY [Minutes]
1859-1879, 1897-1915, 1918—. 11 volumes.
Minutes of the board of directors of the county agricultural society, showing date of meeting, place, names of members present, and a record of business transacted; 1911—, also shows reports of secretary, and copies of all resolutions. Arranged chronologically by dates of meetings. No index. Handwritten and typed. Average 400 pages. 14 x 10 x 2.5. Office of secretary, 709 Reibold Building, Dayton.

576. CASH BOOK
1892—. 45 volumes.
Record of receipts and disbursements of the county agricultural society; receipts, showing date received, amount, and from whom received; disbursements, showing date paid out, to whom paid, purpose, and amount. Arranged chronologically by dates of receipts and disbursements. No index. Handwritten on printed forms. Average 200 pages. 14 x 10 x 2. 43 volumes, 1892-1935, Main administration building, county fairgrounds, 1047 South Main Street, Dayton; 2 volumes, 1936—, Office of secretary, 709 Reibold Building, Dayton.

In 1914 the federal government passed an act providing for co-operative agricultural extension service between the state agricultural colleges of the United States Department of Agriculture. The purpose of the extension service was to give instructions and practical demonstrations in agricultural and home economics to persons not attending college, and to give such information through field demonstrations, publications, and other means. The funds for such work were to be supplied in part by the federal government and part by the state.[1]

A year following the federal legislation, the Ohio legislature accepted the provisions of the act by providing that twenty or more residents of a county organized themselves into a "farmers' institute society for the purpose of teaching better methods of farming, stock raising, fruit culture and business connected with the agriculture," accepted a constitution and bylaws conforming to the rules and regulations prescribed by the trustees of the Ohio State University, and elected proper officers, the institute could be a corporate body. The Ohio State University was required to furnish speakers for their annual meeting. At the close of the session the trustees were authorized to publish the lectures in pamphlet or book form.

Besides maintaining an institute, the society was authorized to maintain a county experiment farm. Furthermore the county commissioners were authorized to select a county agent subject to the approval of the dean of the college of agriculture of the Ohio State University. In the event the county commissioners failed to make such an appointment, the electorate could require them to do so on a referendum vote.[2] The Montgomery County commissioners, however, took action in the same year, 1914, by appointing Mr. A. L. Higgins as the first agent for the county.[3] It is the duty of the county agent to inspect and study agricultural conditions in his county, distribute agricultural literature, and co-operate with the United States Department of Agriculture and the college of agriculture of the Ohio State University.[4]

In 1929 the original legislation was amended as so to authorize the trustees of the Ohio State University to employ home demonstration agents and boys' and girls' club agents and such other employees as they deem necessary, in addition to the agricultural agent.

---

1. *United States Statutes at Large,* XXXVIII, pt. i, 372-374.
2. *Laws of Ohio,* CVI, 356-359.
3. From records on file in the Agricultural Extension Service Office, Ohio State University.
4. *Laws of Ohio,* CVI, 256-359.

At present Montgomery County has an agricultural agent, a home demonstration agent, and a club agent. The county extension agent was given the additional duty of carrying the teachings of the college of agriculture of the Ohio State University in agriculture and home economics to the residents of the county through personal visits, bulletins, and practical demonstrations. Furthermore, it was his duty to render educational service not only in relation to agricultural production, but also in relation to economic problems including marketing, distribution, and utilization of farm products.[5]

The initial legislation contained a clause which required the county commissioners to appropriate annually one thousand dollars if they wish to obtain the services of the agricultural agent. This amount was to be matched by the state. Under the present system the commissioners are empowered to levy a tax and to appropriate money from the proceeds thereof or from the general fund of the county an amount not in excess of three thousand dollars for each agent to be paid into the state treasury to the credit of the agricultural extension fund. Amounts in excess must have the unanimous consent of the commissioners.[6]

---

5. *Laws of Ohio,* CXIII, 82-83; CVIII, pt. i, 364.
6. *Ibid.,* CXIII, 82-83.

Conservation and Crop Control

577. SOIL CONSERVATION
1936—. 20 file boxes. (labeled by names of crops).
Agreements with farmers for conservation of soil, showing date, name of farmer, reports on progress, and type or name of crop planted. Arranged by types or names of crops and alphabetically thereunder by names of farmers. No index. Typed on printed forms. 12 x 15 x 25.5. Agricultural extension agents office, 313 Federal Building, Dayton.

578. CORN AND HOG CONTRACTS
1934-1936. 10 file boxes. Discontinued; law repealed.
Contracts with farmers for corn and hog curtailment under AAA plan, showing date of contract, name of farmer, text of contract and agreement, and record of cash payments. Arranged alphabetically by names of farmers. No index. Handwritten and typed on printed forms. 2 file boxes, 10 x 12.5 x 18; 8 file boxes, 12 x 15 x 25.5. Agricultural extension agents office, 313 Federal Building, Dayton.

579. WHEAT CONTRACTS

1934-1936. 7 file boxes. Discontinued; law repealed.

Copies of contracts between the United States Government and farmers for the purpose of abating proposed wheat crop under AAA program, showing name of farmer, size and location of farm, date of contract, and text and terms of agreement. Arranged alphabetically by names of farmers. No index. Handwritten and typed on printed forms. 12 x 15 x 25.5 Agricultural extension agents office, 313 Federal Building, Dayton.

580. TOBACCO

1934—. 11 file boxes.

Contracts with farmers or curtailment of tobacco production under AAA plan, showing date, name of farmer, location of farm, size, and terms of contracts and agreement. Arranged alphabetically by names of farmers. No index. Handwritten and typed on printed forms. 12 x 15 x 25.5. Agricultural extension agents office, 313 Federal Building, Dayton.

4-H Clubs and Home Demonstration

581. 4-H CLUB RECORDS

1937—. 2 file boxes.

Record of 4-H Club enrollment, showing name and address of member, name of township, names of parents, grade in school, and activity in which engaged. Arranged alphabetically by the names of members. No index. Handwritten and typed on printed forms. 12 x 15 x 25.5. Agricultural extension agents office, 313 Federal Building, Dayton.

582. HOME DEMONSTRATION

1937—. 2 file drawers.

Card record of members of the home demonstration clubs, showing name and address of member, name of township, date of activity, kind or type of activity, as home council, food and nutrition, household management, home beautification, achievement day, camping, child development, household furniture, canning, and fair committee. Arranged alphabetically by names the townships. No index. Handwritten on printed forms. 7.5 x 18 x 20. Agricultural extension agents office, 313 Federal Building, Dayton.

583. REPORTS OF HOME DEMONSTRATION

1937—. 2 file boxes.

Reports of home demonstration activities, showing date, name of township, and record of achievements in child care, clothing, food, nutrition, health, home, and garden activities. Arranged alphabetically by names of townships. No index. Typed and handwritten on printed forms. 12 x 15 x 25.5. Agricultural extension agents office, 313 Federal Building, Dayton.

Correspondence

584. CORRESPONDENCE

1934—. 12 file boxes.

Business correspondence between county agricultural agent and farmers, showing names of correspondents, date of letter, and text of same. Arranged alphabetically by names of correspondents. No index. Handwritten and typed. 12 x 15 x 25.5. Agricultural extension agents office, 313 Federal Building, Dayton.

Archival Materials and Published Documents

Acts of the General Assembly, 1803-1941 (119 volumes, published under state authority).

Baldwin, William Edward, ed., *Throckmorton's Ohio Code* (certified ed., Cleveland, 1936).

Carter, Clarence Edwin, ed., and comp., *Territorial Papers of the United States* (4 volumes, Washington, 1934, in progress). Volumes II and III of this work treat of the Northwest Territory.

Chase, Salmon P., comp., *The Statutes of Ohio and of the Northwest Territory, 1788-1833* (3 volumes, Cincinnati, 1833-1835).

Commissioners' Journal, 1804—. (45 volumes). This journal, as well as the other records listed under the various offices included in the inventory, constitutes the most important source material on the history of Montgomery County.

Common Pleas Record, 1803—. (328 volumes).

County Home Minutes, 1854-1912. (6 volumes).

Curwen, Maskell E., comp., *Public Statues at Large of the State of Ohio* (3 volumes, Cincinnati, 1853-1854).

Hammond, Charles, and others, eds., *Reports of Cases Argued and Determined in the Supreme Court of Ohio in Bank . . .* (20 volumes, Cincinnati, 1824-1852).

Laning, Jay F. Comp., *Revised Statutes of the State of Ohio* (3 volumes, Norwalk, 1905).

Laws of the Territory of the United States Northwest of the River Ohio (3 volumes, Philadelphia and Cincinnati, 1792-1796).

Laws, Treaties and other Documents Having Operation and Respect to the Public Lands (Washington, 1810).

McCook, G. W. and others, eds., *Reports of Cases Argued and Determined in the Supreme Court of Ohio . . .* (137 volumes, Cincinnati, 1852-1940).

Ohio Attorney General, *Opinions,* 1917-1939 (Published under state authority). Published in *Annual Report,* 1846-1914.

Ohio Auditor of State, *Annual Report,* 1836-1939 (published annually under state authority). Printed prior to 1836 in the Senate and House Journals.

Ohio Auditor of State, *Comparative Statistics, Counties of Ohio.* 1906-1939 (published under state authority).

Ohio Department of Agriculture, *Annual Report,* 1846-1936 (published under state authority).

Ohio Secretary of State, *Annual Report,* 1836-1936 (published under state authority). Some volumes titled: *Ohio Statistics.*

Ohio Secretary of State, *Election Statistics,* 1888-1936 (published under state authority).

Ohio Secretary of State, *Official Roster, Federal, State and County Officers and Departmental Information,* 1861-1940 (published biennially under state authority).

Ohio Tax Commission, *Financing State and Local Government in Ohio,* 1900-1932 (mimeographed, Columbus, 1934).

Page, William H., ed., *Page's Ohio General Code, Annotated* (12 volumes, Cincinnati, c1937). Supplements issued periodically for each volume.

Pease, Theodore Calvin, comp., *The Laws of the Northwest Territory, 1788-1800* (Illinois state bar association *Law Series,* Springfield, 1925, I).

[Probate] Journal, 1852——. (223 volumes).

Sayler, J. R. Comp., *The Statutes of the State of Ohio* (4 volumes, Columbus, 1876).

Sherman C. E. *Original Ohio Land Subdivisions, Final Report, III, Ohio Cooperative Topographical Survey* (4 volumes, Mansfield and Columbus 1929).

Smith J. V. Rep., *Official Reports of the Debate and Proceedings of the Ohio State Convention . . . held at Columbus Commencing May 6, 1850, and at Cincinnati, Commencing December 2, 1850* (Columbus, 1851).

The Reorganization of County Government in Ohio: Report of the Governor's Commission on County Government (n. p., December 1934).

Trautwein, George C., ed., *Page's Ohio Cumulative Code Service* (22 volumes, Cincinnati, 1927-1938).

——. *Supplement to Page's Annotated General Code 1926-1935* (Cincinnati, 1935).

United States Statutes at Large, 1789-1941 (54 volumes, United States Government Printing Office).

Diaries and Memoirs

Burnet [Jacob], *Notes on the Early Settlement of the North-western Territory* (Cincinnati, 1847).

Darlington, William M., ed., *Christopher Gist's Journals, with Historical, Geographical and Ethnological Notes and Bibliographies of his Contemporaries* (Pittsburgh, 1893).

General Histories and Reference Works

Adams, George Burton, *Constitutional History of England* (New York, 1921).

Channing, Edward, *A History of the United States* (6 volumes, New York, 1905-1925).

Cross, Arthur Lyon, *A Shorter History of England and Greater Britain* (New York, 1925).

Estrich, Willis, A., ed., *Ohio Jurisprudence* (43 volumes, Rochester, 1928-1938). Henry P. Farnham editor in chief, 1928-1929.

Gwynne, A. E., *A Practical Treatise on the Law of Sheriff and Coroner with Forms and Special Reference to the Statutes of Ohio, Indiana, and Kentucky* (Cincinnati, 1849).

Karraker, Cyrus Herreld, *The Seventeenth Century Sheriff: A Comparative Study of the Sheriff in England and the Chesapeake Colonies, 1607-1689* (Chapel Hill, 1930).

Moley, Raymond, "The Sheriff and the Coroner" (New York, 1926. *The Missouri Crime Survey,* pt. ii, 59-110).

Pollock, Sir Frederick, and Maitland, Frederic William, *The History of English Law Before the Time of Edward I* (2 volumes, Cambridge, 1895).

Robinson, Louis N., *Penology in the United States* (Philadelphia, 1922).

Schapiro J. Salwyn, *Modern and Contemporary European History, 1815-1928* (New York, 1931).

Sutherland, Edwin H., *Principals of Criminology* (Chicago, 1934).

Willoughby, W. F., *Principles Of Judicial Administration* (Washington, 1929).

Regional and Local Histories, Treatises, and Monographs

Amer, Francis J., *The Development of the Judicial System in Ohio from 1787 to 1932* (Johns Hopkins University, Baltimore, 1932. *Institute of Law Bulletin No. 3).*

Beers, W. H., and Company, pub., *History of Montgomery County* (Chicago 1882).

Bond, Beverley W., Jr., *The Civilization of the Old Northwest: A Study of Political, Social, and Economic Development, 1788-1812* (New York, 1934).

Conover, Charlotte Reeve, ed., *Dayton and Montgomery County Resources and People* (4 volumes, New York 1932).

Council of Social Agencies, *Social Service Directory for Dayton and Montgomery County* (3 volumes, Dayton 1930-1938).

Downes, Randolph Chandler, *Frontier Ohio, 1788-1803 (Ohio Historical Collections,* III, Columbus, 1935).

Drake, Daniel, *A Natural and Statistical View of Cincinnati and the Miami Country* (Cincinnati, 1815).

Drury, A. W., *History of the City of Dayton and Montgomery County, Ohio* (2 volumes, Chicago and Dayton, 1909).

Edgar, John F., *Pioneer Life in Dayton and Vicinity* (Dayton, 1896).

Gregory, William M., and Guitteau, William B., *History and Geography of Ohio* (Boston, 1922).

Heiges, R. E., *The Office of Sheriff in the Rural Counties of Ohio* (Findlay, Ohio, 1933).

Hentz, J. P., *History of the Evangelical Lutheran Congregation in Germantown, Ohio* (Dayton 1882).

Hentz, J. P., *Twin Valley* (Dayton, 1883).

Holt, Edgar C., *Party Politics in Ohio, 1840-1850, Ohio Historical Collections* I (Columbus 1931).

Hubbart, Henry G., *The Older Middle West* (New York, 1936).

Kennedy, Aileen Elizabeth, *The Ohio Poor Law and Its Administration* (Sophonisba P. Breckinridge, ed., *Social Service Monographs*, No. 22, University of Chicago Press, Chicago, 1934). A study of the administration of poor relief in Ohio prior to 1932.

Law, Robert O., Company, pub., *Memoirs of the Miami Valley* (3 volumes, Chicago, 1919).

McCarty, Dwight G., *The Territorial Governors of the Old Northwest: A Study in Territorial Administration* (Iowa city, 1910).

Mills, William C., *Archaeological Atlas of Ohio* (Columbus 1914), Contains map showing the location of Ohio mounds, villages, and other remains.

Peters William E., *Ohio Lands and Their Subdivision* (2d ed., Athens, Ohio, 1918).

Porter, George H., *Ohio Politics During the Civil War Period* (New York, 1911).

Roseboom, Eugene Holloway and Weisenburger, Francis Phelps, *A History of Ohio* (New York, 1934).

Sharts, Joseph W., *Biography of Dayton* (Dayton, 1922).

Steele, Robert W., and Mary D. *Early Dayton* (Dayton 1896).

Steele, Robert W., *The Public Schools and Libraries of Dayton* (Dayton, 1889).
The Story of the Miami Conservancy District (Dayton, 1931).
United Brethren Publishing Company, pub., *History of Dayton, Ohio* (Dayton, 1889).

Articles in Periodicals

Atkinson R. C. "County Home Rural Developments in Ohio," *National Municipal Review,* XXXIII (1934), 235.
Atkinson R. C., "Ohio–County Charter Elections," *National Municipal Review,* XXIV (1935), 702-703.
Atkinson, R. C., "Ohio– Optional County Legislation," *National Municipal Review,* XXIV, (1935), 228.
Beaver, R. Pierce, "The Miami Purchase of John Cleaves Symmes," *State Archaeological and Historical Quarterly,* XL (1931), 284-342.
Bond, Beverley W., Jr., "Memoirs of Benjamin Van Cleve," *Quarterly Publications of the Historical and Philosophical Society of Ohio,* XVII (1922), 7-71.
Downes, Randolph Chandler "Evolution of Ohio County Boundaries," *Ohio State Archaeological and Historical Quarterly,* XXXVI (1927), 340-477.
Dykstra, C. A., "Cleveland's Effort for City-County Consolidation," *National Municipal Review,* VIII (1919), 551-556.
Fessler, Mayo, "Secret Political Societies in the North During the Civil War," *Indiana Magazine of History,* XIV, (1918), 183-286.
Gates, Charles M., "The Administration of State Archives," *The Pacific Northwest Quarterly,* XXIX, (January 1938), No. 1.
Goodwin, Frank P., "The Rise of Manufacturers in the Miami Country," *American Historical Review,* XII, (1906-1907), 761-775.
Greenman, E. F., "Excavation of the Coon Mound and an Analysis of the Adena Culture," *Ohio State Archaeological and Historical Quarterly,* XLI, (1932), 367-523.
Hockett, Homer C., *Western Influences on Political Parties to 1825,* Ohio State University *Bulletin,* XXII, No. 3 (1917).
"The Indian Mound, Miamisburg, Ohio," *Ohio State Archaeological and Historical Quarterly,* XIV (1905), 446-447.
Kaplan, H. Eliot, "A Personal Program for County Service," *National Municipal Review,* XXV, (1936), 596-600.

Lambing, A. A., ed., "Celoron's Journal," *Ohio State Archaeological and Historical Quarterly,* XXIX (1920), 335-396.

McAlpine, William, "The Origin of Public Education in Ohio," *Ohio State Archaeological and Historical Quarterly,* XXXVIII (1921), 409-447.

Miller, Edward A., "The History of Educational Legislation in Ohio," *Ohio State Archaeological and Historical Quarterly,* XXVII (1919), 1-271.

Morris, William A., "The Office of Sheriff in the Anglo-Saxon Period," *English Historical Review,* XXXI, (1916), 20-40.

Roseboom, Eugene H., "Ohio in the Presidential Election of 1824," *Ohio State Archaeological and Historical Quarterly,* XXVI, (1917), 153-224.

Shetrone, Henry C., "The Indian in Ohio," *Ohio State Archaeological and Historical Quarterly,* XXVII (1919), 273-510.

Shilling, David C., "Relation of Southern Ohio to the South During the Decade Preceding the Civil War," *Quarterly Publication of the Historical and Philosophical Society of Ohio,* VIII (1913), 3-28.

Stone, Donald C., "The Police Attack Crime," *National Municipal Review,* XXIV, (1935), 39-41.

Symmes, John Cleaves, "The Trenton Circular," *Quarterly Publication of the Historical and Philosophical Society of Ohio,* V (1910).

Van Cleve, John W., "A Brief History of the Settlement of the Town of Dayton," *Journal of Historical and Philosophical Society of Ohio,* No, 1 (1838), 64-70.

Newspapers

Dayton *Journal,* 1936.
Ohio State Journal, 1840, 1933.

1803-1941

Commissioners**

William Brown	1804-1805	Emanuel Gebhart	1840-1843
Samuel Hawkins	1804-1807	Davis Waymire	1842-1851
Edmund Munger	1804-1809	William Worley	1843-1846
John Devor	1805-1811	David Lamme	1844-1853
John Folkerth	1807-1816	John C. Negley	1846-1852
Daniel Hoover	1809-1812	Ezra T. Leggett	1851-1854
John H. Williams	1811-1814	John Yount	1852-1858
Abraham Brower	1812-1815	Frederick Gebhart	1853-1856
David McClure	1814-1817	John Turner	1854-1860
John Miller	1815-1818	John Dryden	1856-1859
Isaac G. Burnett	1816–1822	Henry Shidler	1858-1861
Daniel Yount	1817-1820	Emauel Schultz	1859-1862
Benjamin Maltibie	1818-1824	Daniel Kiser	1860-1863
Henry Brown	1820-1823	John Wheeland	1861-1864
John H. Williams	1822-1825	John Harshman	1862-1865
Chris Taylor	1823-1829	Alfred Iams	1863-1866
Moses Grier	1824-1830	James Applegate	1864-1870
Aaron Baker	1825-1831	Samuel Rohrer	1865-1868
Jacob B. John	1829-1832	George A. Grove	1866-1872
James Russell	1830-1836	Jesse D. Harry	1868-1874
George Olinger	1831-1837	Madison Munday	1870-1876
Aaron Baker	1832-1835	Samuel Martindale	1872-1875
Alexander Grimes	1835-1838	John G. Getter	1874-1880
Chris Emerick	1836-1839	Charles Crook	1875-1878
John Furnas	1837-1840	John R. Brownell	1876-1879
Chris Taylor	1838-1844	Isaac J. Bassett	1878-1884
James A. Riley	1839-1842	George W. Purcell	1879-1885

*Compiled from: Montgomery County Commissioners' Journal, 1804-1941; Common Pleas Record, 1803-1941; Probate Journal, 1852-1941; Ohio Secretary of State, *Annual Report,* 1882-1910; Ohio Secretary of State, *Official Roster, Federal, State, County Officers...* 1908-1940; W. H. Beers and Co., pub., *History of Montgomery County, Ohio* (Chicago, 1882), 535-536.

**The board of county commissioners, with three members each serving a three-year elective term, was established by law in 1804 (2 O. L, 150. In 1906 the term of office was shortened to two years (98 O. L. 271), and in 1920 it was lengthened to its present span of four years (108 O. L. pt. ii, 1300).

Commissioners (continued)

Lewis C. Kimmell	1880-1883	Frank Munger	1906-1913
H. C. Marshall	1883-1889	George W. Fair	1908-1913
John Munger	1884-1890	Richard M. Gebhart	1909-1913
Abraham Troxell	1885-1888	Charles F. Breuner	1913-1919
James B. Hunter	1888-1891	Arthur L. Eberly	1913-1919
Alonzo B. Ridgway	1889-1892	Alonzo Michael	1913-1917
David R. Shroyer	1890-1893	Clem L.Shroyer	1917-1919
Lewis H. Zehring	1891-1894	Herbert A. Shank	1919-1923
James B. Hunter	1892-1898	John J. Baker	1919-1933
Henry W. Kaiser	1894-1900	L. A. Mosby	1919-1933
David A. Dean	1896-1902	J. Mason Prugh	1923-1931
William L. Anderson	1898-1904	Samuel G. Carr	1931-1939
Samuel E. Kemp	1900-196-	Clem L. Shroyer	1933—
Charles W. Haines	1902-1908	John E. Brumbaugh	1933—
L. G. Clagett	1904-1909	Elmer L. Timmerman	1939—

Recorders*

David Reid	1805-1813	Thomas M. Miskelly	1880-1886
Warren Munger, Sr.	1813-1831	Joel O. Shoup	1886-1892
William L. Helfenstein	1831-1835	Jesse R. Lindemuth	1892-1895
David S. Davis	1835-1838	Charles E. Clark	1895-1901
William Potter	1838-1841	John L. Theobald	1901-1907
William Gunckel	1841-1844	Benjamin W. McClary	1907-1911
J. W. Griswold	1844-1850	Elias Van Scoyk	1911-1915
Joseph Hughes	1850-1856	Samuel G. Carr	1915-1919
Daniel G. Fitch	1856-1859	William H. Guckes	1919-1923
David Ecker	1859-1862	T. M. Bookwalter	1923-1929
George W. Owen	1862-1868	Mrs. Mary C. Bookwalter	1929-1931
Johnson Snyder	1868-1874	Bert Badgley	1931-1935
James Hall	1874-1880	Charles A. Pfeiffer	1935—

By statute of 1803 the county recorder was appointed by the associate judges of the court of common pleas for a seven-year term (1 O. L. 136). In 1829 the office became elective for a three-year term (27 O. L. 65), which was changed to a two-year term in 1905 (*Ohio Const. 1851*, Art. XVII, sec. 2, Amendment 1905), and a four-year term in 1936 (116 O. L. pt. ii, 184).

Clerks of the Court of Common Pleas*

Benjamin Van Cleve	1803-1821	John S. Robertson	1876-1882
George Newcom	1821-1822	Owen Britt Brown	1882-1885
C. R. Greene	1822-1833	George W. Knecht	1885-1888
Edward W. Davies	1833-1840	Kemper Flaviues Bowles	1888-1864
Edwin Smith	1840-1847	Calvin W. Hassler	1894-1900
William J. McKinney	1847-1854	Charles W. Bieser	1900-1906
George W. Brown	1854-1855	John M. Ebert	1906-1913
Adam Miller	1855-1858	J. Clarence Schaeffer	1913-1917
David K. Boyer	1858-1864	William H. Hanley	1917-1921
Frederick C. Fox	1864-1870	C. D. Hoffman	1921-1933
John F. Sinks	1870-1876	J. Clarence Schaeffer	1933—

*Under the Ohio Constitution of 1802, the court of common pleas appointed its own clerk for a seven-year term (Art. III, sec. 9). The office of clerk became elective for a three-year term under the constitution of 1851 (Art. IV, sec. 16). In 1905 the term was changed to two years (98 O. L. 641), and to four years in 1936 (116 O. L. pt. ii, 184).

Judges of the Court of Common Pleas**

President judges under the constitution of 1802 for District I which included Montgomery County

Francis Dunlavy	1803-1817	George B. Holt	1843-1850
Joseph H. Crane	1817-1828	John Beers	1850-1851
George B. Holt	1828-1836	Ralph S. Hart	1851-1852
William L. Helfstein	1836-1842		

**The president and associate judges under the first constitution were appointed for seven-year terms by joint ballot of both houses of the general assembly (*Ohio Const. 1802*, Art. II, sec. 8). The constitution of 1851 made the office elective for five-year periods and required the incumbent to be a resident of the district in which elected (*Ohio Const. 1851*, Art. IV. Sec. 12). The amendment of 1912 changed the term to six years and required the election of at least one judge for each county who must be a resident of the county in which elected (*ibid.*, Amendment, 1912).

Associate judges under the constitution of 1802 for District I which included Montgomery County

Isaac Spinning	1803-1826	George Olinger	1837-1844
(Died January)		John Shelby	1840-1847
John Ewing	1803-1810	James Steele	1841
Benjamin Arthur/Archer	1803-1810	(February 20-26)	
Abner Gerard	1814-1818	Vice Thomas Winters; resigned)	
(Resigned December)		Charles G. Swain	1841-1842
Abner Gerard	1814-1818	(Vice James Steele)	
(Died July)		Charles G. Swain	1842-1849
William George	1810-1817	(Resigned April)	
Philip Gunckle	1817-1831	Elias Mathews	1844
James Steele	1818-1820	(March to October; died)	
(Vice A. Gerard)		Amos Irwin	1844-1858
James Steele	1820-1834	Michael Cassady	1844-1851
Benjamin Maltibie	1826-1833	(Resigned April)	
Henry Hipple	1831-1837	George Olinger	1844
(Resigned February)		(Vice Elias Mathews)	
John W. Turner	1833-1840	George Olinger	1844-1851
Thomas Winters	1834-1841	Robert P. Brown	1849-1858
(Resigned February)		Herman Gebhart	1851-1858

Judges under the constitution of 1851 for District II which included Montgomery County

Ralph S. Hart	1852-1857	Alexander F. Hume	1877-1887
Ebenezer Parsons	1857-1867	James A. Gilmore	1879-1874
Ichabod Corwin	1866-1872	John W. Sater	1883-1888
(Died October 1872)		Charles R. White	1885-1890
R. C. Fulton	1872-1873	(Died August 1890)	
(Vice Ichabod Corwin)		Joseph W. O'Neall	1886-1891
John C. McKenny	1866-1872	(Resigned October 1891)	
(Resigned October 1872)		Horace L. Smith	1889-1899
Henderson Elliott	1871-1896	David B. Van Peld	1890-1900
(Died July 1896)		(Vice Charles R. White)	
David L. Meeker	1872-1873	John C. Miller	1890-1895
(Vice John C. McKenny)		J. A. Runyan	1891-1892
David L. Meeker	1873-1883	(Vice Joseph O'Neall)	
Alexander F. Hume	1875-1877		

Judges under the constitution of 1851, (continued)

Walter S. Dillatush	1892-1895	Edward F. Snediker	1906-1912
(Died October 1895)		Charles H. Kyle	1905
George W. Stanky	1895-1896	(January to November	
(Vice Walter S. Dillatush)		Vice Thomas E. Scroggy)	
Charles W. Dustin	1896-1904	Charles H. Kyle	1905-1910
(Resigned 1904)		Edwin P. Matthews	1905
Milton Clark	1896-1906	(November to December	
Albin W.Kumler	1896-1906	resigned December 1905)	
Oren Britt Brown	1896-1906	Ulysses S. Martin	1905-1906
Thomas E. Scroggy	1899-1905	(Vice Edwin P. Matthews)	
(Resigned January 1905)		Warren Gard	1907-1913
William W. Savage	1900-1905	Clarence Murphy	1907-1919
Felix G. Slone	1903-1910	Walter S. Harlan	1912-1917
Edward F. Snediker	1904-1906		
(Vice Charles W. Dustin)			

Resident judges under the constitutional amendment of 1912

Carroll Sprigg	1915-1917	John P. Naas	1928
EdwardT. Snediker	1915-1924	(Part of year, died in office)	
Ulysses S. Martin	1915-1924	Irwin L. Holderman	1929
Roland W. Baggott	1917-1927	(Part of year)	
(Division of Domestic Relations)		Lester L. Cecil	1929—
Robert C. Patterson	1917-1935	Mason Douglas	1930-1936
Alfred McGray	1921-1929	Robert U, Martin	1935—
Edward F. Snediker	1925-1936	Charles Lee Mills	1936—
William W. White	1925-1936	Null M. Hodapp	1937—
Arthur Markey	1927-1940	Franklin G. Krehbiel	1937—
(Division of Domestic Relations)		Frank Nicholas	1941—
John B. Worley	1928	(Division of Domestic Relations)	

Judges of the Probate Court*

Younger V. Wood	1852-1855	John W. Kreitzer	1891-1894
Joseph G. Crane	1855-1858	Obed W. Irwin	1894-1900
James H. Baggott	1858-1861	Benjamin F. McCann	1900-1906
Samuel Boltin	1861-1867	Charles W. Dale	1906-1906
Dennis Dwyer	1867-1876	Roland W. Baggott	1909-1917
John L. H. Frank	1876-1882	Harry N. Routzhon	1917-1929
William D. McKenny	1882-1891	William C. Wiseman	1929—

*The probate court was established in 1852, with a single judge serving a three-year term (*Ohio Const. 1851*, Art. IV, secs. 7, 8). The elective term was increased to its present length of four years in 1012. (*ibid.,* Amendment, 1912).

Prosecuting Attorneys**

Daniel Symmes	1803-1805	Elihu Thompson	1870-1874
Arthur St. Clair	1805-1808	James C. Young	1874-4876
Isaac G. Burnett	1808-1813	John M. Sprigg	1876-1880
Joseph H. Crane	1813-1817	James C. Young	1880-1882
Henry Bacon	1817-1834	John M. Sprigg	1882-1888
Peter P. Lowe	1834-1838	Robert M. Nevin	1888-1891
Joseph H. Crane	1838-1840	John Patterson	1891-1894
William H. Blodget	1840-1841	Charles H. Kumler	1894-1900
George C. Holt	1841	U. S. Martin	1900-1906
Charles Anderson	1841-1843	Carl W. Lenz	1906-1913
Daniel O'Haynes	1843-1847	Robert C. Patterson	1913-1917
Samuel Craighead	1847-1851	Bernard M. Focke	1917-1919
James H. Baggott	1851-1856	H. E. Naw	1919-1923
D. A. Houk	1856-1860	Albert H. Scharrer	1923-1927
Daniel P. Nead	1860-1862	Ralph E. Hoskot	1927-1929
Henderson Elliott	1862-1864	Paul J. Wortman	1929-1931
Younger V. Wood	1864-1866	Calvin C. Crawford	1931-1935
Warren Monger, Jr.	1866-1868	Nicholas F. Nolan	1935—
George V. Nauerth	1868-1870		

**At first appointive by the coourt of common pleas, the office of prosecuting attorney was made elective for a term of two years in 1833 (31 O. L. 13). In 1881 the term was lengthened to three years (78 O. L. 260), in 1906 shortened to two years (98 O. L. 271), and in 1936 increased to four years (116 O. L. pt. ii, 184).

Coroners*

James Miller, Jr.	1803-1807	Ephraim Snyder	1868-1870
Henry Curtner	1807-1809	William R. Bennett	1870-1873
David Squire	1809-1811	Jacob Kuhns	1873-1877
James Wilson	1811-1813	John P. Kline	1877-1879
James Ritchie	1813	James D. Dougherty	1879-1883
(June to October)		W. P. Treen	1883-1887
Aaron Baker	1813-1817	Simon P. Drayer	1887-1891
John Dodson	1817-1831	Gamaliel O. Myers	1891-1895
Phillip Keller	1831-1834	Lee Corbin	1895-1899
Jacob Davis	1834-1836	Harry M. Hatcher	1899-1903
John McClure, Jr.	1836-1837	Walter E. Kline	1903-1907
David Reed	1837-1838	George R. Schuster	1907-1909
Adam Houk	1838-1840	W. Swisher	1909-1913
Ebenezer Henderson	1840-1844	John W. McKenny	1913-1917
Theodore Barlow	1844-1845	Charles J.Otto	1917-1919
Ebenezer Henderson	1845-1851	Edward O. Willoughby	1919-1921
Samuel Richards	1851-1856	Elmer E. Kimmel	1921-1925
David S. Craig	1856-1858	John F. Torrence	1925-1929
George Nauerth	1858-1860	Elmer E. Kimmel	1929-1931
Albert G. Walden	1860-1862	Maurice P. Cooper	1931-1935
William Egry	1862-1864	H. W. Harris	1935-1941
William h. Rouzer	1864-1868	Arthur P. McDonald	1941—

*Under the first constitution the office of corner was made elective for a two-year term (*Ohio Const., 1802*, Art. VI, sec. 1). Since then the only change made was a lengthening of the term to four years in 1936 (116 O. L. pt. ii, 184).

Sheriffs**

George Newcom	1803-1808	Samuel Archer	1816-1820
Jerome Holt	1808-1811	James Henderson	1820-1824
Samuel Archer	1811-1813	George C. Davis	1824-1828
David Squier	1813-1814	Ebenezer Stibbens	1828-1833
John King	1814-1816	James Brown	1833-1836

**Under the first constitution the office of sheriff was made elective for a two-year term (*Ohio Const., 1802*, Art. VI, sec. 1). Since then the only change made was a lengthening of the term to four years in 1936 (116 O. L. pt. ii, 184).

Sheriffs (continued)

Jacob Davis	1836-1838	Louis Mehlberth	1899
Benjamin Hall	1838-1842	(January to September)	
Robert Brown	1842-1846	William C. Kirshner	1899-1903
David Clark	1846-1850	John A. Wright	1903-1907
Ebenezer Henderson	1850-1855	John F. Boes	1907-1909
Samuel C. Emly	1855-1859	Henry Eshbaugh	1909-1913
John Mills	1859-1861	Edward J. Leo	1913-1917
George Wogaman	1861-1865	William C. Oldt	1917-1921
Orion G. H. Davidson	1865-1869	James E. Cusick	1921-1923
Michael J. Swadener	1869-1873	Howard E. Webster	1923-1927
William Patton	1873-1877	Fred S.Wolf	1927-1929
Albert Beebe	1877-1879	Robert M. Blank	1929-1931
Andrew C. Nixon	1879-1883	Fred S. Wolf	1931-1933
Charles T. Freeman	1883-1885	Eugene F. Frick	1933-1935
Frederick Weis	1885-1887	W. L. Case	1935
William H. Snyder	1887-1891	(Part of year; resigned)	
Charles J. Gerdes	1891-1893	P. J. Kloos	1935—
John L. Gusler	1893-1895	(Vice W. L. Case)	
Charles Anderson, Sr.	1895-1899		

Treasurers*

James Patterson	1803-1805	Jonathan Kenney	1856-1860
John Folkerth	1805-1807	David C. Bench	1860-1863
Chris Curtner	1807-1818	Jonathan Kenny	1863-1864
William George	1818-1820	Daniel Staley	1864-1867
William Bomberger	1820-1834	John W. Turner	1867-1871
James Slaght	1834-1838	Daniel H. Dryden	1871-1875
Peter Baer	1838-1840	Henry H. Laubach	1875-1879
Nathaniel Wilson	1840-1844	Jonathan Kenney	
Joseph Davison	1844-1849	(Failed to qualify)	
Smith Davison	1849-1852	Gabriel Herman (Vice)	1879-1880
David Clark	1852-1856	Stephen J. Allen	1880-1884

*The office of treasurer was created by legislative act in 1803 (1 O. L. 98). Appointive by the county commissioners until 1827, the office then became elective for two-year terms (25 O. L. 25-32). The term was lengthened to four years in 1936 (116 O. L. pt ii, 184).

Treasurers (continued)

Louis H. Poock	1884-1888	M. L. Beard	1919-1921
Frank T. Huffman	1888-1892	Charles A. Kline	1921-1923
Thomas B. Minnich	1892-1894	M. L. Beard	1923-1925
Wayland P. Sunderland	1894-1898	William E. Sparks	1925-1929
Thomas A. Selz	1898-1902	Earl A. Welbaum	1929-1933
Charles Anderton, Sr.	1902-1906	A. M. Myers	1933
Clarence S. Wiggin	1906-1909	(Part of year; died in office)	
John V. Lytle	1909-1911	Chester A. Myers	1933-1937
Clarence S. Wiggin	1911-1915	(Vice A. M. Myers)	
George H. Schmidt	1915-1919	Chester A. Myers	1937—

Auditors*

Alexander Grimes	1821-1827	George P. Boyer	1869-1874
Joseph H. Conover	1827-1831	William A. Mays	1874-1878
David C. Baker	1831-1835	Frederick Shutte	1878-1884
James Douglass	1835-1837	John D. Turner	1884-1890
William J. McKinney	1837-1839	Herbert W. Lewis	1890-1896
Isaac Douglass	1839-1841	Alfred G. Feight	1896-1902
John Mills	1841-1853	Thomas J. Kauffman	1902-1908
Jacob Zimmer	1853-1855	John W. Edwards	1908-1913
Daniel H. Dryden	1855-1861	Hugo F. Schneider	1913-1917
Benjamin M. Ayers	1861-1863	George W. Bish	1917-1923
(Died in office)		Joseph A. Lutz	1923-1939
Thomas O. Lowe	1863-1865	Jesse Haines	1939—
Jacob M. Dietrich	1865-1869		

The office of auditor was established by statute in 1820 (18 O. L. 70), and was made elective annually in 1821 (9 O. L. 116). The term was set at two years in 1831 (29 O. L. 280), at three years in 1877 (74 O. L. 381), again at two years in 1906 (98 O. L. 271), and at four years in 1919 (108 O. L. pt. ii, 1294).

Infirmary Directors*

Abraham Darst	1826-1827	Abraham W. Bowen	1859-1862
John Folkerth	1826-1828	I. Donnellan	1860-1866
John C. Negley	1826-1827	George Getter	1862-1865
Abraham Trosell	1826-1827	Daniel Kiser	1865-1868
Henry Oldfather	1826-1827	Michael Moyer	1866-1869
Edmund Munger	1826-1829	William Stansel	1867-1873
John Ehrstine	1826-1827	William H. Rowe	1868-1871
Luther Bruen	1827-1830	John Stephens	1869-1875
Alexander Grimes	1828-1829	David L. Heck	1871-1874
Warren Munger	1828-1832	Richard Lane	1873-1876
Alexander Grimes	1829-1832	Joseph F. Kemp	1874-1877
John Hiser	1830-1831	Adam Snyder	1875-1878
Aaron Baker	1831-1834	William M. Simpson	1876-1879
Jacob Olinger	1831-1837	Frederick Pansing	1877-1883
Peter P. Lowe	1833-1834	Isaac Dissinger	1878-1881
John Shelby	1834-1837	John H. Bell	1879-1885
Job Haines	1835-1837	George W. Kimmel	1881-1884
John Steele	1837-1840	Jacob Clemens	1883-1887
Joseph Barnett	1837-1840	George Rantz	1884-1891
Jacob Witmer	1837-1839	William H. Roberts	1885-1888
John Holler	1839-1840	William A.Klinger	1887-1890
--------------?	1841-1852	John C. Heidinger	1889-1892
C. G. Fitch	1853-1854	Joseph Schultz	1890-1893
Albertus Geiger	1853-1855	Edwin M. Hendrick	1891-1894
C. G. Espick	1853-1854	Levi Baker	1892-1895
D. Carroll	1854-1857	William H. Barbour	1894-1900
J. J. Antrim	1854-1856	Daniel Utz	1893-1896
George Getter	1855-1857	John E. McClary	1895-1898
Zeph Cetrow	1856-1858	(Died November)	
M. N. Kimmel	1857-1858	Hezekiah B. Ulm	1896-1902
David Carrol	1858-1867	William H. Van Riper	1898-1904
		(Vice John B. McClary)	

*A legislative act of 1816 provided for the appointment by the county commissioners of seven directors to have charge of the county infirmary (14 O. L. 447-448). The number of directors was reduced to three in 1831 (29 O. L. 316), and in 1842 they became elective officials serving terms of three years (40 O. L. 45). The board was abolished in 1913 and control of the infirmary was vested in the county commissioners (12 O. L. 133).

Infirmary Directors (continued)

William B. Davis	1900-1906	John C. Nieffer	1906-1913
John P. Pratt	1902-1908	David E. Heeter	1907-1913
A. C. Weaver	1904-1907	V. A. Henkel	1908-1913

Surveyors*

Joseph Wilson	1803-1812	John Hiller	1880-1889
William Kennedy	1812-1823	Herman S. Fox	1889-1895
Samuel Archer	1823-1826	Robert E. Kline	1895-1901
Jesse Ewing	1826-1835	Edwin C. Baird	1901-1907
Fielding Lowery	1835-1838	Howard R. Kepinger	1907-1910
William C. George	1838-1850	Edward A. M–ritz	1910-1913
John Beaver	1850-1856	Victor C. Smith	1913-1917
Joseph B. Johns	1856-1862	Stanley R. Sharts	1917-1919
Jacob S. Binker	1862-1868	Parker S. Bookwalter	1919-1923
Joseph B. Johns	1868-1874	Wesley C. Pease	1923-1933
Frank Snyder	1874-1880	Victor G. Smith	1933-1935

Created by statute of 1803, which made the office appointive by the court of common pleas (1 O. L. 90-93), the surveyor became an elective official serving a three-year term in 1831 (29 O. L,. 399). The term was reduced to two years in 1906 (98 O. L. 145-147), and increased to four years in 1928 (112 O. L. 179)

Engineers**

Victor C. Smith   1935—

**An act of 1935 changed the title of surveyor to engineer (116 O. L. 283).

Governmental

All addresses refer to Dayton unless otherwise noted

Agricultural extension services
451 West Third Street
https://www.mcohio.org/515/County-Agencies

Auditor
451 West Third Street
P. O. Box 972
https://www.mcohio.org/1212/Auditor

Board Of Elections
451 West Third Street
https://www.montgomery.boe.ohio.gov/

Clerk Of Courts
41 North Perry Street
Room 106
https://www.mcclerkofcourts.org/

Coroner
361 West Third Street
https://www.mcohio.org/1213/Coroner

County Commissioners
County Administration Building
451 West Third Street, 10th Floor
Room 1001
https://www.mcohio.org/685/Board-of-County-Commissoners

Engineer
451 West Third Street
P. O. Box 972
https://engineer.mcohio.org/

Juvenile Court
380 West Second Street
https://www.mcjcohio.org/

Probate court
41 North Perry Street
https://www.mcohio.org/1209/Probate-Court

Prosecutor
301 West Third Street
P. O. Box 972
https://www.mcohio.org/1211/Prosecutor

Public Health
117 South Main Street
https://www.phdmc.org/

Recorder
451 West Third Street
https://www.mcohio.org/1210/Recorder

Sheriff
345 West Second Street
https://www.mcohiosheriff.org/

Treasurer
451 West Third Street
https://www.mcohio.org/1207/Treasurer

Veterans services
627 Edwin C. Moses Blvd.
4th Floor, East Medical Plaza
https://mcvsc.org/

Montgomery County has an Historical Records Collection Guide listing records, dates, and format of record being book or microfilm: **mcohio.org/980/Historical-Records-Collection-Guide** housed at the Montgomery County Records Center and Archives.

FamilySearch

https://www.familysearch.org/search/catalog

FamilySearch is a free website with digitized records. Records for Montgomery County include: Auditor, Children's Home, Clerk of Courts, County Commissioners, Correctional Institutions (Jail Register), County Home, Court of Common Pleas, District Court, Probate Judge, Recorder, Sheriff, Soldiers' Home, Soldiers' Relief Commission, Superior Court, and Supreme Court.

Ancestry

https://www.ancestry.com/

A pay site, Ancestry is available at many libraries. Records for Montgomery County include administrators, executors, and inventories. Many other records, in book form with an author, are also available, such as county histories, and church histories. If a specific person is known within the county, it is possible to find more records such as marriage, wills and estates, divorces, tax records, etc.

Montgomery County Records Center and Archives

117 South Main Street

Sixth Floor, Reibold Building

Dayton, Ohio

https://www.mcohio.org/818/Records-Center-Archives

The Center has an extensive listing on their website. The Collection Guide lists the different offices housed at the Center, such as Auditor, Clerk of Courts, Commissioners, County Home, Engineer, Probate Court, Recorder, Sheriff, Stillwater Hospital, Treasurer, and Veteran Service. As always, check all the subheadings available.

AAA records, 578-580

Abstracts

    Land conveyances, 59, 547

    Votes, 128

Accidents, location of, 533

Accounts, *see* each office by name

Administrators, *see* Estates, administrators

Adoptions, minors, 224, 243, 262

Affidavits

    Circuit court cases, 217

    Court of appeals cases, 93

    Court of common pleas cases, 93, 147, 158

    District court cases, 211-213

    Probate court cases, 241, 245, 255, 261

    Superior court cases, 199, 200

    Supreme court cases, 192

Aged, *see* Aid for the aged, board of

Agents licenses, insurance, 87

Agreements

    Corporations, 84

    Partnerships, 84, 127

    Power of attorney, 85

    Traders, 84

Agricultural adjustment administration, 578-580

Agricultural conservation association, 577

Agricultural extension agent entries (records)

    Conservation and crop control 577-580

    4-H club and home demonstration, 581-583

Agricultural society entries (records) 575, 576

Aid for the aged, board of entries (records)

    Applications and investigations, 517-522

    Case records, 523-527

    Miscellaneous, 528, 529

Aid to the blind, *see* Blind Cases

Aid to dependent children, *see* Minors

Aliens, *see* Naturalization cases

Animals, *see* Dogs; Livestock

Appeal bonds, 200, 211

Appearance dockets

    Circuit courts, 214

    Court of appeals, 219

    Court of common pleas, 144

    District court, 209

    Division of domestic relations, 164

    Juvenile court, 169

    Probate court, 237, 238

    Superior court, 194

Applications

    Aliens, 263-266

    Board of aid for the aged, 517-522

    Children's home, 512

    Civilian Conservation Corps, 37

    County home, 6, 494

    Estate settlements, 253, 248-250

    Licenses, vendors, 393

    Lunacy cases, 261

    National Youth Administration, 49

    For relief

        Blind cases, 24

        Minors, 173, 174

        Soldiers, 513, 514

Appointments

    Administration of estates, 227, 235

Appointments (continued)
    Appraisers, 1
    County home, 5, 491
    County officials
        Commissioners, 1
    Deputies to county officials, 400
    Executors, 227, 249
    By governors of Ohio, 117-119
    Guardians, 250
    Notary public, 119
    Notices of, 248, 249, 255
Appraisements
    See also Taxes, Appraisements
    County home property, 14
    Estates, 235, 248-250, 252, 256
    Registered lands 226
Appraisers
    Appointments, 1
    Estates, 230, 252
    Fees, 292, 293
    Minutes of meetings, 351
Appropriations
    To county offices 1, 16, 356
    Election expenses, 449
    Relief, 1, 24, 25, 375, 383
    Schools, 357
Arrest, 93, 241, 299
Assessments, taxes, *see* Taxes,
    assessments
Assessors, board of
    Minutes of meetings, 351
Assignment commissioners entries
    (records), 182-184
Assignments, 235, 259
Assignors, estate settlements, 228
Attorney, power of, 85
Attorneys
    Circuit court cases, 215
    County sheriff's cases, 292, 293,
    304

Attorneys (continued)
    Court of common pleas cases,
    142, 144
    Court of domestic relations,
    165, 166
    District court cases, 208-210
    Probate court cases, 223, 228,
    232, 234, 258
    Receipts for documents
    borrowed, 141
    Receivership cases, 95
    Superior court cases, 195, 197
Auctioneers
    Bonds, 122
Auditor, county entries (records)
    Bonds, 396-398
    Enumeration and statistics, 394,
    395
    financial records, 354-388
    Licenses, 389-393
    Miscellaneous, 400
    Plats, maps, and surveys, 315-
    324
    Property transfers, 313, 314
    Taxes, 325-353
    Weights and measures, 399
Auditor, state, reports to, 358, 365

Banks, *see* Depositories
Bans, marriages, 271
Bar docket, superior court, 197
Bids
    Depositories for county funds,
    439
    Partition fences, 77
    Water lines, construction of, 18
Bills
    County auditors, 379, 380
    County Commissioners, 1, 5,
    379
    County home, 5, 380, 491

Bills (continued)
Of exceptions, 94, 219
Miami Conservancy District, 558
Of particulars, 146, 147, 213
Of sale, 78, 112
Birth, *see* Vital statistics, births
Blind cases
Applications, 24
Appropriations, 1
Payments in, 25, 375, 383
Blotters
County auditor, financial, 361
County treasurers, taxes, 420, 423
Court of common pleas, 142, 152
District court, 208
Juvenile court, 167
Supreme court, 190
Board of aid for the aged, *see* Aid for the aged, board of
Board of county commissioners, *see* board of county
Board of county visitors, *see* visitors, board of county
Board of directors
Agricultural society, *see* Agricultural society
Children's home, *see* Children's home
Conservancy district, *see* Miami Conservancy District
Stillwater Sanatorium
Board of education, *see* Education, board of
Board of Equalization, *see* Revision, board of
Board of health, *see* Health, board of
Board of revision, *see* Revision board of

Board of state charities, 503, 512
Bonds
Administrators, 230, 247, 248
Appeal, 200, 211
Auctioneers, 122
Contractors, 18, 77
County officials, 437, 438
Justices of the peace, 118
Mayors, 118
Trustees of the sinking fund, 444
Executors, 229, 247, 249
Guardians, 247, 250, 251
Issued for
Improvements in county, 397, 398
Relief, 397, 398
Schools, 370
Township officials, 367, 437
Bridges
Construction of, 1, 536, 537, 540, 542
Maps, 537, 564
Budget commissioners
Entries (records), 440
Budgets
County Commissioners 1
Relief, 1, 25
Taxing districts, 354, 355
Buildings, county
Appraisements, 326
Bonds for improvement of, 397
Children's home, *see* Children's home
County home, *see* County home
Courthouse, *see* Courthouse
Jails, *see* Jails
Railroad property, 351
Schools, 73

Burials
> Inmates of county home, 495, 497
> Soldiers, *see* Soldiers

Calendars
> Clerk of courts, 90
> Probate court, 223, 236

Capias, 193

Cashbooks
> Agricultural society, 576
> Board of Elections, 450
> Clerk of courts, 129
> County sheriffs, 302
> County treasurers, 427
> Miami Conservancy District, 424
> Probate court, 278
> Probation department, 188

Certificates
> Births. *See* Vital statistics, births
> Deaths, *see* Vital statistics, deaths
> Election officials, 240
> For employment
>> NYA, 36, 38, 39
>> WPA, 36
> Inheritance taxes certified by county auditor, 350
> Medical, 37, 260, 261, 274, 275
> Midwives, 276
> Teachers, 453
> Titles, motor vehicles, 115
> Titles, registered land, 74

Chattel mortgages, *see* Mortgages

Children, *see* Minors

Children's home, board of trustees
> Accounts with county auditor, 360
> County commissioners records, 1, 7

Children's home, board of trustees (continued)
> Entries (records)
>> Case records, 505-507
>> Financial records, 508-510
>> Minutes, 504
>> Miscellaneous, 511, 512

Cigarettes
> Licenses, 391
> Tax on, 352, 353, 418

Circuit court, 214*218

Cities
> Indebtedness, 365
> Maps, 318, 319, 322, 324

Citizenships *see* Naturalization cases

Civil docket, 143, 224, 297

Civilian Conservation Corps, 37

Claims
> Damage to livestock, 11, 13, 311, 381
> Damage to property, 1
> Estate settlements, 227, 253
> Soldiers burial commission, 8

Clerk, county, *see* Clerk of courts

Clerk of courts, entries (records)
> Commissions and licenses, 117-126
> Coroners inquest, 137-139
> Court proceedings, 90-95
> Elections, 128
> Financial records, 129-136
> Judgments and executions, 96-107
> Jury and witness records, 108-111
> Miscellaneous, 140, 141
> Motor Vehicles, 112-116
> Partnerships, 127

Clerks
 Superior court, 194
Clubs
 4-H, 301, 581
Commissioner, children's home, 511
Commissioners, budget, *see* Budget
 commissioners
Commissioners, board of county
 Bills, 380, 399
 Entries (records)
  Aid for the blind, 24,
  25
  Financial records, 11,
  12
  Institutions and relief,
  5-10
  Minutes of meetings, 1-
  4
  Miscellaneous, 13, 1 4
  Relief administration,
  25-55
  Sanitary department,
  15-23
 Reports, county officials *see*
 Reports
Commissions, *see* Appointments
Common pleas court, *see* Court of
 common pleas
Complete records
 Circuit court, 218
 Court of appeals, 221
 Court of common pleas, 234
 District court, 212, 213
 Superior court, 199
 Supreme court, 192
 Probate court, 240
Conservancy district, *see* Miami
 Conservancy District
Constables, 144
Contractors
 Bonds, 18, 77

Contractors (continued)
 Liens, 69
 Projects under construction, 371
Contracts
 Agricultural Adjustment
 Administration, 578-580
 Agricultural Conservation
 Association, 577
 Board of health, 467
 County commissioners, 1
 County engineers, 542, 543
 Miami Conservancy District,
 569
Coroner, county
 Bonds, 437, 438
 Entries (records) 291-309
 Reports of inquest, 137-139, 282
Corporations
 Agreements, 84
 Plats, 531
 Taxes, 340
Correspondence
 Agricultural extension agent,
 584
 Agricultural society, 575
 Aid to dependent children, 181
 Board of aid for the aged, 529
 Board of health, 472
 County engineer, 546
 Miami Conservancy District,
 563, 572-574
 Probation department, 186
 Relief administration, 35
 Soldiers relief commission, 516
Cosmetic dealers licenses, 390
Costs
 Children's home, 7
 Circuit court cases, 217
 Clerk of courts, 105, 130, 132,
 133, 135
 County home, 5

Costs (continued)

    County prosecuting attorneys cases, 287

    County sheriff's reports, 292, 293, 300, 301, 304, 305

    Court of appeals, 92, 93, 100

    Court of common pleas, 92, 93, 100, 106, 133, 142, 143, 153-157

    Court of domestic relations, 164

    District court cases, 209, 211

    Justices of the peace court, 143, 366

    Probate court cases, 235, 236-238, 243, 256, 258, 279

    Projects, county, 1, 16, 371.

    Projects, N. Y. A., 49, 50, 54

    Relief

        Emergency cases, 1, 8-10, 33, 34

    Soldiers burial, 373

    Superior court cases, 194, 200, 204

    Supreme court cases, 190

    Stillwater Sanatorium, 488

Councilman of city wards, duties relative to soldier relief, 271

County home

    County commissioner records, 1, 5, 6, 14

    Entries (records)

        Case records, 492-499

        Financial records, 500

        Minutes, 491

        Miscellaneous, 502, 503

        Personnel, 501

Court of appeals

    Entries (records), 219-222

    History, 191

Court of common pleas

    Entries (records)

        Civil cases, 142-151

        Criminal cases, 152-159

        Division of domestic relations, 164-166

        Juvenile court records, 167-171

        Naturalization, 160-163

        Probation department, 185-189

Court dockets

    Circuit court, 215

    Court of common pleas, 145

    District court, 210

    Superior court, 195

Court of domestic relations

    Entries (records), 164-166

Court orders, *see also* Writs

    Clerk of courts, 92

    Court of appeals, 92, 191, 194, 213, 214, 216, 221

    Court of common pleas, 92, 144, 146, 147, 150

    Probate court, 224, 237-240, 260

    Superior court, 194

Court reporters, 123, 179

Court writs, *see* Writs

Court of appeal, *see* Circuit court; Court of appeals; District courts; Superior court; Supreme court

Crabbe Act, violation of, 245

Criminal cases, *see also* prosecuting attorney

    County sheriff's, 303

    Court of appeals, 93

    Court of common pleas, 152-157

    Clerk of courts, 105, 136

Criminal cases (continued)
    Probate court, 236-238, 240, 241
Cripples, 459
Crops, *see* Agricultural extension agent
Culverts, 542

Dairies
    Inspections, 467
    Permits, 468
Dayton, city of
    Taxes, 331, 343-345, 347
Deaths
    See also Vital statistics, deaths inmates, county home
    Old age pensioners, 527
    Reports, coroners, 137-139, 291
Decisions
    District court cases, 209, 212, 213
    Grand jury cases, 287
    Superior court cases, 199
    Supreme court cases, 192
Decrees
    Circuit court cases, 214
    Court of appeals, 221
    Court of common pleas, 146, 147
    Probate court cases, 237
Deeds
    Property sold for delinquent taxes, 314
    Registered lands, 226
    Titles to real property, by 6
    Uncalled for, 60
Delinquency
    Minors, *see* Minors
    Taxes *see* Taxes
Demurrers
    Circuit court, 217
    Court of common pleas, 146

Demurrers (continued)
    District court, 211, 212
    Superior court, 199, 200
    Supreme court, 192
Dispositions
    Cases filed and clerk of courts office, 94
    Supreme court cases, 200
Depositories, county funds, 439
Deposits, unclaimed, 280
Deputies
    To county officials
        Appointments, 400
        Bonds, 437
Diseases, *see* Health, board of
District court
    Entries (records), 208-213
Division of aid for the aged, *see* Aid for the aged
Division of charities, 512
Division of domestic relations, *see* Court of domestic relations
Divorce cases, 146, 166, 193
Dockets
    Aid to dependent children, 172
    Assignment commission, 182
    Circuit court, 214, 215
    Clerk of courts, 90, 91, 96, 99, 100, 104, 105, 108, 110, 111
    County auditors, 379, 380
    County sheriff's, 292, 293, 295-297, 301
    Court of appeals, 219
    Court of common pleas, 143-145
    Court of domestic relations, 164, 165
    District court, 209, 210
    Juvenile court, 169
    Probate court, 224, 226, 228-230, 232, 237, 238, 259

Dockets (continued)
Superior court, 194-197, 202, 205
Dogs
Licenses, 310, 389
Livestock injured by, 311, 381
Persons bitten by, 465
Strays, 312
Dog warden, county
Bonds, 438
Entries (records), 310-312
Reports, 1, 13, 311, 312, 465
Domestic relations, *see* Court of domestic relations

Education, board of
Entries (records), 452-456
History, 243-245
Reports to county auditor, 395
Elections, *See also* Elections, board of
General, 446, 448
Reports to Secretary of State, 448
Votes in, 128
Elections, board of
Financial records, 449-451
Minutes of meetings, 445
Registrations and votes, 446-448
Embalmers licenses, 124
Employees, 1, 9, 10, 26-35
See also clerks
Children's home, 7
County home, 5, 501
Stillwater sanatorium, 490
Employment
Civilian Conservation Corps, 37
National Youth Administration, 36, 38-50, 52
Students, 36, 38-55, 456

Employment (continued)
Works Progress Administration, 36
Engineer (surveyor), county
Entries (records)
Financial records, 544
Improvements, 534-543
Miscellaneous, 545, 546
Surveys, plats, and maps, 530-533
Reports to county commissioners, 1
Enrollments, *see* Registrations
Entry dockets, 196, 296
Epileptics, 261
Equalization board, *see* Revision, board of
Estates
Administrators
Accounts, 235, 253, 254, 258
Appointments, 227, 248
Bonds, 230, 247-251
Dockets, 228, 230
Fees, 258
Inventories, 235, 252
Letters of fiduciary, 248-250
Notices, 248, 255
Oaths, 253
Appraisers, 230, 252
Appraisements, 235, 248-250, 252
Assignments, 235, 259
Claims, 227, 253
Cost, 235
Executors
Accounts, 235, 253, 254, 258

Estates, Executors (continued)
Appointments, 227, 249
Bonds, 229, 247, 249
Dockets, 228
Fees, 258
Inventory, 235, 252
Oaths, 253
Guardians, *see* Guardians
Heirs at law, 248, 256, 258
Journal entries, 243
Petitions, registered lands, 227, 235
Sales, 252
Taxes, *see* Taxes, inheritance
Wills 224, 235, 246
Estimates, *see also* Bids; Contracts
Construction work in county, 1, 18
Injuries to livestock, 311
Examinations, medical, 179, 480, 507
Examiners, county treasury, 281
Excise taxes, *see* Taxes, excise
Execution dockets, 205, 292, 293
Executions to satisfy judgments, 102-106, 205, 244, 292, 293
Evidence court, court cases, 150, 192, 199

Fairs, *see* Agricultural society
Federal relief, *see* Relief
Federal tax liens, 71
Feeble-minded cases, 162, 203, 260
Fees, *see also* Salaries
Appraisers, 292, 293
Attorneys, 132, 258, 304
Candidates, elections, 450, 451
County officials
Auditors, 358, 364
Clerk of courts, 104, 105, 115, 129, 130, 194

Fees (continued)
Commissioners, 16
Recorders, 83, 88
Reports to county auditor, 369
Sheriff's, 129, 130, 144, 194, 278, 292-295, 297, 298, 300, 301, 303-307
Jurors, 108, 109, 201, 385, 388
Licenses, 120-123, 310, 359
Printers, 278, 292, 293
Soldiers burial committees, 373
Witnesses, 110, 111, 129, 131, 202, 278, 385, 388, 436
Felonies, 154
Fence partition cases, 77
Ferry licenses, 123
Finances, *see* each office by name
Fines, criminal cases, 136, 366
Fiscal accounts, *see* each office by name
Fishing licenses, 121
Foreign execution docket, 293
Foreign writs, 293, 298
4-H clubs, 481

Gas leases, 62, 63
Governors, Ohio
Appointments made by, 117-119
Grand jury
Entries (records), 109, 111, 283-285, 287
Guardians (Guardianships)
Accounts, 254
Bonds, 247, 250, 251
Dockets, 232
Estate settlements, 228, 232, 235, 252
Journal entries, 243
Letters, 235, 250

Guardians (continued)
Of minors, 169, 176, 178, 228, 269

Health, county board of
Entries (records)
Case records, 458-460
Contagious diseases, 462
Immunizations, 461
Inspections, 463-468
Minutes, 457
Miscellaneous, 471, 472
Vital statistics, 469, 470
Nurses, 458, or 60
Stillwater Sanatorium records, 473-490
Hearings
Circuit court, 216
Court of appeals, 220
Court of common pleas, 156
Court of domestic relations, 165
Probate court, 226
Heirs-at-law, estates, 248, 256, 258
Home demonstration agent, 582, 583
Hospital
Tuberculosis, 473-490
Hunters licenses, 120

Idiots, *see* Insanity cases
Indentures, minors, 491, 505
Indictments
County prosecuting attorneys cases, 290
Court of common pleas, 158
Infirmary, *see* County home
Inheritance taxes, *see* Taxes, inheritance
Injunctions, 193

Inquest
County coroners records, 137-139, 282, 291
Insanity cases
Housing in county home of, 498
Probate court cases, 243
Inspections
Board of health, 458, 463-468
County treasury, 281
Inspectors, *see* Examiners
Institutions, *see also* ; County home; Stillwater Sanatorium
Reports to board of health, 463
Warrants, commitments to penal, 241
Inventories
County coroners, 282
County property, 1
Estates, 235, 252
N. Y. A. 53
Personal property, 337, 339
Sale of tax stamps, 419
Investigations
Board of health, 465
Civilian Conservation Corps, 37
County prosecuting attorney, 290
Dog wardens, 13, 311
Juvenile court cases, 167
Miami Conservancy District, 573
Probation department, 186
Relief
Blind cases, 24
Board of aid for the aged, 519, 522
Emergency cases, 27, 28, 35
Road supervisors, 545

Invoices
  Commissary, children home, 511
  Stillwater Sanatorium, 489
Insurance agents licenses, 87
Insurance companies, 86

Jails
  Prisoners records, 300, 301
Journal entries
  Court of appeals, 92, 220
  Court of common pleas, 92, 144, 146
  Probate court, 243
  Superior court, 194, 200
  Supreme court, 191
Journals
  County auditors, 363, 384
  County commissioners, 1, 5
  County home, 5
  County sheriff, 308
  County Treasurers, 428, 434
  Court of common pleas, 146
  Juvenile court, 170
  Sanitary Department, 15-17
  Trustees of the sinking fund, 444
Judges
  Circuit court, 215
Judgments
  Costs, 106, 133
  Executions to satisfy, 102-104, 106, 205, 292, 293
  Levies in, 107, 207
  Superior court, 203, 204
  Supreme court, 190
Juries (jurors)
  Clerk of courts records 108, 109
  Court of common pleas, 142
  Fees, 108, 109, 201, 385, 388
  Superior court cases, 201
  Supreme court cases, 190, 191

Jury commissioners
  Entries (records), 283-285
Justices of the peace
  Bonds, 18
  Commissions, 18
  Courts, 143
Juvenile court, see Minors
  Aid to dependent children, 172-181
  Entries (records), 167-181
Juveniles see Minors

Kennel licenses, 310, 389

Landmarks, 530
Lands
  Registered, 74
Leases, 62, 63
Ledgers
  Board of Elections, 449
  County auditors, 356
  County home, 372
  Miami Conservancy District, 552
Letters, fiduciary, 235, 248-250
Levies, tax, see Taxes, levies
Licenses
  Auctioneers, 122
  Cigarettes, 391
  Cosmetic dealers, 390
  Dogs, 310, 389
  Embalmers, 124
  Fees, 120-123, 310, 359
  Ferry, 123
  Fishing, 121
  Hunters, 120
  Insurance agents, 87
  Kennel, 310, 389
  Limited practitioners, 275
  Marriage, 269
  Midwives, 276

Licenses (continued)
    Ministers, 272, 273
    Nurses, 277
    Optometrist, 125
    Peddlers, 123, 392
    Physicians, 274
    Real estate brokers, 126
    Real estate salesmen, 126
Liens
    Contractors, 69
    Judgments rendered, 96
    Mechanics, 68, 70
    Personal property, 115
    Tax, 64, 71-73
Liquor cases, 245
Liquor traffic taxes, 352, 417
Livestock
    Children's home, 7
    Claims, 11, 13, 311, 381
    Contracts, AAA, 578
    County home, 14
    Strays, 140
    Taxes, 339
Lunacy cases, 260, 261, 299

Maps
    Accident spots, 533
    Cities, 318, 319, 322, 324
    Miami Conservancy District, 564, 566
    Relief districts, 180
    Sewer, water lines, 22, 23
    Taxing districts, 315, 316, 318-322
    Township, 315, 316
Marines, *see* Soldiers
Marriages, *see* Vital statistics, marriages
Matrons
    Children's home, 7
Mayors
    Bonds, 118

Mayors (continued)
    Commissions, 118
Measures, reports on, 399
Mechanics liens, 68, 70
Medical certificates, 260, 261, 274, 275
Medical examinations, 179, 480, 507
Miami Conservancy District
    Entries (records)
        Financial records, 552-563
        Maps and photographs, 564-567
        Miscellaneous, 571-574
        Orders and contracts, 568-570
        Property and tax records, 547-551
Miamisburg city of, 467
Military records, *see* Soldiers
Ministers licenses, 272, 273
Minors *See also* Juvenile court; Schools
    Adoptions, 224, 243, 262
    Aid to, 172-181, 376, 377
    Cripples, 459
    Custody of, 165
    Health records, 179, 459, 460
    Housed in county home, 491
    Marriages, 269
    School age, 394
Minutes
    Agricultural society, 575
    Board of appraisers, 351
    Board of directors, county home, 5, 491
    Board of education, 452
    Board of Elections, 445
    Board of health, 457
    Board of revision, 441
    Board of trustees, children home, 504
    Budget commissioners, 440

Minutes (continued)
Circuit court, 216
County commissioners, 1, 5, 15
Correct of common pleas, 146
Soldiers relief commission, 513
Superior court, 198
Supreme court, 191
Trustees of the sinking fund, 444
Mortgages
Personal property, 78, 79, 83
Real property, 64, 66, 67
Mothers' pensions, 172, 376, 377
Motions
Court of appeals, 220
Court of common pleas, 145, 147, 165
Court of domestic relations, 165
District court, 212, 213
Probate court, 226
Superior court, 199
Supreme court, 192
Motor Vehicles, 112, 115, 359
Municipal corporations, plats, 531

Narcotics, Stillwater Sanatorium, 481
National Youth Administration, 36, 38-55
Naturalization cases, ,42, 161-163, 263-266
Newspapers
Sheriff's sales, 309
Notaries public, commissions, 119
Notices
County commissioners to dog warden, 311
County sheriff, 244
Estates, settlement of, 248, 249, 255
National Youth Administration, 41, 50
Sales, county sheriff's, 309
Tax, 64

Nurses
Children's home, 265
Health, 458, 460
Registered, 277

Oakwood City
Assessments, 332
Maps, 322
Oaths
Administrators, 253
Aliens, 163
Deputies, county officials, 400
Executors, 253
Inspectors of county treasury, 281
Justices of the peace, 118
Mayors, 118
Notaries public, 119
Offenses, criminal cases, 236, 241
Oil leases, 62, 63
Old age pensions, see Pensions
Options
District court cases, 212
Superior court cases, 199
Supreme court cases, 192
Optometrist licenses, 125
Orders See also Court orders
Miami Conservancy District, 568, 571
Relief, 9, 10, 31, 32
Of sales, property, 196, 296
To transfer property, 55
Original papers
Circuit court, 217
Court of appeals, 92, 93, 222
Court of common pleas, 92, 93
Court of domestic relations, 166
District court, 211
Juvenile court cases, 171
Probate court cases, 235, 241, 261

Original papers (continued)
    Superior court cases, 200
    Supreme court cases, 193
Orphans home, *see* Children's home
Orphans, *see* Minors

Partnerships, agreements, 84, 127
Pay-in orders, 427, 428, 431
Pay rolls, 460
Peddlers licenses, 123, 392
Penal institutions, 93
Penalties, tax, *see* Taxes, penalties
Pending court cases
    Clerk of courts, 90, 103
    County prosecuting attorney, 86
Pensions
    Blind cases, *see* Blind cases
    Mothers, 172, 376, 377
    Old age, 517-529
    Soldiers, *see* Soldiers
Permits
    Construction work in county, 20
    Dairies, 468
    Employment, students, 456
Personal property
    Appraisements, county home, 14
    Assignments, 259
    County, 1
    Domestic animals, 140, 339
    Estates, 248-250, 252, 256, 258
    Levies, 107, 207
    Livestock, *see* Livestock
    Mortgages, 78, 79, 83
    Motor vehicles, *see* Motor vehicles
    Orders for transfer of, 55
    Taxes, *see* Taxes
    Transfers, 53, 55, 78-83, 259
Petitions
    Circuit court, 214, 217

Petitions (continued)
    For construction work in county, 1
    Court of common pleas, 146, 147
    District court cases, 211-213
    Estates, 227, 235
    Naturalization cases, 163
    Superior court, 199, 200
    Supreme court, 192, 193
Petit jury
    Entries (records), 109, 283-285
Photographs
    Miami Conservancy District, 567
    X-rays, Stillwater Sanatorium, 479, 480
Physicians
    Licenses, 274
    Reports, blind cases, 24
Plans, 540
Plats, 75, 317, 320, 321, 531, 534, 537
Pleas
    Clerk of court cases, 93
    Court of appeals cases, 220
    Court of common pleas case, 147, 156
    District court cases, 212, 213
    Probate court cases, 212, 213
    Superior court cases, 199
    Supreme court cases, 192
Politics, *see* Elections
Poorhouse, *see* County home
Poor relief, *see* Relief
Pound of keepers, *see* Dog warden
Power of attorney, 85
Practitioners licenses, 274, 275
Praecipes, 91, 92
Primary elections, 446, or 448
Printers fees, 92, 93

Prisoners
 Jail records, 300, 301
 On probation, 185-187
Probate court Entries (records)
 Assignments, 259
 Civil cases, 223-235
 County sheriff's cases, 305, 306
 Criminal cases, 236-241
 Dependents, 260-262
 Estates, guardianships, 246-258
 Financial records, 278-280
 General court proceedings, 242-245
 Licenses and certificates, 272-277
 Miscellaneous, 281, 282
 Naturalization, 263-266
 Vital statistics, 267-271
Probation Department
 Entries (records), 185-189
Proof of publication, 255
Prosecuting attorney, county
 Entries (records), 286-290
 Bonds, 437, 438
Publications, *see* Notices
Public improvements
 Assessments, 328, 403
Public schools, *see* Schools
Public utilities, 365

Quarantine, 462

Railroads
 Appraisements of property, 351
 Maps of, 564
 Policemen for, 117
Rails, guard, 538
Rates, tax, *see* Taxes, rates
Real estate brokers, licenses, 126
Real estate salesmen, licenses, 126

Real property *See also* Estates; Taxes
 Appraisements
  County home, 14
 Assignments, 259
 Claims, 1
 Deeds, 56, 60
 Foreclosures, 289
 Levies, 107, 207, 325, 358, 402, 549
 Liens, 64, 68-73
 Maps, 315, 316, 318, 322, 532
 Mortgages, 64, 66, 67
 Partition cases, 77, 196
 Plats, 75, 317, 320, 321, 531, 534, 537, 540
 Lots, 59, 323, 324
 Registered lands, 74, 226, 227
 Sales, 296, 304, 309
 Surveys, 75, 443, 530
 Titles, 56, 59, 74, 226, 227
 Transfers, 259, 313, 314, 334
Receiverships, 95
Recorder, county
 Bonds, 437, 438
 Entries (records)
  Grants of authority, 85-87
  Incorporations and Partnerships, 84
  Miscellaneous, 88, 89
  Personal property transfers, 78-83
  Real property transfers, 56-77
Relief
 Administration of, 26-55
 Bonds, 397, 398
 Budgets, 1
 Civilian Conservation Corps, 37
 Emergency, 1, 9, 10, 26-35
 Maps, 180

Relief (continued)
    Minors, *see* Minors aid to
    Mothers pensions, 172, 376, 377
    National Youth Administration,
    36, 38-55
    Outdoors, 378
    Soldiers, 1, 8, 374, 513-516
    Transients, 378
    Vouchers, 377, 382, 383
    Warrants issued for, 386, 434
    Works Progress Administration,
    36
Registrations
    Board of health, 459
    Children's home, 505
    Civilian Conservation Corps, 37
    4H club members, 581
    Home demonstration members,
    582
    Land titles, 74, 226, 227
    Limited practitioners, 275
    National Youth Administration,
    38
    Schools, 395, 455
    Stillwater Sanatorium, 473, 475,
    476
    Vital statistics, 469, 470
    Voters, 283, 447
    Visitors to county home, 502
    Works Progress Administration,
    36
Reports
    Board of education, 395
    Board of health, 458, 460, 463,
    465, 466, 468, 471
    Children's home, 5, 512
    Civilian Conservation Corps, 37
    County home, 1, 5, 7, 503
    County officials
        Auditor, 365, 368
    Clerk of courts, 136

Reports (continued)
    Coroners, 137, 139, 282, 291
    Dog wardens, 13, 311, 312, 465
    Engineers, 1
    Prosecuting attorneys, 290
    Elections, 448, 451
    Financial status of county home,
    1, 12, 500
    Home demonstration, 583
    Justices of the peace, 366
    Juvenile court cases, 167
    Miami Conservancy District,
    551, 571
    National Youth Administration,
    54
    Relief, 1, 8, 24, 27, 28, 175,
    179, 513
    Roads, 1, 545
    Sealer of weights, measures 399
    Schools, 394, 460, 464
    Soldiers burials, 8
    Soldiers relief commission, 513
    Stillwater Sanatorium, 484-486
    Teachers, 454
    Townships, 360, 365, 367
    Treasury inspectors, 281
Resolutions, *see* Minutes
Returns, elections, 448
Returns, taxes, *see* Taxes, returns
Returns on writs, *see* Writs, returns
Revision, board of
    Entries (records), 441-443
Rivers, 540, 564
Roads
    Assessments for, 329, 330, 336,
    402
    Bonds for improvement of, 397,
    398
    Construction of, 1, 534, 536,
    542, 545
    Contracts, 402, 542

Roads (continued)
  Guard rails for, 538
  Maps, 564
  Taxes, 329, 330, 336, 402
  Road supervisors reports, 545
  Road viewers reports, 1

Sailors, *see* Soldiers
Salaries *See also* Fees; Pay rolls
  Board of directors, Miami Conservancy District, 559
  Employees
    County home, 5, 500, 501
    National Youth Administration, 43, 52
  Superintendent, Children's home, 509
  Teachers, 370, 395
Sales
  Bonds, 370
  Personal property
    Dogs, 312
    Estates, 252
    Livestock, Children's home, 7
    Motor vehicles, 112
  Real property
    Estates, 126, 252
    By county sheriff, 296, 304, 309
    For delinquent taxes, 349
  Tax receipts, 419
  Tax stamps, 419
  Tuberculosis, *see* Stillwater Sanatorium
Sanitary department, 1, 15-23
Sanitation, reports on, 463, 465
Schick tests, 461.

Schools, *see also* Education, board of
  Bonds, sale of, 370
  Budgets, 354, 355, 357
  Enumeration reports, 394, 455
  Inspections, health, 460, 464
  Levies, 358
  Property, 395
  Settlements of accounts, 357, 358
  Students
    Attendance records, 370, 454
    Employment permits, 456
    Enrollments, 395
  Teachers, 370, 395, 453, 454
  Tuition, 370
Sealer, weights, measures, 399
Secretary of state
  Of Elections, 448
Sentences
  Court of appeals, 93
  Court of common pleas, 93, 142
  District court, 212
  Superior court, 199
  Supreme court, 192
Sewerage system, inspections, 463
Sewers
  Assessments, 328, 331
  Construction of, 18, 19, 539
  Inspections, board of health, 463
Sheriff, county
  Entries (records)
    Court orders, 292-299
    Financial records, 302-308
    Jail records, 300, 301
    Miscellaneous, 309
  Fees, 129, 130, 194, 278
  Returns on writs, 92, 144, 156-158, 194, 200, 211, 217, 260

Sinking fund, *see* Trustees of the sinking
          fund
Soldiers (sailors, marines)
          Burial committees, 8, 373
          Citizenship papers, 265
          Military records, 89
          Relief, 1, 8, 374, 513-516
Specifications, construction work on
          county, 1, 18
          Tax stamp, 419
State board of Equalization, 351
State division of charities, 503, 512
State medical board, 274, 275
Statement of accounts
          County auditor to county
          commissioners, 12, 368
          County auditor to state auditor,
          365
          Justices of the peace to county
          auditor, 366
          Ownership of motor vehicles, 12
          Soldiers burial commission, 8
State secretary, *see* Secretary of State
Statistics on population, *see* Census
Stillwater Sanatorium
          Entries (records)
                    Admission   and
                    registers, 473-476
                    Case records, 477-483
                    Financial records, 487-
                    489
                    Statistics, 484-486
Strays, livestock, 140
Streams, 530
Streets
          Assessments, 328, 329, 331, 341
          Plats, 531, 540
Students, *see* Schools, students
Subpoenas
          County sheriffs, 295
          Court of appeals, 93

Subpoenas (continued)
          Court of common pleas, 93
Superior courts, Entries (records)
          General court proceedings, 194-
          200
          Judgments and executions, 203-
          207
          Jury and witness records, 201,
          202
Superintendent, Children's home, *see*
          Children's home
Superior court
          Entries (records), 190-193
Sureties to bonds, 230, 241, 247-251
Surgeons certificates, 274
Surveyors, *see* Engineers, county
Surveys, 75, 443, 530

Tally sheets, 446
Taxes, *see also* Revision, board of
          Additions, 288, 341, 351, 409,
          441
          Appraisements, 289, 326, 327,
          349, 351, 443
          Cigarette traffic, 352, 353, 418
          Classified, 338, 340, 358, 408,
          415
          Collections, 353, 420-427, 431,
          550, 551
          Complaints, 442, 443
          City of Dayton, 342-345, 347
          Cost, 330
          Deductions, 341, 351, 441
          Delinquent, 288, 289, 314, 334,
          335, 341-349, 404, 411-415,
          427
          Duplicates, 334-336, 341, 402-
          404, 407, 408, 415, 549
          Exemptions, 257, 258, 350
          Excise, 352, 353, 417-419

Taxes (continued)

Inheritance, 256-258, 350, 416, 422, 431

Intangibles, 340, 406, 408

Levies, 325, 358, 402, 549

Liens, 64, 71-73

Liquor traffic, 417

List, 401, 405, 414

Miami Conservancy District, 333, 336, 346, 405, 423, 424, 549

Notices, 64, 309

Penalties, 288, 289, 334-336, 339-342, 344, 346-348, 353, 401, 411-413, 415

Personal property, 256-258, 337-340, 342, 343, 345, 350, 351-401, 405-408, 414, 415, 442

Property sold for, 314, 349

Railroad property, 351

Rates, 331, 337

Remittance, 410

Returns, 337, 345, 412

Roads, 329, 330, 336, 402

Settlements, 358, 412

Special, 19, 288, 289, 328, 329, 331, 332, 336, 341, 365, 403, 411, 412

Vendors, 352, 353

Waivers, state tax commission, 258

Tax maps, 315, 318, 322

Tax receipts, 419

Taxing districts

Budgets, 289, 354, 355

Inheritance taxes, 416

Settlements, 358

Tax stamps

Vendors, 419

Teachers

Certificates, 453

Reports, 454

Salaries, 370, 395

Testimonial letters, 229, 235, 248, 249

Testimony

Clerk of courts cases, 94

Court of common pleas, 150

District court, 212, 213

Supreme court cases, 192

Tests

Analysis of water, 466, 467

Of dogs, 465

Schick, 461

Sewage, 463

Titles

Motor vehicles, 115

Real property, 56, 59, 74, 226, 227

Tobacco, contracts, 580

Townships

Accounts, 358, 360, 365, 367

Assessments, 342

Clerks, 343

Levies, 325, 358

Official bonds, 367, 437

Roads, 545

Traders, 84

Transfers

Personal property, 78-83

Real property, 56, 59-67, 259, 313, 314, 334

Transience, relief to, 378

Treasury, county

Entries (records)

Bonds, 437, 438

Financial records, 427-436

Miscellaneous, 439

Taxes, 401-426

Trial docket, assignment commissioners, 182

Trustees
Children's home, 263-265
Of estates, 223, 232, 235, 243, 258
Of sinking fund
Entries (records), 444
Tuberculosis hospitals, 1, 473-490
Turnpikes, *see* Roads

Unclaimed deposits, 307
United States
Oaths of allegiance, 163
Soldiers, *see* Soldiers

Vendors
Cigarette taxes, 352, 353, 417, 418, 419
Licenses, 393
Vendors, jurors, 109, 201
Verdicts
County coroners, 137, 138
Court of common pleas, 157, 159
District court, 212
Superior court, 199
Supreme court, 192
Veterans, *see* Soldiers
Villages
Assessments, tax, 332
Levies, school, 358
Tax maps, 315, 316
Visitors, board of county, 5
Vital statistics
Births, 267, 469
Deaths, 268, 470
Marriage bans, 271
Voters, 283, or 447
Votes, 446, 448

Vouchers
Children's home, 510
For mothers pensions, 377
Miami Conservancy District, 555, 556, 558, 563
National Youth Administration, officials, 51
For relief, 9, 10, 377, 382, 383

Wages *see* Salaries
Warrants, *see also* Writs
Issued on county treasurer, 384, 387, 427, 432
Issued on relief, 386, 434
Water
Analysis test, 466, 467
Assessments, 331
Construction of lines, 16, 18-23
Weights, inspection of, 399
Wells, inspection of, 467
Wills, 224, 229, 235, 246
Works Progress Administration, 36
Witnesses
Adoption cases, 262
Circuit court cases, 214, 217
County coroner inquests, 138, 139, 291
Court of common pleas, 110, 142
Court of domestic relations, 164
Fees, 110, 111, 129, 131, 202, 278, 385, 388, 436
Grand jury cases, 111
Probate court cases, 246, 385, 388
Superior court cases, 202
Supreme court cases, 190
Wills, 246
Writs
Clerk of courts, 91, 104

Writs (continued)
Court of appeals, 92, 93, 155, 156
   Court of common pleas, 92, 93,
   144, 156-158
   County sheriffs, 292-295, 297,
   298, 303, 308
   Probate court cases, 224, 241,
   245, 261, 299
   Returns on, 92, 144, 156-158,
   194, 200, 211, 217, 260
   Superior court cases, 194, 200
X-ray photographs, Stillwater
   Sanatorium, 479, 480

The Historical Records Survey Project

Sargent B. Child, National Director
Willard N. Hogan, Regional Supervisor
Lillian Kessler, State Supervisor
James L. Graham, District Supervisor

Division of Community Service Programs

Florence Kerr, Assistant Commissioner
Mary Gillette Moon, Chief Regional Supervisor
Ruth Neighbors, State Director
Hazel B. Weeks, District Director

WORK PROJECTS ADMINISTRATION

Howard O. Hunter, Commissioner
George Field, Regional Director
Carl Watson, State Administrator
L. A. Gillett, District Manager

Sponsors

The Ohio State Archaeological and Historical Society
The Board of County Commissioners of Montgomery County:

Clem L. Shroyer
John E. Brumbaugh
Elmer F. Timmerman

Heritage Books by Jana Sloan Broglin:

*Additions and Corrections to the W.P.A. Inventory
of Adams County, Ohio: West Union*

*Additions and Corrections to the W.P.A. Inventory
of Allen County, Ohio: Lima*

*Additions and Corrections to the W.P.A. Inventory
of Ashland County, Ohio: Ashland*

*Additions and Corrections to the W.P.A. Inventory
of Athens County, Ohio: Athens*

*Additions and Corrections to the W.P.A. Inventory
of Belmont County, Ohio: St. Clairsville*

*Additions and Corrections to the W.P.A. Inventory
of Cuyahoga County, Ohio: Cleveland*

*Additions and Corrections to the W.P.A. Inventory
of Fulton County, Ohio: Wauseon*

*Additions and Corrections to the W.P.A. Inventory
of Geauga County, Ohio: Chardon*

*Additions and Corrections to the W.P.A. Inventory
of Hamilton County, Ohio: Cincinnati*

*Additions and Corrections to the W.P.A. Inventory
of Hancock County, Ohio: Findlay*

*Additions and Corrections to the W.P.A. Inventory
of Lake County, Ohio: Painesville*

*Additions and Corrections to the W.P.A. Inventory
of Lorain County, Ohio: Elyria*

*Additions and Corrections to the W.P.A. Inventory
of Lucas County, Ohio: Toledo*

*Additions and Corrections to the W.P.A. Inventory
of Medina County, Ohio: Medina*

*Additions and Corrections to the W.P.A. Inventory
of Montgomery County, Ohio: Dayton*

*Additions and Corrections to the W.P.A. Inventory
of Muskingum County, Ohio: Zanesville*

*Additions and Corrections to the W.P.A. Inventory
of Seneca County, Ohio: Tiffin*

*Additions and Corrections to the W.P.A. Inventory
of Trumbull County, Ohio: Warren*

*Additions and Corrections to the W.P.A. Inventory
of Washington County, Ohio: Marietta*

*Additions and Corrections to the W.P.A. Inventory
of Wayne County, Ohio: Wooster*

Hookers, Crooks and Kooks, Part I: Hookers

Hookers, Crooks and Kooks, Part II: Crooks and Kooks

Lucas County, Ohio, Index to Deaths, 1867–1908

Mason County, Kentucky Wills and Estates, 1791–1832, Second Edition